Honorifics Explained

Throughout the Del Rey Manga books, you will find Japanese honorifics left intact in the translations. For those not familiar with how the Japanese use honorifics and, more important, how they differ from American honorifics, we present this brief overview.

Politeness has always been a critical facet of Japanese culture. Ever since the feudal era, when Japan was a highly stratified society, use of honorifics—which can be defined as polite speech that indicates relationship or status—has played an essential role in the Japanese language. When addressing someone in Japanese, an honorific usually takes the form of a suffix attached to one's name (example: "Asuna-san"), is used as a title at the end of one's name, or appears in place of the name itself (example: "Negi-sensei," or simply "Sensei!").

Honorifics can be expressions of respect or endearment. In the context of manga and anime, honorifics give insight into the nature of the relationship between characters. Many English translations leave out these important honorifics and therefore distort the feel of the original Japanese. Because Japanese honorifics contain nuances that English honorifics lack, it is our policy at Del Rey not to translate them. Here, instead, is a guide to some of the honorifics you may encounter in Del Rey Manga.

-san: This is the most common honorific and is equivalent to Mr., Miss, Ms., or Mrs. It is the all-purpose honorific and can be used in any situation where politeness is required.

-sama: This is one level higher than "-san" and is used to confer great respect.

-dono: This comes from the word "tono," which means "lord." It is an even higher level than "-sama" and confers utmost respect.

-kun: This suffix is used at the end of boys' names to express familiarity or endearment. It is also sometimes used by men

among friends, or when addressing someone younger or of a lower station.

-chan: This is used to express endearment, mostly toward girls. It is also used for little boys, pets, and even among lovers. It gives a sense of childish cuteness.

Bōzu: This is an informal way to refer to a boy, similar to the English terms "kid" and "squirt."

Sempai/Senpai: This title suggests that the addressee is one's senior in a group or organization. It is most often used in a school setting, where underclassmen refer to their upperclassmen as "sempai." It can also be used in the workplace, such as when a newer employee addresses an employee who has seniority in the company.

Kohai: This is the opposite of "sempai" and is used toward underclassmen in school or newcomers in the workplace. It connotes that the addressee is of a lower station.

Sensei: Literally meaning "one who has come before," this title is used for teachers, doctors, or masters of any profession or art.

Anesan (or *nesan*): A generic term for a girl, usually older, that means "sister."

Ojōsama: A way of referring to the daughter or sister of someone with high political or social status.

-[blank]: This is usually forgotten in these lists, but it is perhaps the most significant difference between Japanese and English. The lack of honorific means that the speaker has permission to address the person in a very intimate way. Usually, only family, spouses, or very close friends have this kind of permission. Known as *yobisute,* it can be gratifying when someone who has earned the intimacy starts to call one by one's name without an honorific. But when that intimacy hasn't been earned, it can be very insulting.

NEGIMA!

24

Ken Akamatsu

TRANSLATED AND ADAPTED BY
Alethea Nibley and Athena Nibley

LETTERING AND RETOUCH BY
Steve Palmer

BALLANTINE BOOKS • NEW YORK

Negima! volume 24 is a work of fiction. Names, characters, places, and incidents are the products of the author's imagination or are used fictitiously. Any resemblance to actual events, locales, or persons, living or dead, is entirely coincidental.

A Del Rey Manga/Kodansha Trade Paperback Original

Published in the United States by Del Rey, an imprint of The Random House Publishing Group, a division of Random House, Inc., New York.

DEL REY is a registered trademark and the Del Rey colophon is a trademark of Random House, Inc.

Publication rights arranged through Kodansha Ltd.

First published in Japan in 2008 by Kodansha Ltd., Tokyo

ISBN 978-0-345-51427-1

Printed in the United States of America

www.delreymanga.com

9 8 7 6 5 4 3 2 1

Translators/adapters: Alethea Nibley and Athena Nibley
Lettering and retouch: Steve Palmer

A Word from the Author

Presenting *Negima!* volume 24!

Every member of the Negi party has super-powered up. The time has finally come for the real fighting.

Will Negi really use his dark magic?!

And where are the members who haven't been found yet?!

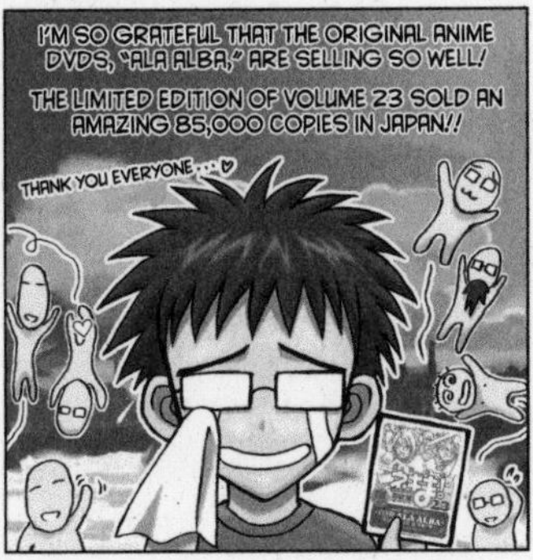
I'M SO GRATEFUL THAT THE ORIGINAL ANIME DVDS, "ALA ALBA," ARE SELLING SO WELL!
THE LIMITED EDITION OF VOLUME 23 SOLD AN AMAZING 85,000 COPIES IN JAPAN!!
THANK YOU EVERYONE...♥

And Fate's adorable backup squad arrives, and the Magical World arc is thrown into big confusion. Is the climax still a long way off?!

The new, all-manga-based anime series, *Magister Negi Magi ~ Ala Alba ~*, has started on Japanese TV. For details, check my home page.

Ken Akamatsu
www.ailove.net

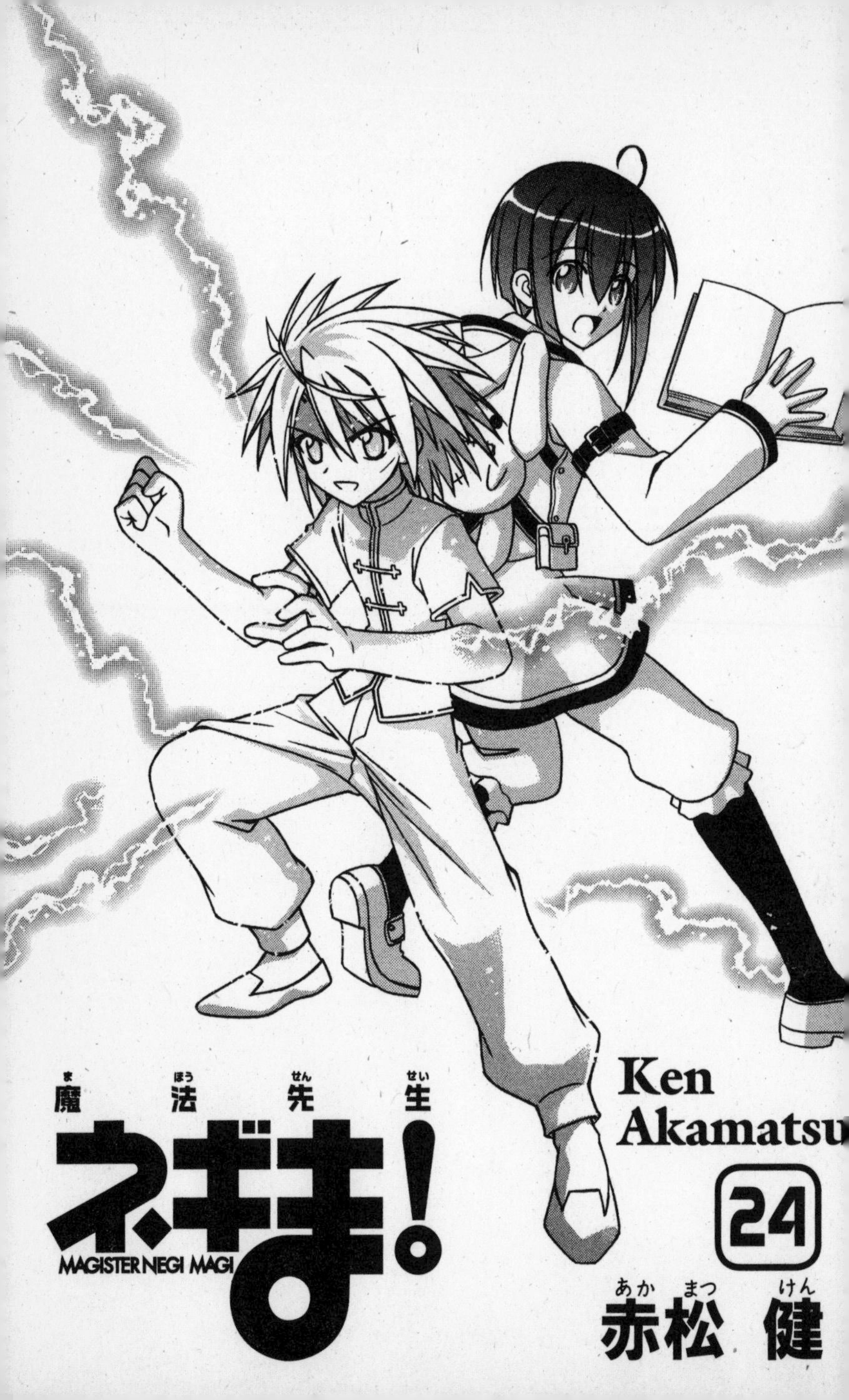

魔法先生ネギま！

MAGISTER NEGI MAGI

Ken Akamatsu

24

赤松 健

CONTENTS

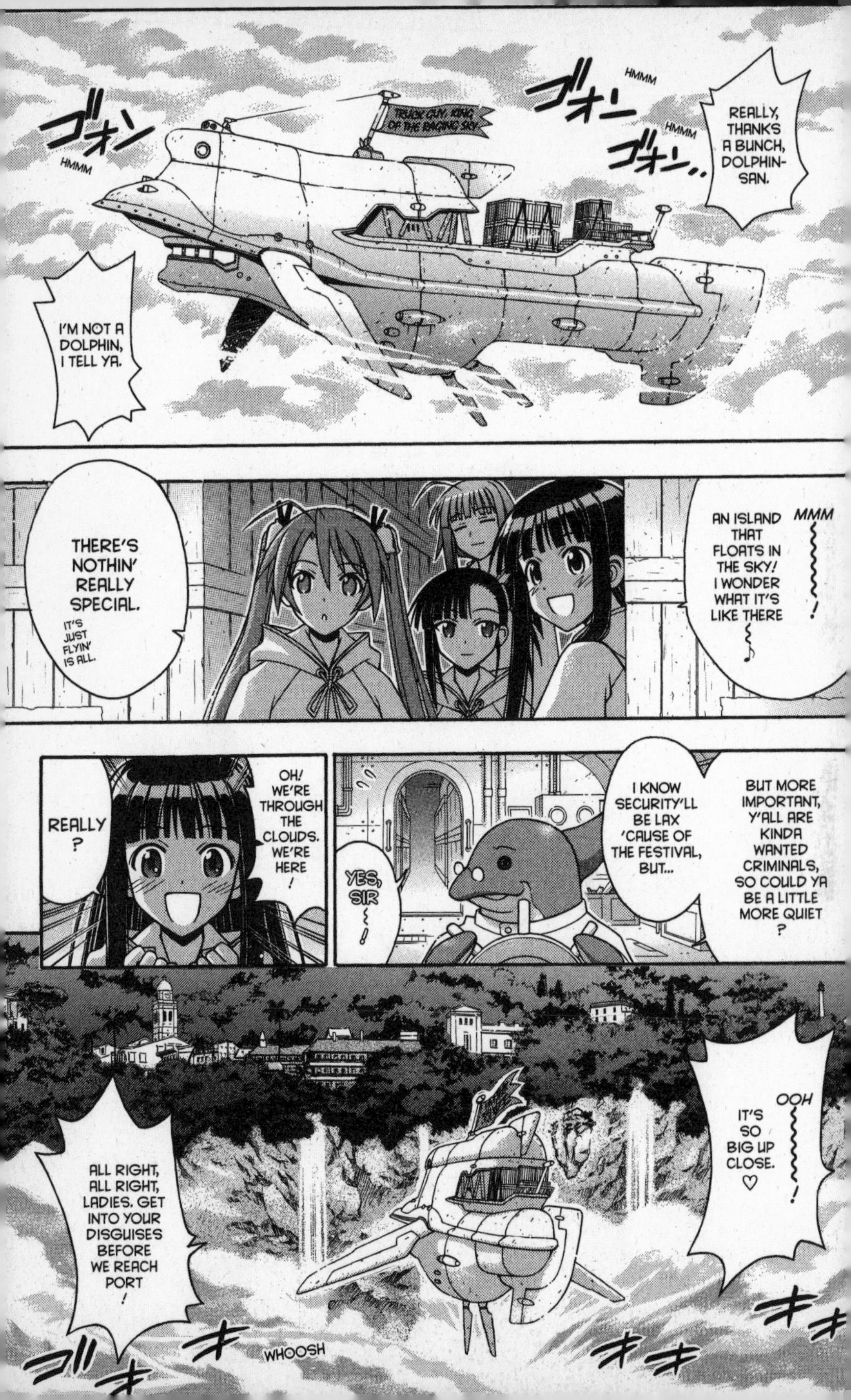
HMMM
HMMM
REALLY, THANKS A BUNCH, DOLPHIN-SAN.
TRUCK GUY, KING OF THE RAGING SKY
HMMM
I'M NOT A DOLPHIN, I TELL YA.
MMM~!
AN ISLAND THAT FLOATS IN THE SKY! I WONDER WHAT IT'S LIKE THERE~♪
THERE'S NOTHIN' REALLY SPECIAL.
IT'S JUST FLYIN' IS ALL.
BUT MORE IMPORTANT, Y'ALL ARE KINDA WANTED CRIMINALS, SO COULD YA BE A LITTLE MORE QUIET?
I KNOW SECURITY'LL BE LAX 'CAUSE OF THE FESTIVAL, BUT...
YES, SIR~!
OH! WE'RE THROUGH THE CLOUDS. WE'RE HERE!
REALLY?
OOH~!
IT'S SO BIG UP CLOSE. ♡
ALL RIGHT, ALL RIGHT, LADIES. GET INTO YOUR DISGUISES BEFORE WE REACH PORT!
WHOOSH

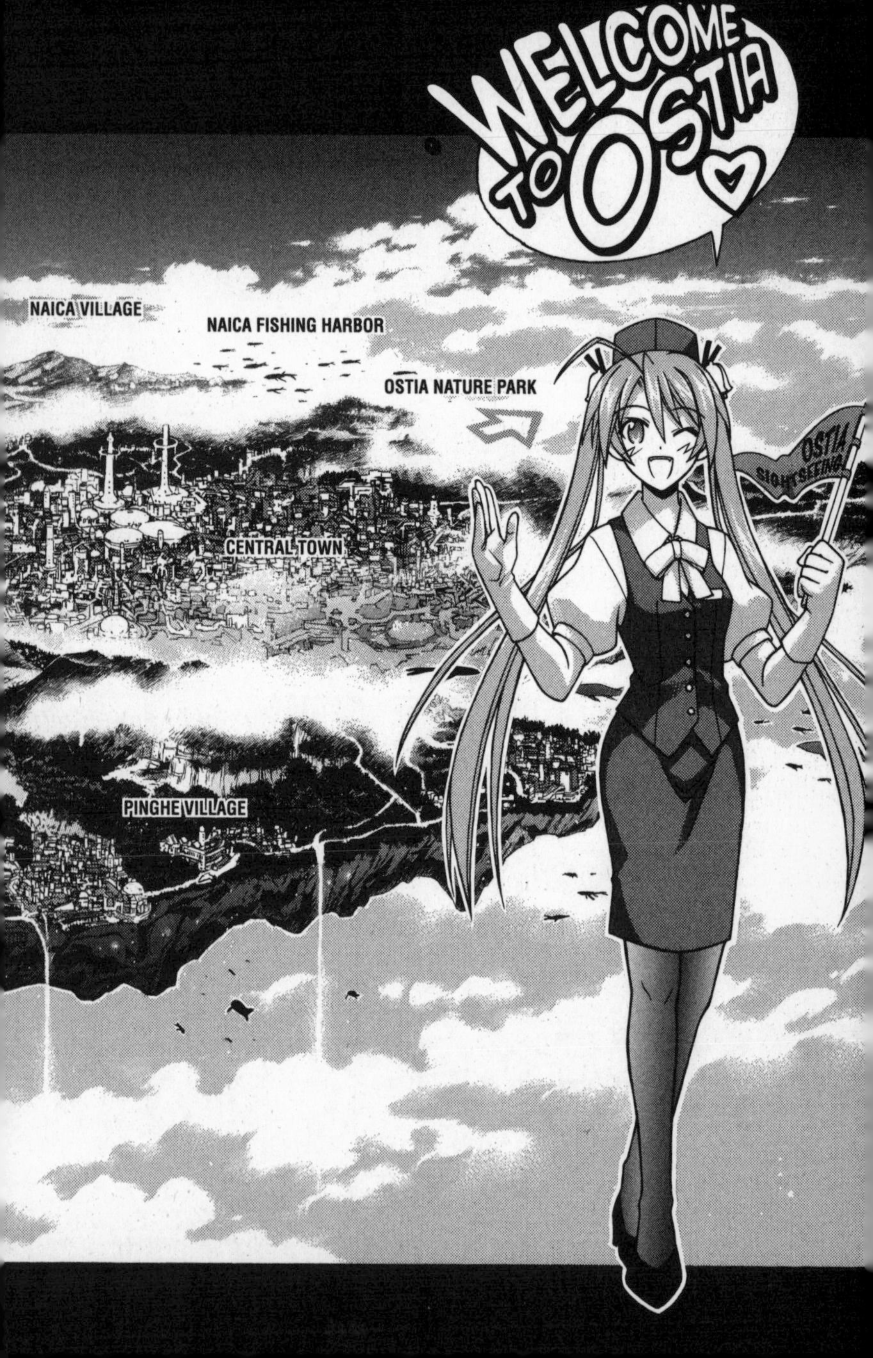
WELCOME TO OSTIA
NAICA VILLAGE
NAICA FISHING HARBOR
OSTIA NATURE PARK
OSTIA SIGHTSEEING
CENTRAL TOWN
PINGHE VILLAGE

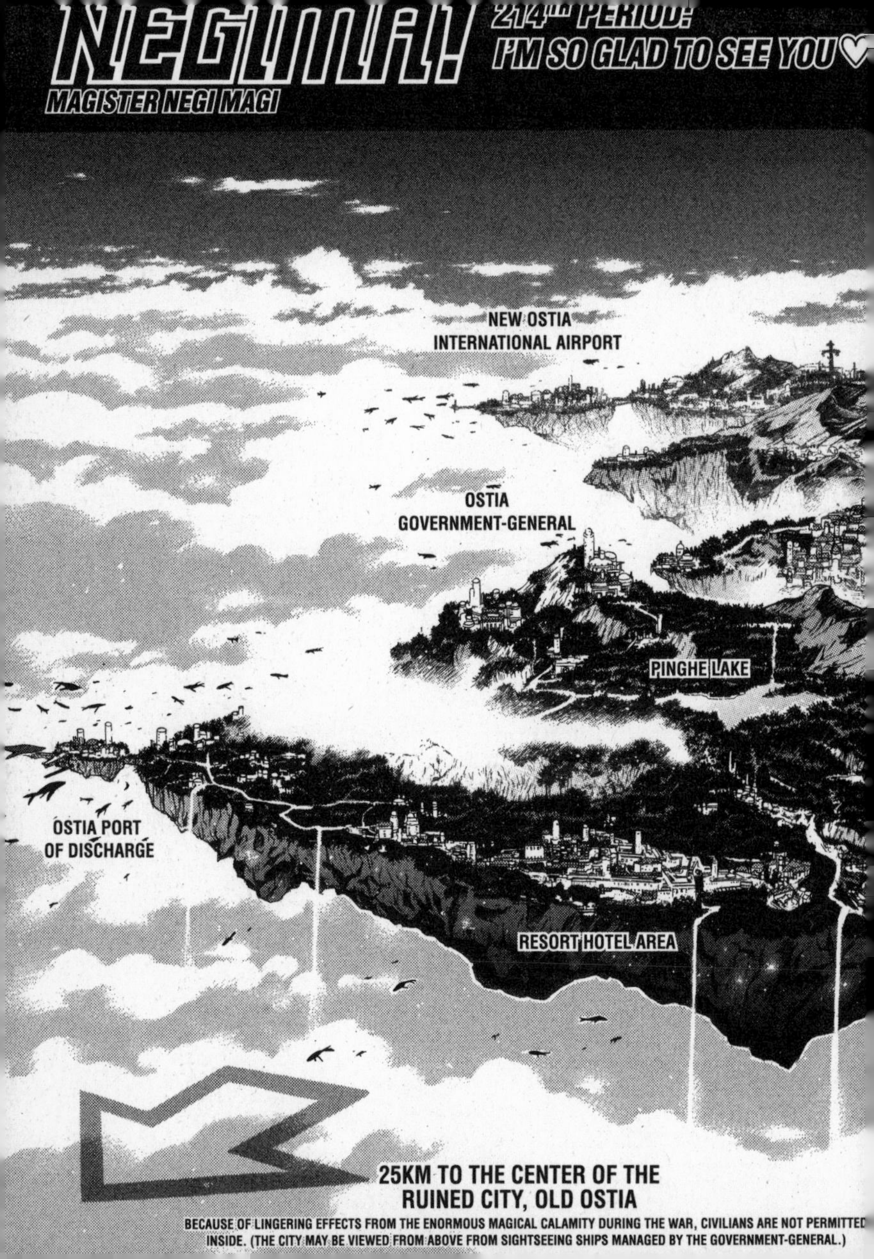
NEGIMA!
MAGISTER NEGI MAGI
214th PERIOD:
I'M SO GLAD TO SEE YOU♡
NEW OSTIA
INTERNATIONAL AIRPORT
OSTIA
GOVERNMENT-GENERAL
PINGHE LAKE
OSTIA PORT
OF DISCHARGE
RESORT HOTEL AREA
25KM TO THE CENTER OF THE
RUINED CITY, OLD OSTIA
BECAUSE OF LINGERING EFFECTS FROM THE ENORMOUS MAGICAL CALAMITY DURING THE WAR, CIVILIANS ARE NOT PERMITTED INSIDE. (THE CITY MAY BE VIEWED FROM ABOVE FROM SIGHTSEEING SHIPS MANAGED BY THE GOVERNMENT-GENERAL.)

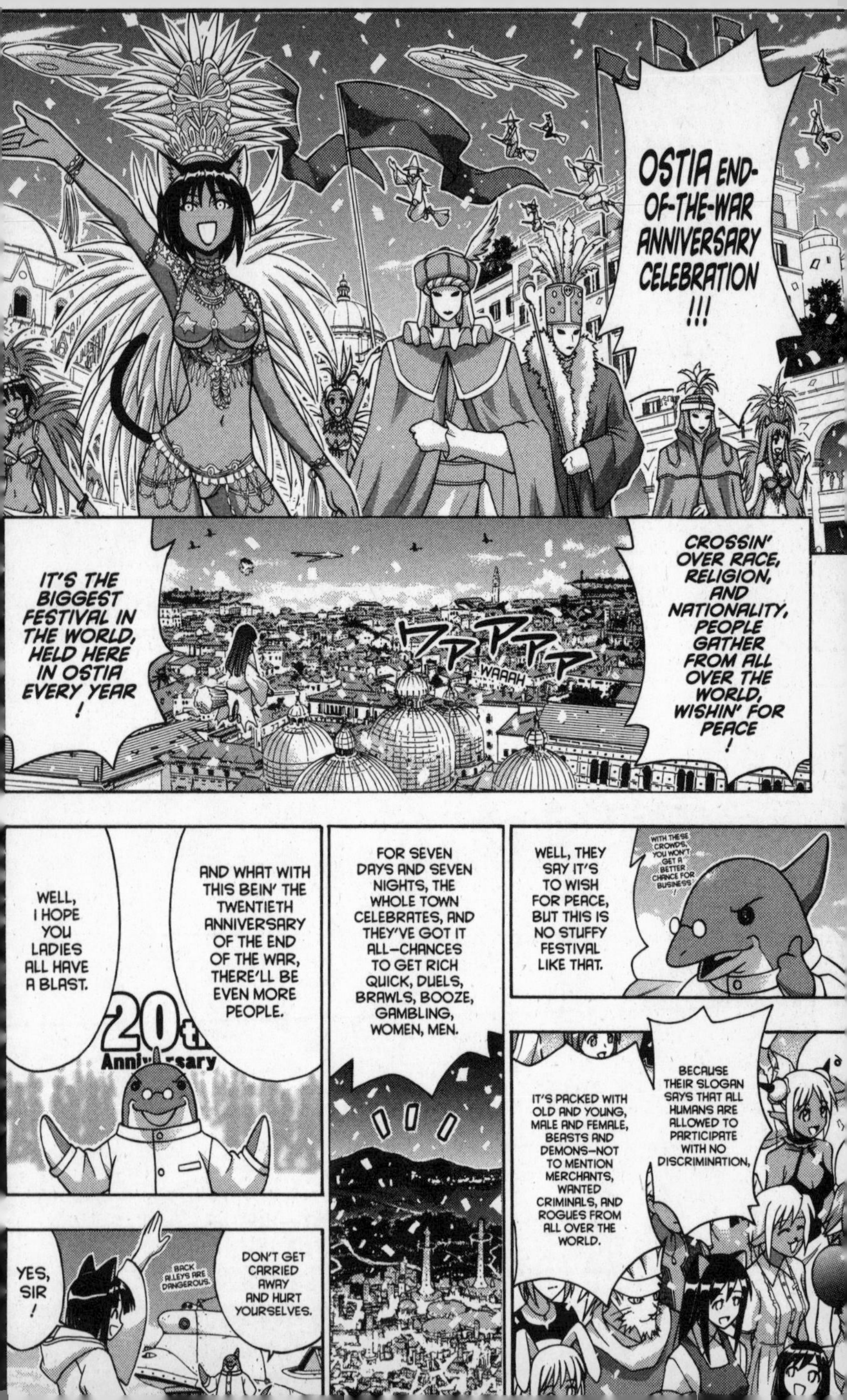
OSTIA END-OF-THE-WAR ANNIVERSARY CELEBRATION!!!
CROSSIN' OVER RACE, RELIGION, AND NATIONALITY, PEOPLE GATHER FROM ALL OVER THE WORLD, WISHIN' FOR PEACE!
WAAAH
IT'S THE BIGGEST FESTIVAL IN THE WORLD, HELD HERE IN OSTIA EVERY YEAR!
WITH THESE CROWDS, YOU WON'T GET A BETTER CHANCE FOR BUSINESS!
WELL, THEY SAY IT'S TO WISH FOR PEACE, BUT THIS IS NO STUFFY FESTIVAL LIKE THAT.
BECAUSE THEIR SLOGAN SAYS THAT ALL HUMANS ARE ALLOWED TO PARTICIPATE WITH NO DISCRIMINATION,
IT'S PACKED WITH OLD AND YOUNG, MALE AND FEMALE, BEASTS AND DEMONS—NOT TO MENTION MERCHANTS, WANTED CRIMINALS, AND ROGUES FROM ALL OVER THE WORLD.
FOR SEVEN DAYS AND SEVEN NIGHTS, THE WHOLE TOWN CELEBRATES, AND THEY'VE GOT IT ALL—CHANCES TO GET RICH QUICK, DUELS, BRAWLS, BOOZE, GAMBLING, WOMEN, MEN.
AND WHAT WITH THIS BEIN' THE TWENTIETH ANNIVERSARY OF THE END OF THE WAR, THERE'LL BE EVEN MORE PEOPLE.
WELL, I HOPE YOU LADIES ALL HAVE A BLAST.
DON'T GET CARRIED AWAY AND HURT YOURSELVES.
BACK ALLEYS ARE DANGEROUS.
YES, SIR!

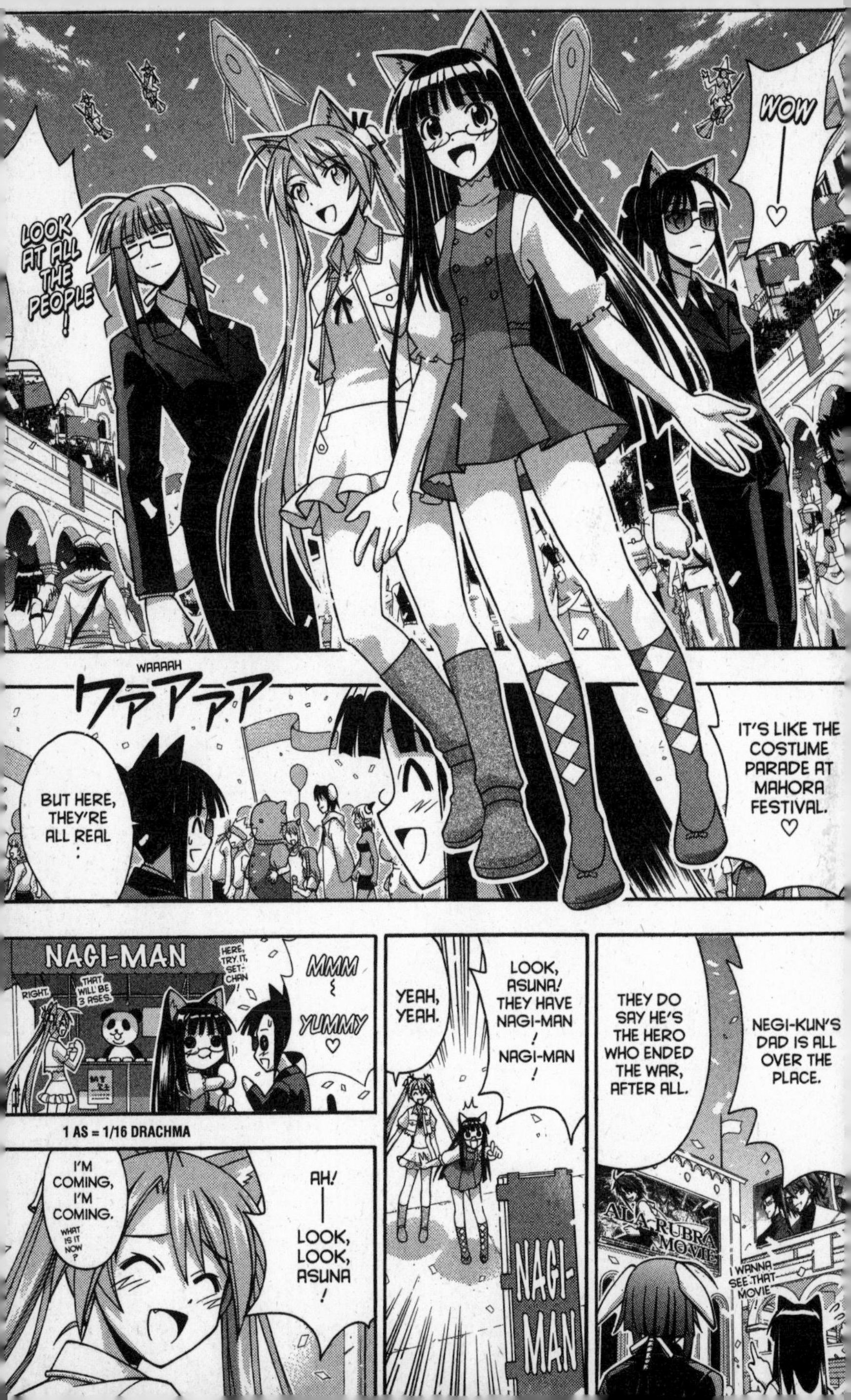
WOW — ♡
LOOK AT ALL THE PEOPLE!
IT'S LIKE THE COSTUME PARADE AT MAHORA FESTIVAL. ♡
WAAAAH ワァアァア
BUT HERE, THEY'RE ALL REAL..
NEGI-KUN'S DAD IS ALL OVER THE PLACE.
THEY DO SAY HE'S THE HERO WHO ENDED THE WAR, AFTER ALL.
ALA RUBRA MOVIE
I WANNA SEE THAT MOVIE
LOOK, ASUNA! THEY HAVE NAGI-MAN! NAGI-MAN!
YEAH, YEAH.
NAGI-MAN
MMM~ YUMMY ♡
HERE, TRY IT, SET-CHAN!
THAT WILL BE 3 ASES.
RIGHT.
NAGI-MAN
1 AS = 1/16 DRACHMA
AH! — LOOK, LOOK, ASUNA!
I'M COMING, I'M COMING.
WHAT IS IT NOW?

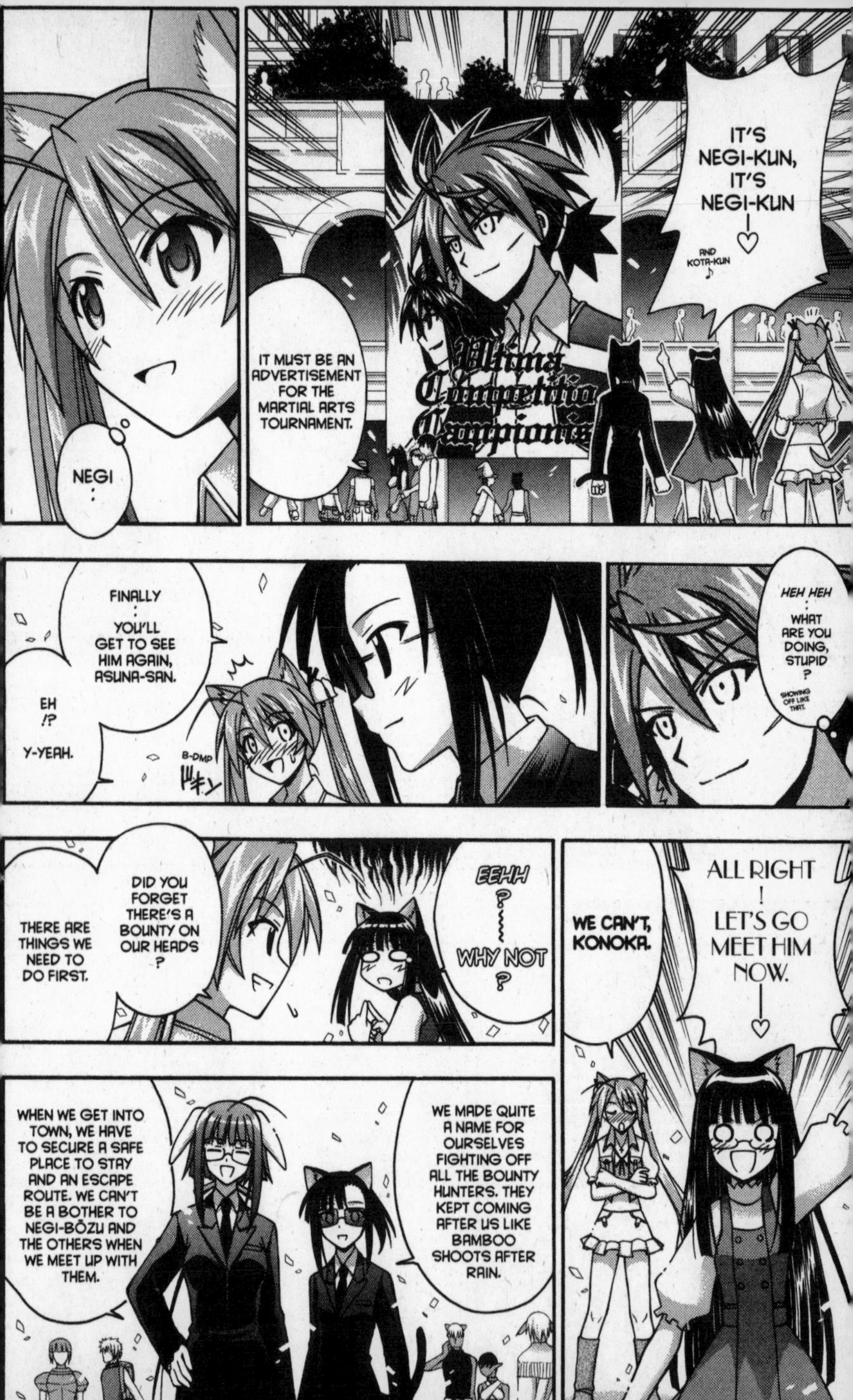
IT'S NEGI-KUN, IT'S NEGI-KUN ♡
AND KOTA-KUN ♪
IT MUST BE AN ADVERTISEMENT FOR THE MARTIAL ARTS TOURNAMENT.
NEGI...
HEH HEH... WHAT ARE YOU DOING, STUPID?
SHOWING OFF LIKE THAT.
FINALLY... YOU'LL GET TO SEE HIM AGAIN, ASUNA-SAN.
EH!?
Y-YEAH.
B-DMP
ドキン
ALL RIGHT! LET'S GO MEET HIM NOW. ♡
WE CAN'T, KONOKA.
EEHH?... WHY NOT?
DID YOU FORGET THERE'S A BOUNTY ON OUR HEADS?
THERE ARE THINGS WE NEED TO DO FIRST.
WE MADE QUITE A NAME FOR OURSELVES FIGHTING OFF ALL THE BOUNTY HUNTERS. THEY KEPT COMING AFTER US LIKE BAMBOO SHOOTS AFTER RAIN.
WHEN WE GET INTO TOWN, WE HAVE TO SECURE A SAFE PLACE TO STAY AND AN ESCAPE ROUTE. WE CAN'T BE A BOTHER TO NEGI-BŌZU AND THE OTHERS WHEN WE MEET UP WITH THEM.

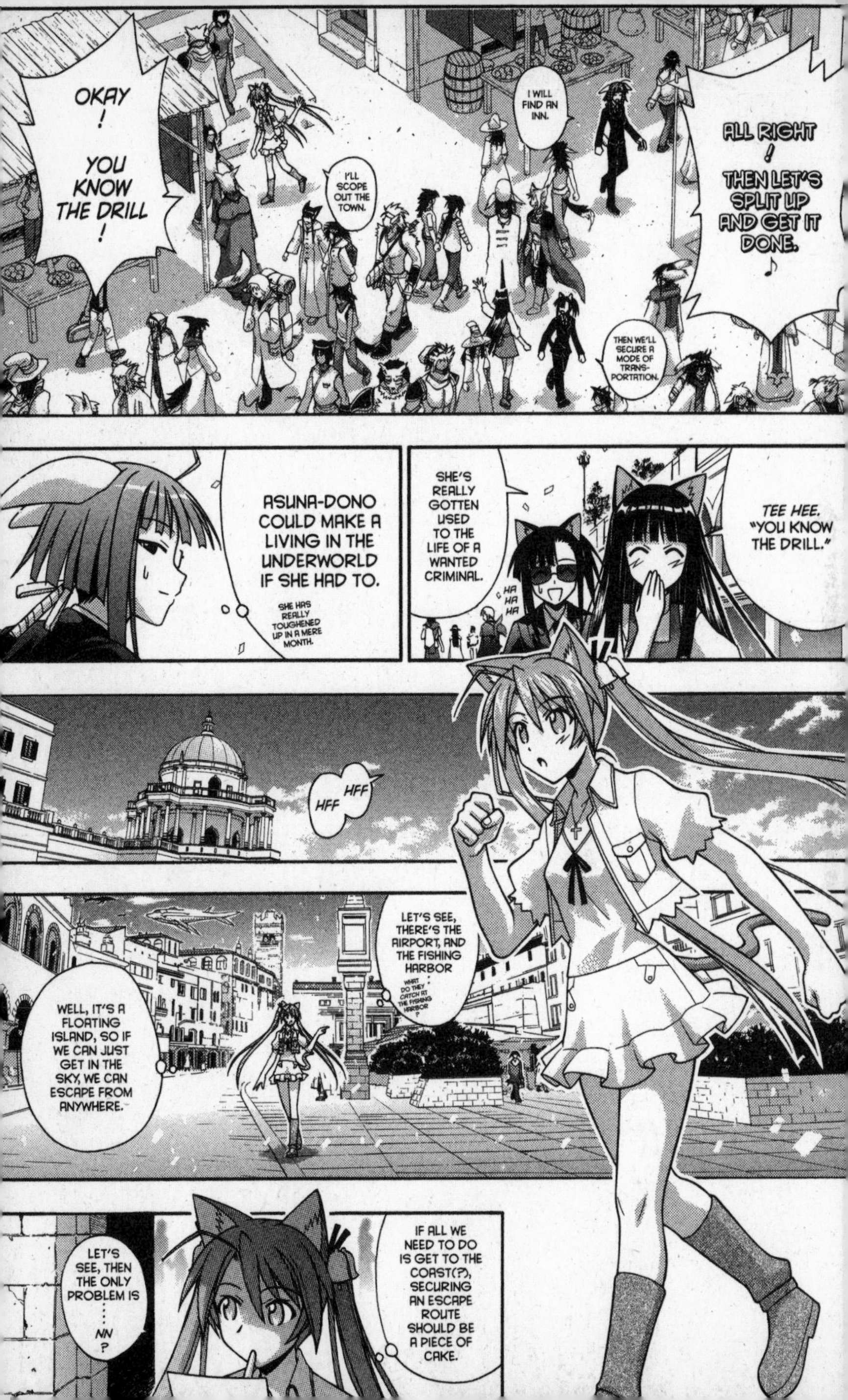
ALL RIGHT! THEN LET'S SPLIT UP AND GET IT DONE. ♪
I WILL FIND AN INN.
THEN WE'LL SECURE A MODE OF TRANS-PORTATION.
I'LL SCOPE OUT THE TOWN.
OKAY! YOU KNOW THE DRILL!
TEE HEE. "YOU KNOW THE DRILL."
SHE'S REALLY GOTTEN USED TO THE LIFE OF A WANTED CRIMINAL.
HA HA HA
ASUNA-DONO COULD MAKE A LIVING IN THE UNDERWORLD IF SHE HAD TO.
SHE HAS REALLY TOUGHENED UP IN A MERE MONTH.
HFF HFF
LET'S SEE, THERE'S THE AIRPORT, AND THE FISHING HARBOR
WHAT DO THEY CATCH AT THE FISHING HARBOR?
WELL, IT'S A FLOATING ISLAND, SO IF WE CAN JUST GET IN THE SKY, WE CAN ESCAPE FROM ANYWHERE.
IF ALL WE NEED TO DO IS GET TO THE COAST(?), SECURING AN ESCAPE ROUTE SHOULD BE A PIECE OF CAKE.
LET'S SEE, THEN THE ONLY PROBLEM IS......
NN?

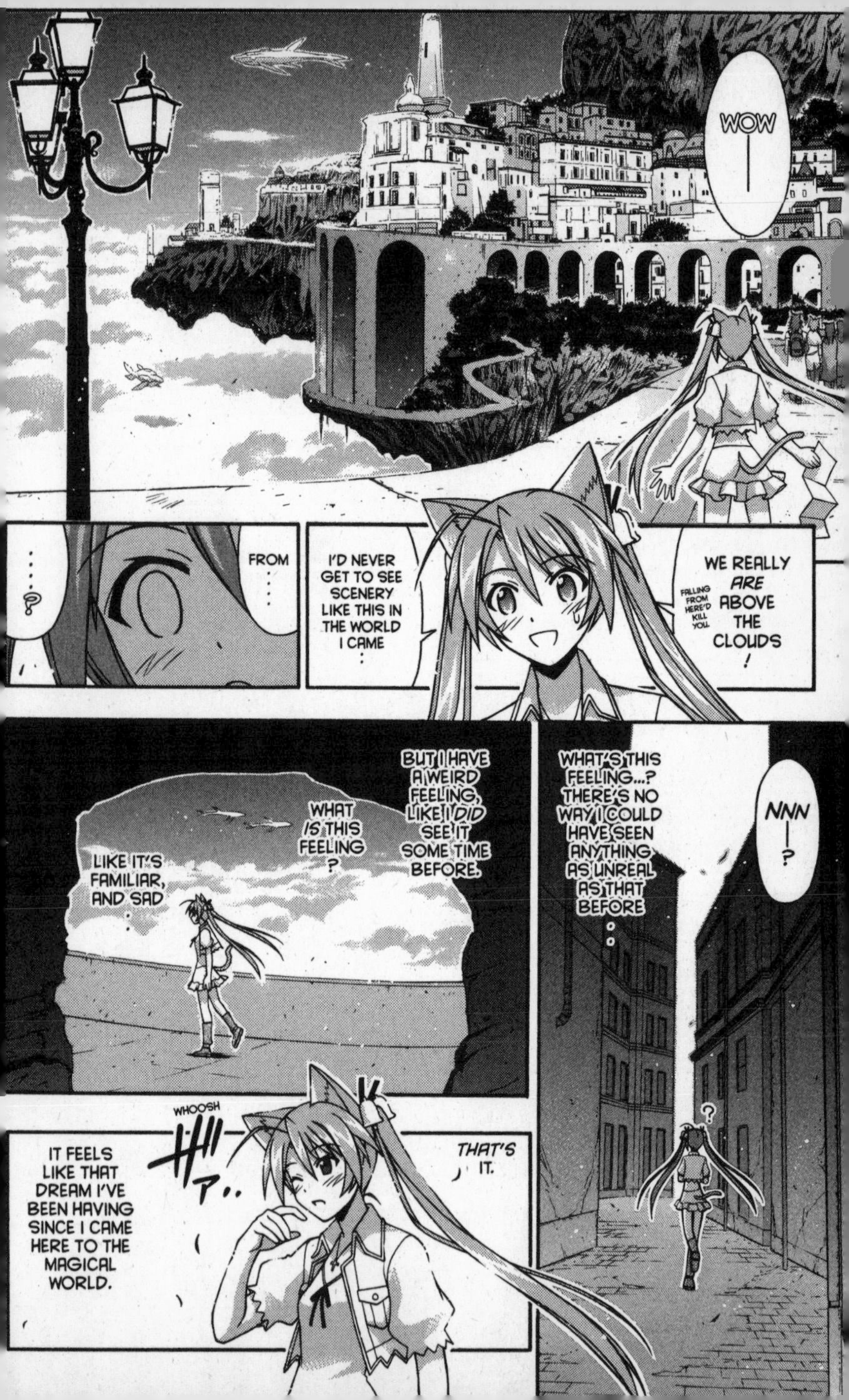
WOW—
WE REALLY ARE ABOVE THE CLOUDS!
FALLING FROM HERE'D KILL YOU.
I'D NEVER GET TO SEE SCENERY LIKE THIS IN THE WORLD I CAME...
FROM...
...?
NNN—?
WHAT'S THIS FEELING...? THERE'S NO WAY I COULD HAVE SEEN ANYTHING AS UNREAL AS THAT BEFORE...
BUT I HAVE A WEIRD FEELING, LIKE I DID SEE IT SOME TIME BEFORE.
WHAT IS THIS FEELING?
LIKE IT'S FAMILIAR, AND SAD.
THAT'S IT.
WHOOSH
ア..
IT FEELS LIKE THAT DREAM I'VE BEEN HAVING SINCE I CAME HERE TO THE MAGICAL WORLD.

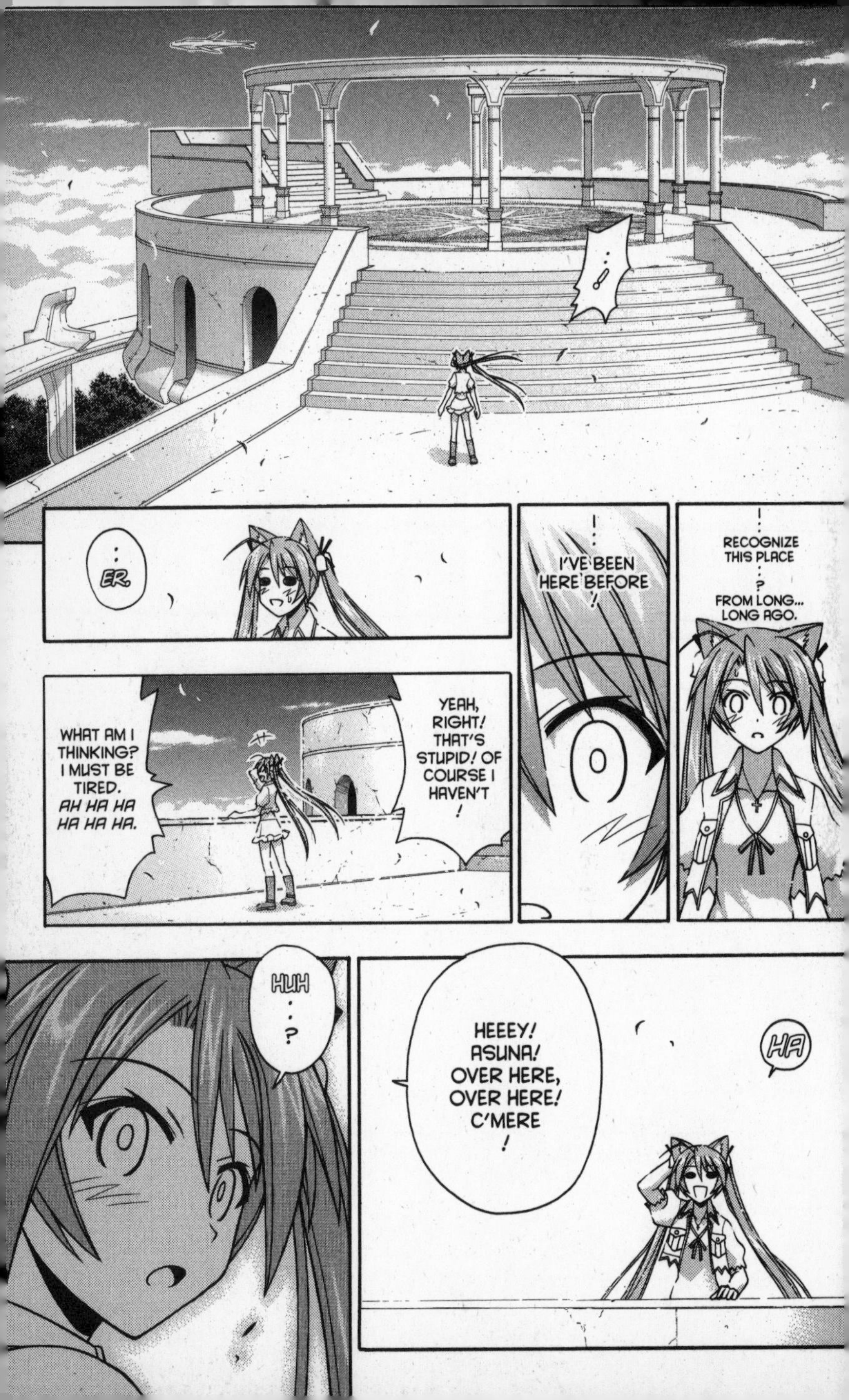
...!
...! RECOGNIZE THIS PLACE...? FROM LONG... LONG AGO.
...! I'VE BEEN HERE BEFORE!
...ER.
YEAH, RIGHT! THAT'S STUPID! OF COURSE I HAVEN'T!
WHAT AM I THINKING? I MUST BE TIRED. AH HA HA HA HA HA.
HA
HEEEY! ASUNA! OVER HERE, OVER HERE! C'MERE!
HUH...?

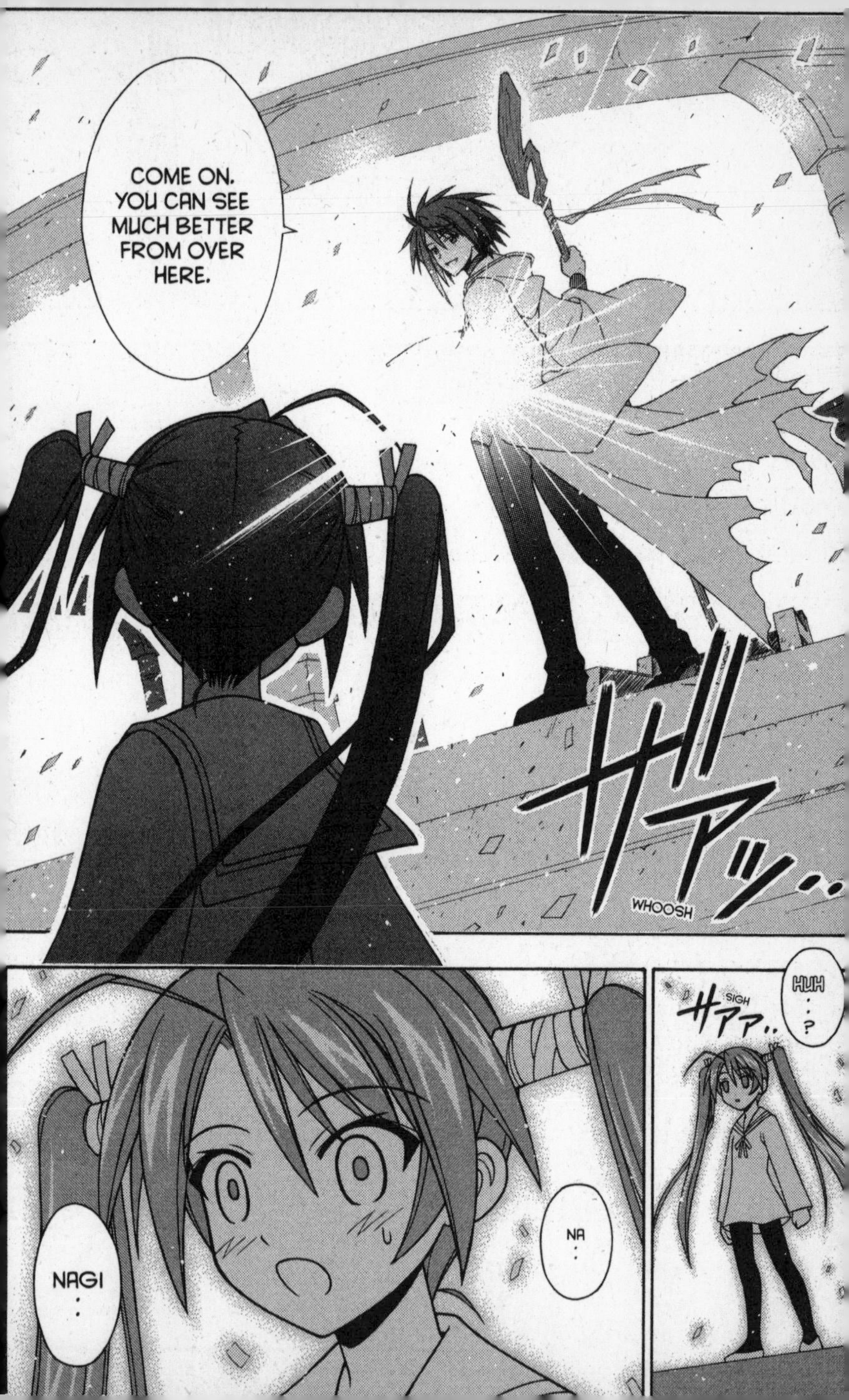
COME ON. YOU CAN SEE MUCH BETTER FROM OVER HERE.
ザアッ..
WHOOSH
サアア..
SIGH
HUH...?
NA..
NAGI...

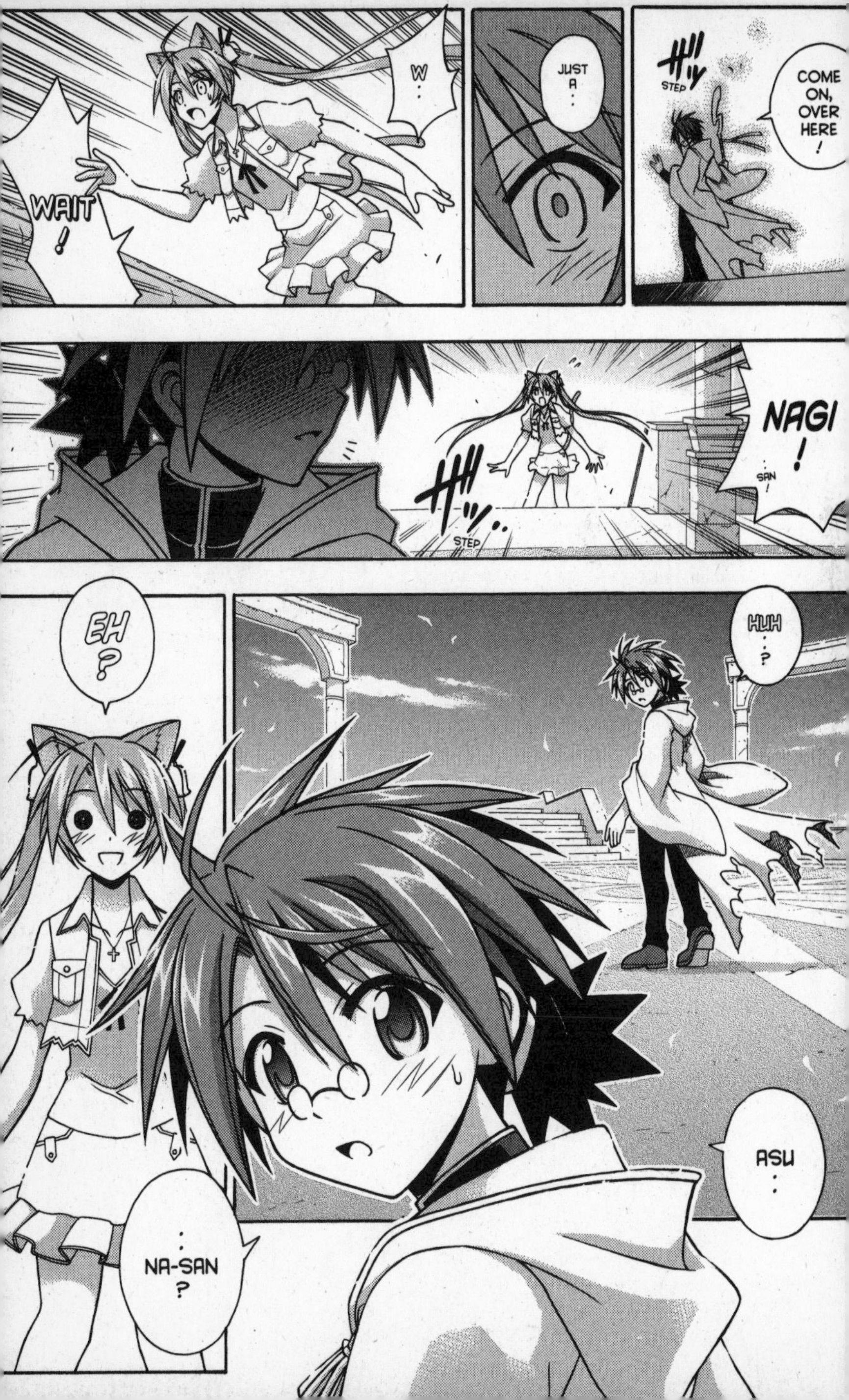
STEP
COME ON, OVER HERE!
JUST A...
W...
WAIT!
NAGI!
...SAN!
STEP
HUH...?
ASU...
EH?
...NA-SAN?

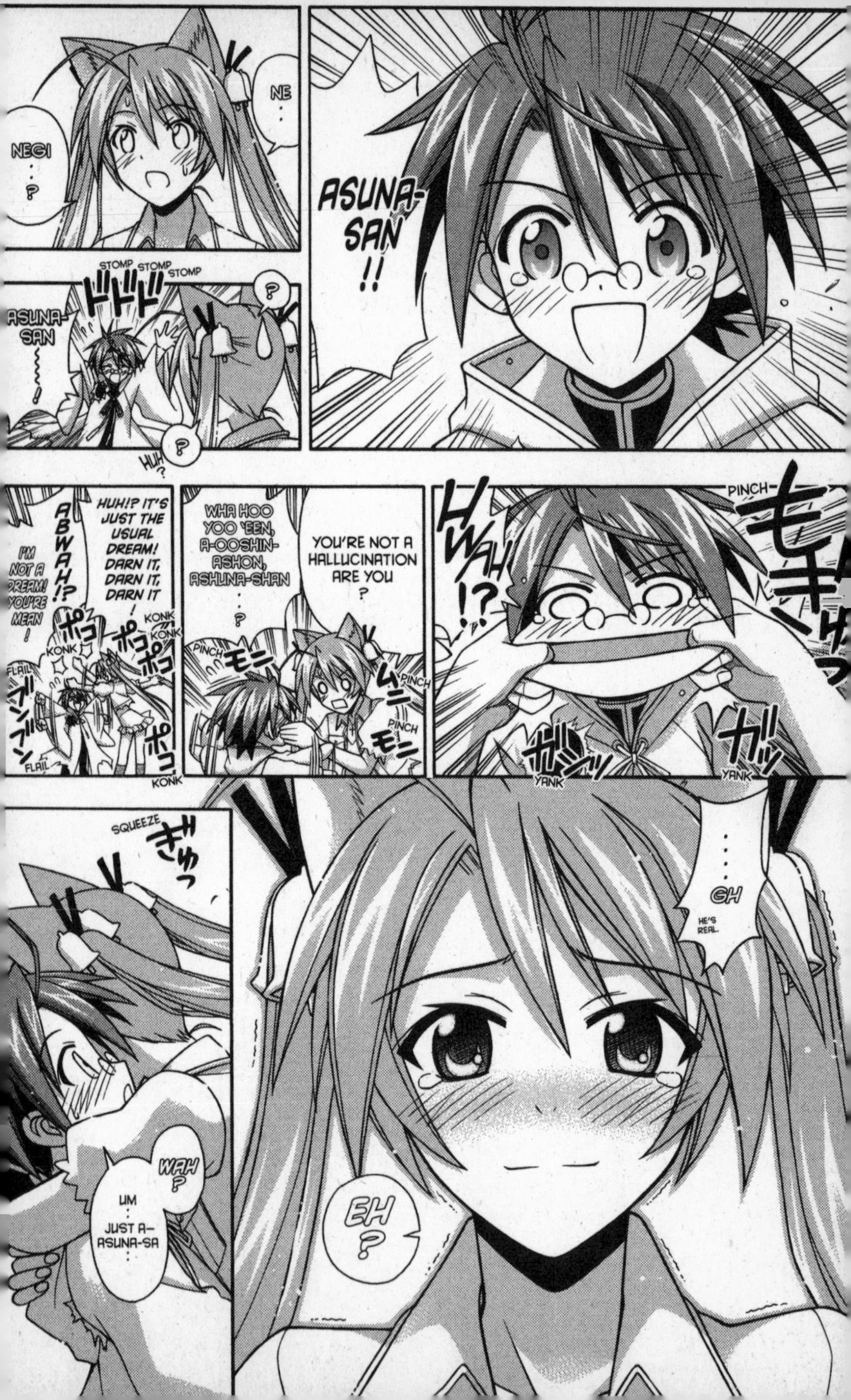
ASUNA-SAN!!
NE . . .
NEGI . . . ?
STOMP STOMP STOMP
ドドド
?
ASUNA-SAN~~~!
?
HUH?
PINCH
HWAH!?
ガッ
YANK
YANK
YOU'RE NOT A HALLUCINATION ARE YOU?
WHA HOO YOO 'EEN, A-OOSHIN-ASHON, ASHUNA-SHAN . . . ?
ムニ
PINCH
PINCH
モニ
PINCH
モニ
HUH!? IT'S JUST THE USUAL DREAM! DARN IT, DARN IT, DARN IT!
ABWAH!?
I'M NOT A DREAM! YOU'RE MEAN!
ポコ
KONK
ポコ
KONK
ポコ
KONK
ポコ
KONK
FLAIL
FLAIL
. . . . GH
HE'S REAL.
EH?
SQUEEZE
ぎゅっ
WAH?
UM . . . JUST A- ASUNA-SA . . .

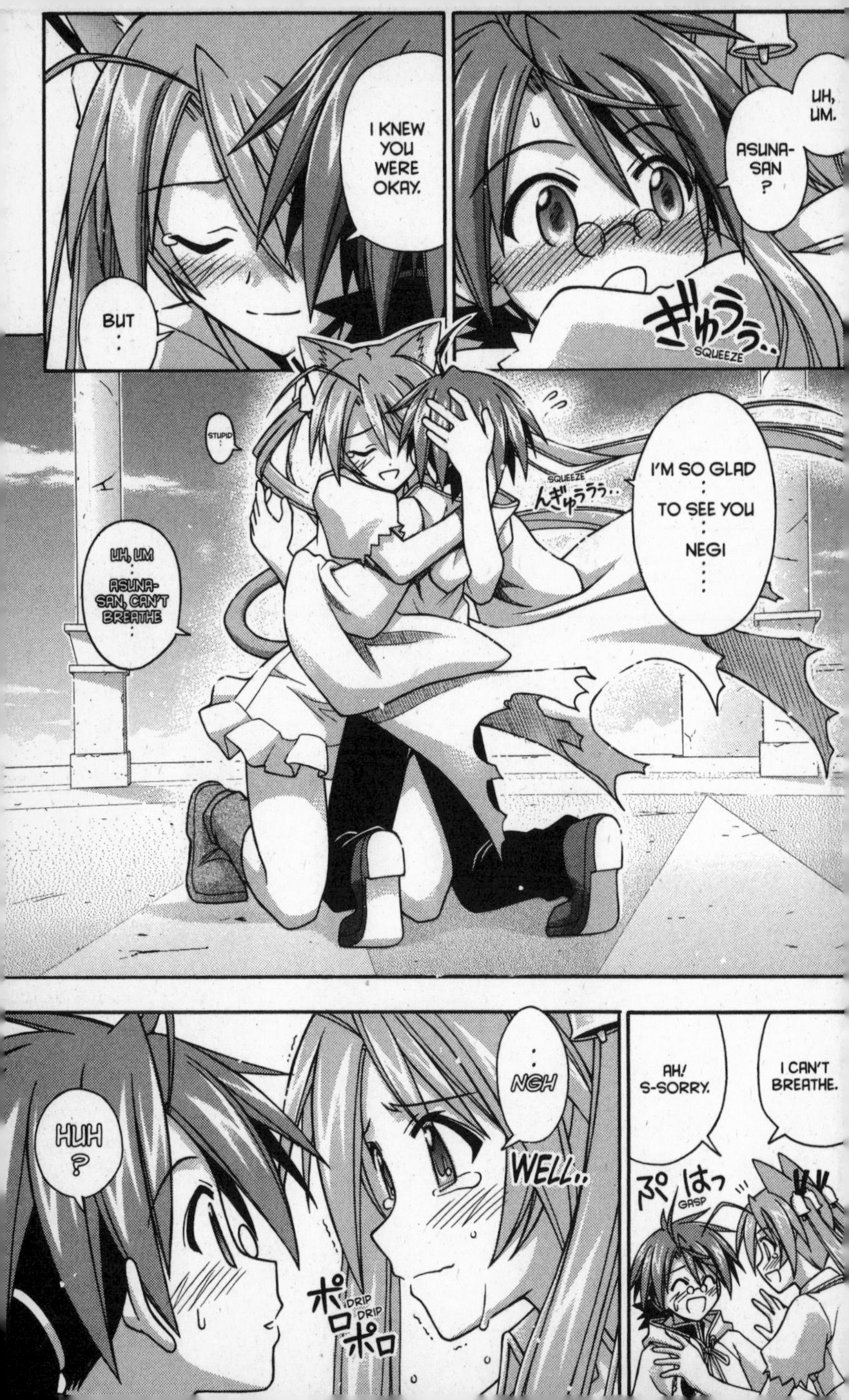
UH, UM. ASUNA-SAN?
ぎゅうう..
SQUEEZE
I KNEW YOU WERE OKAY.
BUT . .
I'M SO GLAD . . . TO SEE YOU . . . NEGI . . . . . .
SQUEEZE
んぎゅううう..
STUPID . .
UH, UM . . . ASUNA-SAN, CAN'T BREATHE . . .
I CAN'T BREATHE.
AH! S-SORRY.
ぷはっ
GASP
. . . NGH
WELL..
HUH?
ポロポロ
DRIP DRIP

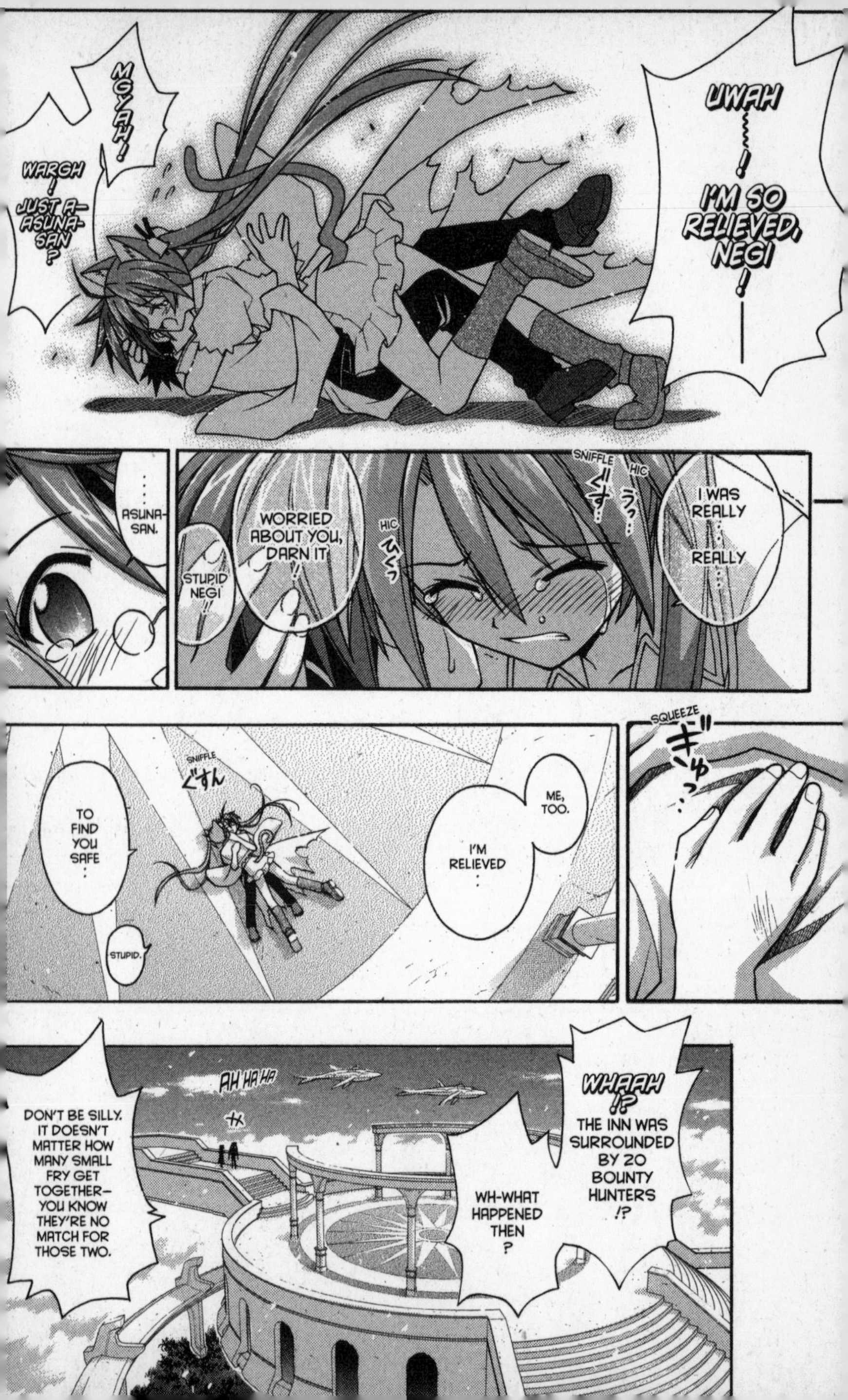
UWAH~~~! I'M SO RELIEVED, NEGI!——
MGYAH!
WARGH! JUST A-ASUNA-SAN?
I WAS REALLY... REALLY...
SNIFFLE
HIC
HIC
WORRIED ABOUT YOU, DARN IT!
STUPID NEGI!!
...ASUNA-SAN.
SQUEEZE
ME, TOO.
I'M RELIEVED...
SNIFFLE
TO FIND YOU SAFE...
STUPID.
WHAAAH!? THE INN WAS SURROUNDED BY 20 BOUNTY HUNTERS!?
WH-WHAT HAPPENED THEN?
AH HA HA
DON'T BE SILLY. IT DOESN'T MATTER HOW MANY SMALL FRY GET TOGETHER— YOU KNOW THEY'RE NO MATCH FOR THOSE TWO.

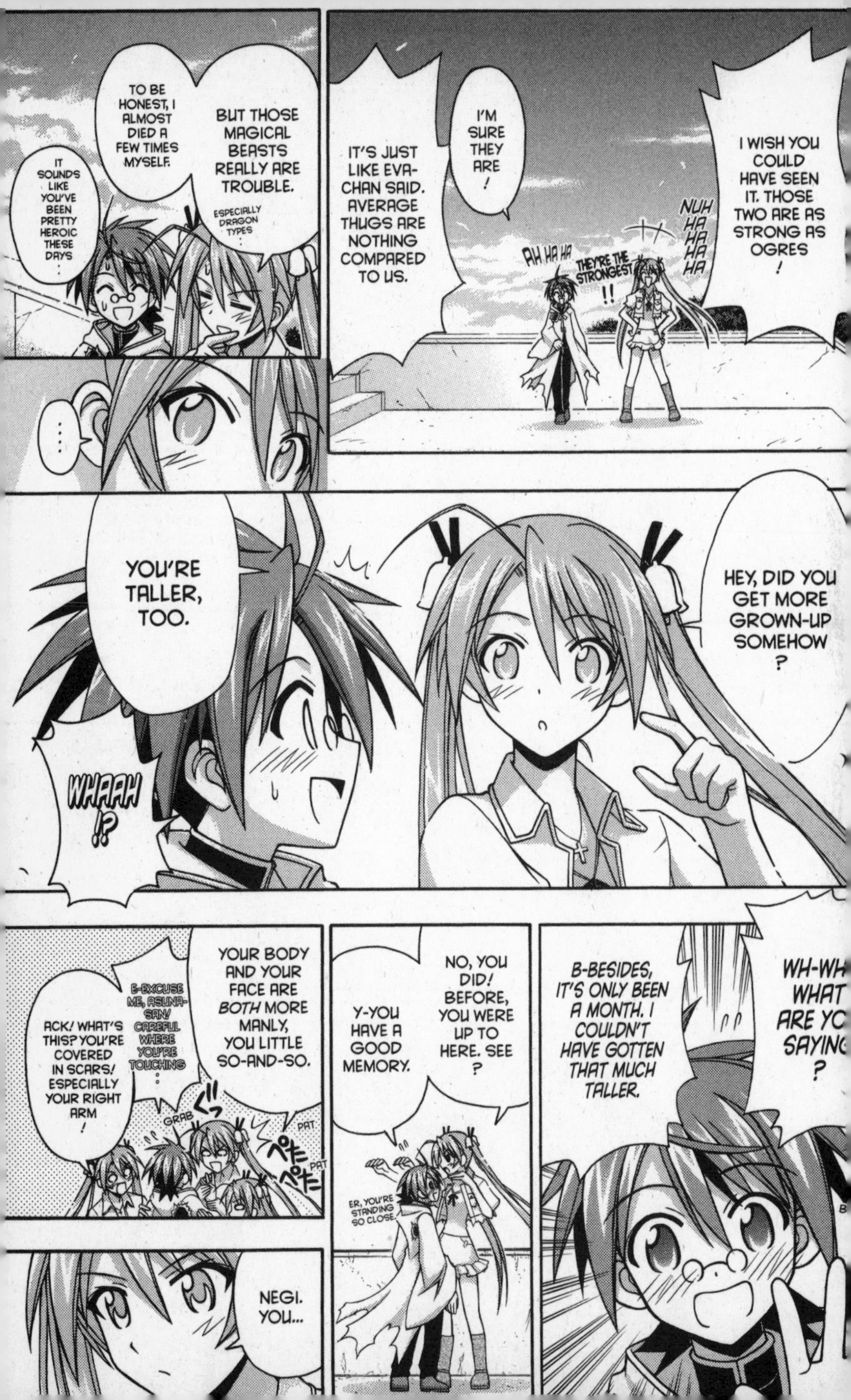
I WISH YOU COULD HAVE SEEN IT. THOSE TWO ARE AS STRONG AS OGRES!
NUH HA HA HA HA
THEY'RE THE STRONGEST!!
AH HA HA
I'M SURE THEY ARE!
IT'S JUST LIKE EVA-CHAN SAID. AVERAGE THUGS ARE NOTHING COMPARED TO US.
BUT THOSE MAGICAL BEASTS REALLY ARE TROUBLE.
TO BE HONEST, I ALMOST DIED A FEW TIMES MYSELF.
ESPECIALLY DRAGON TYPES...
IT SOUNDS LIKE YOU'VE BEEN PRETTY HEROIC THESE DAYS...
...
HEY, DID YOU GET MORE GROWN-UP SOMEHOW?
YOU'RE TALLER, TOO.
WHAAH!?
WH-WH WHAT ARE YO SAYING?
B-BESIDES, IT'S ONLY BEEN A MONTH. I COULDN'T HAVE GOTTEN THAT MUCH TALLER.
NO, YOU DID! BEFORE, YOU WERE UP TO HERE. SEE?
Y-YOU HAVE A GOOD MEMORY.
ER, YOU'RE STANDING SO CLOSE.
YOUR BODY AND YOUR FACE ARE BOTH MORE MANLY, YOU LITTLE SO-AND-SO.
B-EXCUSE ME, ASUNA-SAN! CAREFUL WHERE YOU'RE TOUCHING...
ACK! WHAT'S THIS? YOU'RE COVERED IN SCARS! ESPECIALLY YOUR RIGHT ARM!
ぐっ GRAB
ぺたぺた PAT PAT
NEGI. YOU...

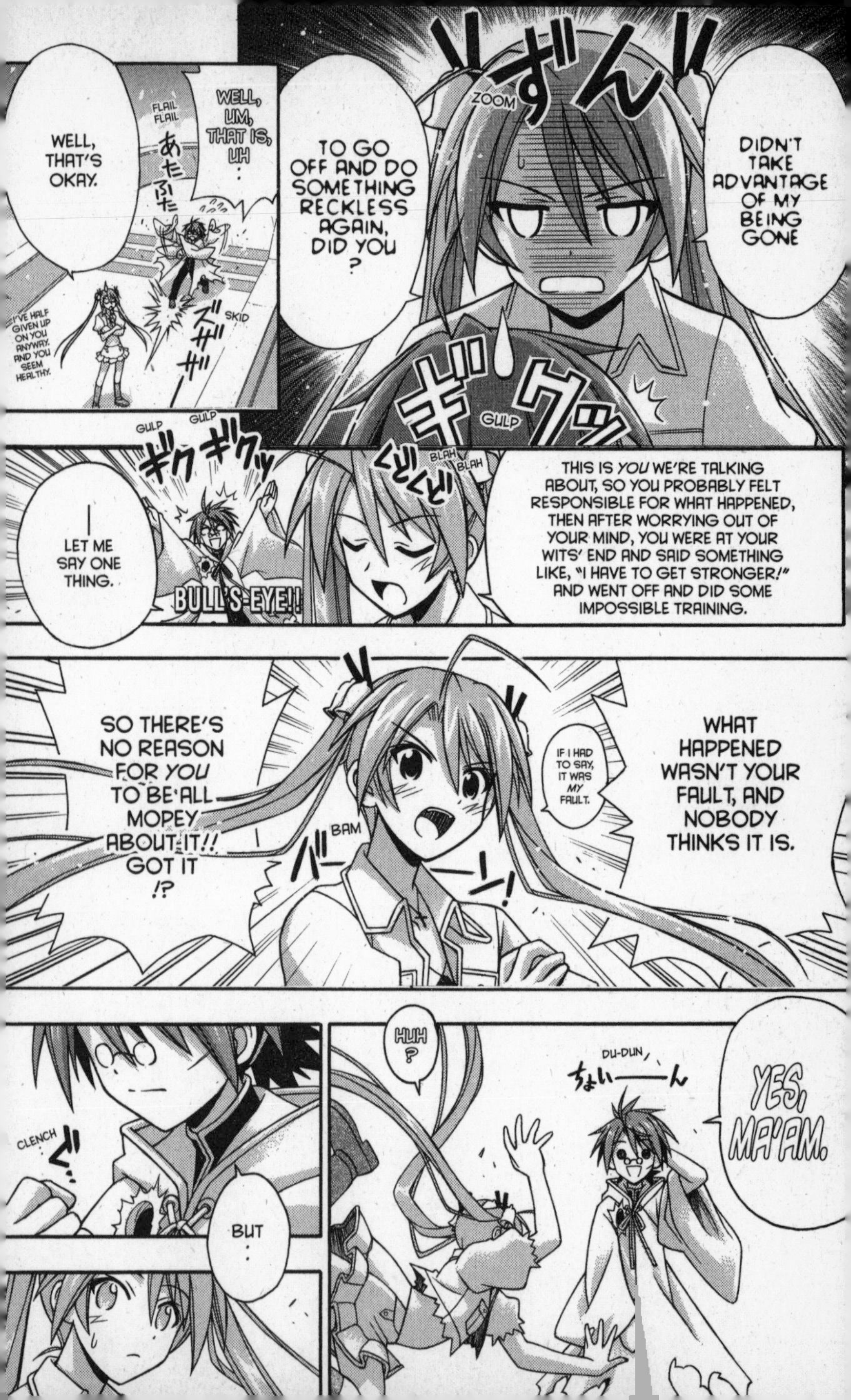
DIDN'T TAKE ADVANTAGE OF MY BEING GONE
ZOOM
TO GO OFF AND DO SOMETHING RECKLESS AGAIN, DID YOU?
GULP
WELL, UM, THAT IS, UH...
FLAIL FLAIL
SKID
WELL, THAT'S OKAY.
I'VE HALF GIVEN UP ON YOU ANYWAY. AND YOU SEEM HEALTHY.
THIS IS YOU WE'RE TALKING ABOUT, SO YOU PROBABLY FELT RESPONSIBLE FOR WHAT HAPPENED, THEN AFTER WORRYING OUT OF YOUR MIND, YOU WERE AT YOUR WITS' END AND SAID SOMETHING LIKE, "I HAVE TO GET STRONGER!" AND WENT OFF AND DID SOME IMPOSSIBLE TRAINING.
BLAH BLAH
GULP GULP
BULL'S-EYE!!
I LET ME SAY ONE THING.
WHAT HAPPENED WASN'T YOUR FAULT, AND NOBODY THINKS IT IS.
IF I HAD TO SAY, IT WAS MY FAULT.
BAM
SO THERE'S NO REASON FOR YOU TO BE ALL MOPEY ABOUT IT!! GOT IT!?
YES, MA'AM.
DU-DUN
HUH?
BUT...
CLENCH

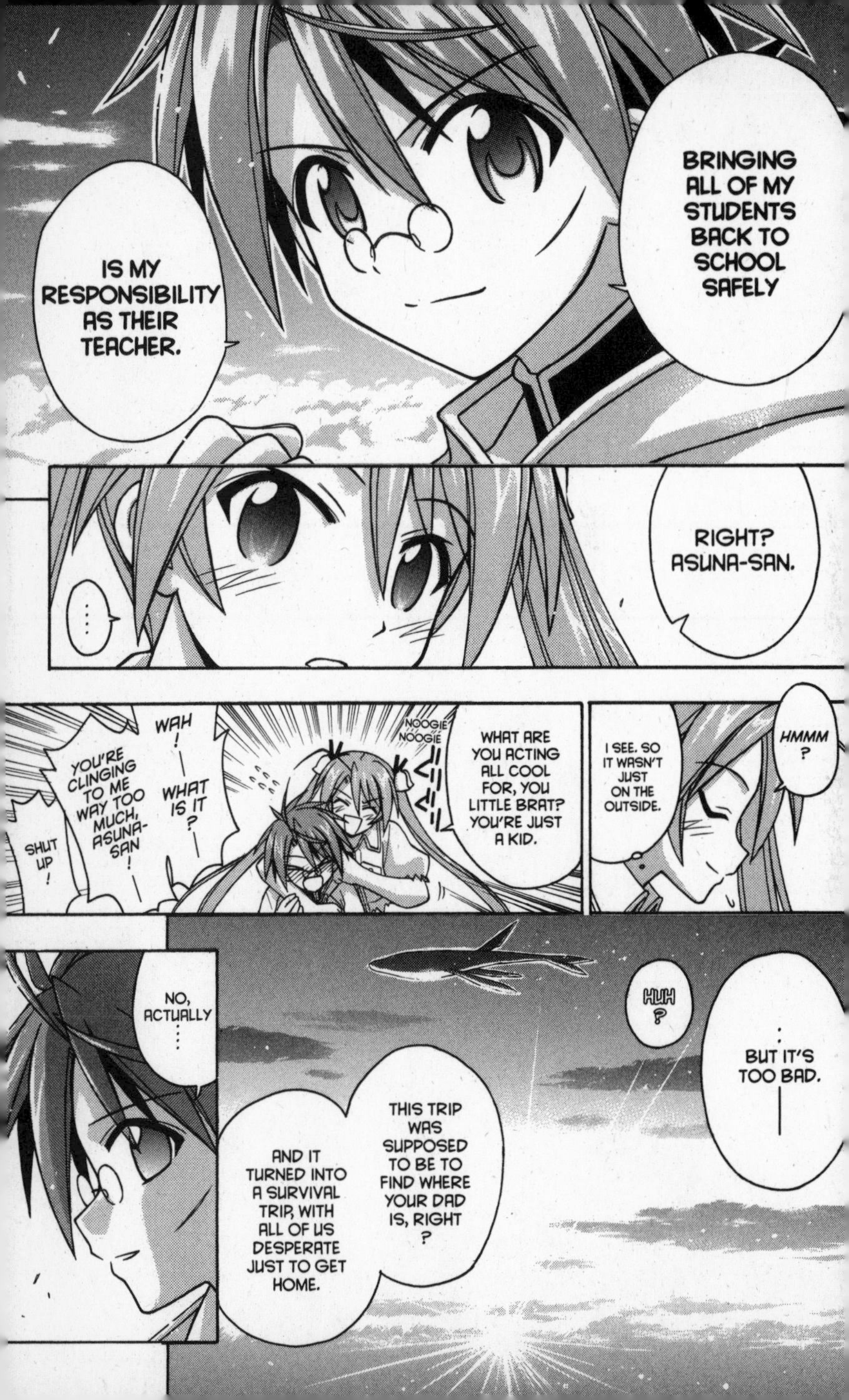
BRINGING ALL OF MY STUDENTS BACK TO SCHOOL SAFELY
IS MY RESPONSIBILITY AS THEIR TEACHER.
RIGHT? ASUNA-SAN.
......
HMMM ?
I SEE. SO IT WASN'T JUST ON THE OUTSIDE.
NOOGIE NOOGIE
WHAT ARE YOU ACTING ALL COOL FOR, YOU LITTLE BRAT? YOU'RE JUST A KID.
WAH! WHAT IS IT?
YOU'RE CLINGING TO ME WAY TOO MUCH, ASUNA-SAN!
SHUT UP!
...BUT IT'S TOO BAD.
HUH ?
THIS TRIP WAS SUPPOSED TO BE TO FIND WHERE YOUR DAD IS, RIGHT?
AND IT TURNED INTO A SURVIVAL TRIP, WITH ALL OF US DESPERATE JUST TO GET HOME.
NO, ACTUALLY......

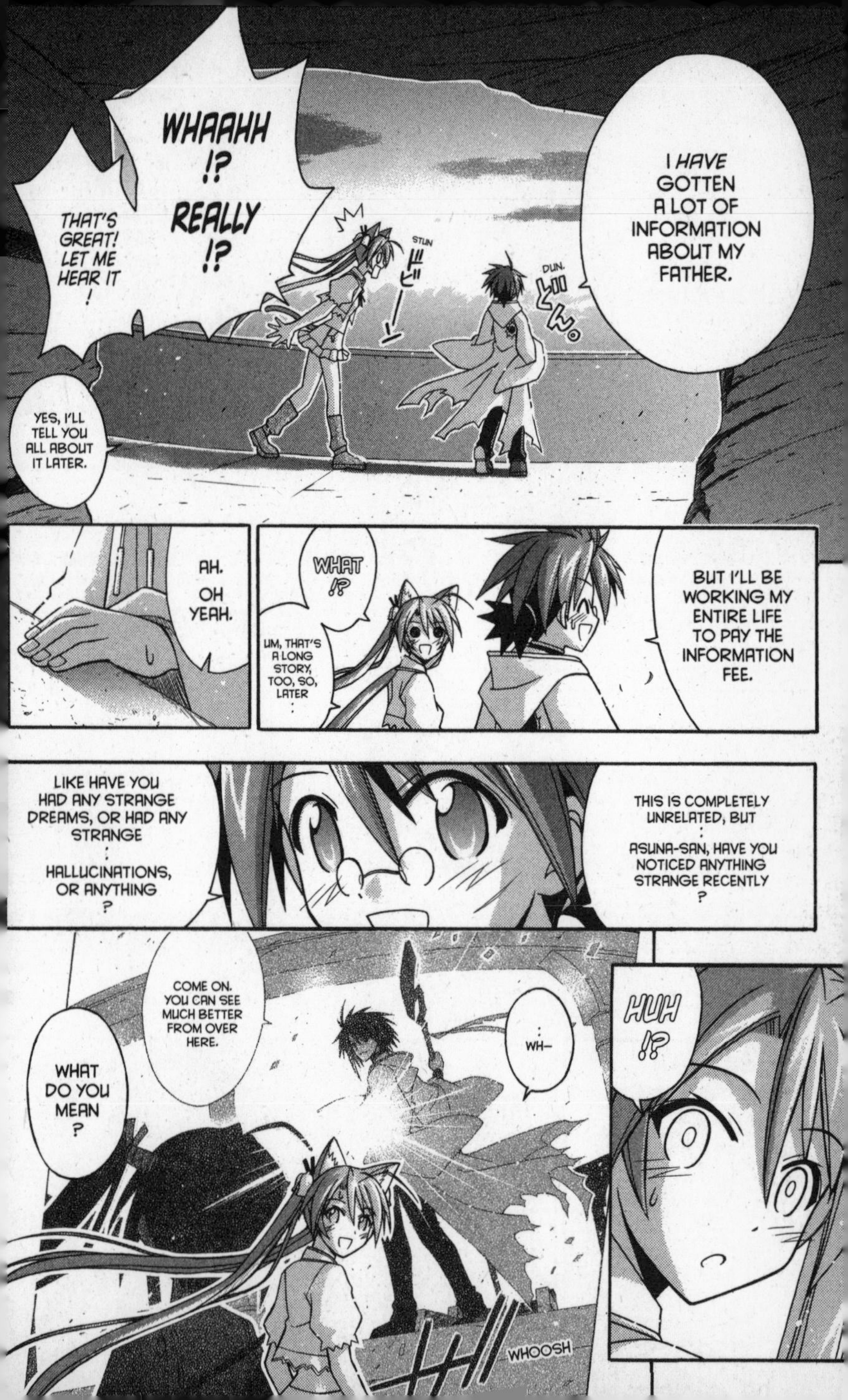
I HAVE GOTTEN A LOT OF INFORMATION ABOUT MY FATHER.
DUN.
STUN
WHAAHH !? REALLY !?
THAT'S GREAT! LET ME HEAR IT !
YES, I'LL TELL YOU ALL ABOUT IT LATER.
BUT I'LL BE WORKING MY ENTIRE LIFE TO PAY THE INFORMATION FEE.
WHAT !?
UM, THAT'S A LONG STORY, TOO, SO, LATER :
AH. OH YEAH.
THIS IS COMPLETELY UNRELATED, BUT : ASUNA-SAN, HAVE YOU NOTICED ANYTHING STRANGE RECENTLY ?
LIKE HAVE YOU HAD ANY STRANGE DREAMS, OR HAD ANY STRANGE : HALLUCINATIONS, OR ANYTHING ?
HUH !?
: WH–
COME ON. YOU CAN SEE MUCH BETTER FROM OVER HERE.
WHAT DO YOU MEAN ?
WHOOSH

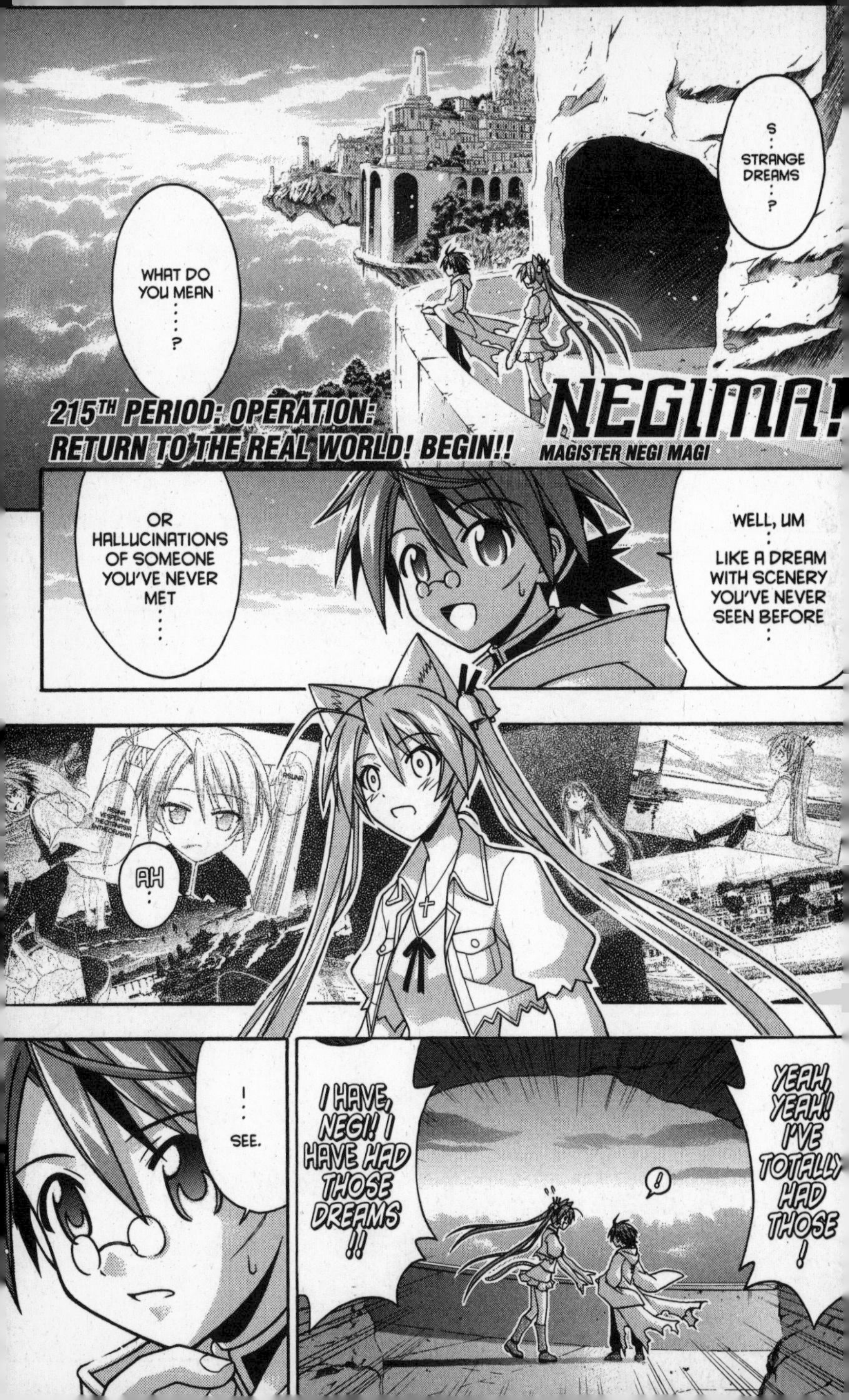
S... STRANGE DREAMS...?
WHAT DO YOU MEAN.....?
NEGIMA! MAGISTER NEGI MAGI
215TH PERIOD: OPERATION: RETURN TO THE REAL WORLD! BEGIN!!
WELL, UM.. LIKE A DREAM WITH SCENERY YOU'VE NEVER SEEN BEFORE..
OR HALLUCINATIONS OF SOMEONE YOU'VE NEVER MET....
AH..
YEAH, YEAH! I'VE TOTALLY HAD THOSE!
!
I HAVE, NEGI! I HAVE HAD THOSE DREAMS!!
I.. SEE.

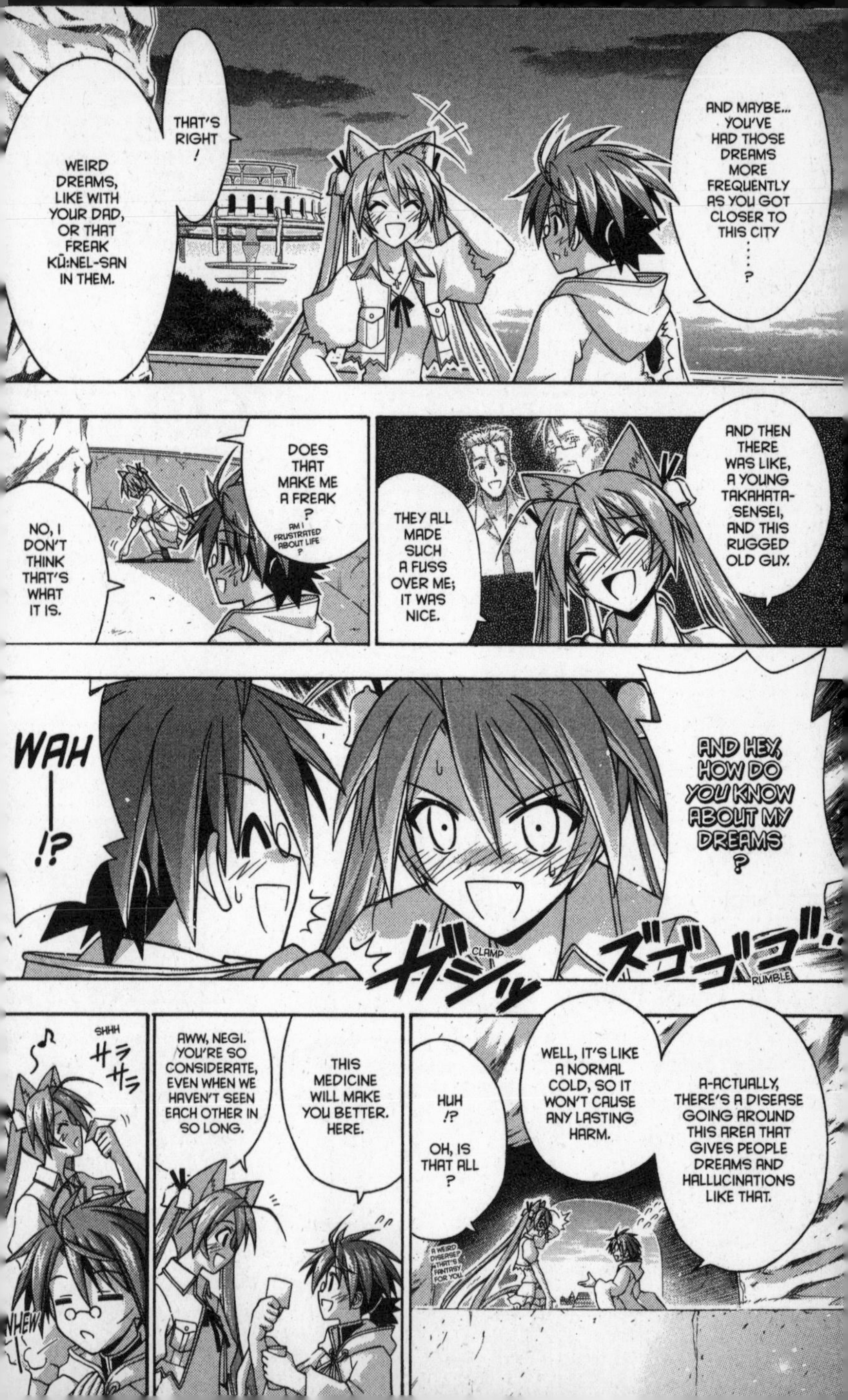
AND MAYBE... YOU'VE HAD THOSE DREAMS MORE FREQUENTLY AS YOU GOT CLOSER TO THIS CITY....?
THAT'S RIGHT!
WEIRD DREAMS, LIKE WITH YOUR DAD, OR THAT FREAK KŪ:NEL-SAN IN THEM.
AND THEN THERE WAS LIKE, A YOUNG TAKAHATA-SENSEI, AND THIS RUGGED OLD GUY.
THEY ALL MADE SUCH A FUSS OVER ME; IT WAS NICE.
DOES THAT MAKE ME A FREAK?
AM I FRUSTRATED ABOUT LIFE?
NO, I DON'T THINK THAT'S WHAT IT IS.
AND HEY, HOW DO YOU KNOW ABOUT MY DREAMS?
ズゴゴゴ RUMBLE
ガシッ CLAMP
WAH—!?
A-ACTUALLY, THERE'S A DISEASE GOING AROUND THIS AREA THAT GIVES PEOPLE DREAMS AND HALLUCINATIONS LIKE THAT.
WELL, IT'S LIKE A NORMAL COLD, SO IT WON'T CAUSE ANY LASTING HARM.
HUH!? OH, IS THAT ALL?
A WEIRD DISEASE? THAT'S FANTASY FOR YOU.
THIS MEDICINE WILL MAKE YOU BETTER. HERE.
AWW, NEGI. YOU'RE SO CONSIDERATE, EVEN WHEN WE HAVEN'T SEEN EACH OTHER IN SO LONG.
SHHH サラサラ

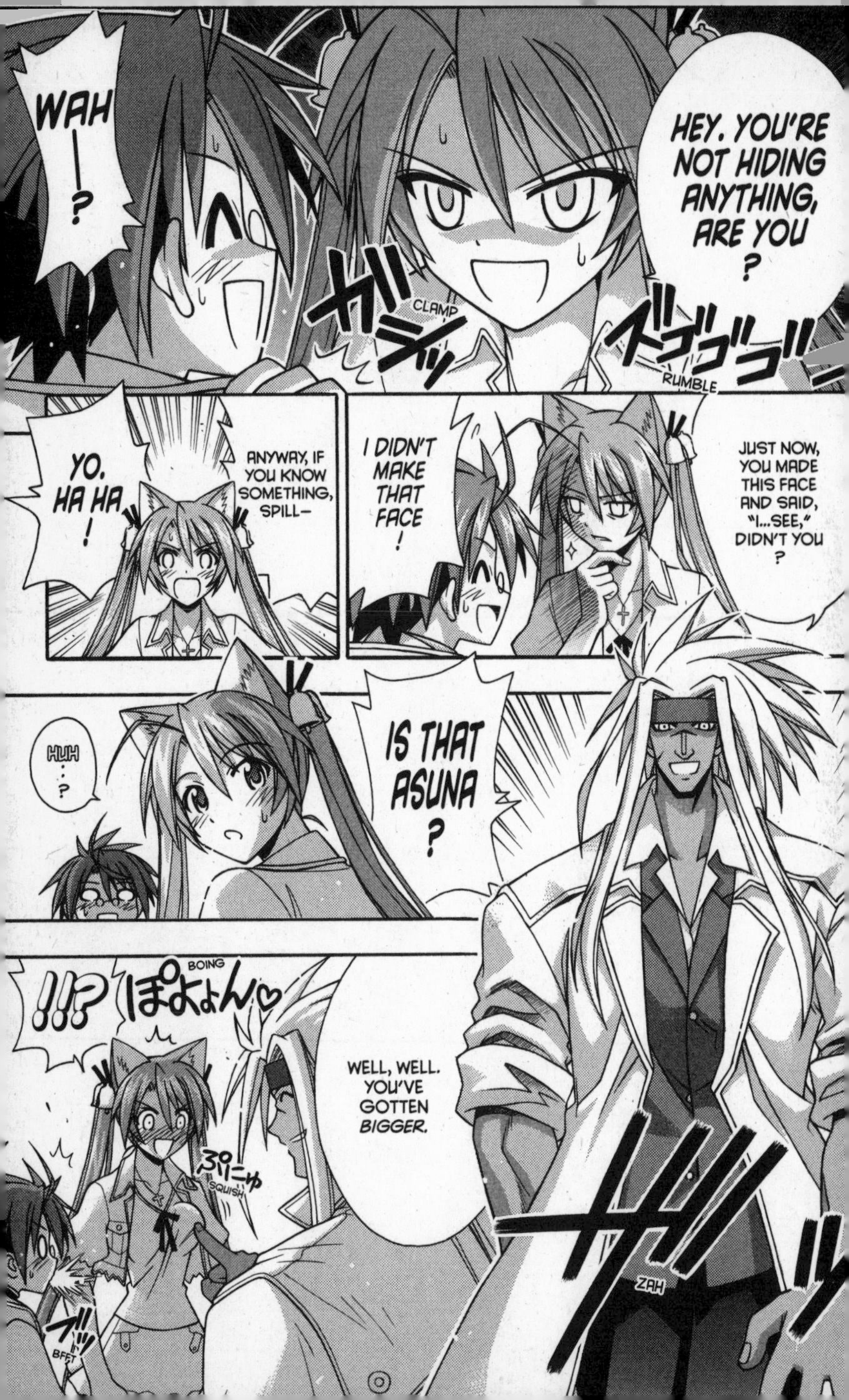
HEY. YOU'RE NOT HIDING ANYTHING, ARE YOU?
WAH—?
ゴゴゴゴ
RUMBLE
ガシッ
CLAMP
JUST NOW, YOU MADE THIS FACE AND SAID, "I...SEE," DIDN'T YOU?
I DIDN'T MAKE THAT FACE!
ANYWAY, IF YOU KNOW SOMETHING, SPILL—
YO. HA HA!
IS THAT ASUNA?
ザッ
ZAH
HUH...?
WELL, WELL. YOU'VE GOTTEN *BIGGER.*
ぽよよん♡
BOING
!!!?
ぷにゅ
SQUISH
ブッ
BFFT

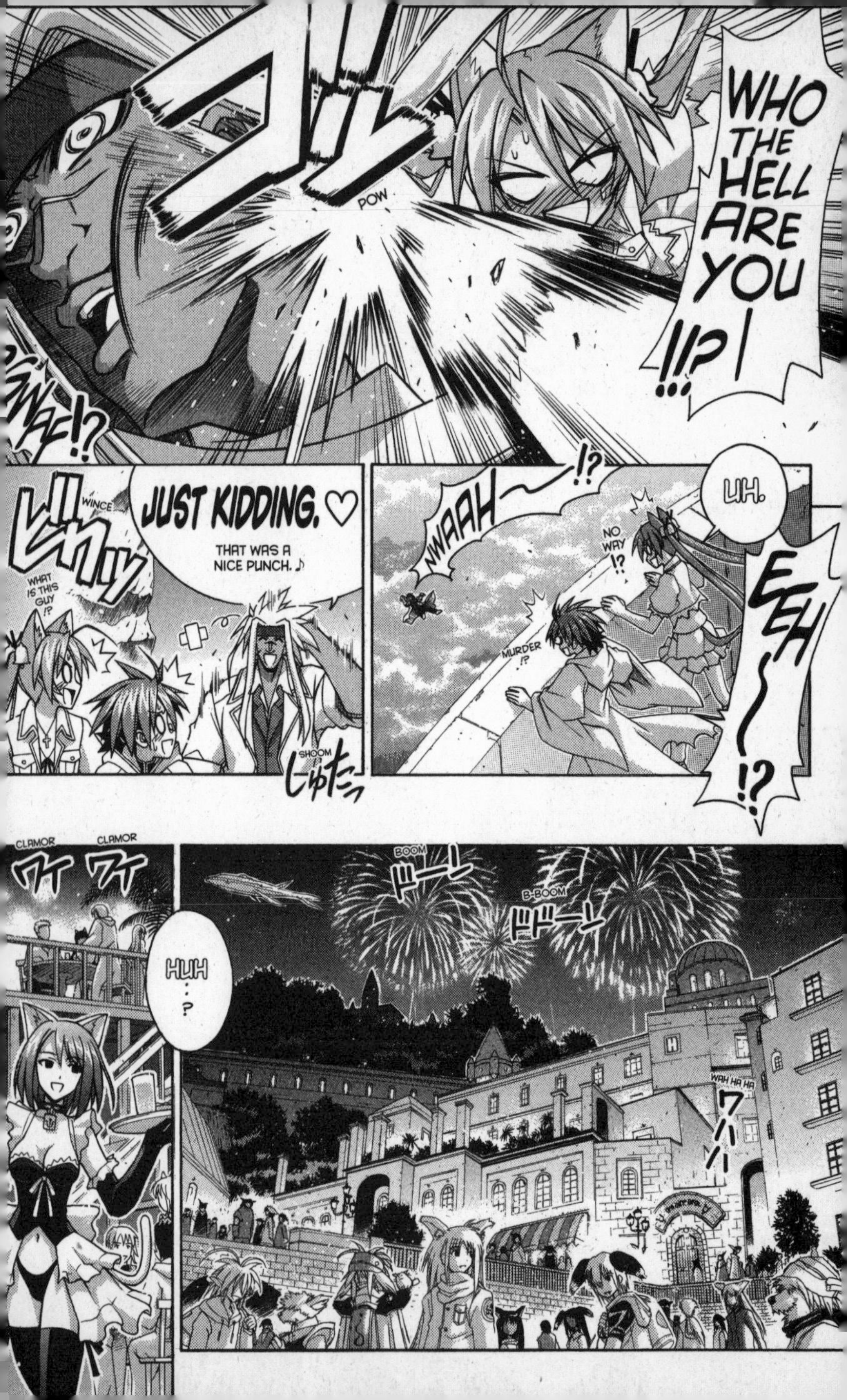
WHO THE HELL ARE YOU !!?
POW
UH.
EEH~~!?
NWAAH~~!?
NO WAY !?
MURDER !?
JUST KIDDING.♡
THAT WAS A NICE PUNCH.♪
WINCE
WHAT IS THIS GUY !?
SHOOM
BOOM
B-BOOM
WAH HA HA
CLAMOR
CLAMOR
HUH...?

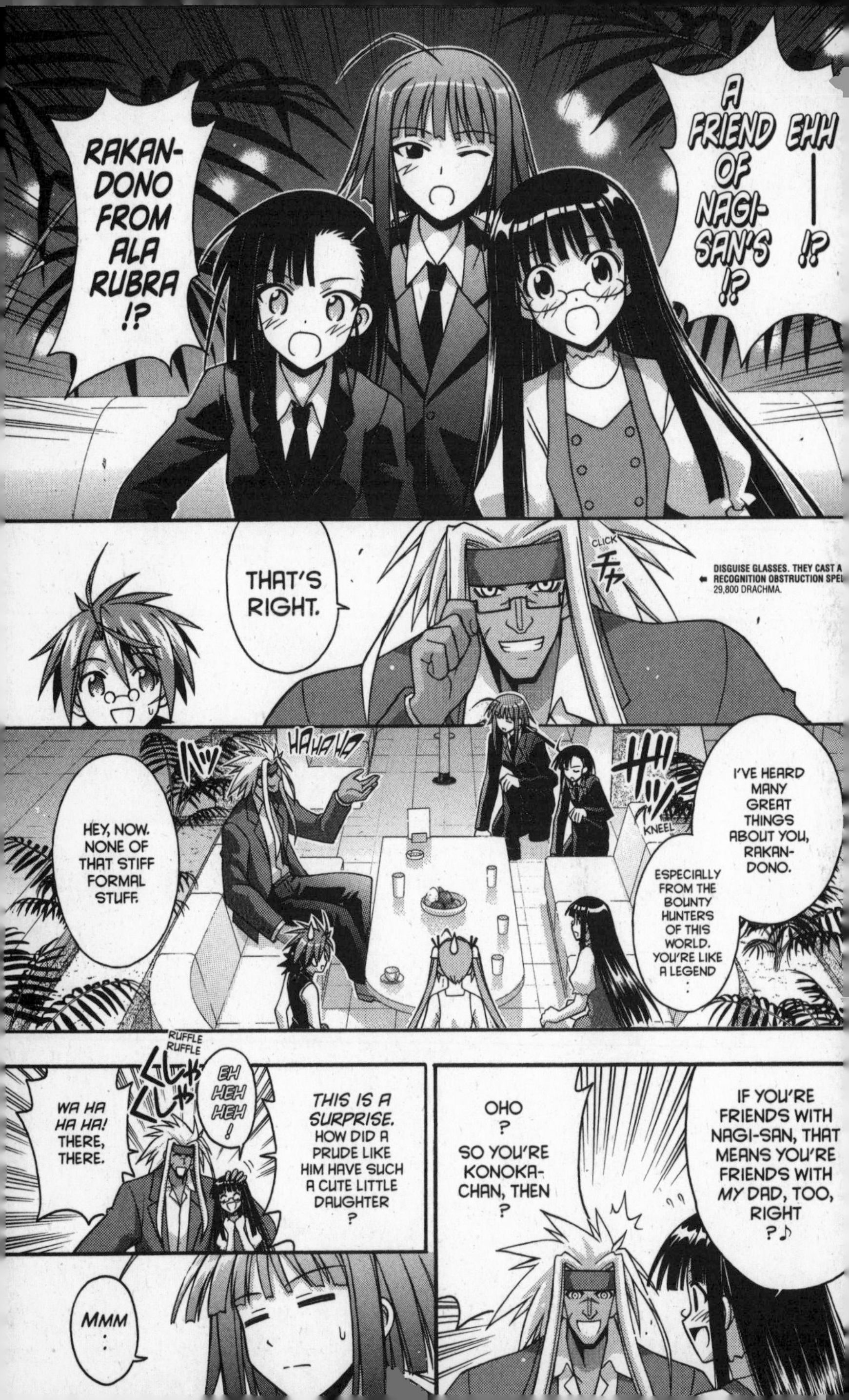

EHH—!?
A FRIEND OF NAGI-SAN'S!?
RAKAN-DONO FROM ALA RUBRA!?
DISGUISE GLASSES. THEY CAST A RECOGNITION OBSTRUCTION SPEL 29,800 DRACHMA.
CLICK
THAT'S RIGHT.
KNEEL
I'VE HEARD MANY GREAT THINGS ABOUT YOU, RAKAN-DONO.
ESPECIALLY FROM THE BOUNTY HUNTERS OF THIS WORLD. YOU'RE LIKE A LEGEND :
HAHAHA
HEY, NOW. NONE OF THAT STIFF FORMAL STUFF.
IF YOU'RE FRIENDS WITH NAGI-SAN, THAT MEANS YOU'RE FRIENDS WITH MY DAD, TOO, RIGHT ?♪
OHO ? SO YOU'RE KONOKA-CHAN, THEN ?
THIS IS A SURPRISE. HOW DID A PRUDE LIKE HIM HAVE SUCH A CUTE LITTLE DAUGHTER ?
EH HEH HEH !
RUFFLE RUFFLE
WA HA HA HA! THERE, THERE.
MMM :

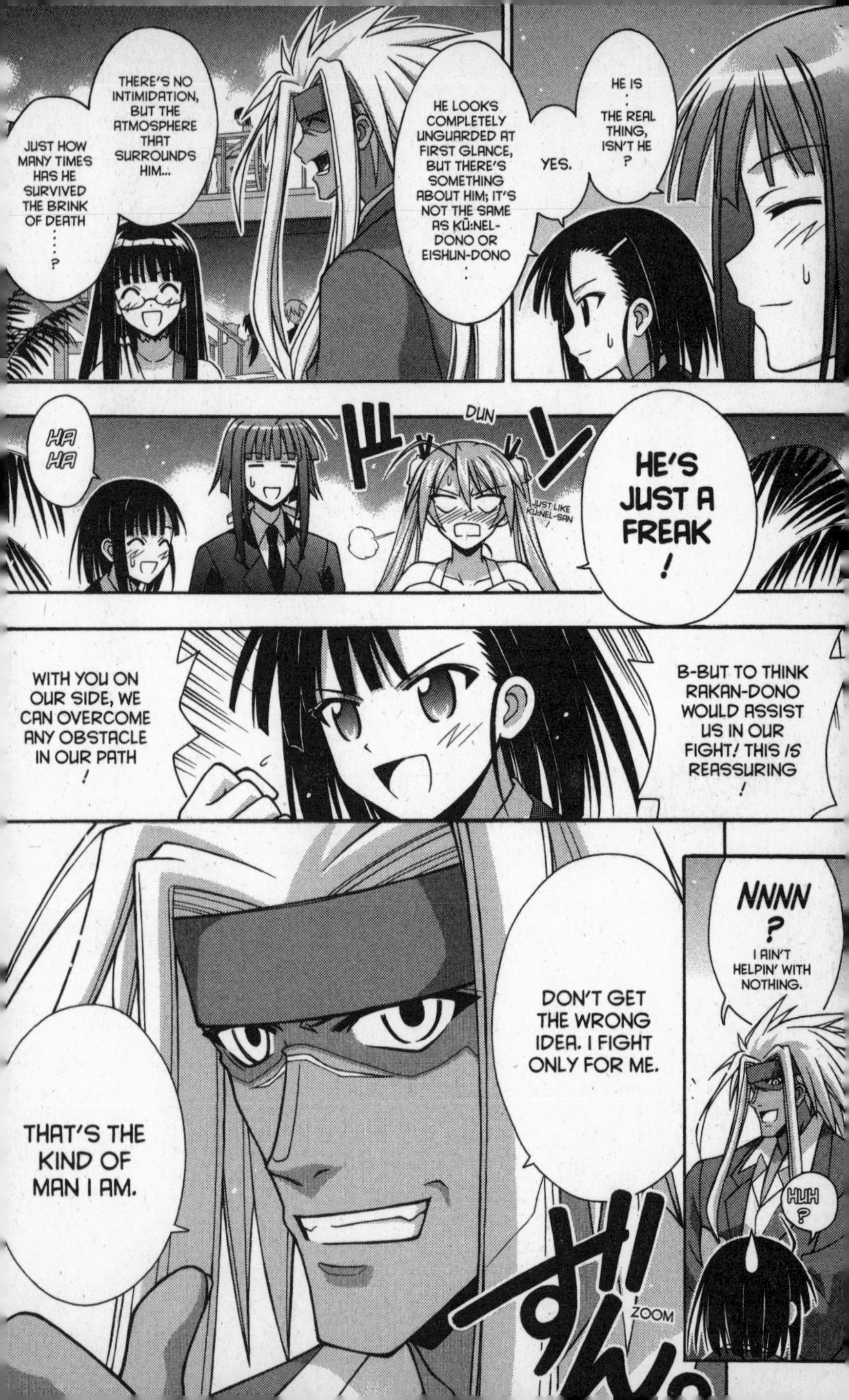
HE IS... THE REAL THING, ISN'T HE?
YES.
HE LOOKS COMPLETELY UNGUARDED AT FIRST GLANCE, BUT THERE'S SOMETHING ABOUT HIM; IT'S NOT THE SAME AS KŪ:NEL-DONO OR EISHUN-DONO...
THERE'S NO INTIMIDATION, BUT THE ATMOSPHERE THAT SURROUNDS HIM...
JUST HOW MANY TIMES HAS HE SURVIVED THE BRINK OF DEATH.....?
HE'S JUST A FREAK!
DUN
JUST LIKE KŪ:NEL-SAN
HA HA
B-BUT TO THINK RAKAN-DONO WOULD ASSIST US IN OUR FIGHT! THIS *IS* REASSURING!
WITH YOU ON OUR SIDE, WE CAN OVERCOME ANY OBSTACLE IN OUR PATH!
NNNN? I AIN'T HELPIN' WITH NOTHING.
HUH?
DON'T GET THE WRONG IDEA. I FIGHT ONLY FOR ME.
THAT'S THE KIND OF MAN I AM.
ZOOM

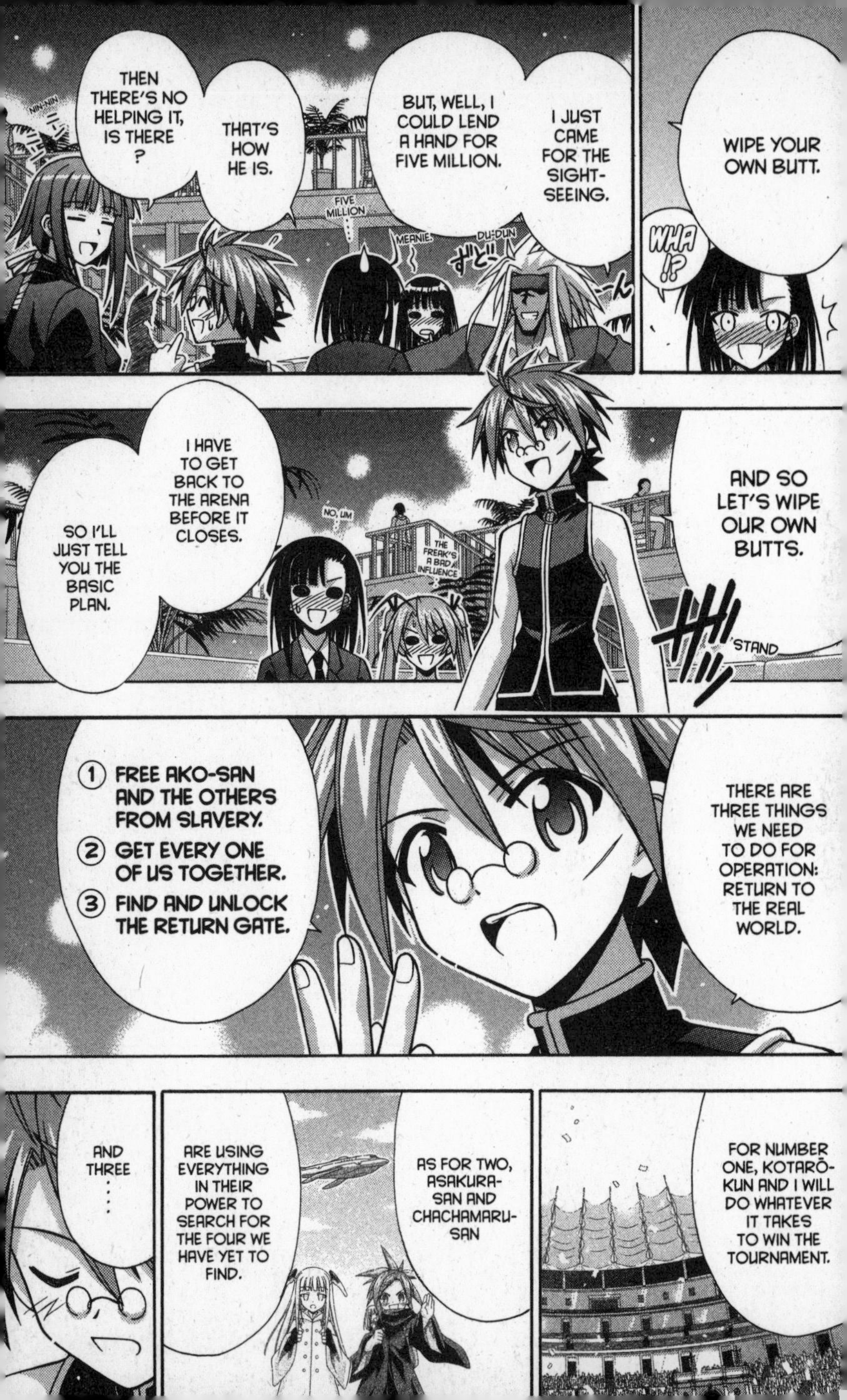
WIPE YOUR OWN BUTT.
WHA !?
I JUST CAME FOR THE SIGHT-SEEING.
BUT, WELL, I COULD LEND A HAND FOR FIVE MILLION.
DU-DUN
MEANIE.
FIVE MILLION . . .
THAT'S HOW HE IS.
THEN THERE'S NO HELPING IT, IS THERE ?
NIN-NIN
AND SO LET'S WIPE OUR OWN BUTTS.
STAND
THE FREAK'S A BAD INFLUENCE
NO, UM
I HAVE TO GET BACK TO THE ARENA BEFORE IT CLOSES.
SO I'LL JUST TELL YOU THE BASIC PLAN.
THERE ARE THREE THINGS WE NEED TO DO FOR OPERATION: RETURN TO THE REAL WORLD.
1 FREE AKO-SAN AND THE OTHERS FROM SLAVERY.
2 GET EVERY ONE OF US TOGETHER.
3 FIND AND UNLOCK THE RETURN GATE.
FOR NUMBER ONE, KOTARŌ-KUN AND I WILL DO WHATEVER IT TAKES TO WIN THE TOURNAMENT.
AS FOR TWO, ASAKURA-SAN AND CHACHAMARU-SAN
ARE USING EVERYTHING IN THEIR POWER TO SEARCH FOR THE FOUR WE HAVE YET TO FIND.
AND THREE . . .

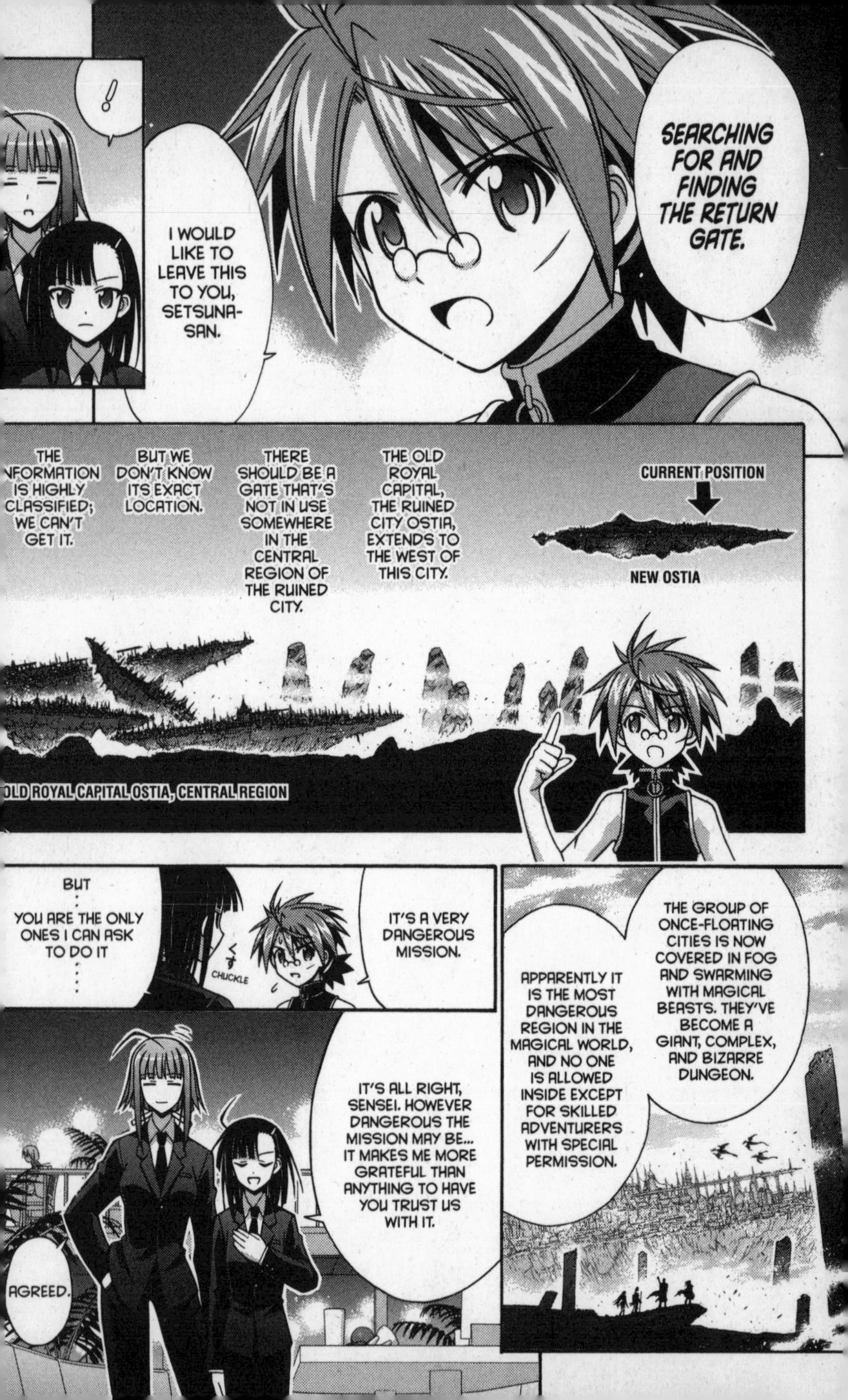
SEARCHING FOR AND FINDING THE RETURN GATE.
I WOULD LIKE TO LEAVE THIS TO YOU, SETSUNA-SAN.
!
CURRENT POSITION
NEW OSTIA
THE OLD ROYAL CAPITAL, THE RUINED CITY OSTIA, EXTENDS TO THE WEST OF THIS CITY.
THERE SHOULD BE A GATE THAT'S NOT IN USE SOMEWHERE IN THE CENTRAL REGION OF THE RUINED CITY.
BUT WE DON'T KNOW ITS EXACT LOCATION.
THE NFORMATION IS HIGHLY CLASSIFIED; WE CAN'T GET IT.
OLD ROYAL CAPITAL OSTIA, CENTRAL REGION
THE GROUP OF ONCE-FLOATING CITIES IS NOW COVERED IN FOG AND SWARMING WITH MAGICAL BEASTS. THEY'VE BECOME A GIANT, COMPLEX, AND BIZARRE DUNGEON.
APPARENTLY IT IS THE MOST DANGEROUS REGION IN THE MAGICAL WORLD, AND NO ONE IS ALLOWED INSIDE EXCEPT FOR SKILLED ADVENTURERS WITH SPECIAL PERMISSION.
IT'S A VERY DANGEROUS MISSION.
くす
CHUCKLE
BUT... YOU ARE THE ONLY ONES I CAN ASK TO DO IT...
IT'S ALL RIGHT, SENSEI. HOWEVER DANGEROUS THE MISSION MAY BE... IT MAKES ME MORE GRATEFUL THAN ANYTHING TO HAVE YOU TRUST US WITH IT.
AGREED.

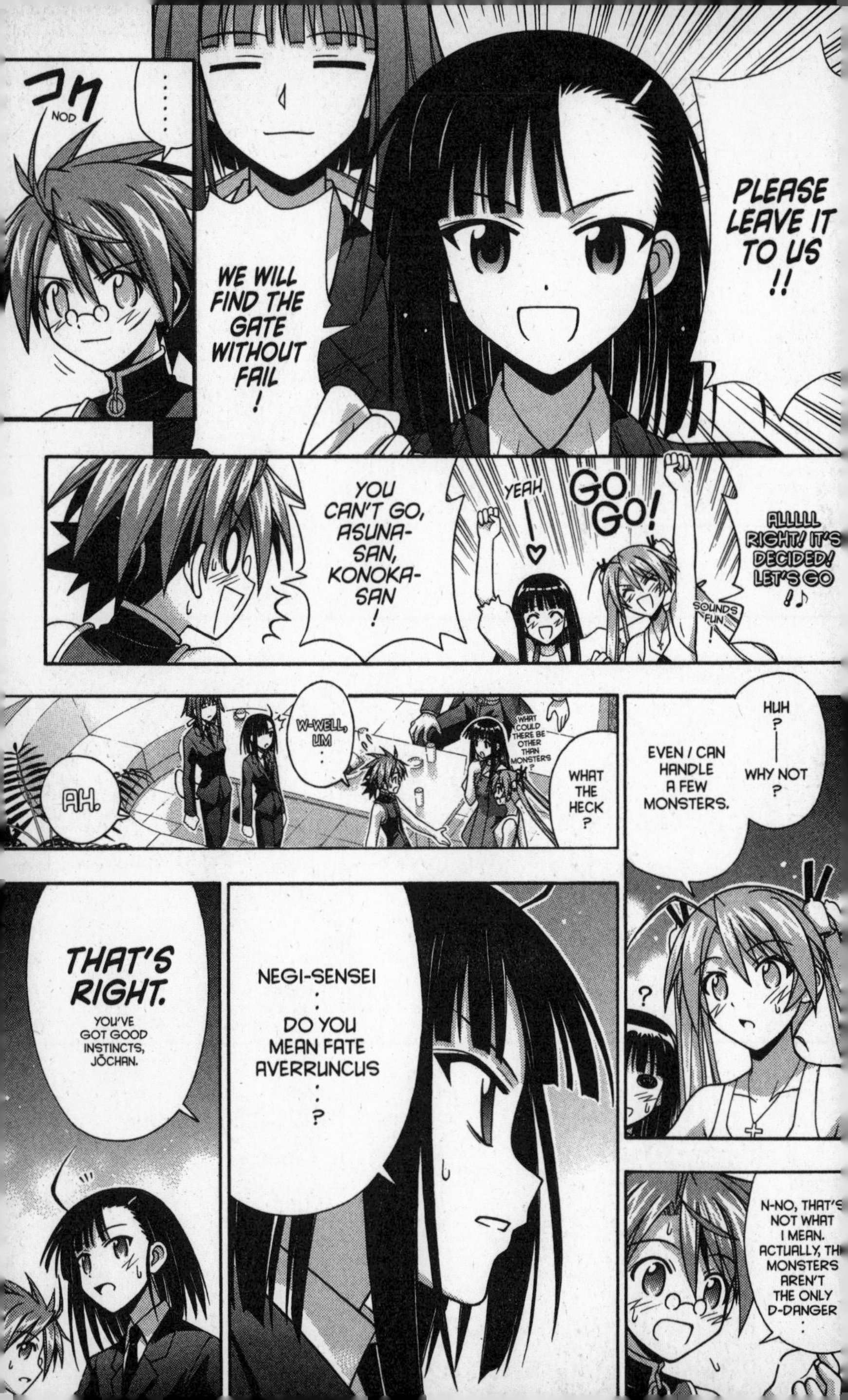
PLEASE LEAVE IT TO US !!
WE WILL FIND THE GATE WITHOUT FAIL !
......
コク NOD
ALLLLLL RIGHT! IT'S DECIDED! LET'S GO !!♪
SOUNDS FUN !
GO GO!
YEAH ! ♥
YOU CAN'T GO, ASUNA-SAN, KONOKA-SAN !
HUH ? — WHY NOT ?
EVEN I CAN HANDLE A FEW MONSTERS.
WHAT THE HECK ?
WHAT COULD THERE BE OTHER THAN MONSTERS ?
W-WELL, UM . . .
AH.
?
N-NO, THAT'S NOT WHAT I MEAN. ACTUALLY, TH MONSTERS AREN'T THE ONLY D-DANGER . . .
NEGI-SENSEI . . . DO YOU MEAN FATE AVERRUNCUS . . . ?
THAT'S RIGHT.
YOU'VE GOT GOOD INSTINCTS, JŌCHAN.

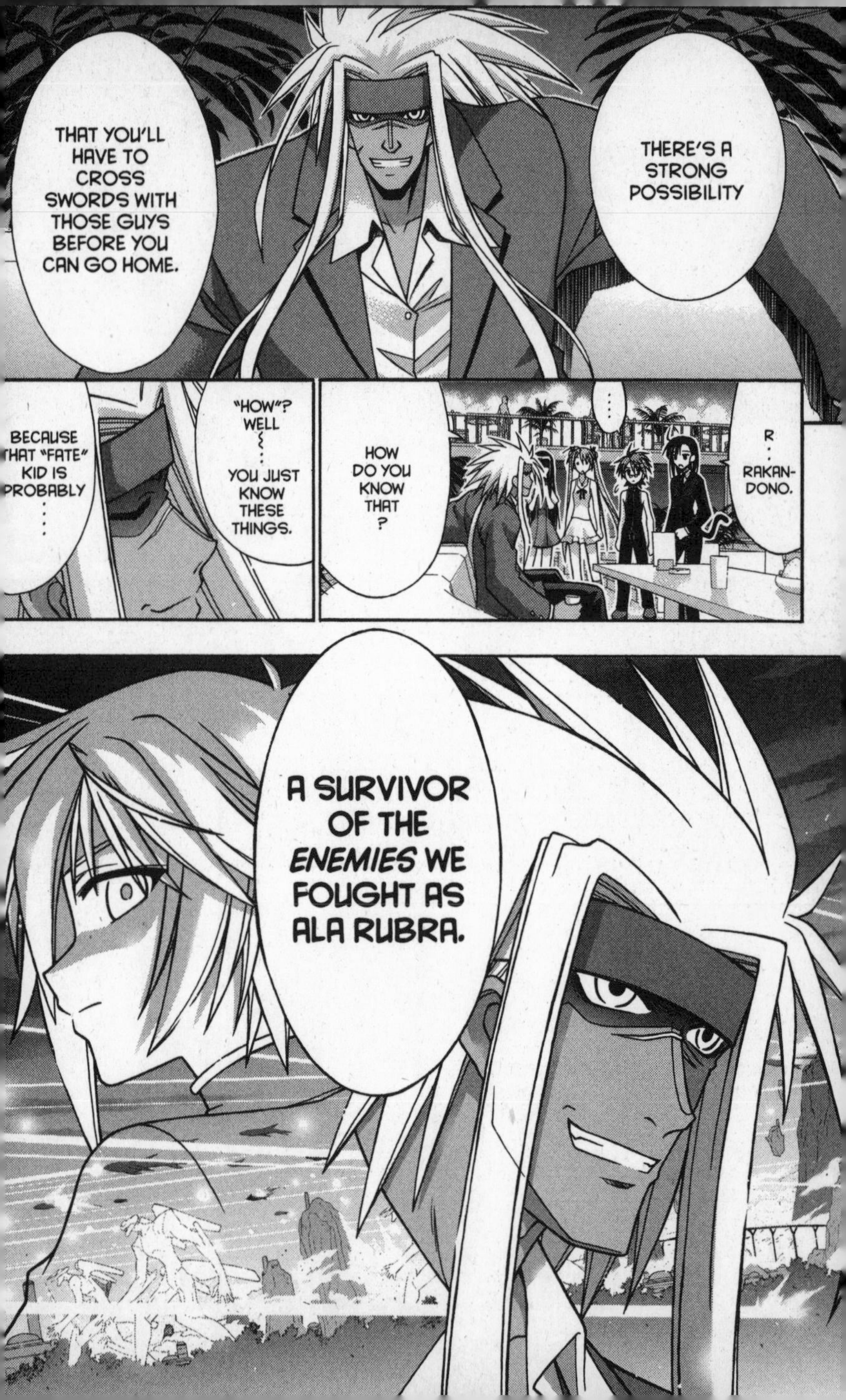
THERE'S A STRONG POSSIBILITY
THAT YOU'LL HAVE TO CROSS SWORDS WITH THOSE GUYS BEFORE YOU CAN GO HOME.
R... RAKAN-DONO.
...
HOW DO YOU KNOW THAT?
"HOW"? WELL ~... YOU JUST KNOW THESE THINGS.
BECAUSE THAT "FATE" KID IS PROBABLY...
A SURVIVOR OF THE ENEMIES WE FOUGHT AS ALA RUBRA.

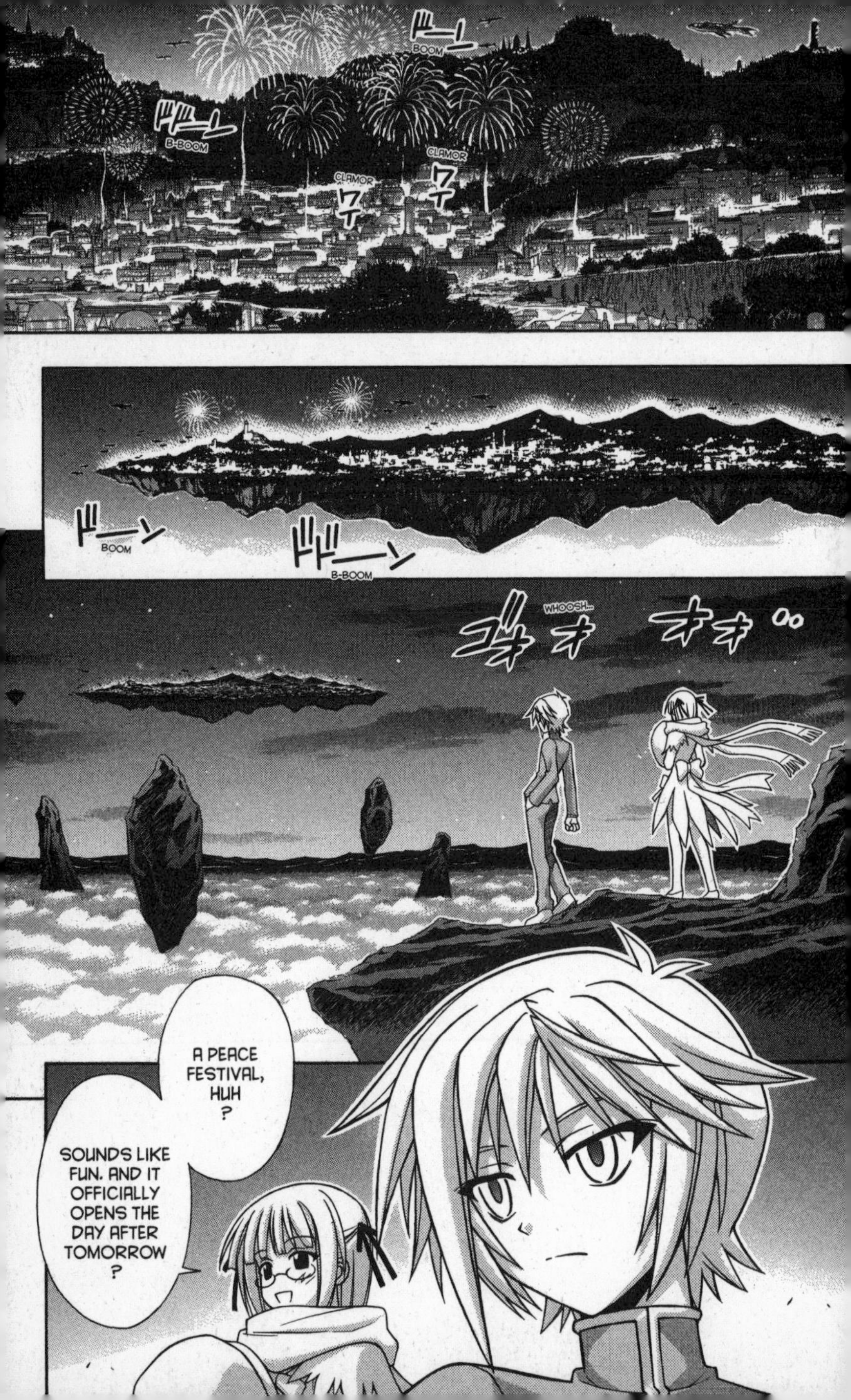
ドーン
BOOM
ドドーン
B-BOOM
ワイ
CLAMOR
ワイ
CLAMOR
ドーン
BOOM
ドドーン
B-BOOM
ゴォォ オォォ。。
WHOOSH...
A PEACE FESTIVAL, HUH?
SOUNDS LIKE FUN. AND IT OFFICIALLY OPENS THE DAY AFTER TOMORROW?

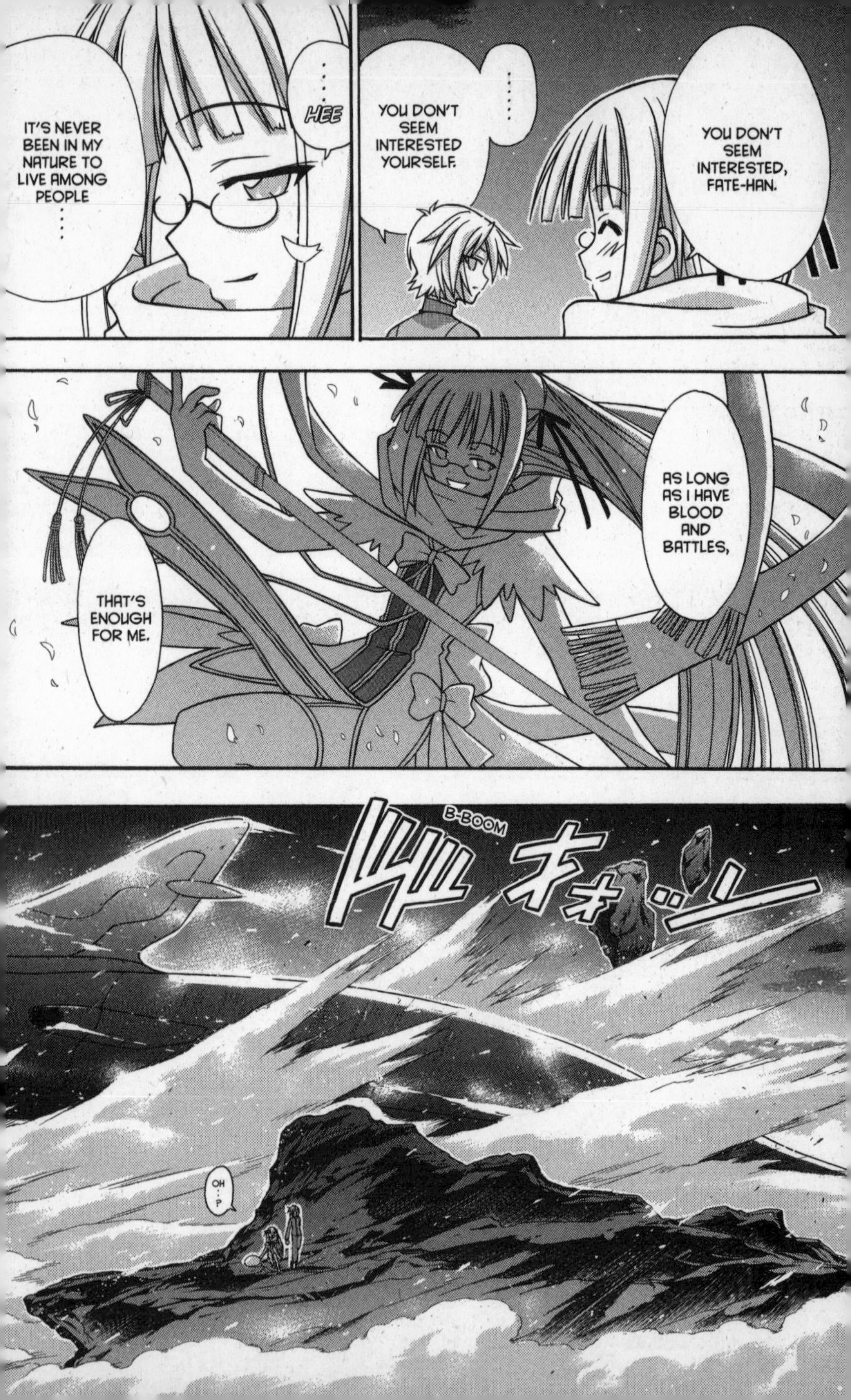

YOU DON'T SEEM INTERESTED, FATE-HAN.
.....
YOU DON'T SEEM INTERESTED YOURSELF.
.....
HEE
IT'S NEVER BEEN IN MY NATURE TO LIVE AMONG PEOPLE .....
AS LONG AS I HAVE BLOOD AND BATTLES,
THAT'S ENOUGH FOR ME.
B-BOOM
OH...?

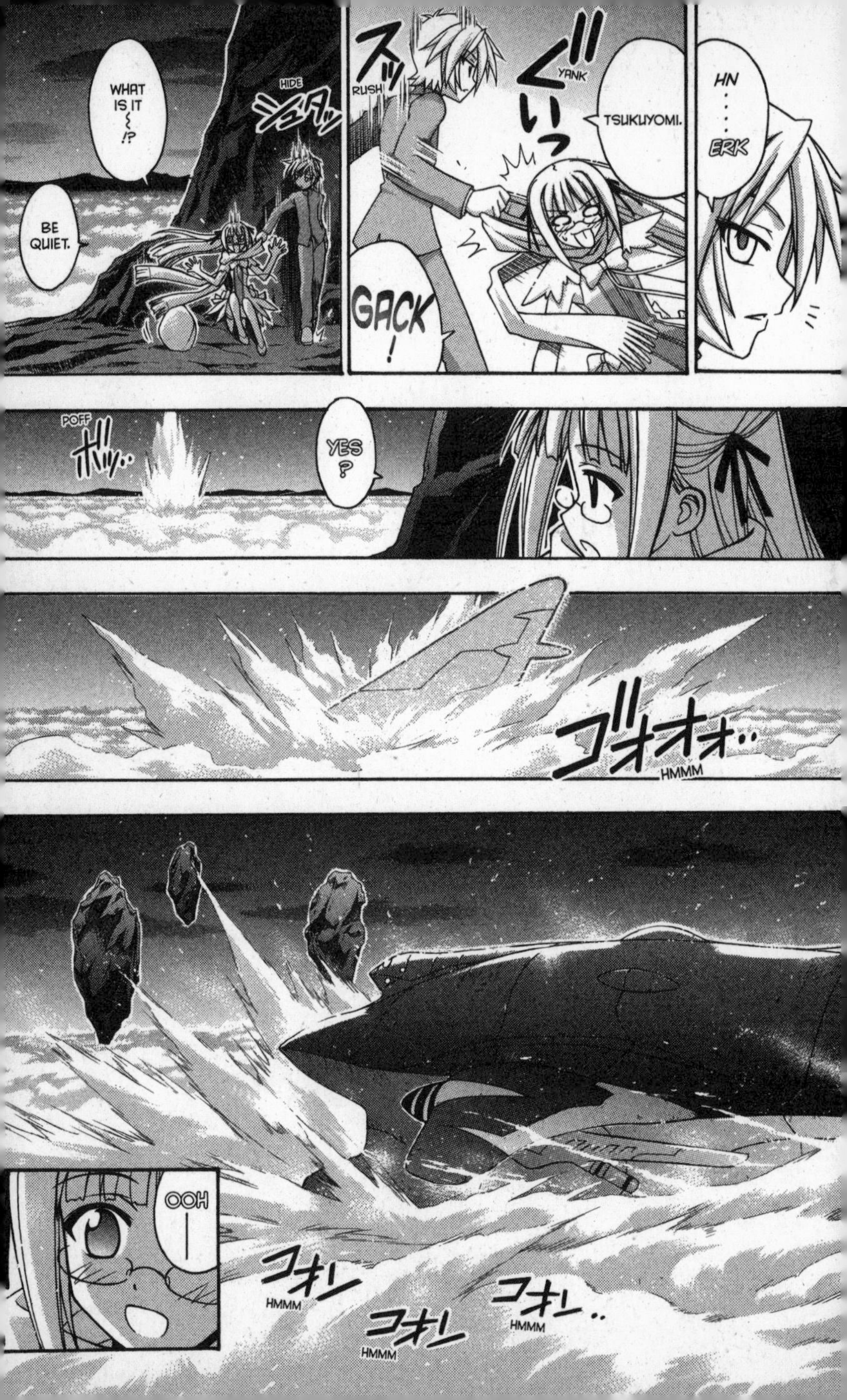
HN... ERK
TSUKUYOMI.
YANK
RUSH
GACK!
HIDE
WHAT IS IT~!?
BE QUIET.
YES?
POFF
HMMM
OOH—
HMMM
HMMM
HMMM

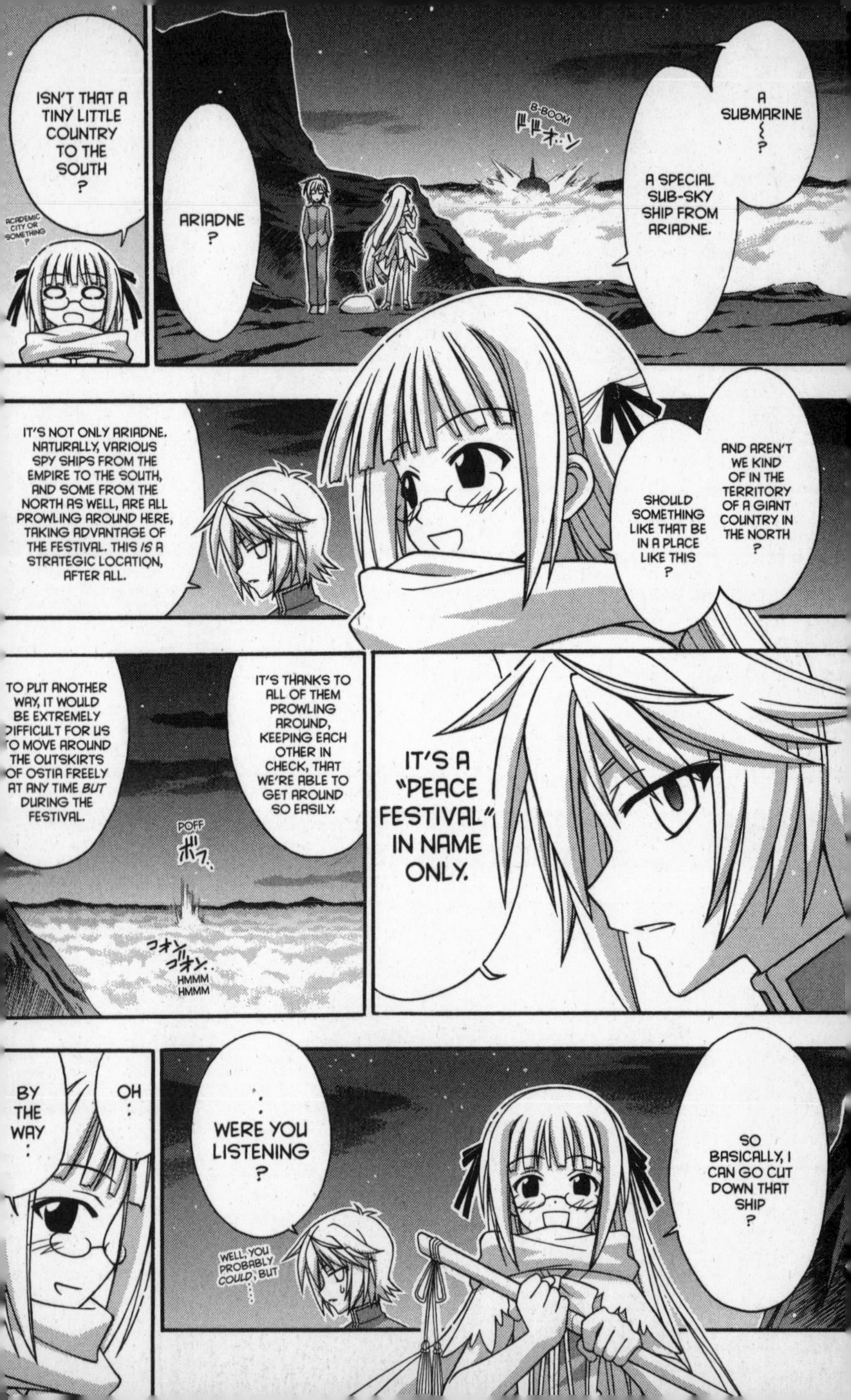
B-BOOM
A SUBMARINE ?
A SPECIAL SUB-SKY SHIP FROM ARIADNE.
ARIADNE ?
ISN'T THAT A TINY LITTLE COUNTRY TO THE SOUTH ?
ACADEMIC CITY OR SOMETHING ?
SHOULD SOMETHING LIKE THAT BE IN A PLACE LIKE THIS ?
AND AREN'T WE KIND OF IN THE TERRITORY OF A GIANT COUNTRY IN THE NORTH ?
IT'S NOT ONLY ARIADNE. NATURALLY, VARIOUS SPY SHIPS FROM THE EMPIRE TO THE SOUTH, AND SOME FROM THE NORTH AS WELL, ARE ALL PROWLING AROUND HERE, TAKING ADVANTAGE OF THE FESTIVAL. THIS *IS* A STRATEGIC LOCATION, AFTER ALL.
IT'S A "PEACE FESTIVAL" IN NAME ONLY.
IT'S THANKS TO ALL OF THEM PROWLING AROUND, KEEPING EACH OTHER IN CHECK, THAT WE'RE ABLE TO GET AROUND SO EASILY.
TO PUT ANOTHER WAY, IT WOULD BE EXTREMELY DIFFICULT FOR US TO MOVE AROUND THE OUTSKIRTS OF OSTIA FREELY AT ANY TIME *BUT* DURING THE FESTIVAL.
POFF
HMMM HMMM
SO BASICALLY, I CAN GO CUT DOWN THAT SHIP ?
... WERE YOU LISTENING ?
WELL, YOU PROBABLY *COULD*, BUT ...
OH ...
BY THE WAY ...

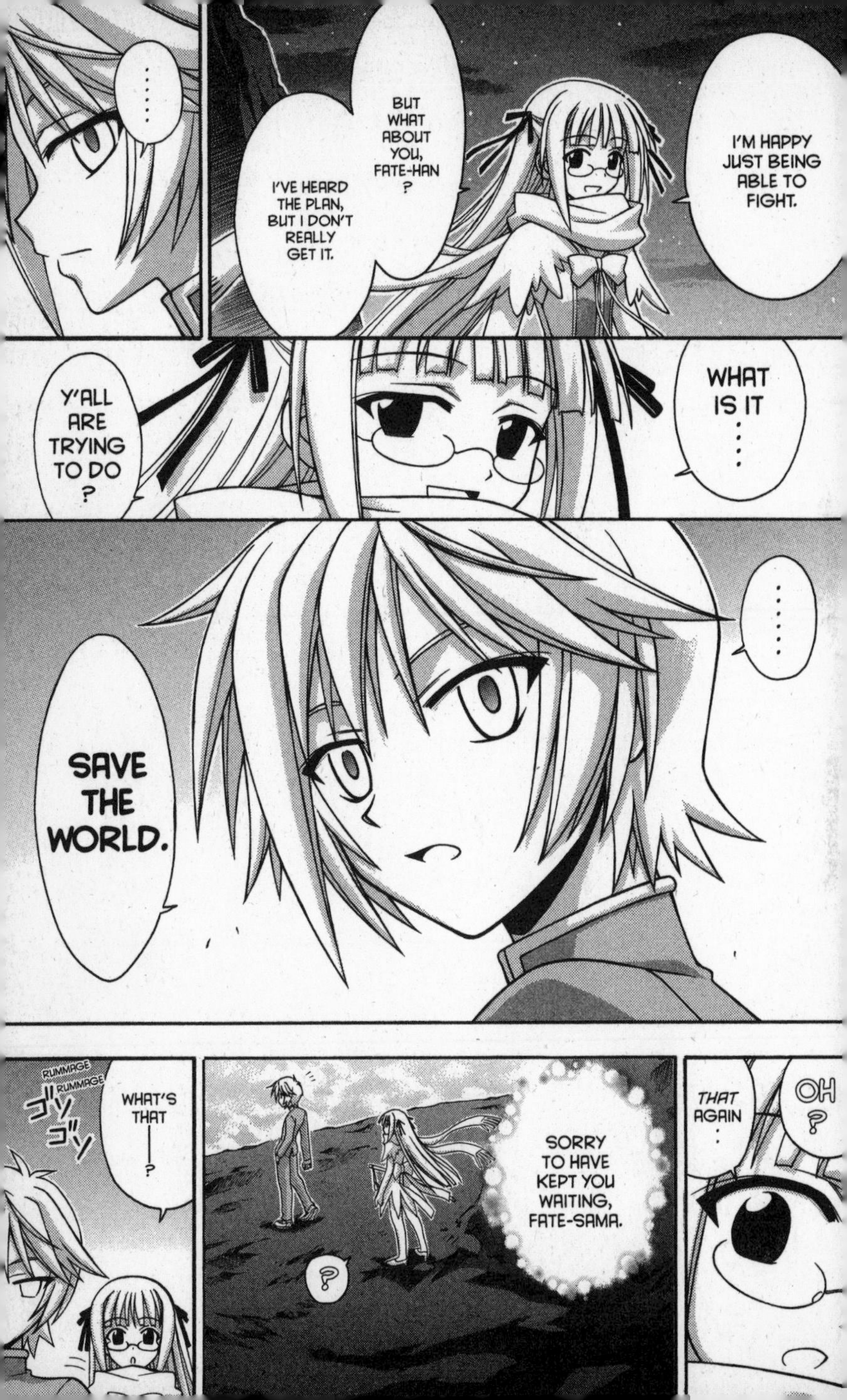
I'M HAPPY JUST BEING ABLE TO FIGHT.
BUT WHAT ABOUT YOU, FATE-HAN?
I'VE HEARD THE PLAN, BUT I DON'T REALLY GET IT.
......
WHAT IS IT ....
Y'ALL ARE TRYING TO DO?
......
SAVE THE WORLD.
OH?
THAT AGAIN :
SORRY TO HAVE KEPT YOU WAITING, FATE-SAMA.
?
RUMMAGE RUMMAGE
ゴソ ゴソ
WHAT'S THAT—?

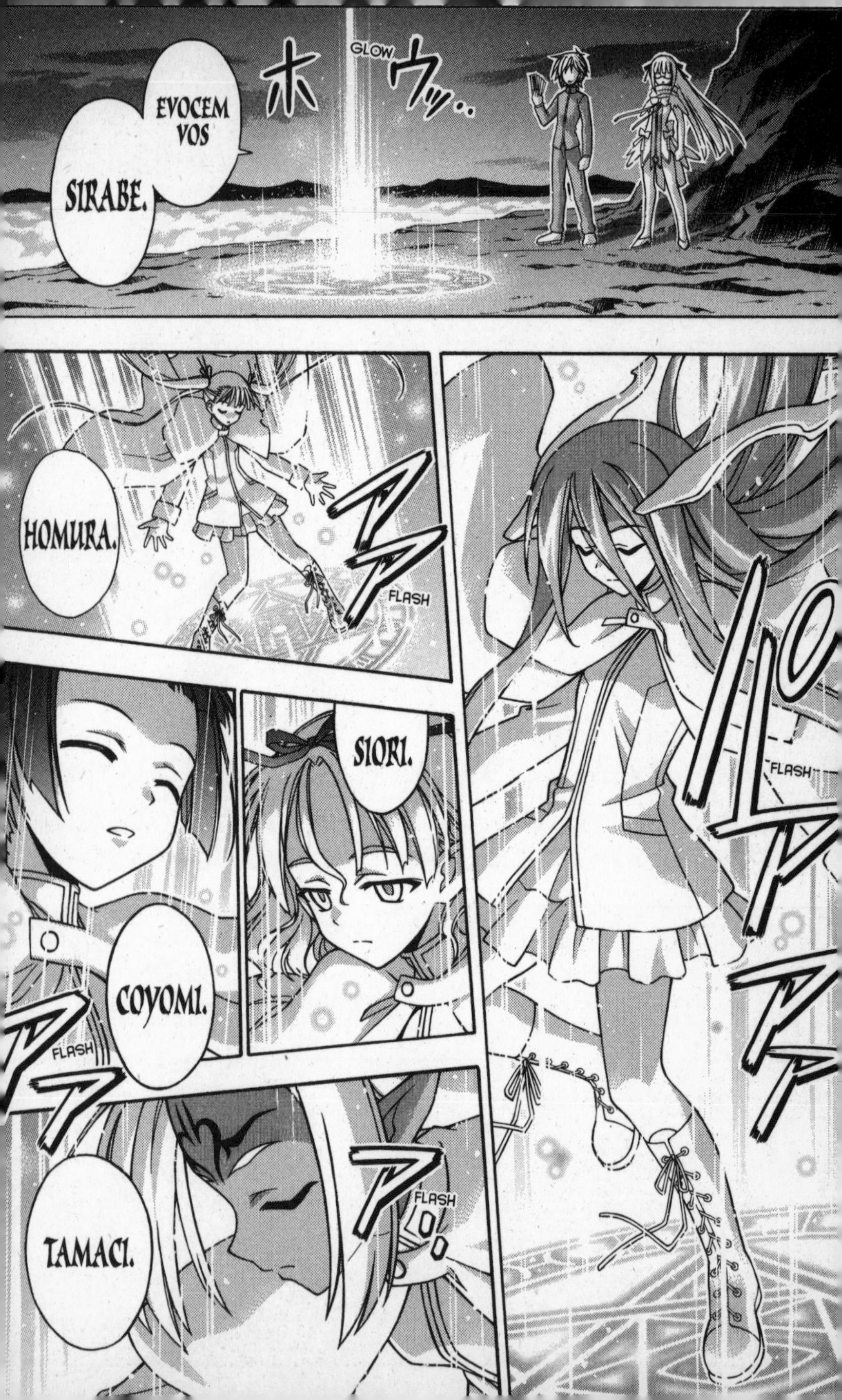
ホウッ..
GLOW
EVOCEM VOS
SIRABE.
パアア
FLASH
HOMURA.
FLASH
SIORI.
COYOMI.
FLASH
TAMACI.
FLASH

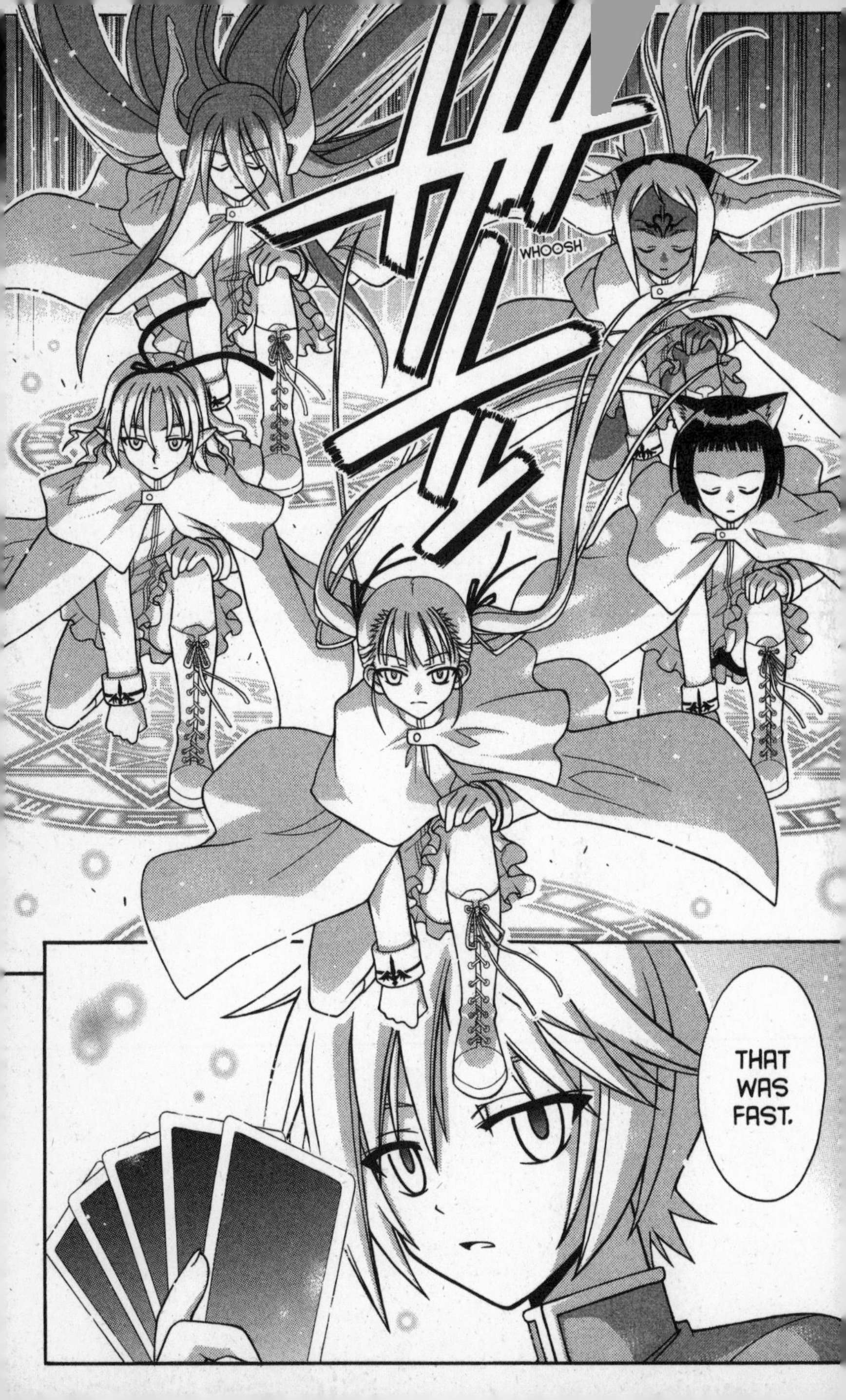
WHOOSH
THAT WAS FAST.

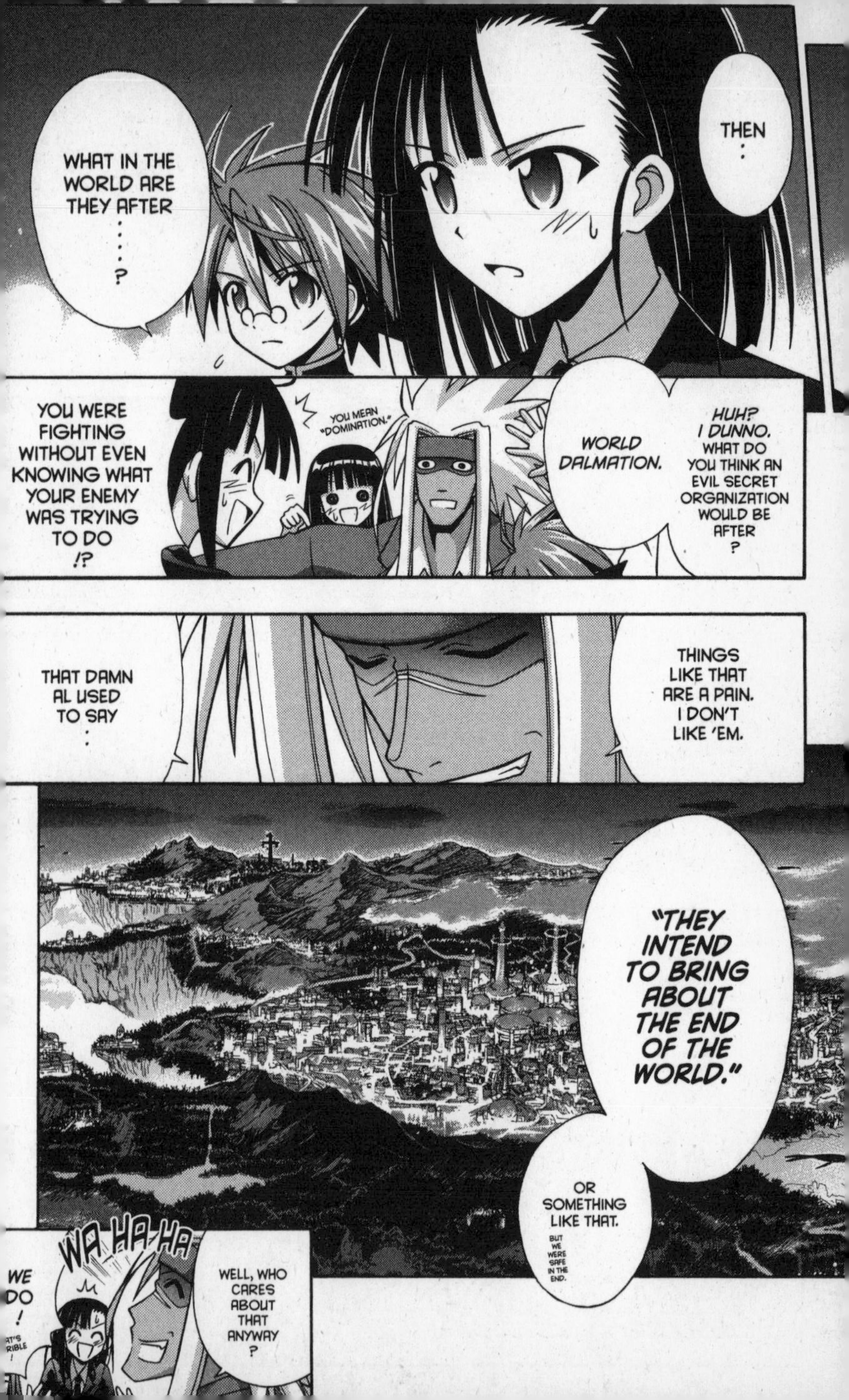
THEN:
WHAT IN THE WORLD ARE THEY AFTER.....?
HUH? I DUNNO. WHAT DO YOU THINK AN EVIL SECRET ORGANIZATION WOULD BE AFTER?
WORLD DALMATION.
YOU MEAN "DOMINATION."
YOU WERE FIGHTING WITHOUT EVEN KNOWING WHAT YOUR ENEMY WAS TRYING TO DO!?
THINGS LIKE THAT ARE A PAIN. I DON'T LIKE 'EM.
THAT DAMN AL USED TO SAY:
"THEY INTEND TO BRING ABOUT THE END OF THE WORLD."
OR SOMETHING LIKE THAT.
BUT WE WERE SAFE IN THE END.
WELL, WHO CARES ABOUT THAT ANYWAY?
WA HA HA
WE DO!

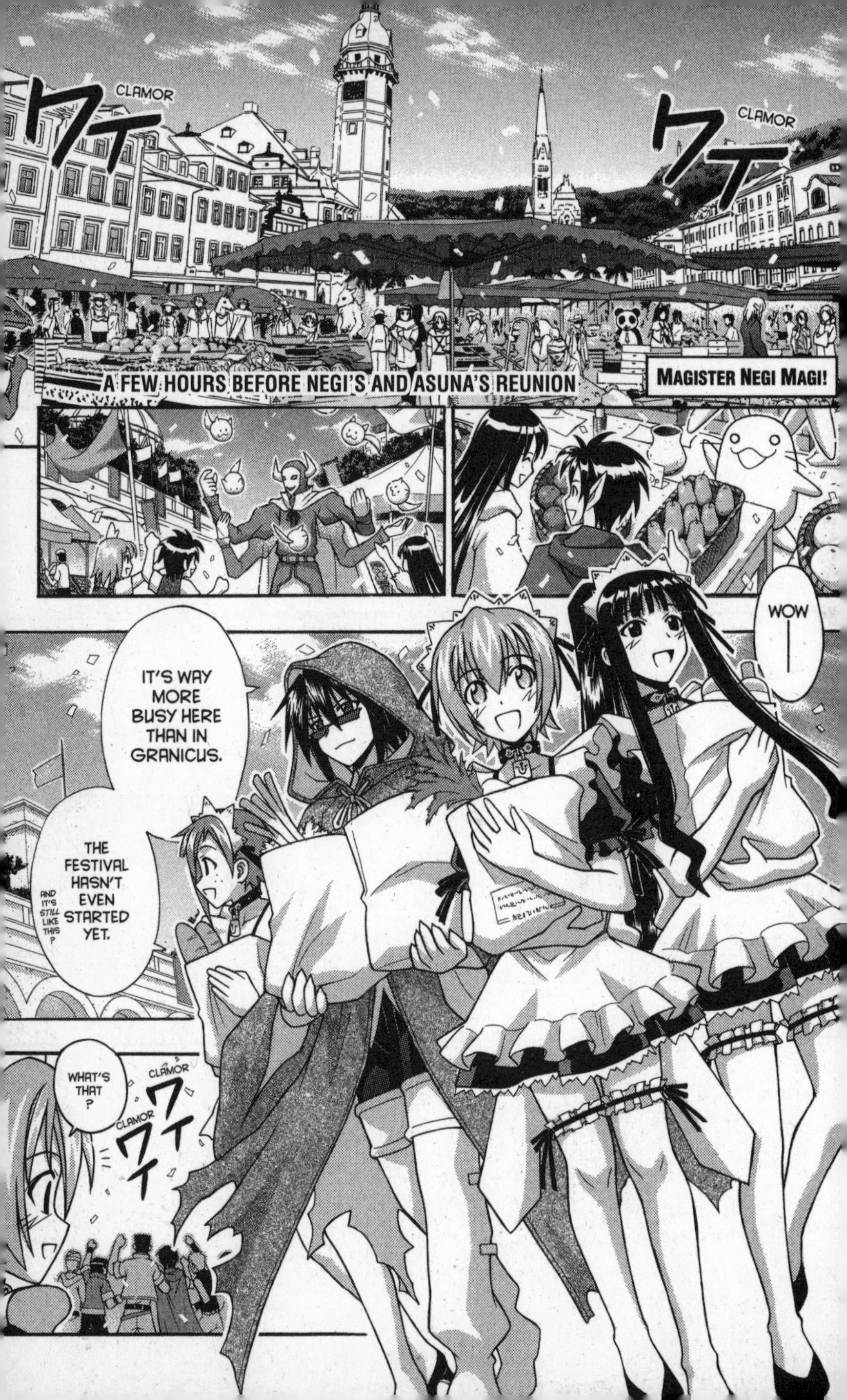
CLAMOR
CLAMOR
MAGISTER NEGI MAGI!
A FEW HOURS BEFORE NEGI'S AND ASUNA'S REUNION
WOW
IT'S WAY MORE BUSY HERE THAN IN GRANICUS.
THE FESTIVAL HASN'T EVEN STARTED YET.
AND IT'S STILL LIKE THIS?
CLAMOR
WHAT'S THAT?
CLAMOR

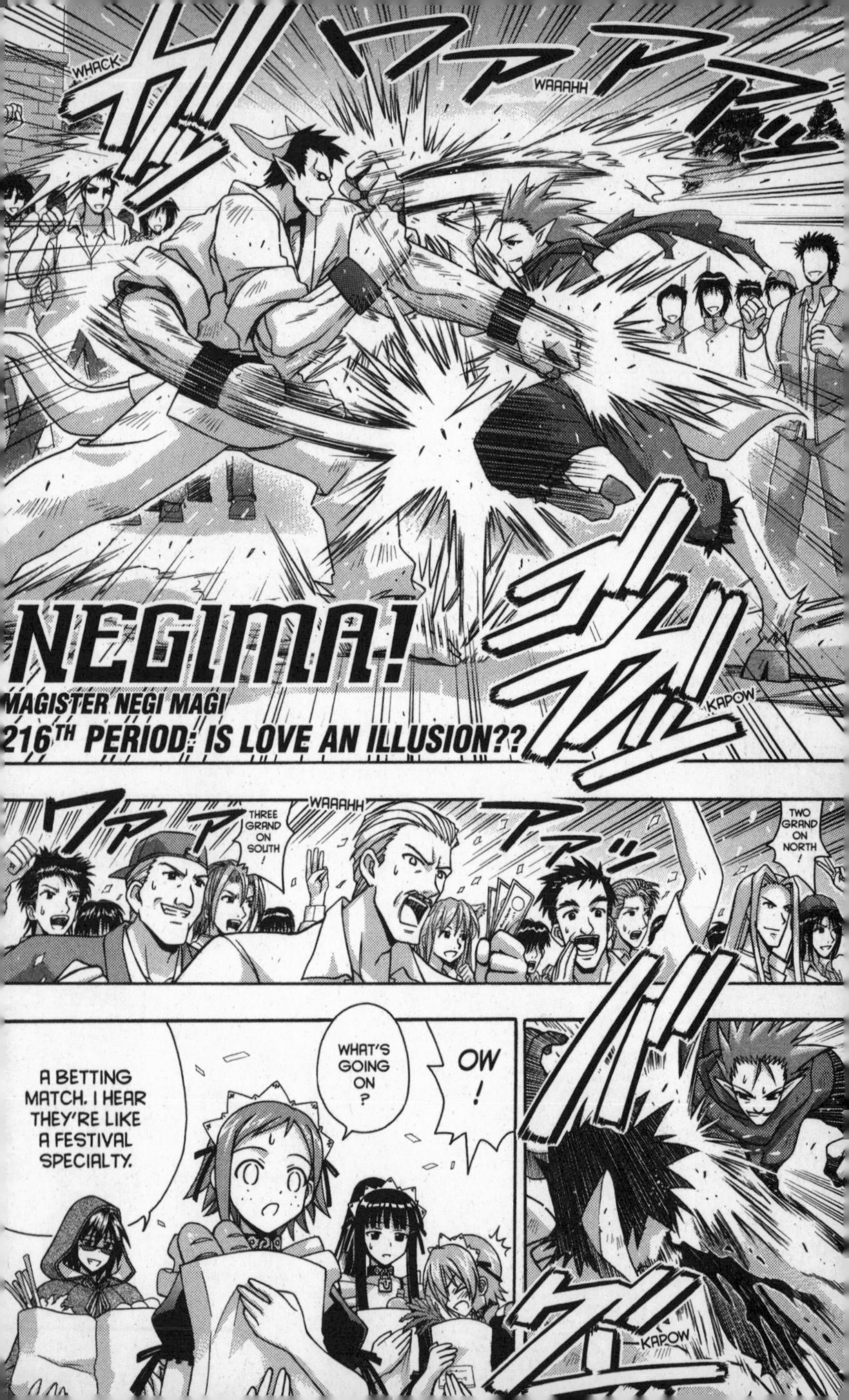
WAAAHH
WHACK
NEGIMA!
MAGISTER NEGI MAGI
216TH PERIOD: IS LOVE AN ILLUSION??
KAPOW
TWO GRAND ON NORTH!
WAAAHH
THREE GRAND ON SOUTH!
KAPOW
OW!
WHAT'S GOING ON?
A BETTING MATCH. I HEAR THEY'RE LIKE A FESTIVAL SPECIALTY.

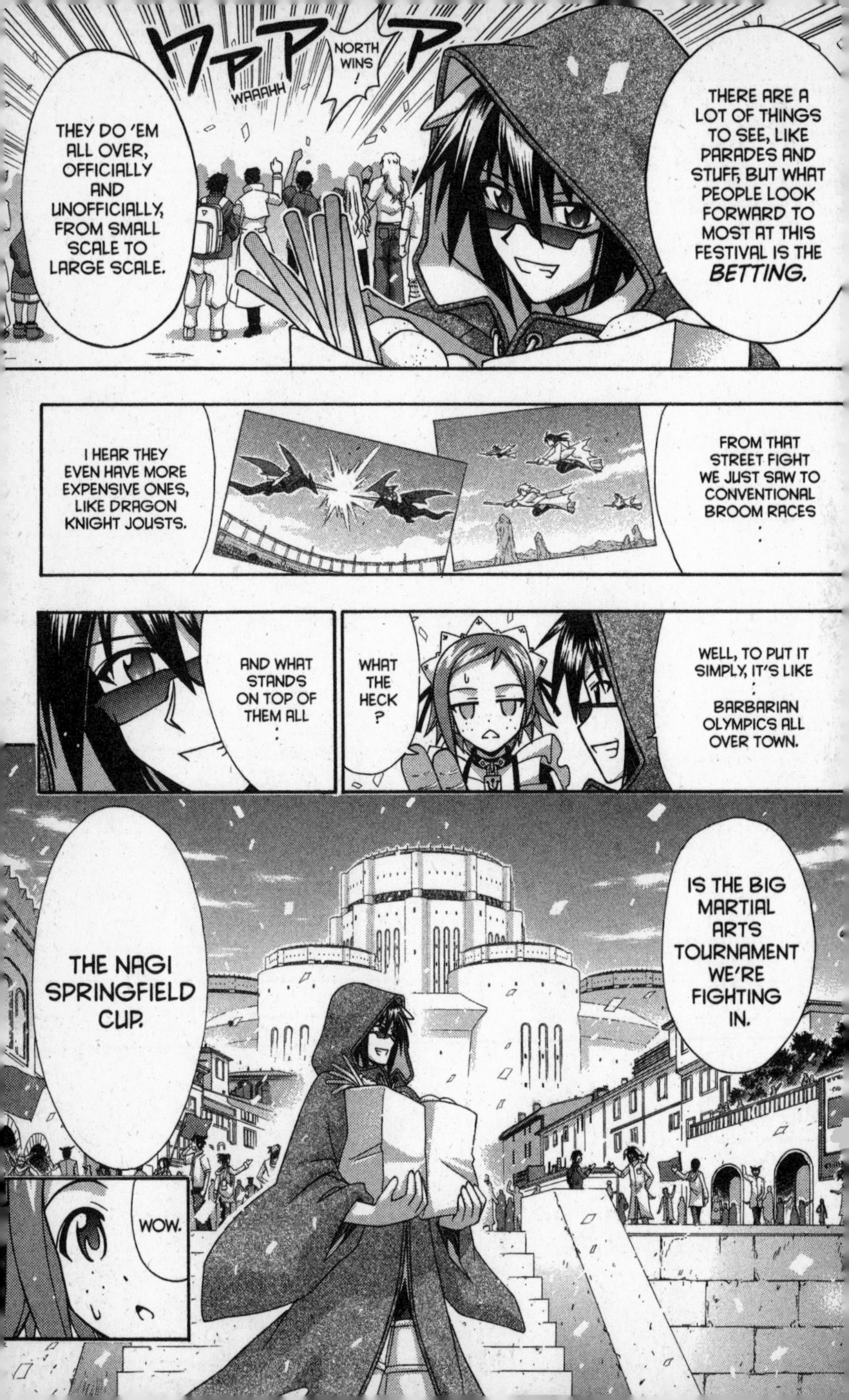
NORTH WINS!
WAAAHH
THERE ARE A LOT OF THINGS TO SEE, LIKE PARADES AND STUFF, BUT WHAT PEOPLE LOOK FORWARD TO MOST AT THIS FESTIVAL IS THE *BETTING.*
THEY DO 'EM ALL OVER, OFFICIALLY AND UNOFFICIALLY, FROM SMALL SCALE TO LARGE SCALE.
FROM THAT STREET FIGHT WE JUST SAW TO CONVENTIONAL BROOM RACES...
I HEAR THEY EVEN HAVE MORE EXPENSIVE ONES, LIKE DRAGON KNIGHT JOUSTS.
WELL, TO PUT IT SIMPLY, IT'S LIKE... BARBARIAN OLYMPICS ALL OVER TOWN.
WHAT THE HECK?
AND WHAT STANDS ON TOP OF THEM ALL...
IS THE BIG MARTIAL ARTS TOURNAMENT WE'RE FIGHTING IN.
THE NAGI SPRINGFIELD CUP.
WOW.

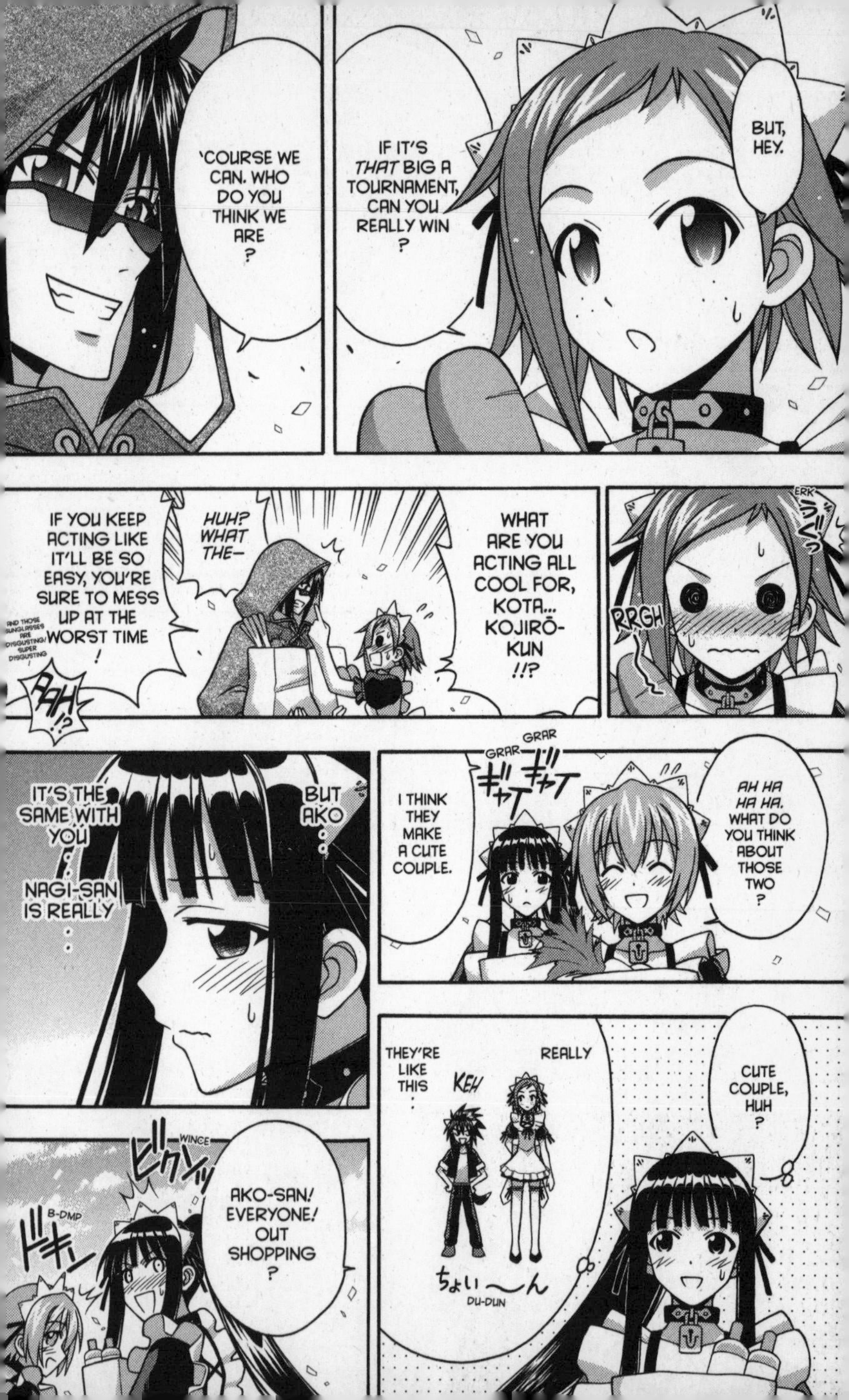
BUT, HEY.
IF IT'S *THAT* BIG A TOURNAMENT, CAN YOU REALLY WIN?
'COURSE WE CAN. WHO DO YOU THINK WE ARE?
ERK
RRGH
WHAT ARE YOU ACTING ALL COOL FOR, KOTA... KOJIRŌ-KUN!!?
HUH? WHAT THE–
IF YOU KEEP ACTING LIKE IT'LL BE SO EASY, YOU'RE SURE TO MESS UP AT THE WORST TIME!
AND THOSE SUNGLASSES ARE DISGUSTING! SUPER DISGUSTING!
AAH!!?
AH HA HA HA. WHAT DO YOU THINK ABOUT THOSE TWO?
GRAR GRAR
I THINK THEY MAKE A CUTE COUPLE.
CUTE COUPLE, HUH?
REALLY
THEY'RE LIKE THIS:
KEH
ちょい～ん
DU-DUN
BUT AKO...
IT'S THE SAME WITH YOU...
NAGI-SAN IS REALLY...
WINCE
AKO-SAN! EVERYONE! OUT SHOPPING?
B-DMP

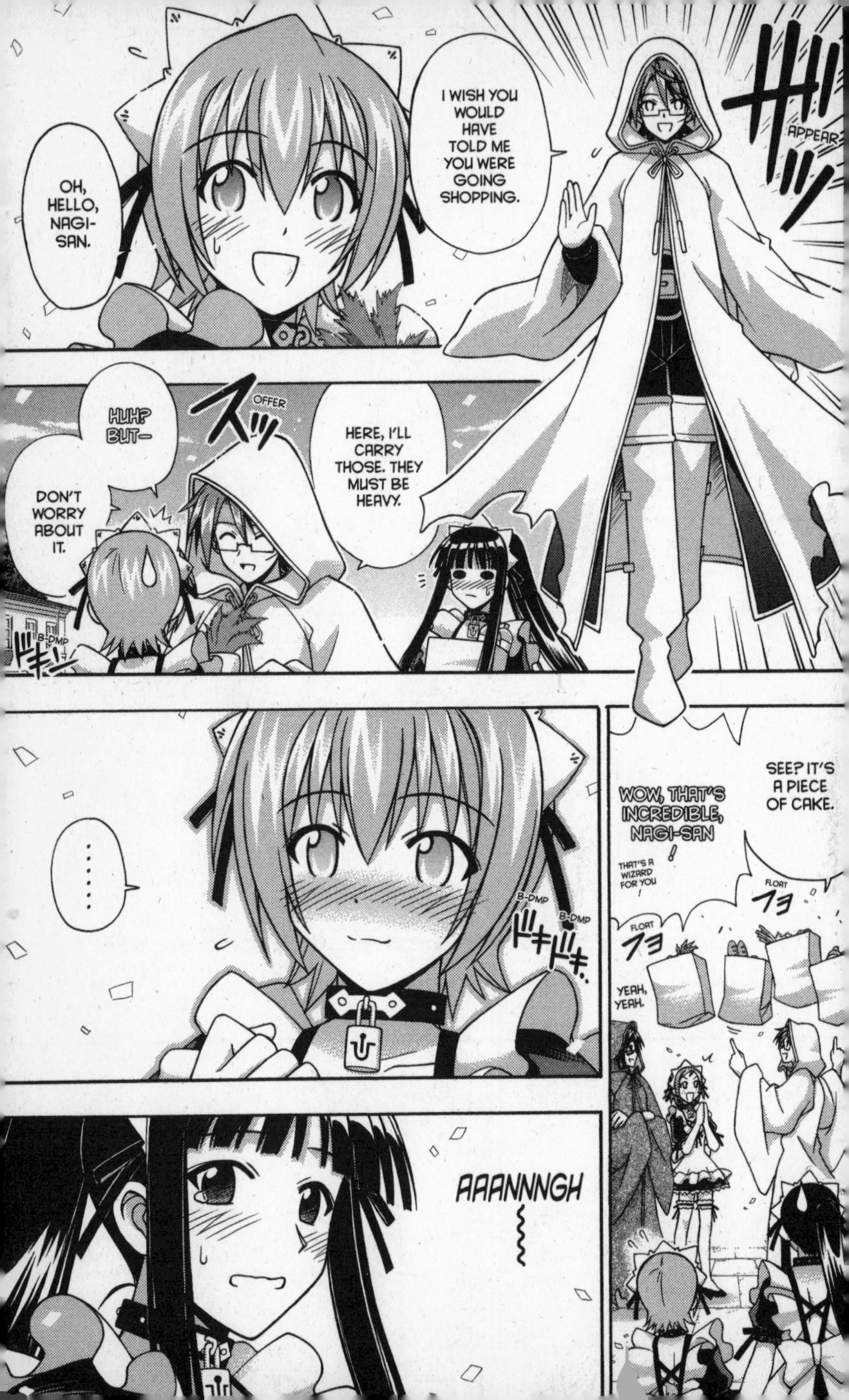
APPEAR
I WISH YOU WOULD HAVE TOLD ME YOU WERE GOING SHOPPING.
OH, HELLO, NAGI-SAN.
OFFER
HERE, I'LL CARRY THOSE. THEY MUST BE HEAVY.
HUH? BUT—
DON'T WORRY ABOUT IT.
B-DMP
SEE? IT'S A PIECE OF CAKE.
WOW, THAT'S INCREDIBLE, NAGI-SAN!
THAT'S A WIZARD FOR YOU!
FLOAT
FLOAT
YEAH, YEAH.
......
B-DMP
B-DMP
AAANNNGH

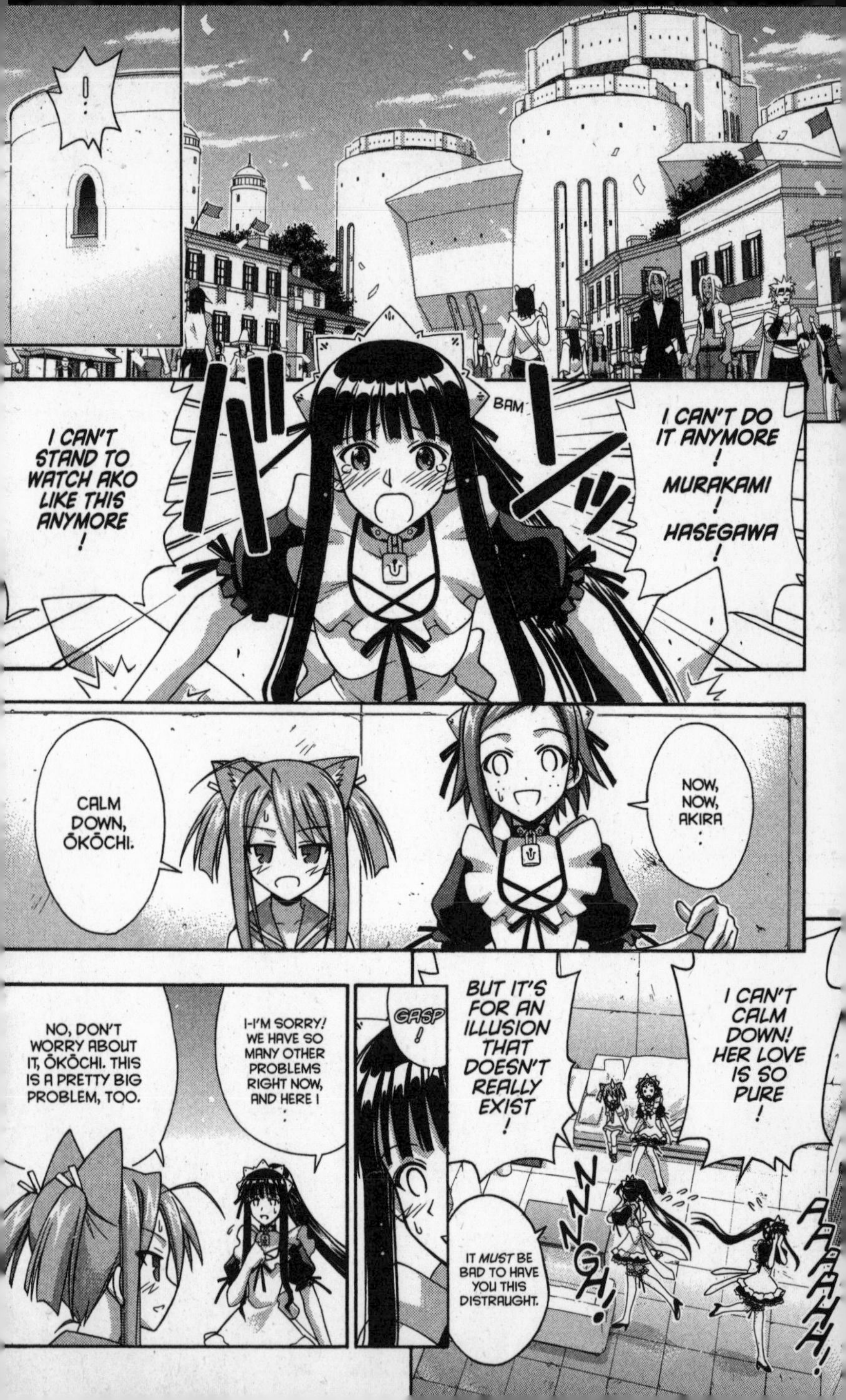
!
BAM
I CAN'T DO IT ANYMORE! MURAKAMI! HASEGAWA!
I CAN'T STAND TO WATCH AKO LIKE THIS ANYMORE!
NOW, NOW, AKIRA...
CALM DOWN, ŌKŌCHI.
I CAN'T CALM DOWN! HER LOVE IS SO PURE!
BUT IT'S FOR AN ILLUSION THAT DOESN'T REALLY EXIST!
AAAAHH!
NNNGH!
GASP!
IT *MUST* BE BAD TO HAVE YOU THIS DISTRAUGHT.
I-I'M SORRY! WE HAVE SO MANY OTHER PROBLEMS RIGHT NOW, AND HERE I...
NO, DON'T WORRY ABOUT IT, ŌKŌCHI. THIS IS A PRETTY BIG PROBLEM, TOO.

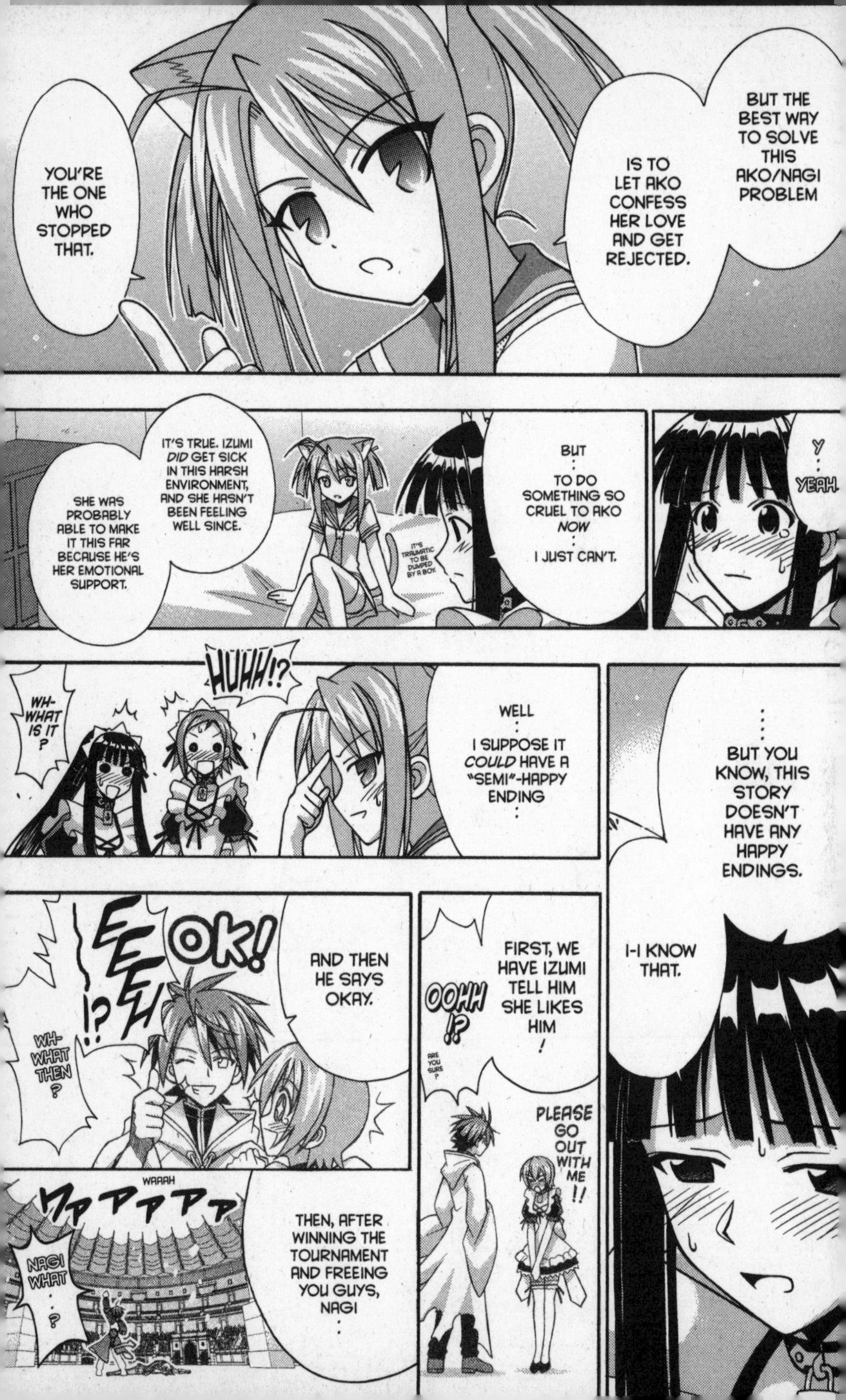
BUT THE BEST WAY TO SOLVE THIS AKO/NAGI PROBLEM
IS TO LET AKO CONFESS HER LOVE AND GET REJECTED.
YOU'RE THE ONE WHO STOPPED THAT.
Y... YEAH.
BUT... TO DO SOMETHING SO CRUEL TO AKO *NOW*... I JUST CAN'T.
IT'S TRAUMATIC TO BE DUMPED BY A BOY.
IT'S TRUE. IZUMI *DID* GET SICK IN THIS HARSH ENVIRONMENT, AND SHE HASN'T BEEN FEELING WELL SINCE.
SHE WAS PROBABLY ABLE TO MAKE IT THIS FAR BECAUSE HE'S HER EMOTIONAL SUPPORT.
... BUT YOU KNOW, THIS STORY DOESN'T HAVE ANY HAPPY ENDINGS.
I-I KNOW THAT.
WELL... I SUPPOSE IT *COULD* HAVE A "SEMI"-HAPPY ENDING...
HUHH!?
WH-WHAT IS IT?
FIRST, WE HAVE IZUMI TELL HIM SHE LIKES HIM!
OOHH!?
ARE YOU SURE?
PLEASE GO OUT WITH ME!!
AND THEN HE SAYS OKAY.
EEEEH!?
OK!
WH-WHAT THEN?
THEN, AFTER WINNING THE TOURNAMENT AND FREEING YOU GUYS, NAGI...
WAAAH
NAGI WHAT...?

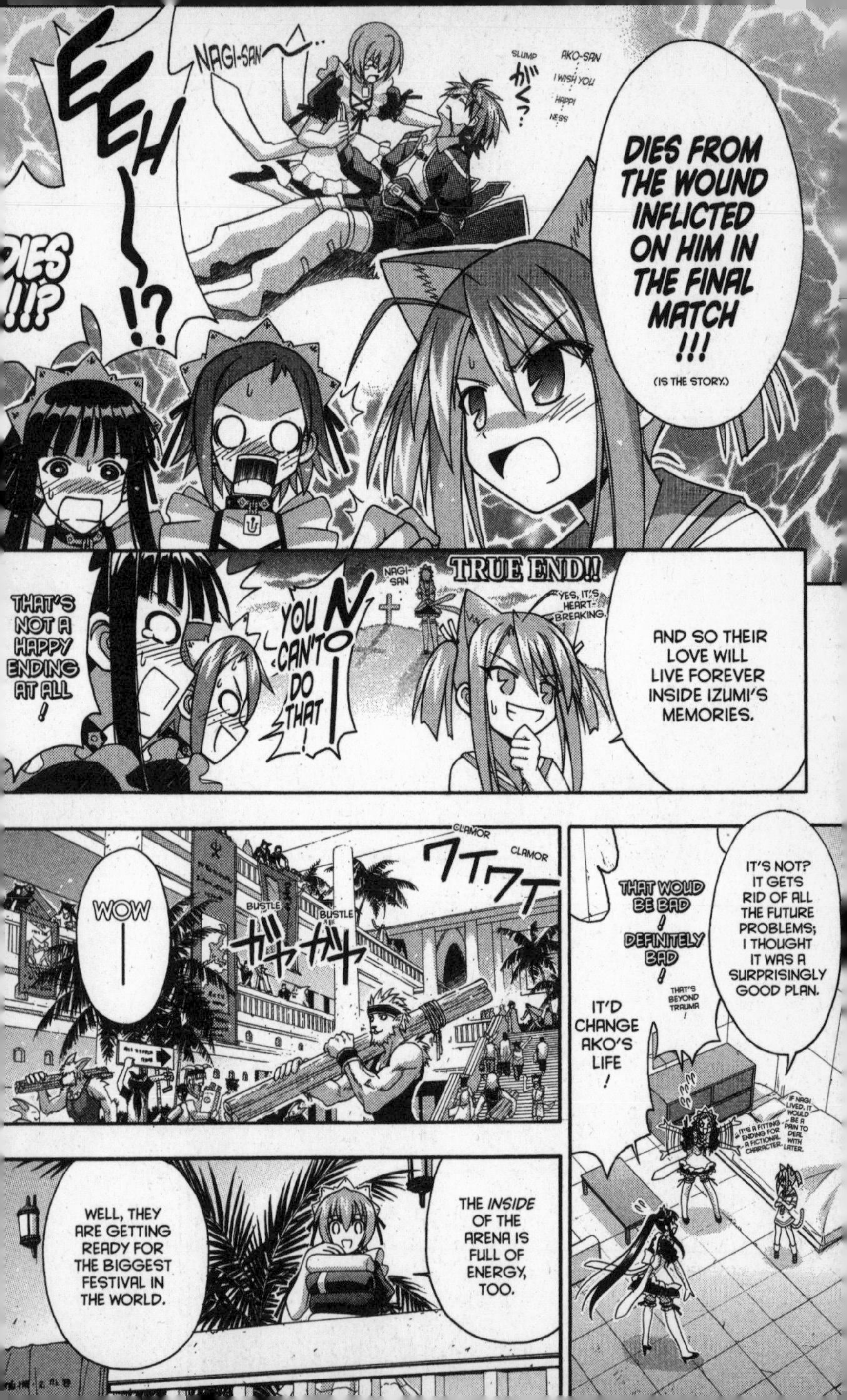
DIES FROM THE WOUND INFLICTED ON HIM IN THE FINAL MATCH !!!
(IS THE STORY.)
AKO-SAN I WISH YOU HAPPI NESS
SLUMP がくっ
NAGI-SAN～～..
EEEH～～!?
DIES !!!?
AND SO THEIR LOVE WILL LIVE FOREVER INSIDE IZUMI'S MEMORIES.
YES, IT'S HEART-BREAKING.
TRUE END!!
NAGI-SAN
NO—! YOU CAN'T DO THAT!
THAT'S NOT A HAPPY ENDING AT ALL!
IT'S NOT? IT GETS RID OF ALL THE FUTURE PROBLEMS; I THOUGHT IT WAS A SURPRISINGLY GOOD PLAN.
THAT WOULD BE BAD! DEFINITELY BAD!
THAT'S BEYOND TRAUMA!
IT'D CHANGE AKO'S LIFE!
IF NAGI LIVED, IT WOULD BE A PAIN TO DEAL WITH LATER.
IT'S A FITTING ENDING FOR A FICTIONAL CHARACTER.
CLAMOR CLAMOR
ワァワァ
BUSTLE BUSTLE
ガヤガヤ
WOW—
THE *INSIDE* OF THE ARENA IS FULL OF ENERGY, TOO.
WELL, THEY ARE GETTING READY FOR THE BIGGEST FESTIVAL IN THE WORLD.

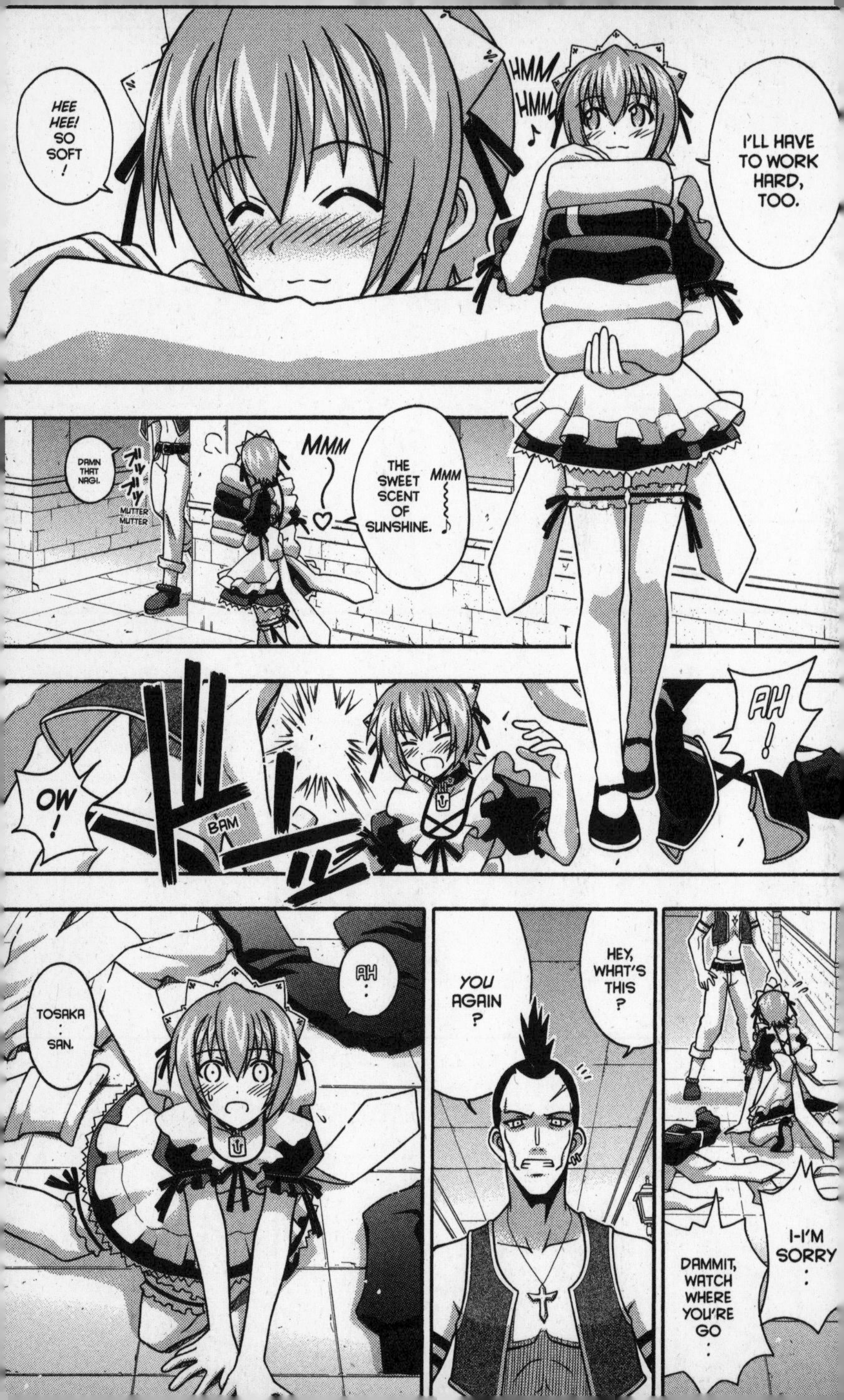
HMM HMM
I'LL HAVE TO WORK HARD, TOO.
HEE HEE! SO SOFT!
MMM
THE SWEET SCENT OF SUNSHINE.
MMM
DAMN THAT NAGI.
MUTTER MUTTER
AH!
BAM
OW!
I-I'M SORRY..
DAMMIT, WATCH WHERE YOU'RE GO..
HEY, WHAT'S THIS?
YOU AGAIN?
AH..
TOSAKA.. SAN.

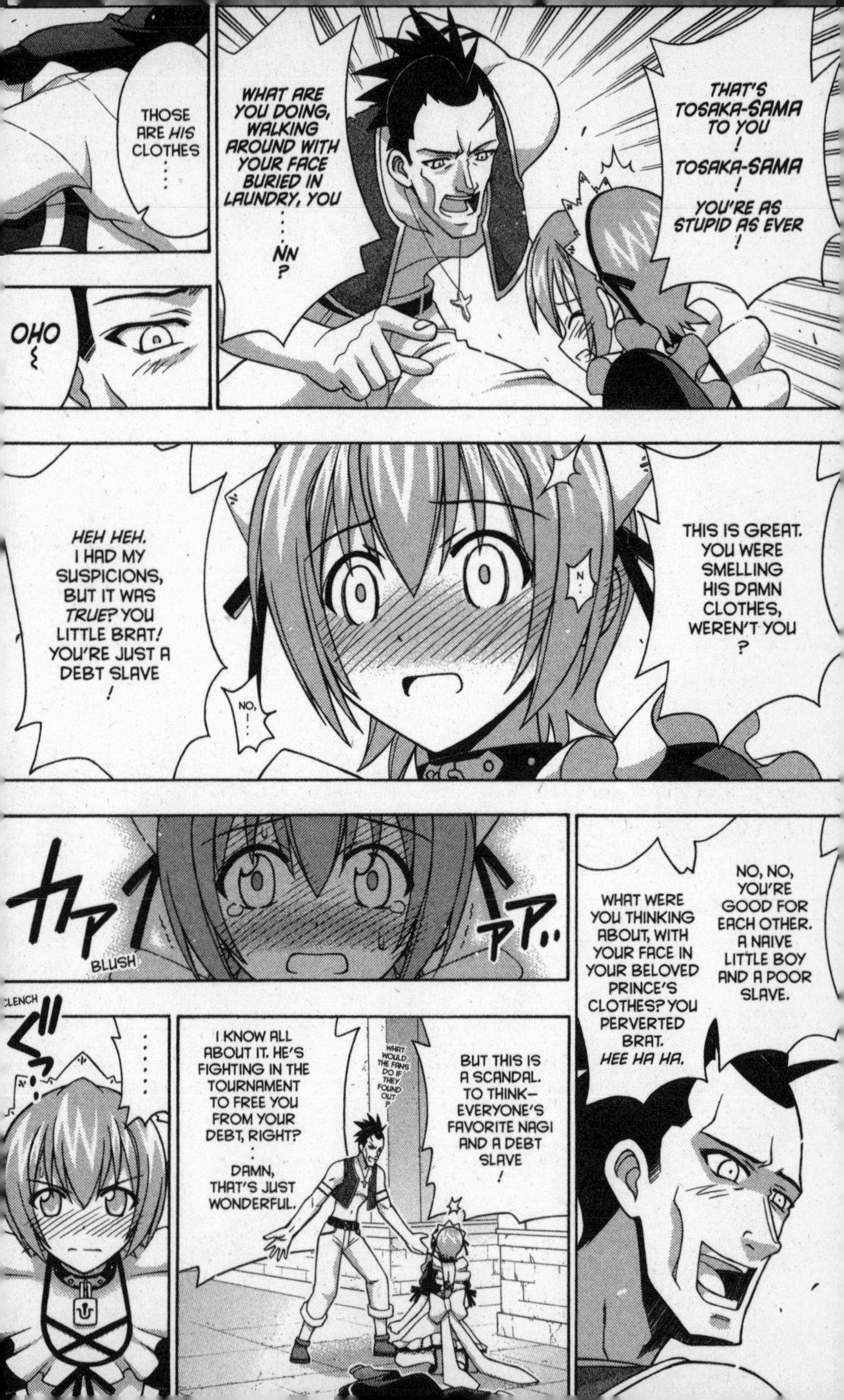
THAT'S TOSAKA-SAMA TO YOU! TOSAKA-SAMA! YOU'RE AS STUPID AS EVER!
WHAT ARE YOU DOING, WALKING AROUND WITH YOUR FACE BURIED IN LAUNDRY, YOU... ...NN?
THOSE ARE HIS CLOTHES...
OHO
THIS IS GREAT. YOU WERE SMELLING HIS DAMN CLOTHES, WEREN'T YOU?
N...
HEH HEH. I HAD MY SUSPICIONS, BUT IT WAS TRUE? YOU LITTLE BRAT! YOU'RE JUST A DEBT SLAVE!
NO, !...
NO, NO, YOU'RE GOOD FOR EACH OTHER. A NAIVE LITTLE BOY AND A POOR SLAVE.
WHAT WERE YOU THINKING ABOUT, WITH YOUR FACE IN YOUR BELOVED PRINCE'S CLOTHES? YOU PERVERTED BRAT. HEE HA HA.
BLUSH
BUT THIS IS A SCANDAL. TO THINK—EVERYONE'S FAVORITE NAGI AND A DEBT SLAVE!
WHAT WOULD THE FANS DO IF THEY FOUND OUT?
I KNOW ALL ABOUT IT. HE'S FIGHTING IN THE TOURNAMENT TO FREE YOU FROM YOUR DEBT, RIGHT? ...
DAMN, THAT'S JUST WONDERFUL.
CLENCH
......

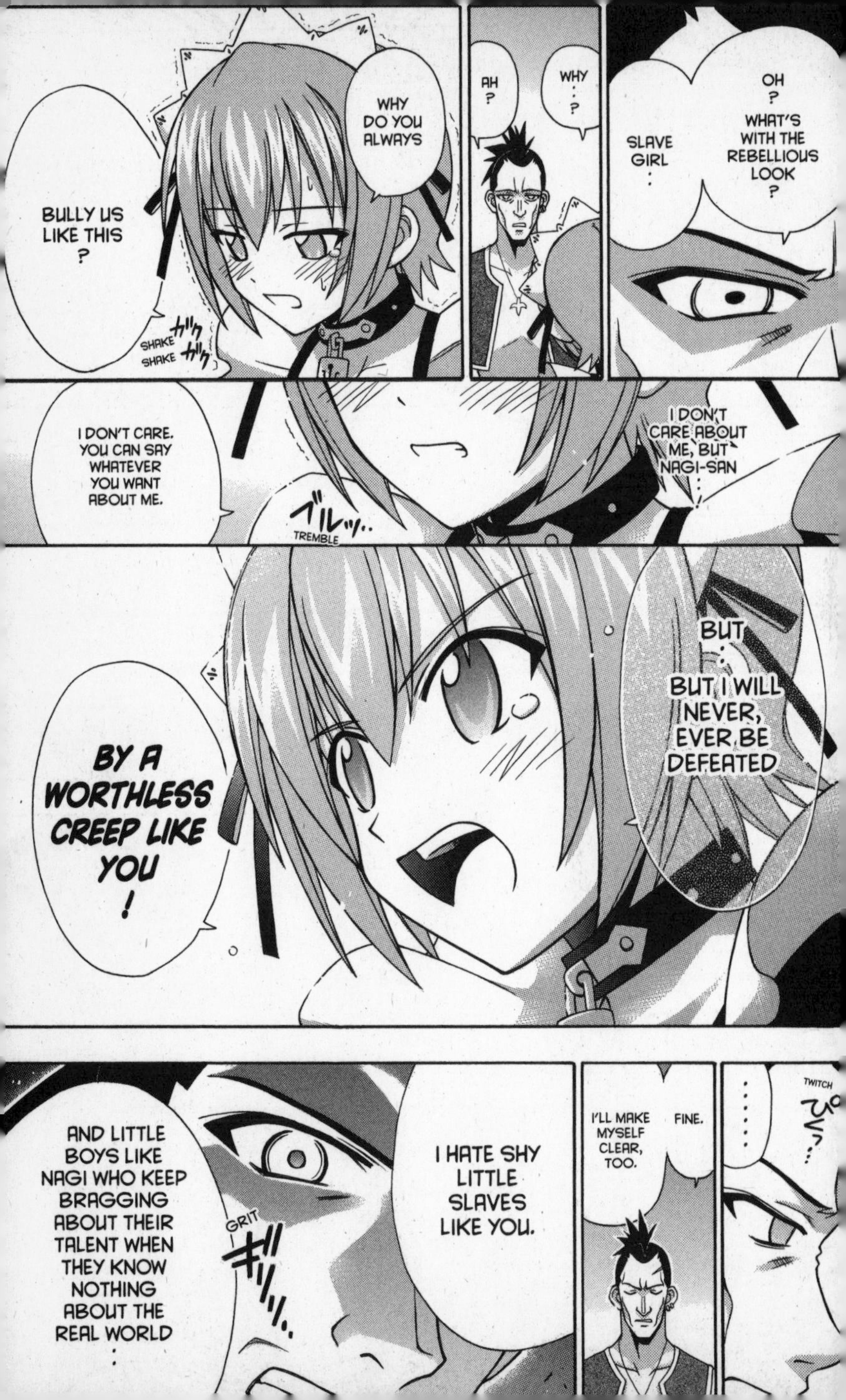
OH? WHAT'S WITH THE REBELLIOUS LOOK?
SLAVE GIRL...
WHY...?
AH?
WHY DO YOU ALWAYS
BULLY US LIKE THIS?
SHAKE SHAKE
I DON'T CARE ABOUT ME, BUT NAGI-SAN...
TREMBLE
I DON'T CARE. YOU CAN SAY WHATEVER YOU WANT ABOUT ME.
BUT... BUT I WILL NEVER, EVER BE DEFEATED
BY A WORTHLESS CREEP LIKE YOU!
TWITCH
......
FINE.
I'LL MAKE MYSELF CLEAR, TOO.
I HATE SHY LITTLE SLAVES LIKE YOU.
AND LITTLE BOYS LIKE NAGI WHO KEEP BRAGGING ABOUT THEIR TALENT WHEN THEY KNOW NOTHING ABOUT THE REAL WORLD...
GRIT

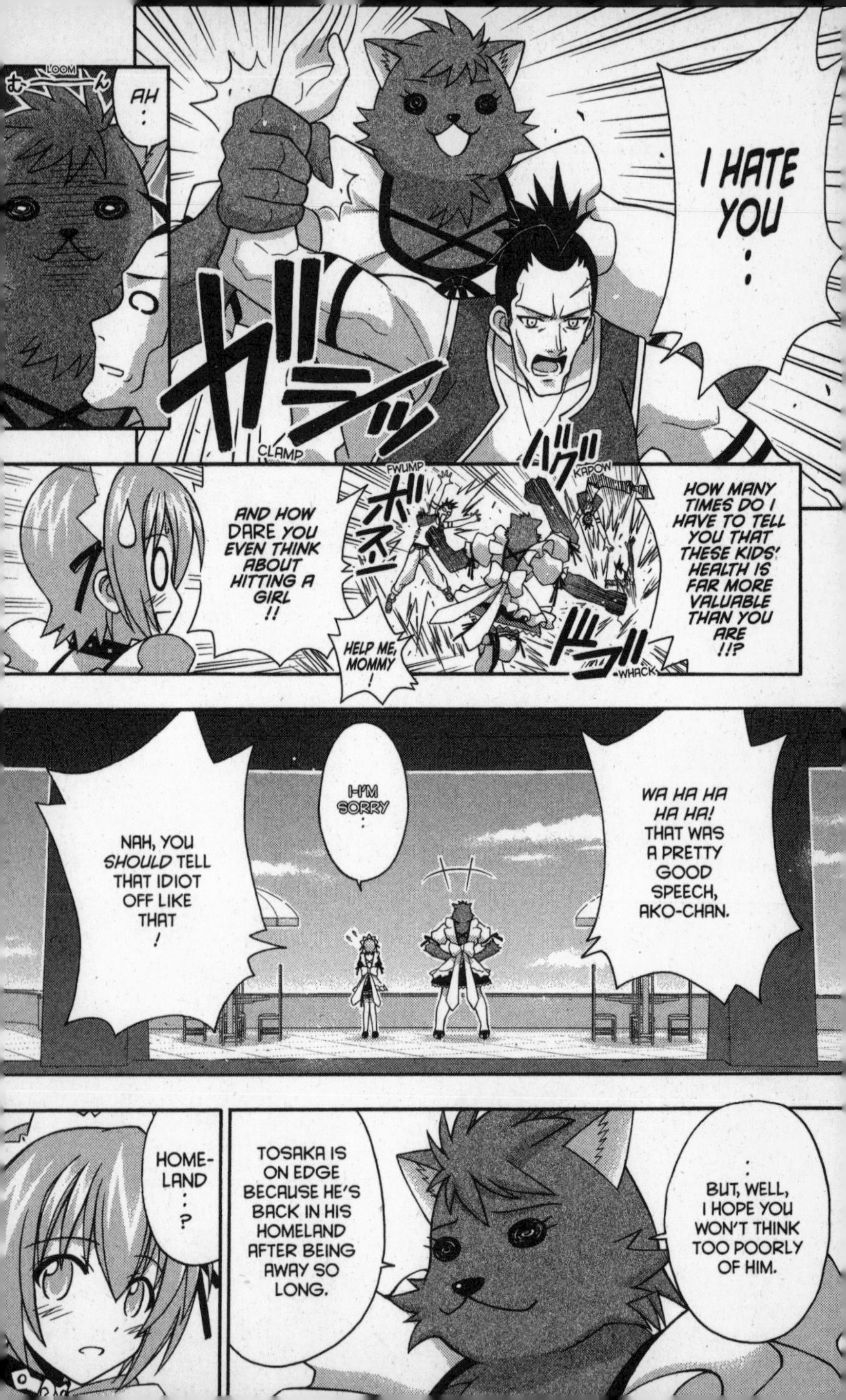

I HATE YOU :
CLAMP
LOOM
AH . .
HOW MANY TIMES DO I HAVE TO TELL YOU THAT THESE KIDS' HEALTH IS FAR MORE VALUABLE THAN YOU ARE !!?
WHACK
KAPOW
FWUMP
HELP ME, MOMMY !
AND HOW DARE YOU EVEN THINK ABOUT HITTING A GIRL !!
WA HA HA HA HA! THAT WAS A PRETTY GOOD SPEECH, AKO-CHAN.
I-I'M SORRY . .
NAH, YOU SHOULD TELL THAT IDIOT OFF LIKE THAT !
: BUT, WELL, I HOPE YOU WON'T THINK TOO POORLY OF HIM.
TOSAKA IS ON EDGE BECAUSE HE'S BACK IN HIS HOMELAND AFTER BEING AWAY SO LONG.
HOME-LAND . . ?

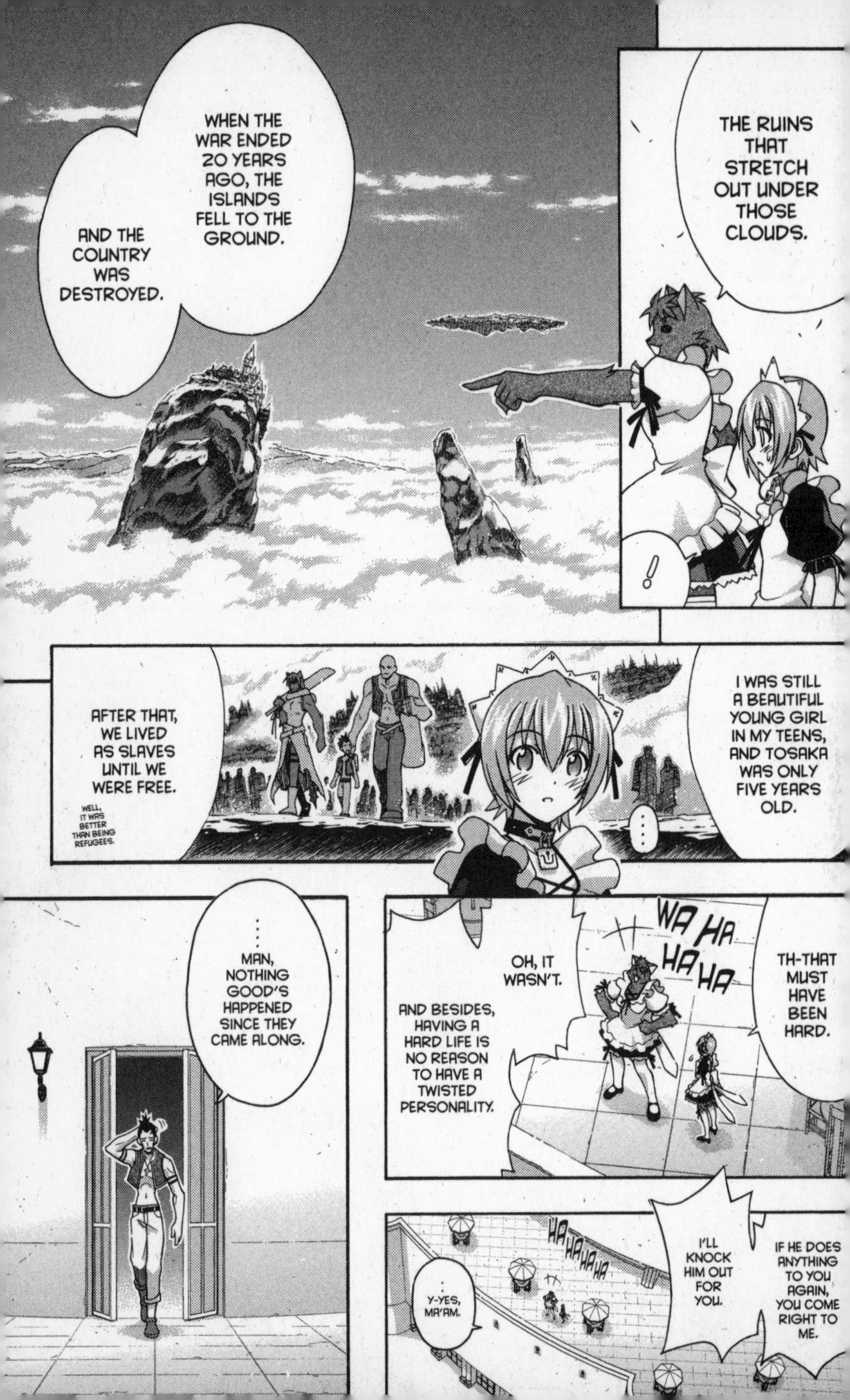
THE RUINS THAT STRETCH OUT UNDER THOSE CLOUDS.
!
WHEN THE WAR ENDED 20 YEARS AGO, THE ISLANDS FELL TO THE GROUND.
AND THE COUNTRY WAS DESTROYED.
I WAS STILL A BEAUTIFUL YOUNG GIRL IN MY TEENS, AND TOSAKA WAS ONLY FIVE YEARS OLD.
...
AFTER THAT, WE LIVED AS SLAVES UNTIL WE WERE FREE.
WELL, IT WAS BETTER THAN BEING REFUGEES.
TH-THAT MUST HAVE BEEN HARD.
WA HA HA HA HA
OH, IT WASN'T.
AND BESIDES, HAVING A HARD LIFE IS NO REASON TO HAVE A TWISTED PERSONALITY.
IF HE DOES ANYTHING TO YOU AGAIN, YOU COME RIGHT TO ME.
I'LL KNOCK HIM OUT FOR YOU.
HA HA HA HA HA
...Y-YES, MA'AM.
... MAN, NOTHING GOOD'S HAPPENED SINCE THEY CAME ALONG.

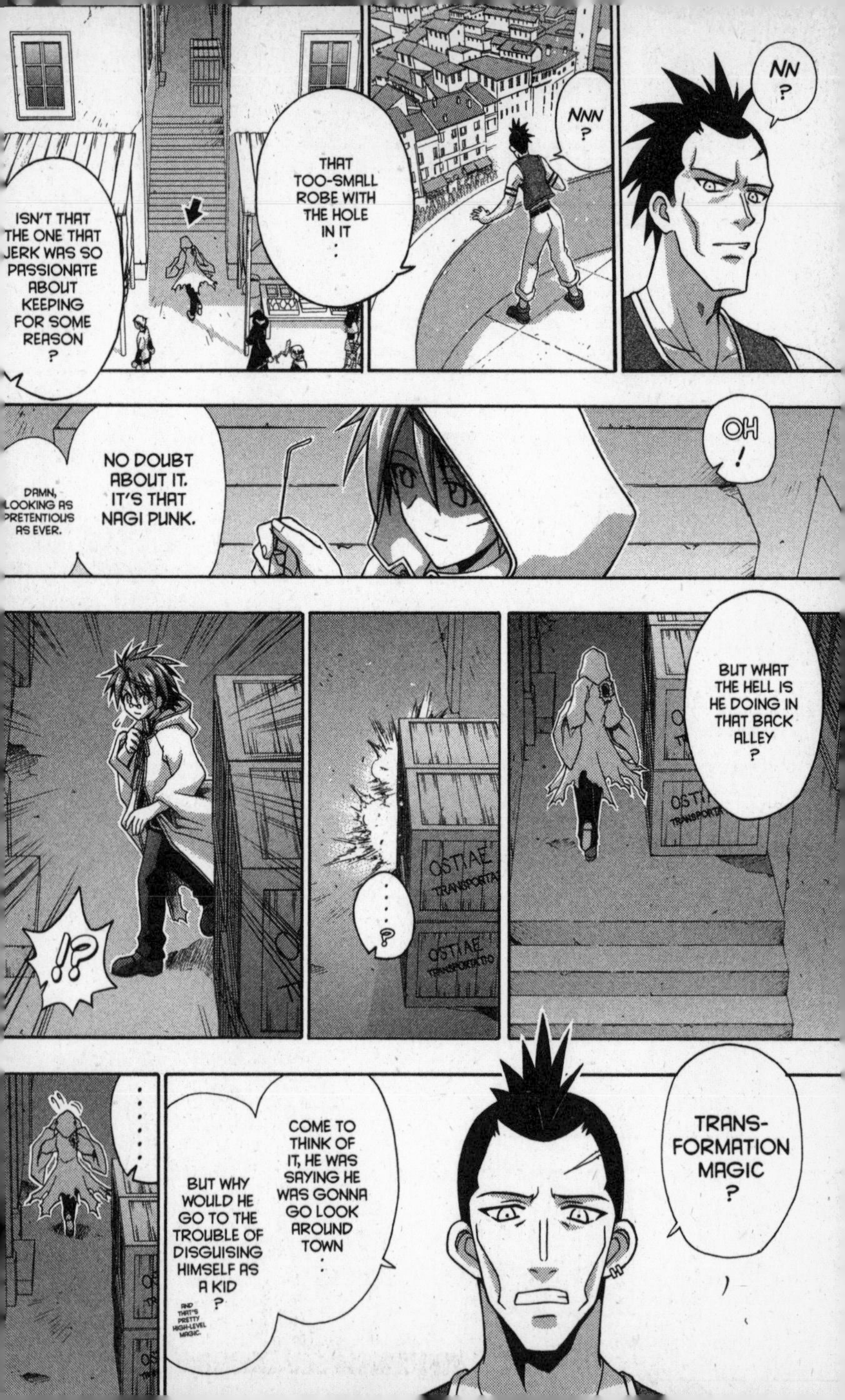
NN ?
NNN ?
THAT TOO-SMALL ROBE WITH THE HOLE IN IT :
ISN'T THAT THE ONE THAT JERK WAS SO PASSIONATE ABOUT KEEPING FOR SOME REASON ?
OH !
NO DOUBT ABOUT IT. IT'S THAT NAGI PUNK.
DAMN, LOOKING AS PRETENTIOUS AS EVER.
BUT WHAT THE HELL IS HE DOING IN THAT BACK ALLEY ?
OSTIAE
.... ?
!?
TRANS-FORMATION MAGIC ?
COME TO THINK OF IT, HE WAS SAYING HE WAS GONNA GO LOOK AROUND TOWN :
BUT WHY WOULD HE GO TO THE TROUBLE OF DISGUISING HIMSELF AS A KID ?
AND THAT'S PRETTY HIGH-LEVEL MAGIC.
......

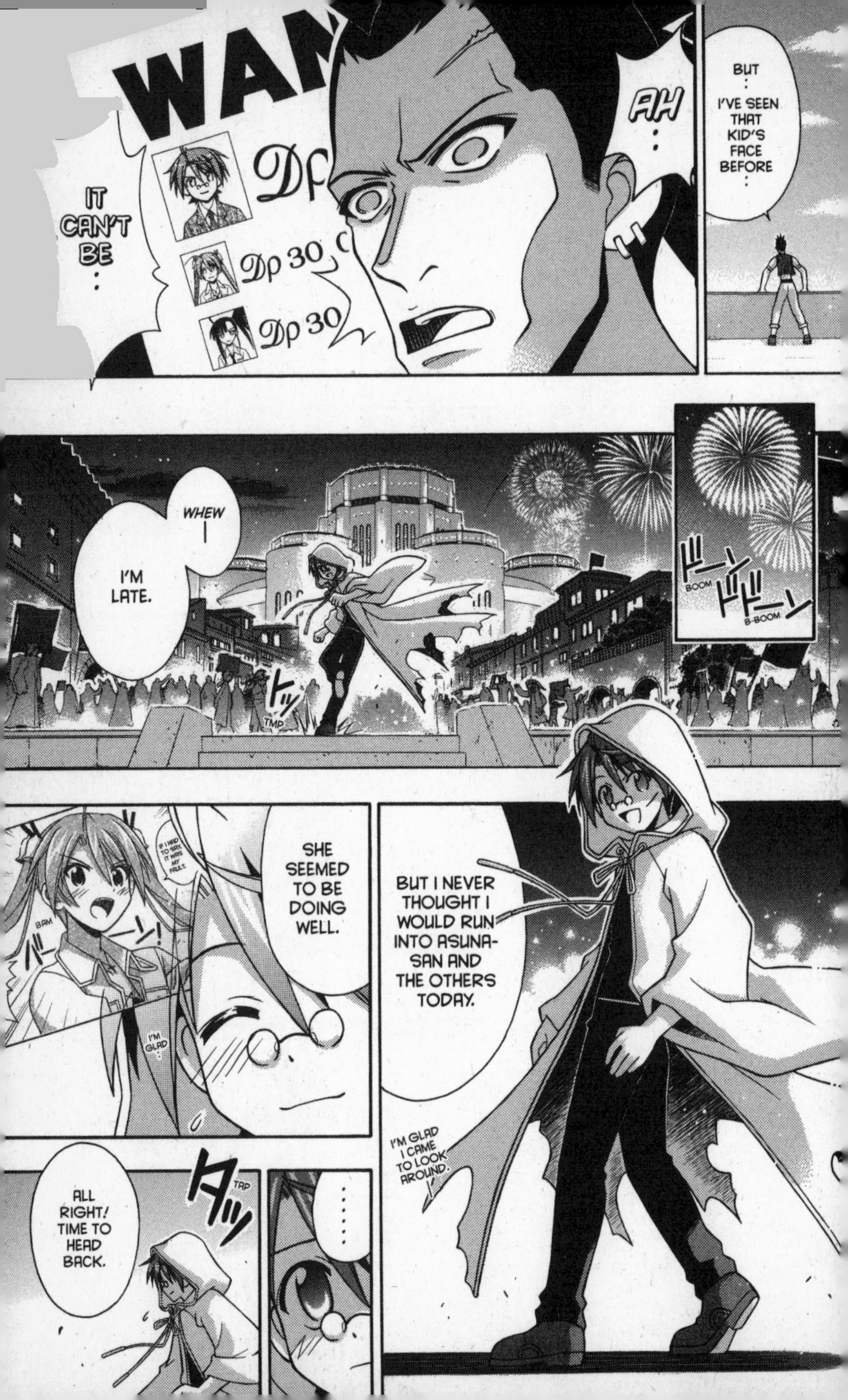
BUT... I'VE SEEN THAT KID'S FACE BEFORE...
AH...
WAN
Dp 30
Dp 30
IT CAN'T BE...
BOOM
B-BOOM
WHEW
I'M LATE.
TMP
BUT I NEVER THOUGHT I WOULD RUN INTO ASUNA-SAN AND THE OTHERS TODAY.
I'M GLAD I CAME TO LOOK AROUND.
SHE SEEMED TO BE DOING WELL.
IF I HAD TO SAY, IT WAS MY FAULT.
BAM
I'M GLAD...
......
TAP
ALL RIGHT! TIME TO HEAD BACK.

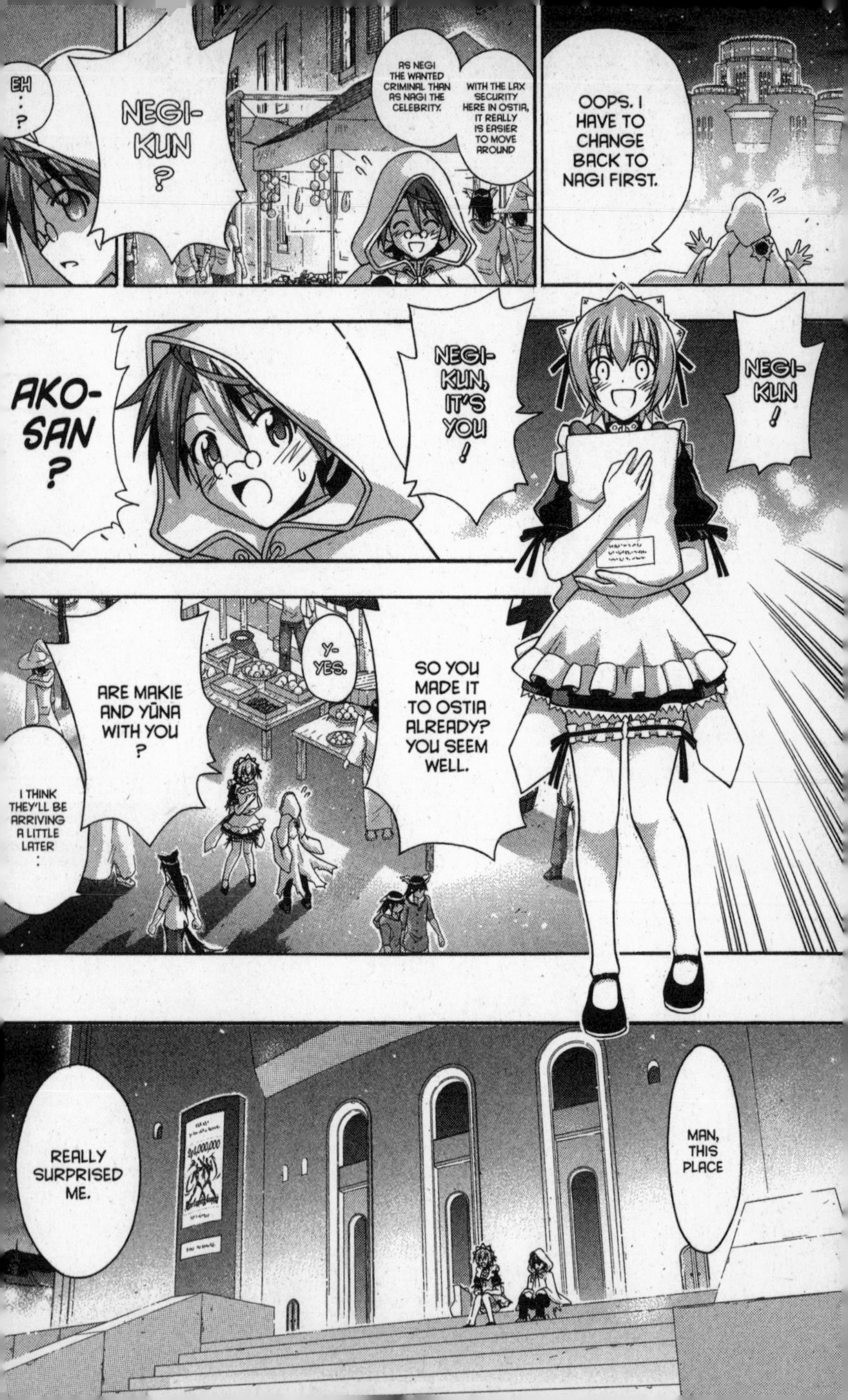
OOPS. I HAVE TO CHANGE BACK TO NAGI FIRST.
WITH THE LAX SECURITY HERE IN OSTIA, IT REALLY IS EASIER TO MOVE AROUND
AS NEGI THE WANTED CRIMINAL THAN AS NAGI THE CELEBRITY.
NEGI-KUN?
EH...?
NEGI-KUN!
NEGI-KUN, IT'S YOU!
AKO-SAN?
SO YOU MADE IT TO OSTIA ALREADY? YOU SEEM WELL.
Y-YES.
ARE MAKIE AND YŪNA WITH YOU?
I THINK THEY'LL BE ARRIVING A LITTLE LATER...
MAN, THIS PLACE
REALLY SURPRISED ME.

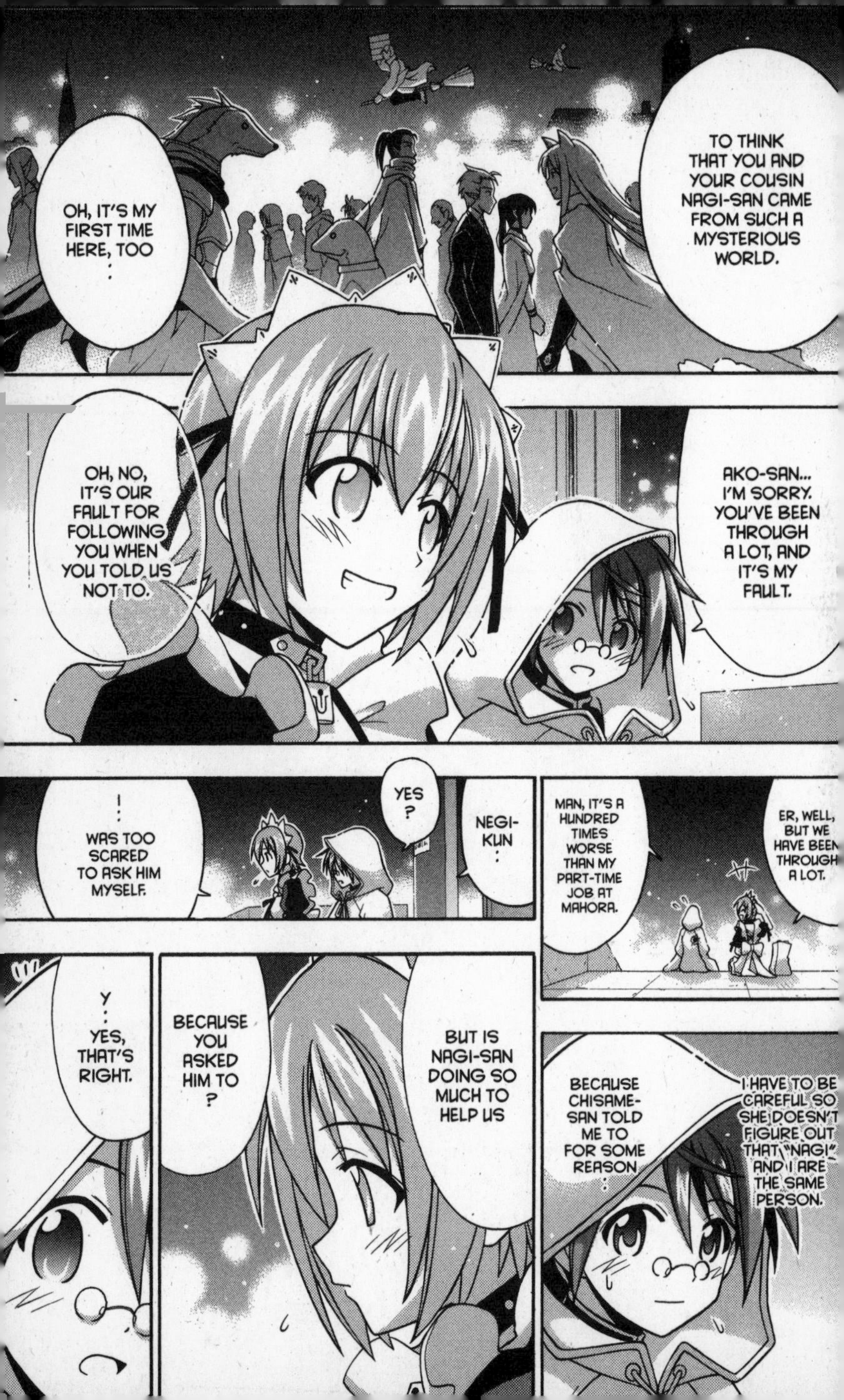
TO THINK THAT YOU AND YOUR COUSIN NAGI-SAN CAME FROM SUCH A MYSTERIOUS WORLD.
OH, IT'S MY FIRST TIME HERE, TOO...
AKO-SAN... I'M SORRY. YOU'VE BEEN THROUGH A LOT, AND IT'S MY FAULT.
OH, NO, IT'S OUR FAULT FOR FOLLOWING YOU WHEN YOU TOLD US NOT TO.
ER, WELL, BUT WE HAVE BEEN THROUGH A LOT.
MAN, IT'S A HUNDRED TIMES WORSE THAN MY PART-TIME JOB AT MAHORA.
NEGI-KUN...
YES?
!... WAS TOO SCARED TO ASK HIM MYSELF.
I HAVE TO BE CAREFUL SO SHE DOESN'T FIGURE OUT THAT "NAGI" AND I ARE THE SAME PERSON.
BECAUSE CHISAME-SAN TOLD ME TO FOR SOME REASON...
BUT IS NAGI-SAN DOING SO MUCH TO HELP US
BECAUSE YOU ASKED HIM TO?
Y... YES, THAT'S RIGHT.

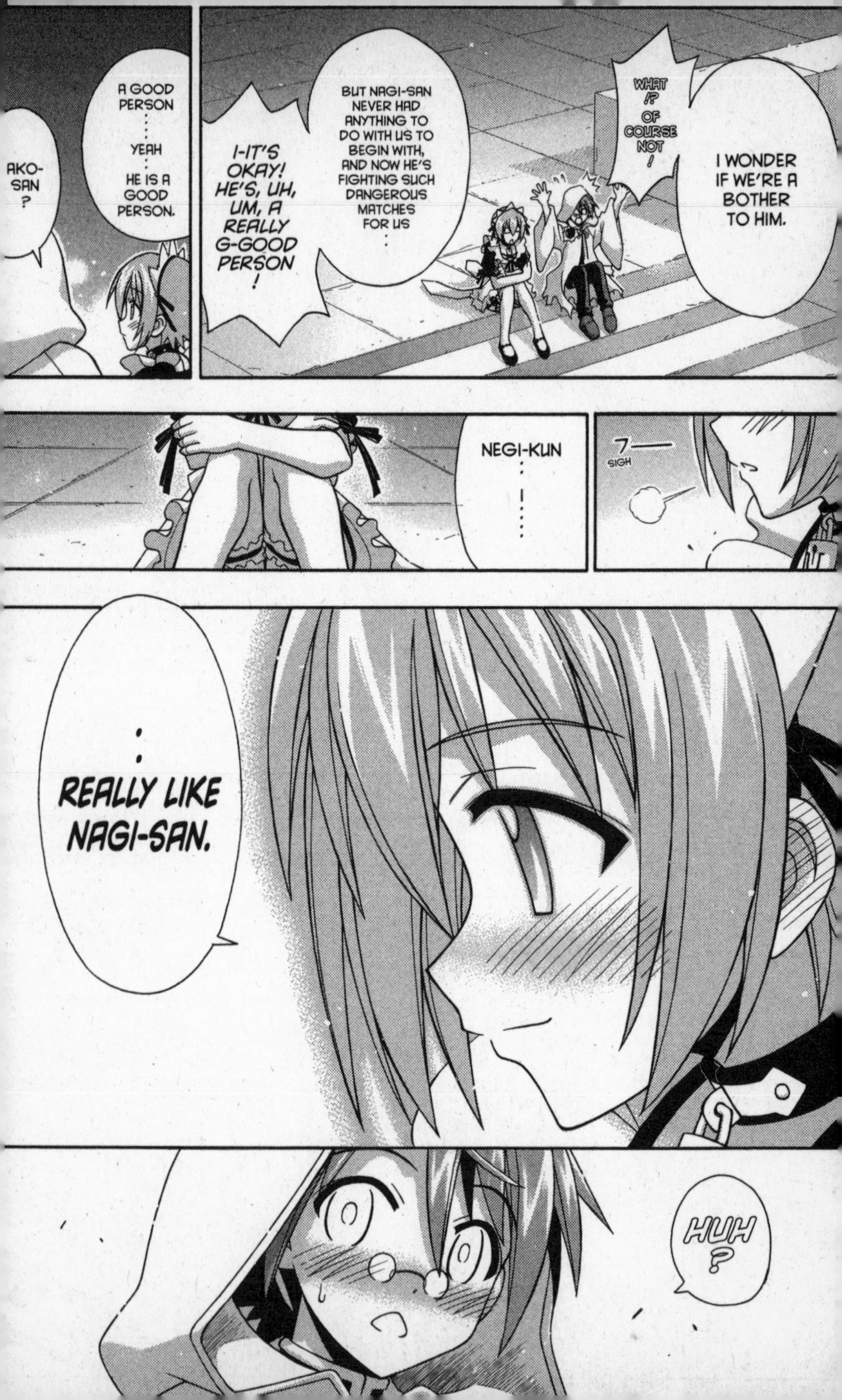

I WONDER IF WE'RE A BOTHER TO HIM.
WHAT!? OF COURSE NOT!
BUT NAGI-SAN NEVER HAD ANYTHING TO DO WITH US TO BEGIN WITH, AND NOW HE'S FIGHTING SUCH DANGEROUS MATCHES FOR US...
I-IT'S OKAY! HE'S, UH, UM, A REALLY G-GOOD PERSON!
A GOOD PERSON... YEAH... HE IS A GOOD PERSON.
AKO-SAN?
SIGH
NEGI-KUN... I......
...REALLY LIKE NAGI-SAN.
HUH?

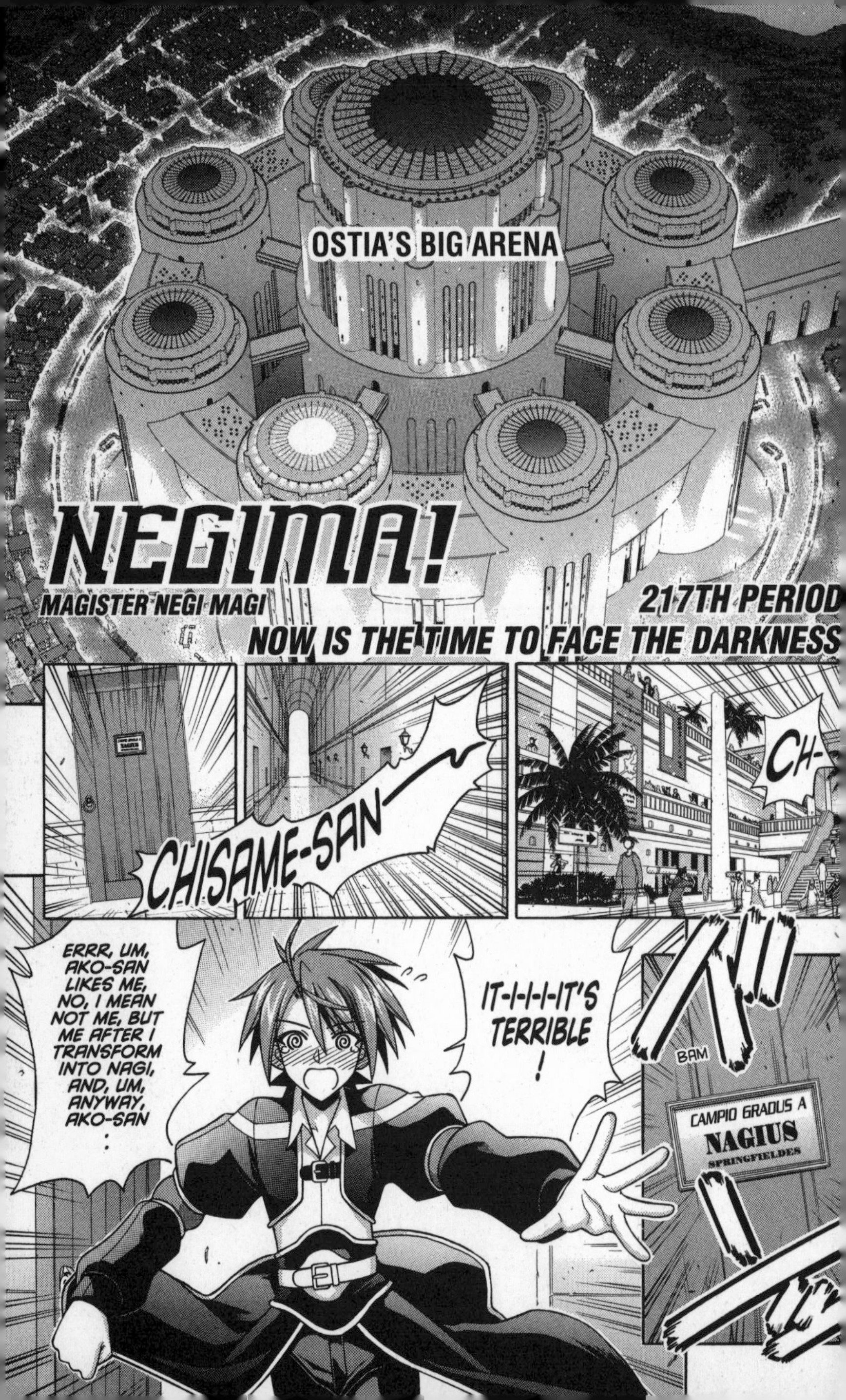
OSTIA'S BIG ARENA
NEGIMA!
MAGISTER NEGI MAGI
217TH PERIOD
NOW IS THE TIME TO FACE THE DARKNESS
CH-
CHISAME-SAN
BAM
CAMPIO GRADUS A
NAGIUS
SPRINGFIELDES
IT-I-I-I-IT'S TERRIBLE!
ERRR, UM, AKO-SAN LIKES ME, NO, I MEAN NOT ME, BUT ME AFTER I TRANSFORM INTO NAGI, AND, UM, ANYWAY, AKO-SAN...

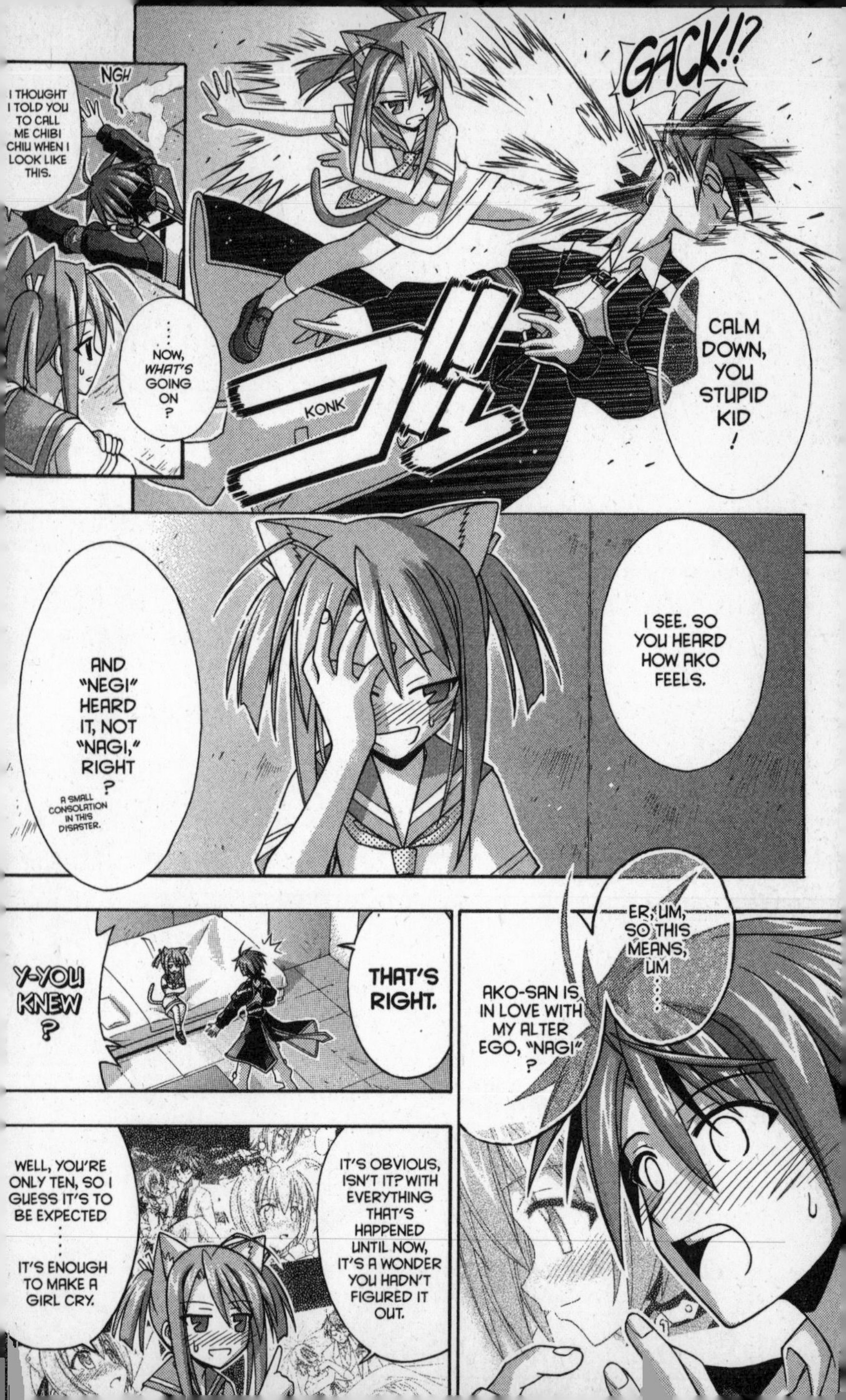
GACK!!?
CALM DOWN, YOU STUPID KID!
KONK
NGH
I THOUGHT I TOLD YOU TO CALL ME CHIBI CHIU WHEN I LOOK LIKE THIS.
... NOW, WHAT'S GOING ON?
I SEE. SO YOU HEARD HOW AKO FEELS.
AND "NEGI" HEARD IT, NOT "NAGI," RIGHT?
A SMALL CONSOLATION IN THIS DISASTER.
ER, UM, SO THIS MEANS, UM.....
AKO-SAN IS IN LOVE WITH MY ALTER EGO, "NAGI"?
THAT'S RIGHT.
Y-YOU KNEW?
IT'S OBVIOUS, ISN'T IT? WITH EVERYTHING THAT'S HAPPENED UNTIL NOW, IT'S A WONDER YOU HADN'T FIGURED IT OUT.
WELL, YOU'RE ONLY TEN, SO I GUESS IT'S TO BE EXPECTED...
IT'S ENOUGH TO MAKE A GIRL CRY.

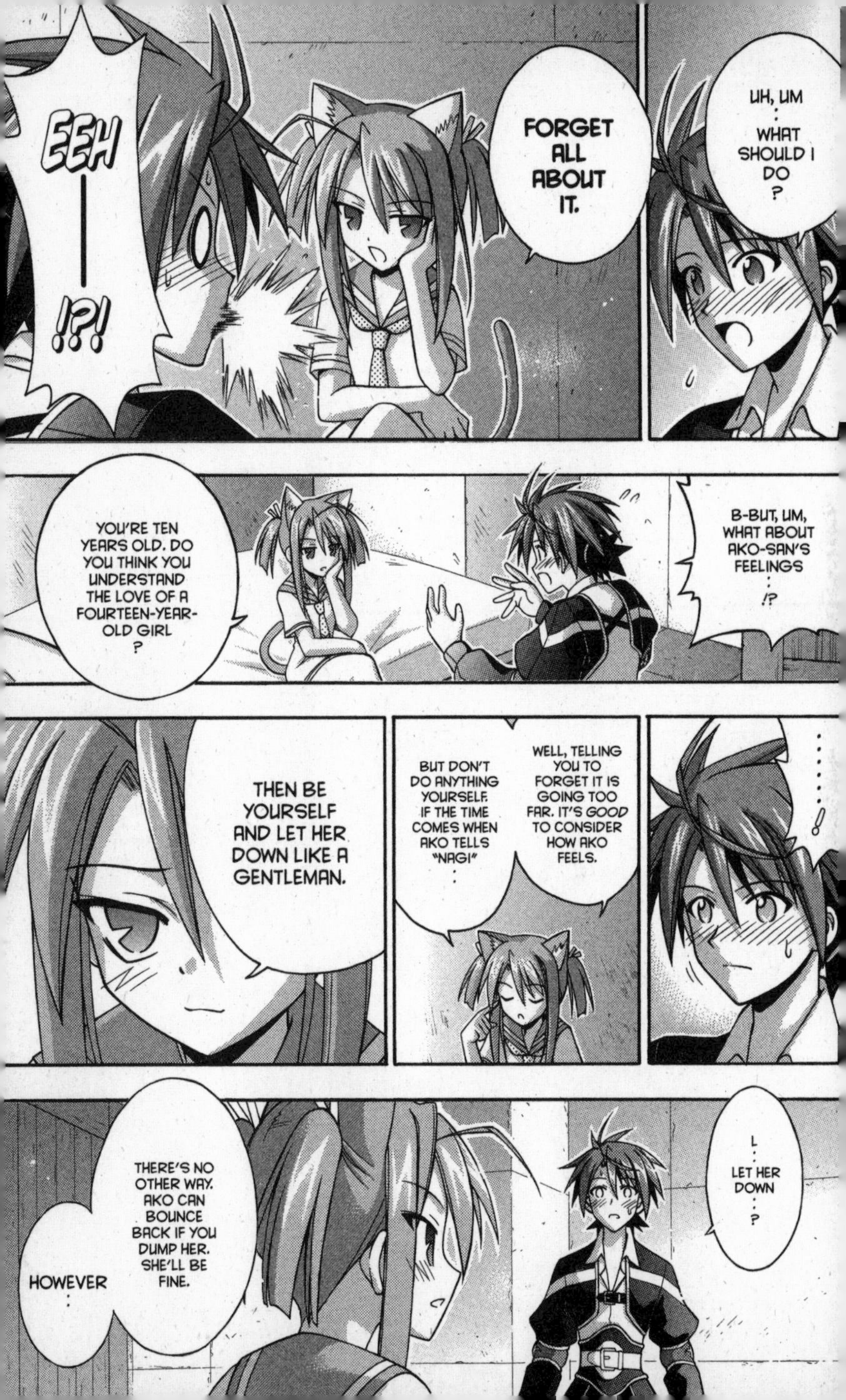
UH, UM... WHAT SHOULD I DO?
FORGET ALL ABOUT IT.
EEH—!?!
B-BUT, UM, WHAT ABOUT AKO-SAN'S FEELINGS...!?
YOU'RE TEN YEARS OLD. DO YOU THINK YOU UNDERSTAND THE LOVE OF A FOURTEEN-YEAR-OLD GIRL?
......!
WELL, TELLING YOU TO FORGET IT IS GOING TOO FAR. IT'S *GOOD* TO CONSIDER HOW AKO FEELS.
BUT DON'T DO ANYTHING YOURSELF. IF THE TIME COMES WHEN AKO TELLS "NAGI"...
THEN BE YOURSELF AND LET HER DOWN LIKE A GENTLEMAN.
L... LET HER DOWN...?
THERE'S NO OTHER WAY. AKO CAN BOUNCE BACK IF YOU DUMP HER. SHE'LL BE FINE.
HOWEVER...

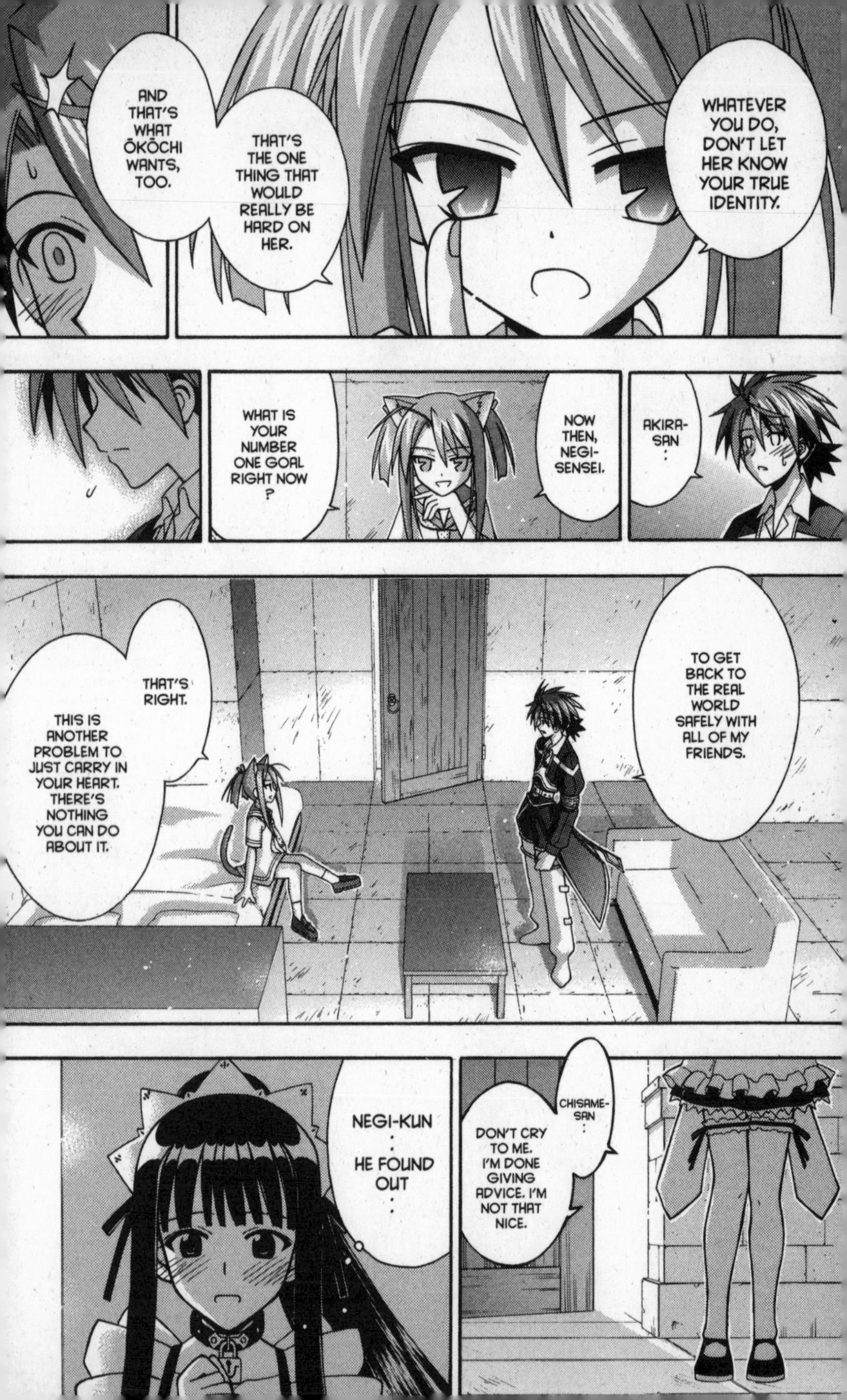
WHATEVER YOU DO, DON'T LET HER KNOW YOUR TRUE IDENTITY.
THAT'S THE ONE THING THAT WOULD REALLY BE HARD ON HER.
AND THAT'S WHAT ŌKŌCHI WANTS, TOO.
AKIRA-SAN…
NOW THEN, NEGI-SENSEI.
WHAT IS YOUR NUMBER ONE GOAL RIGHT NOW?
TO GET BACK TO THE REAL WORLD SAFELY WITH ALL OF MY FRIENDS.
THAT'S RIGHT.
THIS IS ANOTHER PROBLEM TO JUST CARRY IN YOUR HEART. THERE'S NOTHING YOU CAN DO ABOUT IT.
CHISAME-SAN…
DON'T CRY TO ME. I'M DONE GIVING ADVICE. I'M NOT THAT NICE.
NEGI-KUN… HE FOUND OUT…

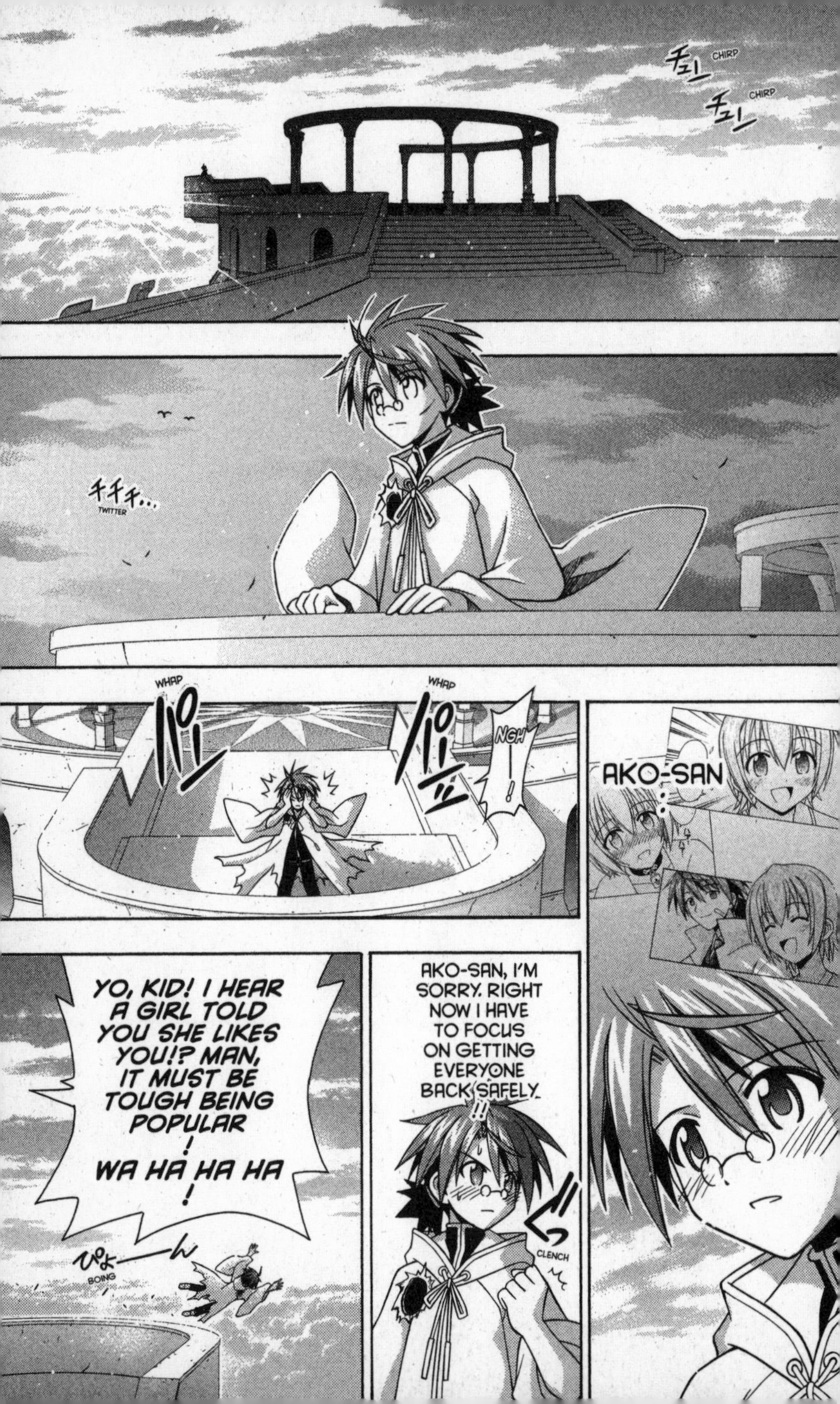

チュン
CHIRP
チュン
CHIRP
チチチ…
TWITTER
AKO-SAN…
WHAP
パン
WHAP
パンッ
NGH!!
AKO-SAN, I'M SORRY. RIGHT NOW I HAVE TO FOCUS ON GETTING EVERYONE BACK SAFELY.
!!
ぐっ
CLENCH
YO, KID! I HEAR A GIRL TOLD YOU SHE LIKES YOU!? MAN, IT MUST BE TOUGH BEING POPULAR! WA HA HA HA!
ぴよーん
BOING

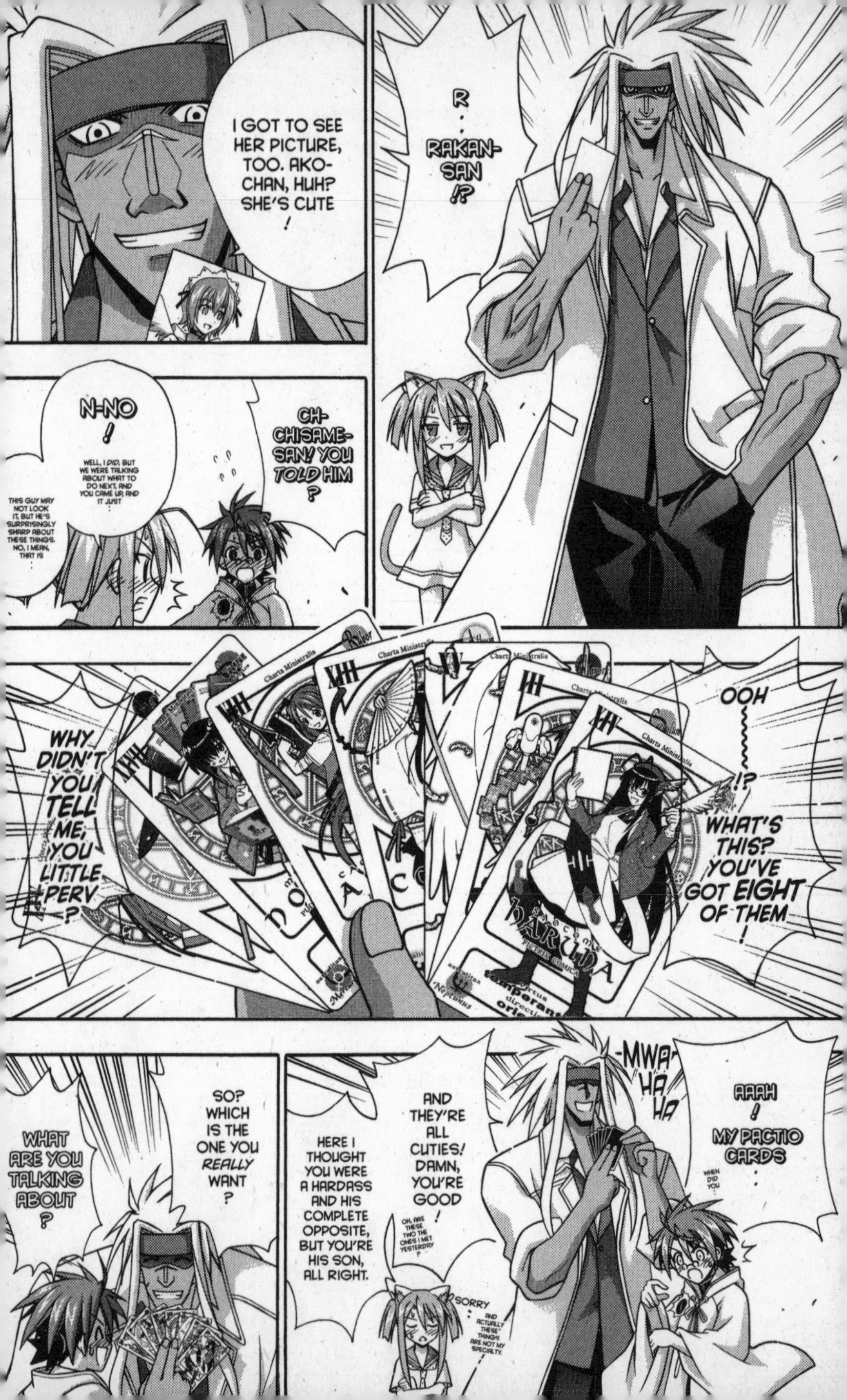
R... RAKAN-SAN!?
I GOT TO SEE HER PICTURE, TOO. AKO-CHAN, HUH? SHE'S CUTE!
CH-CHISAME-SAN! YOU *TOLD* HIM?
N-NO!
WELL, I *DID*, BUT WE WERE TALKING ABOUT WHAT TO DO NEXT, AND YOU CAME UP, AND IT JUST...
THIS GUY MAY NOT LOOK IT, BUT HE'S SURPRISINGLY SHARP ABOUT THESE THINGS. NO, I MEAN, THAT IS...
OOH~~!? WHAT'S THIS? YOU'VE GOT **EIGHT** OF THEM!
WHY DIDN'T YOU TELL ME, YOU LITTLE PERV?
Charta Ministralis
HARUNA
-MWA-HA HA
AAAH! MY PACTIO CARDS!
WHEN DID YOU
AND THEY'RE ALL CUTIES! DAMN, YOU'RE GOOD!
HERE I THOUGHT YOU WERE A HARDASS AND HIS COMPLETE OPPOSITE, BUT YOU'RE HIS SON, ALL RIGHT.
OH, ARE THESE TWO THE ONES I MET YESTERDAY?
SORRY...
AND ACTUALLY THESE THINGS ARE NOT MY SPECIALTY.
SO? WHICH IS THE ONE YOU *REALLY* WANT?
WHAT ARE YOU TALKING ABOUT?

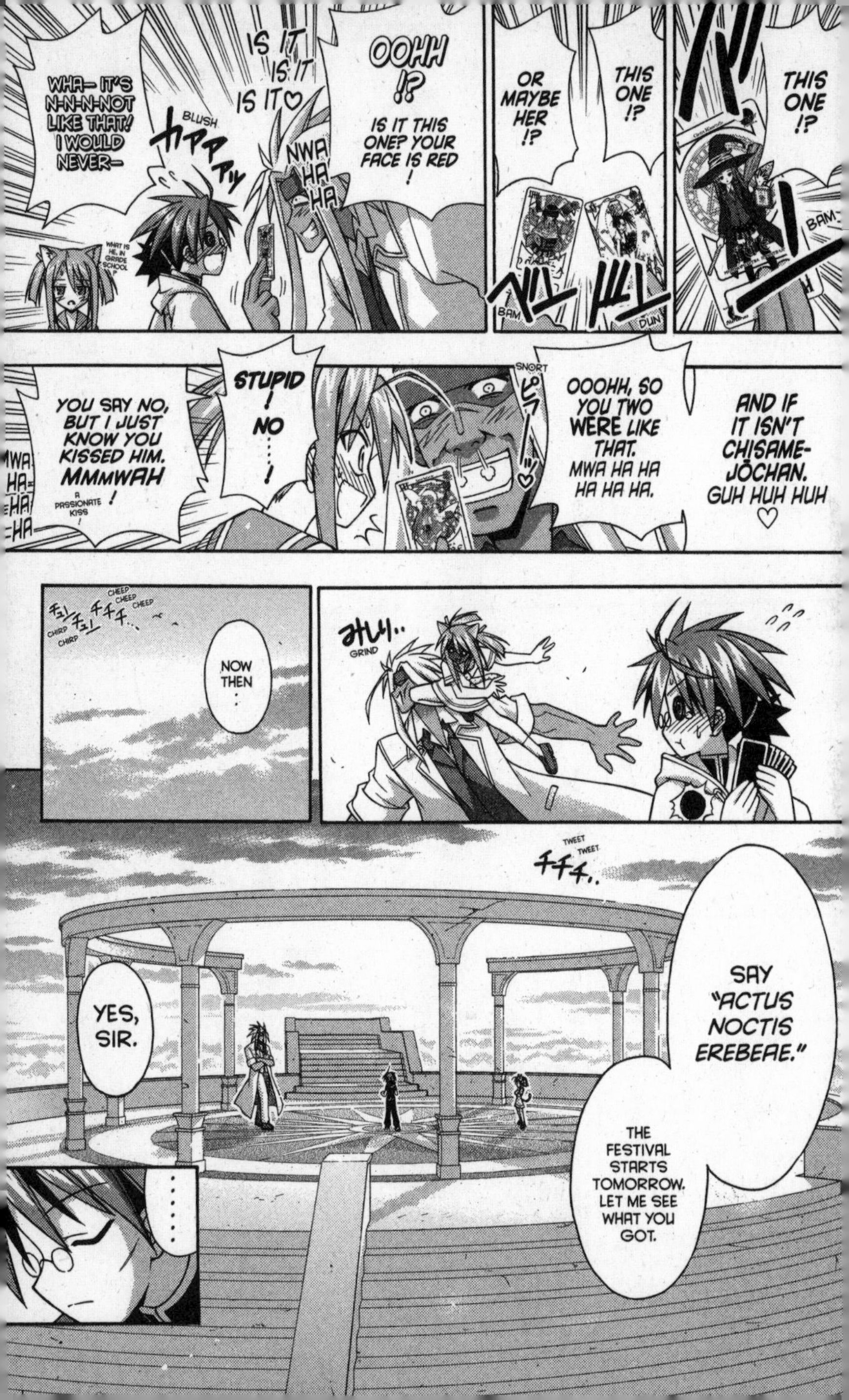
THIS ONE!?
BAM
THIS ONE!?
OR MAYBE HER!?
DUN
BAM
OOHH!?
IS IT THIS ONE? YOUR FACE IS RED!
IS IT IS IT IS IT♡
NWA HA HA
BLUSH
WHA- IT'S N-N-N-NOT LIKE THAT! I WOULD NEVER-
WHAT IS HE, IN GRADE SCHOOL?
AND IF IT ISN'T CHISAME-JŌCHAN. GUH HUH HUH ♡
OOOHH, SO YOU TWO WERE LIKE THAT. MWA HA HA HA HA HA.
SNORT
STUPID! NO...!
YOU SAY NO, BUT I JUST KNOW YOU KISSED HIM. MMMWAH!
A PASSIONATE KISS!
MWA HA HA HA
GRIND
CHEEP CHEEP CHEEP
CHIRP CHIRP
NOW THEN...
TWEET TWEET
SAY "ACTUS NOCTIS EREBEAE."
THE FESTIVAL STARTS TOMORROW. LET ME SEE WHAT YOU GOT.
YES, SIR.
......

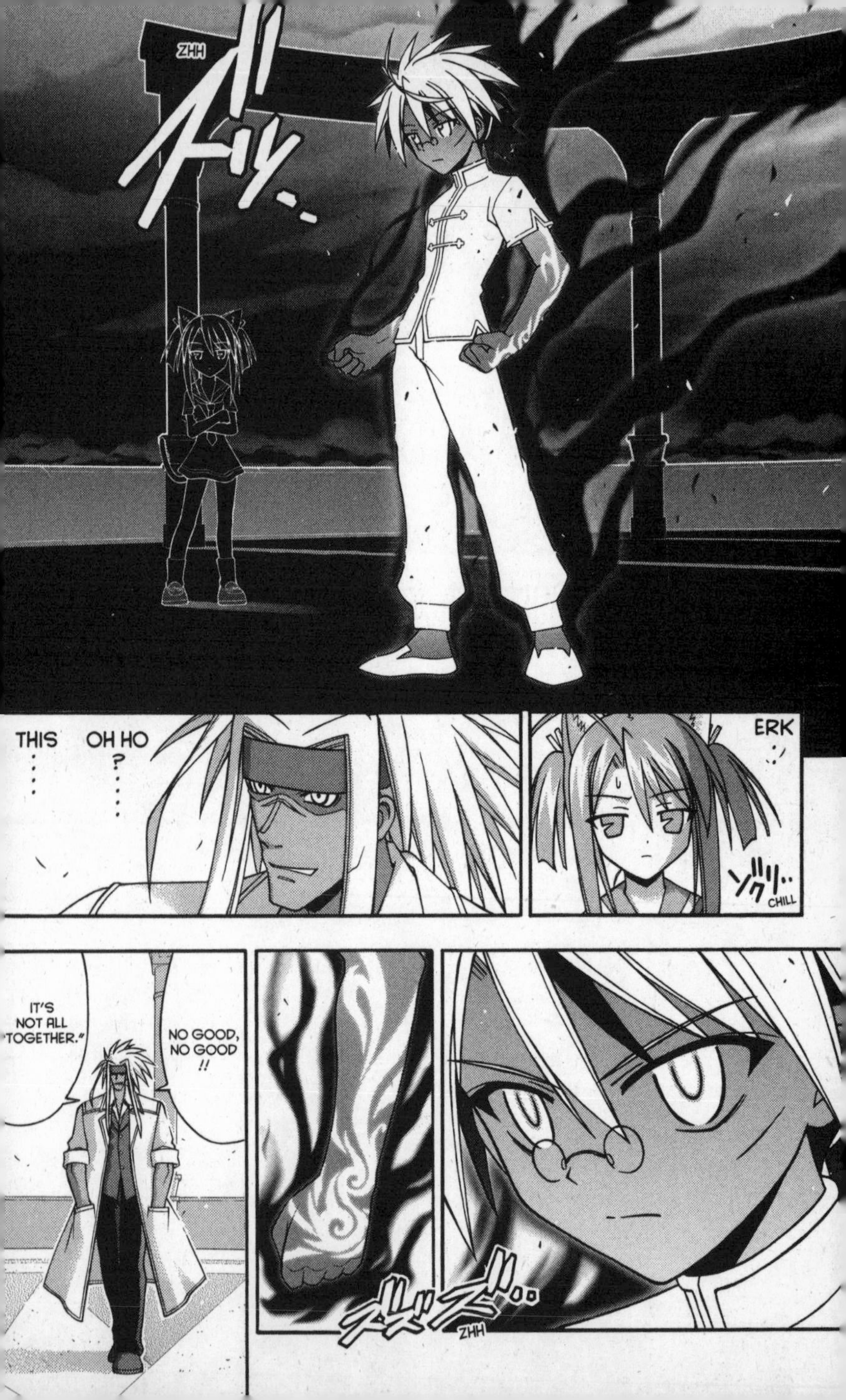
ZHH
ERK
CHILL
OH HO?....
THIS....
ZHH
NO GOOD, NO GOOD!!
IT'S NOT ALL TOGETHER."

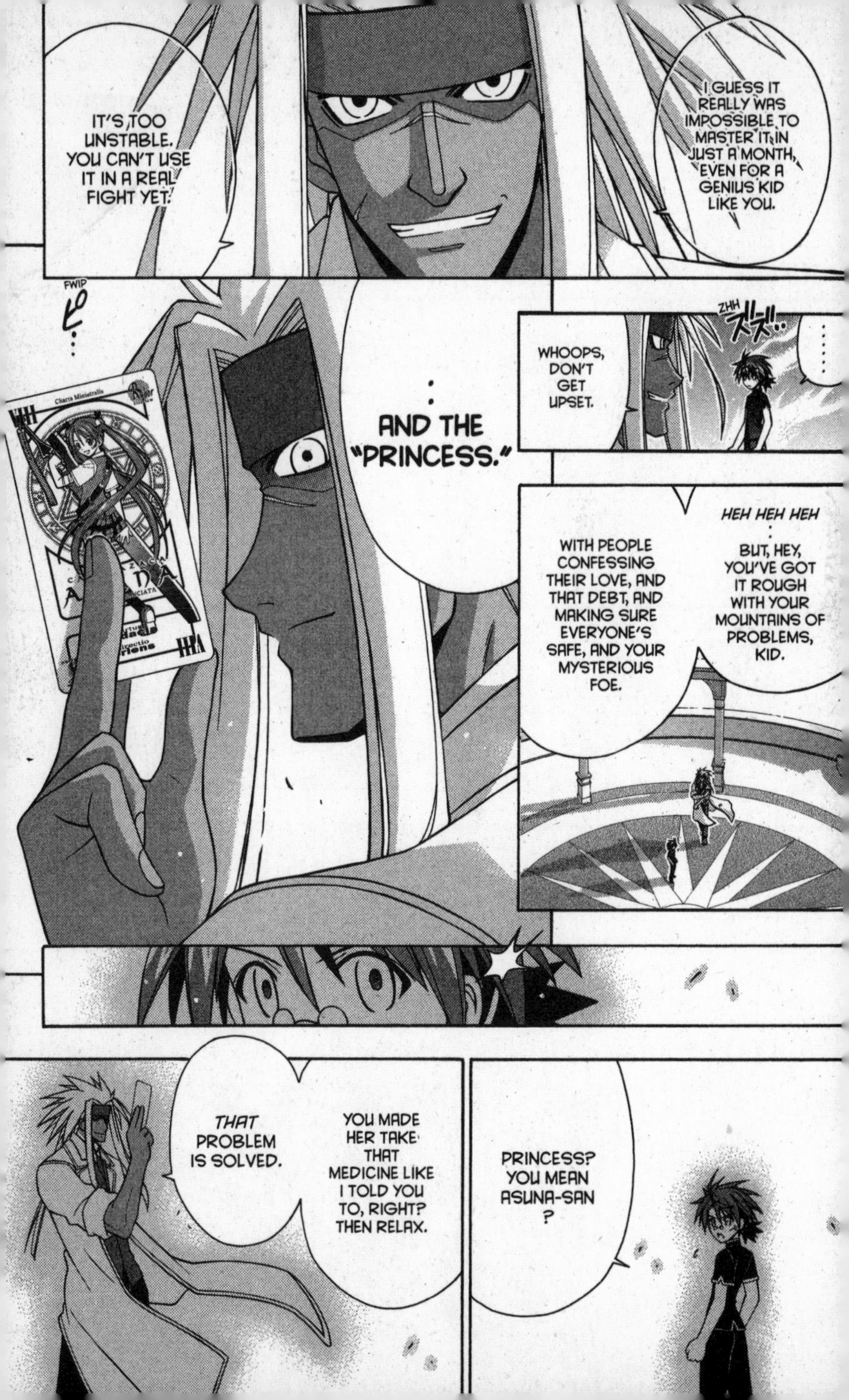
I GUESS IT REALLY WAS IMPOSSIBLE TO MASTER IT IN JUST A MONTH, EVEN FOR A GENIUS KID LIKE YOU.
IT'S TOO UNSTABLE. YOU CAN'T USE IT IN A REAL FIGHT YET.
......
ZHH
ズズ..
WHOOPS, DON'T GET UPSET.
HEH HEH HEH
: BUT, HEY, YOU'VE GOT IT ROUGH WITH YOUR MOUNTAINS OF PROBLEMS, KID.
WITH PEOPLE CONFESSING THEIR LOVE, AND THAT DEBT, AND MAKING SURE EVERYONE'S SAFE, AND YOUR MYSTERIOUS FOE.
FWIP
ピ...
: AND THE "PRINCESS."
PRINCESS? YOU MEAN ASUNA-SAN ?
YOU MADE HER TAKE THAT MEDICINE LIKE I TOLD YOU TO, RIGHT? THEN RELAX.
THAT PROBLEM IS SOLVED.

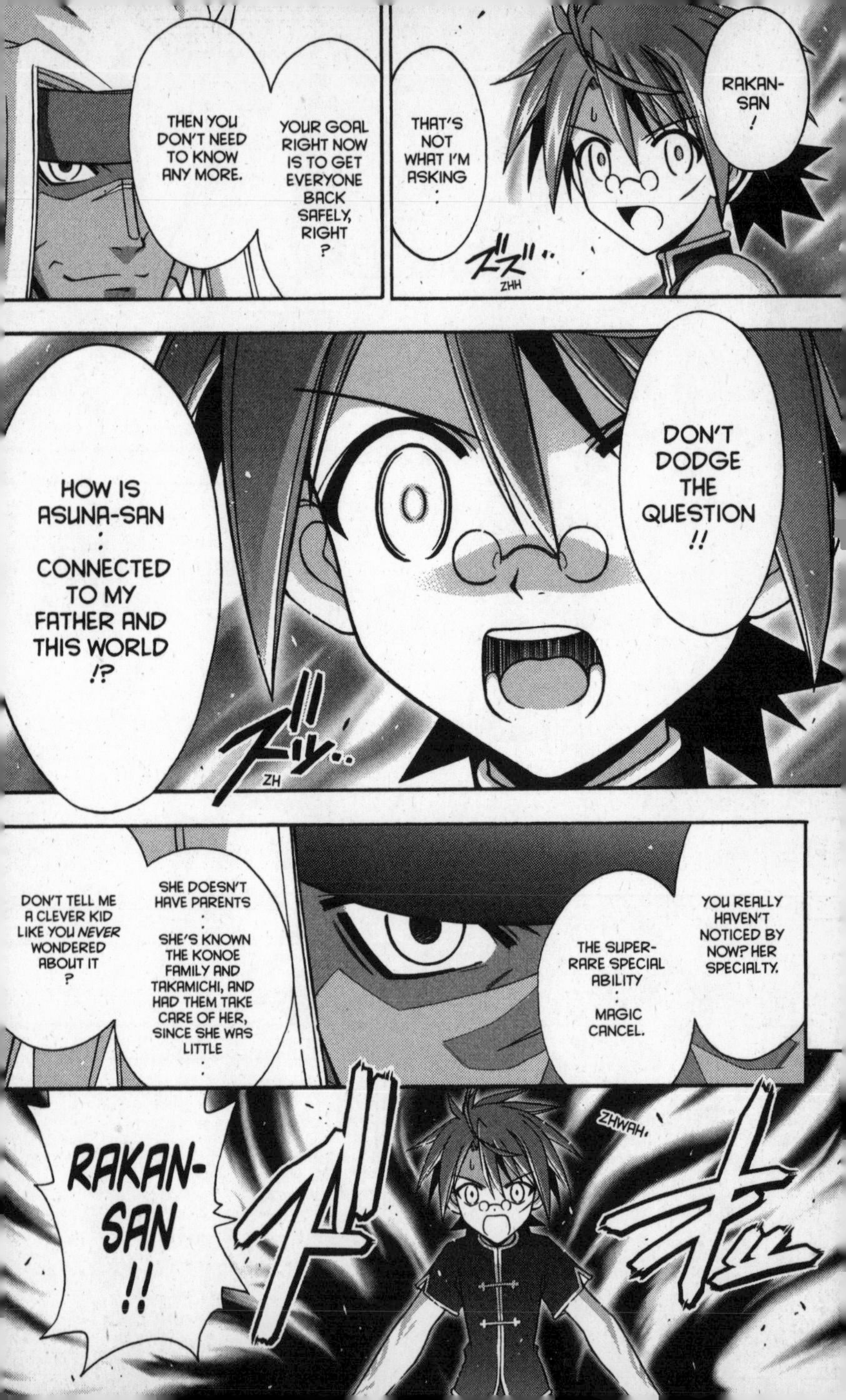
RAKAN-SAN !
THAT'S NOT WHAT I'M ASKING :
ZHH
YOUR GOAL RIGHT NOW IS TO GET EVERYONE BACK SAFELY, RIGHT ?
THEN YOU DON'T NEED TO KNOW ANY MORE.
DON'T DODGE THE QUESTION !!
HOW IS ASUNA-SAN : CONNECTED TO MY FATHER AND THIS WORLD !?
ZH
YOU REALLY HAVEN'T NOTICED BY NOW? HER SPECIALTY.
THE SUPER-RARE SPECIAL ABILITY : MAGIC CANCEL.
SHE DOESN'T HAVE PARENTS : SHE'S KNOWN THE KONOE FAMILY AND TAKAMICHI, AND HAD THEM TAKE CARE OF HER, SINCE SHE WAS LITTLE :
DON'T TELL ME A CLEVER KID LIKE YOU *NEVER* WONDERED ABOUT IT ?
ZHWAH
RAKAN-SAN !!

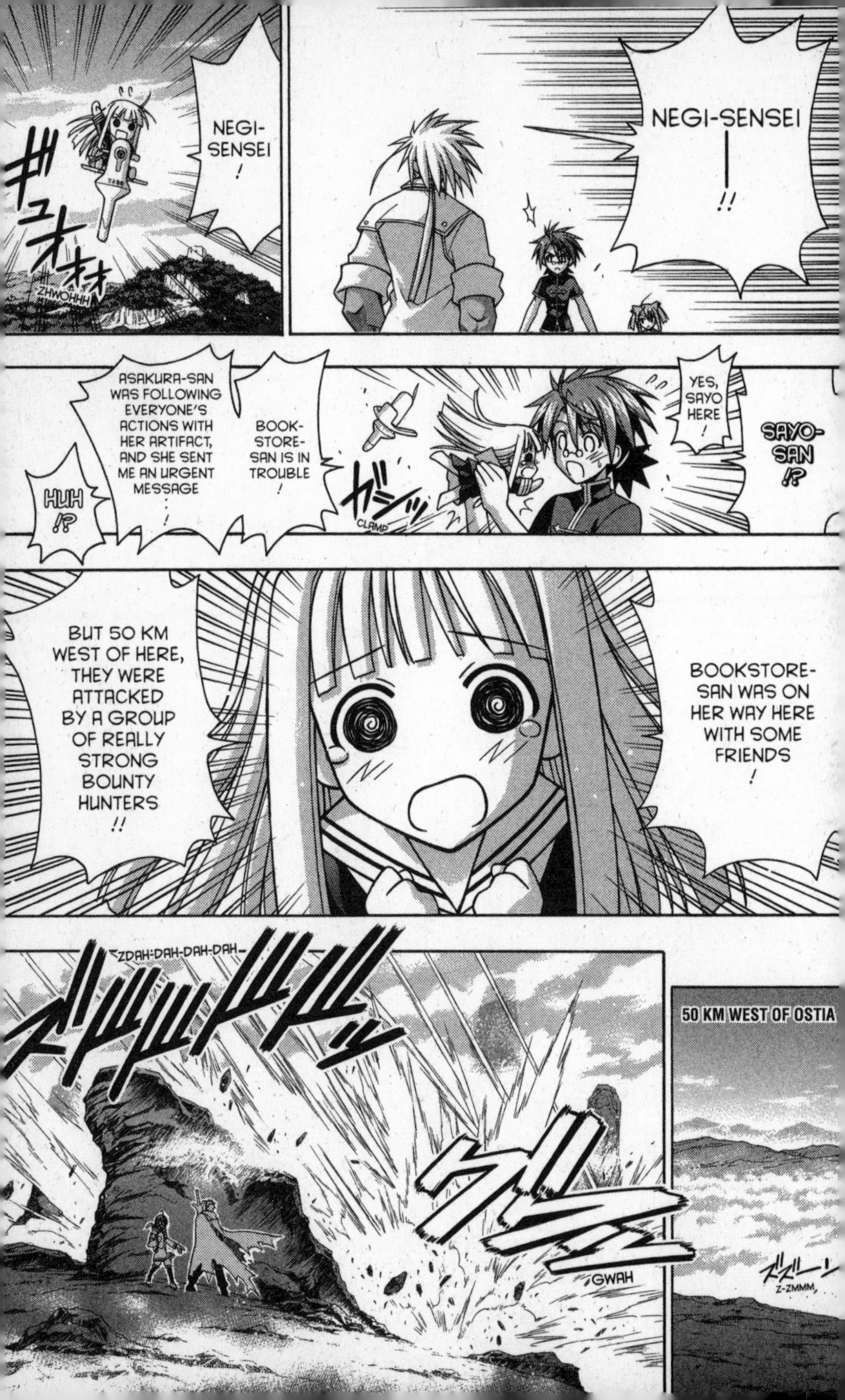
NEGI-SENSEI—!!
NEGI-SENSEI!
ZHWOHHH
SAYO-SAN!?
YES, SAYO HERE!
CLAMP
BOOKSTORE-SAN IS IN TROUBLE!
ASAKURA-SAN WAS FOLLOWING EVERYONE'S ACTIONS WITH HER ARTIFACT, AND SHE SENT ME AN URGENT MESSAGE...!
HUH!?
BOOKSTORE-SAN WAS ON HER WAY HERE WITH SOME FRIENDS!
BUT 50 KM WEST OF HERE, THEY WERE ATTACKED BY A GROUP OF REALLY STRONG BOUNTY HUNTERS!!
50 KM WEST OF OSTIA
Z-ZMMM,
ZDAH-DAH-DAH-DAH
GWAH

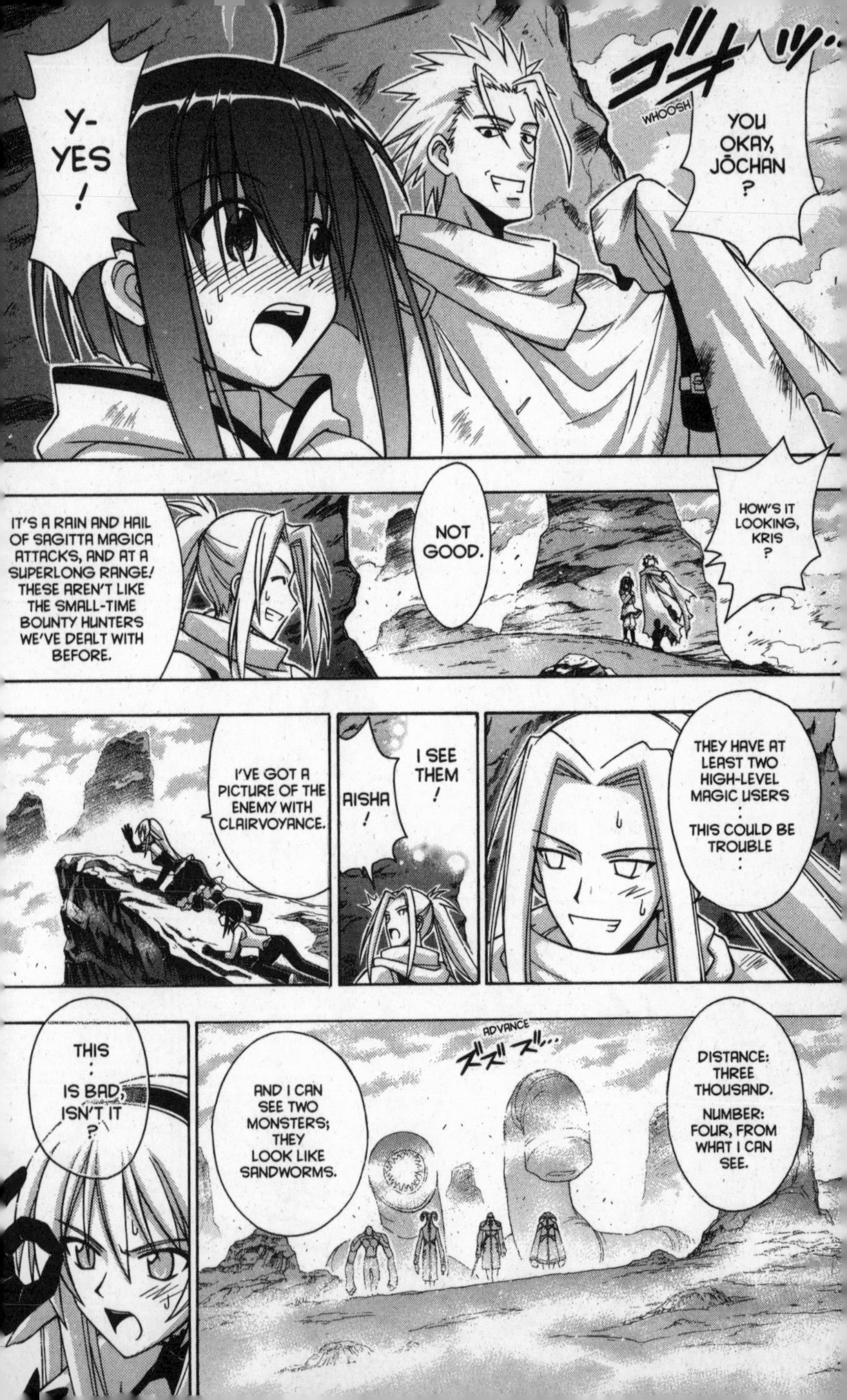
WHOOSH
YOU OKAY, JŌCHAN?
Y-YES!
HOW'S IT LOOKING, KRIS?
NOT GOOD.
IT'S A RAIN AND HAIL OF SAGITTA MAGICA ATTACKS, AND AT A SUPERLONG RANGE! THESE AREN'T LIKE THE SMALL-TIME BOUNTY HUNTERS WE'VE DEALT WITH BEFORE.
THEY HAVE AT LEAST TWO HIGH-LEVEL MAGIC USERS... THIS COULD BE TROUBLE...
I SEE THEM!
AISHA!
I'VE GOT A PICTURE OF THE ENEMY WITH CLAIRVOYANCE.
DISTANCE: THREE THOUSAND.
NUMBER: FOUR, FROM WHAT I CAN SEE.
ADVANCE
AND I CAN SEE TWO MONSTERS; THEY LOOK LIKE SANDWORMS.
THIS... IS BAD, ISN'T IT?

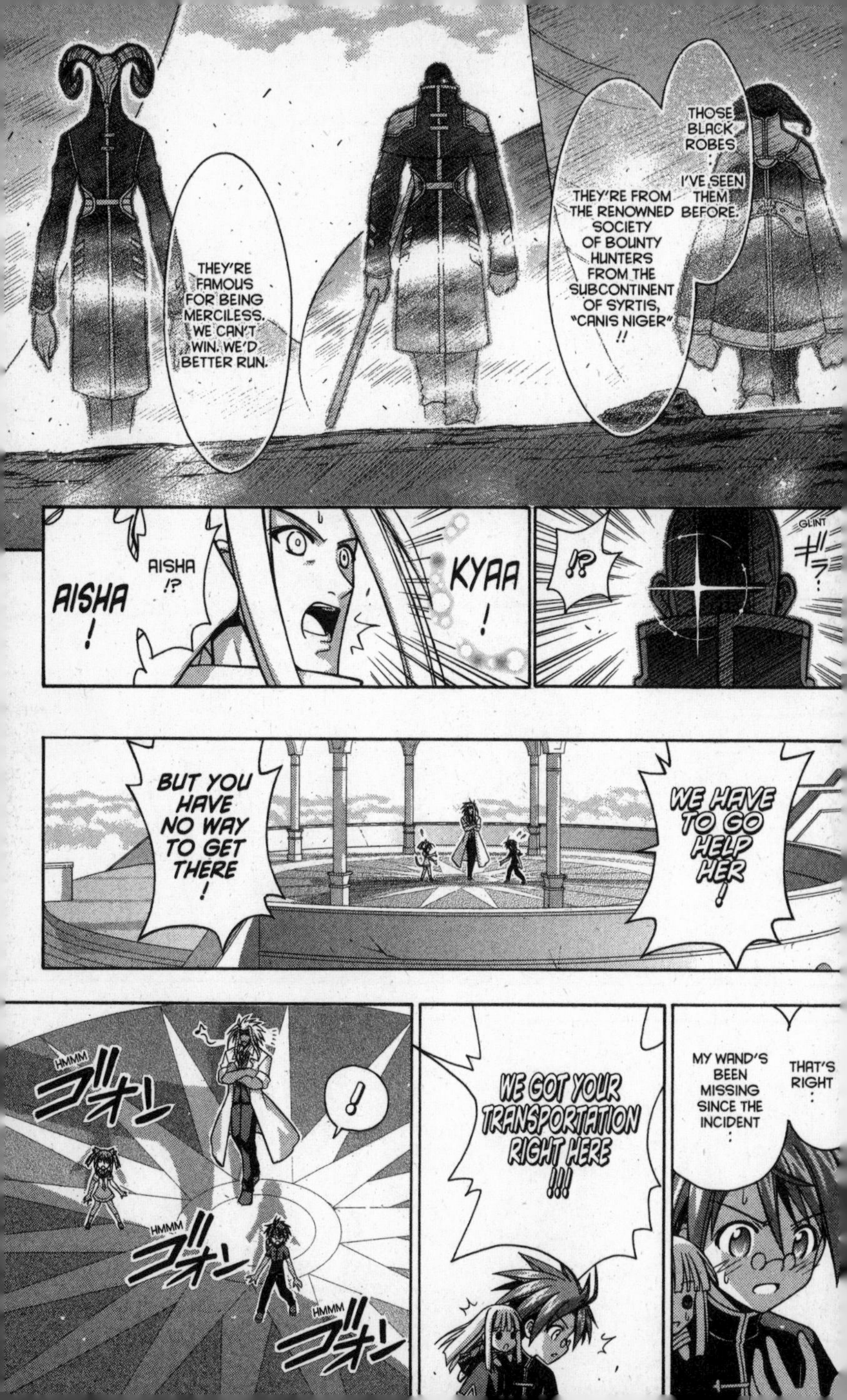

THOSE BLACK ROBES... I'VE SEEN THEM BEFORE.
THEY'RE FROM THE RENOWNED SOCIETY OF BOUNTY HUNTERS FROM THE SUBCONTINENT OF SYRTIS, "CANIS NIGER"!!
THEY'RE FAMOUS FOR BEING MERCILESS. WE CAN'T WIN. WE'D BETTER RUN.
GLINT
ギラ
!?
KYAA!
AISHA!?
AISHA!
WE HAVE TO GO HELP HER!
BUT YOU HAVE NO WAY TO GET THERE!
THAT'S RIGHT...
MY WAND'S BEEN MISSING SINCE THE INCIDENT...
WE GOT YOUR TRANSPORTATION RIGHT HERE!!!
!
HMMM
ゴオン
HMMM
ゴオン
HMMM
ゴオン

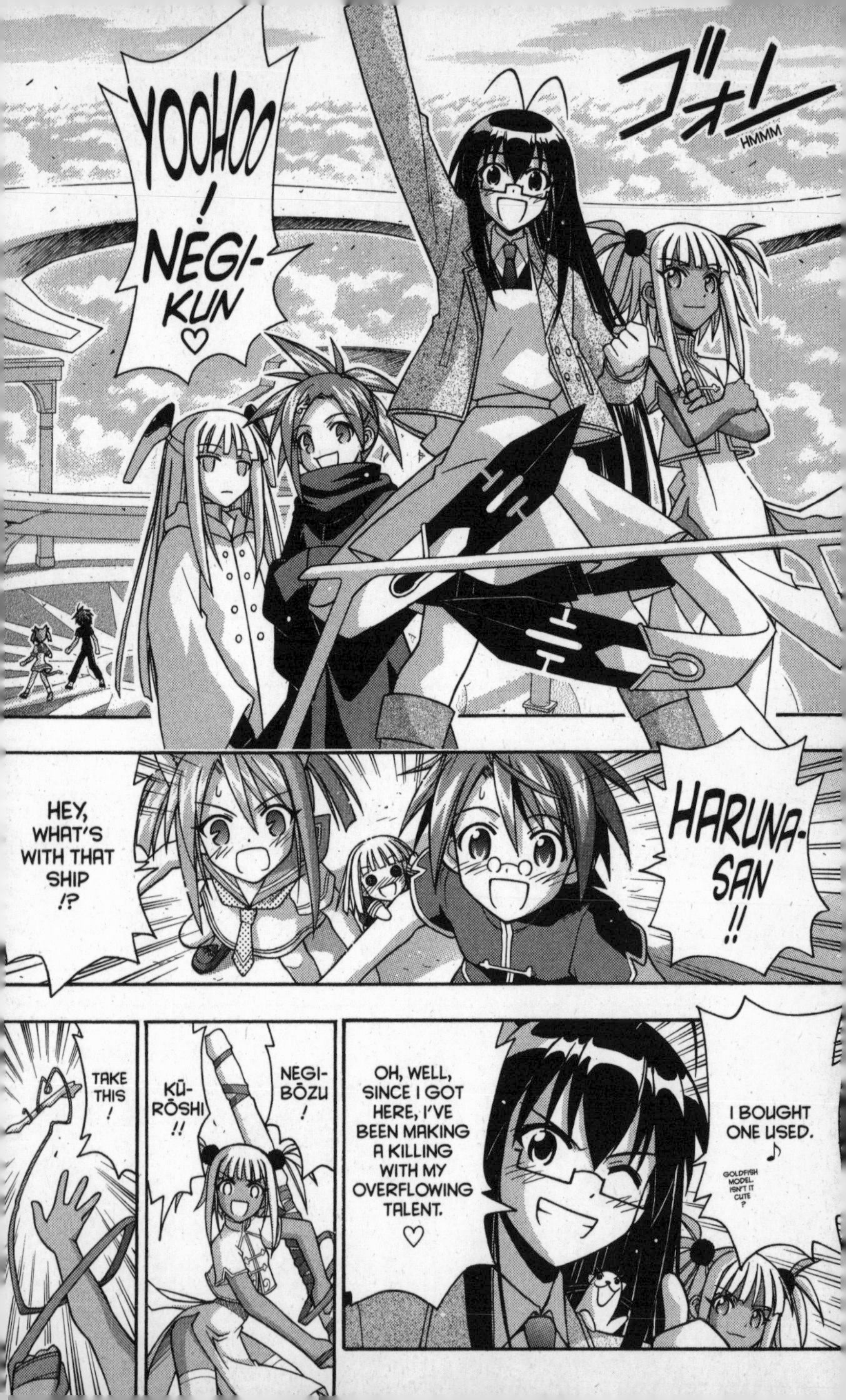
ゴォン
HMMM
YOOHOO! NEGI-KUN ♡
HARUNA-SAN!!
HEY, WHAT'S WITH THAT SHIP!?
I BOUGHT ONE USED. ♪
GOLDFISH MODEL. ISN'T IT CUTE?
OH, WELL, SINCE I GOT HERE, I'VE BEEN MAKING A KILLING WITH MY OVERFLOWING TALENT. ♡
NEGI-BŌZU!
KŪ-RŌSHI!!
TAKE THIS!

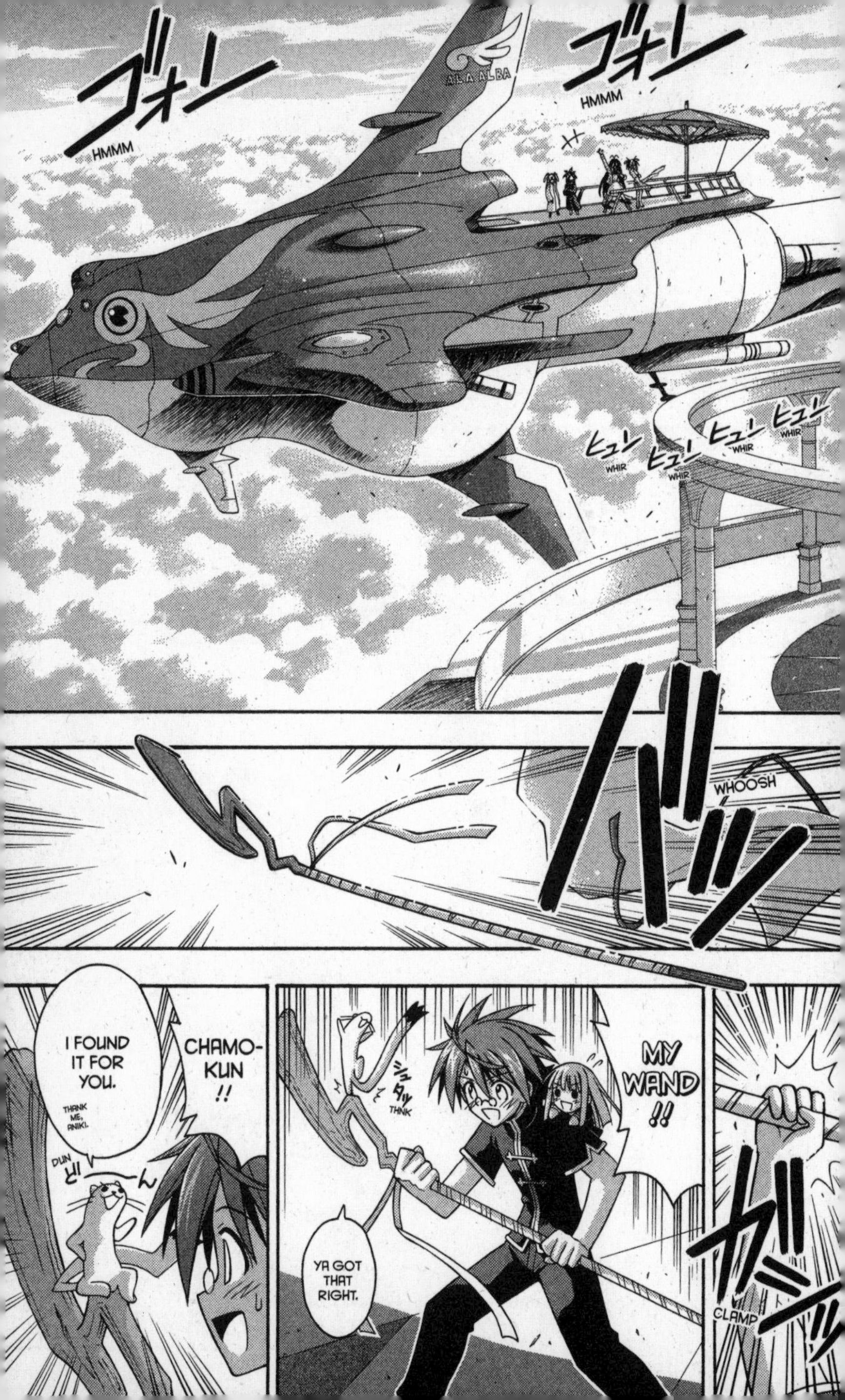

ゴォン
HMMM
ゴォン
HMMM
ALA ALBA
ヒュン
WHIR
ヒュン
WHIR
ヒュン
WHIR
ヒュン
WHIR
WHOOSH
CLAMP
MY WAND !!
THNK
YA GOT THAT RIGHT.
CHAMO-KUN !!
I FOUND IT FOR YOU.
THANK ME, ANIKI.
DUN

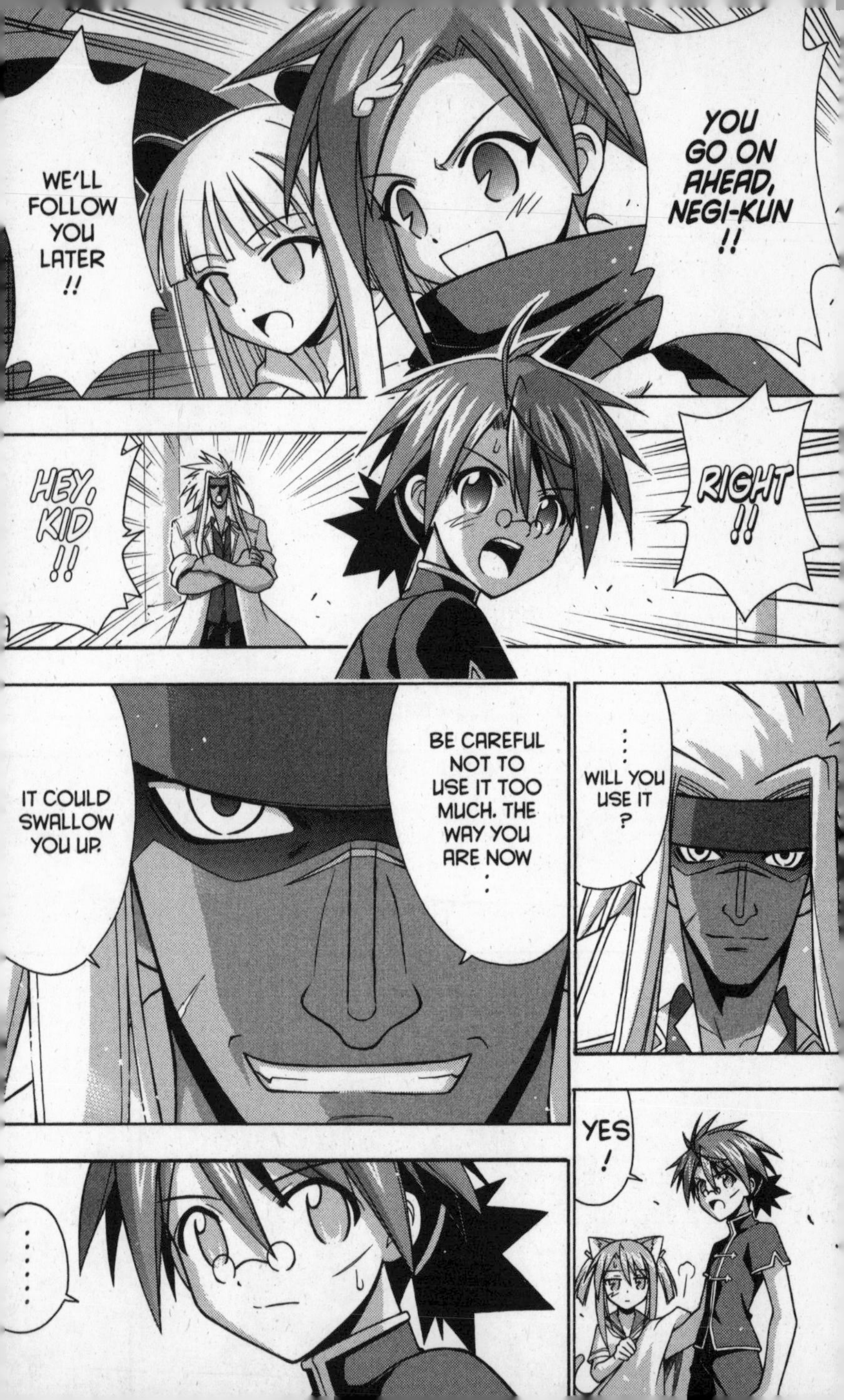
YOU GO ON AHEAD, NEGI-KUN!!
WE'LL FOLLOW YOU LATER!!
RIGHT!!
HEY, KID!!
...WILL YOU USE IT?
BE CAREFUL NOT TO USE IT TOO MUCH. THE WAY YOU ARE NOW...
IT COULD SWALLOW YOU UP.
YES!
......

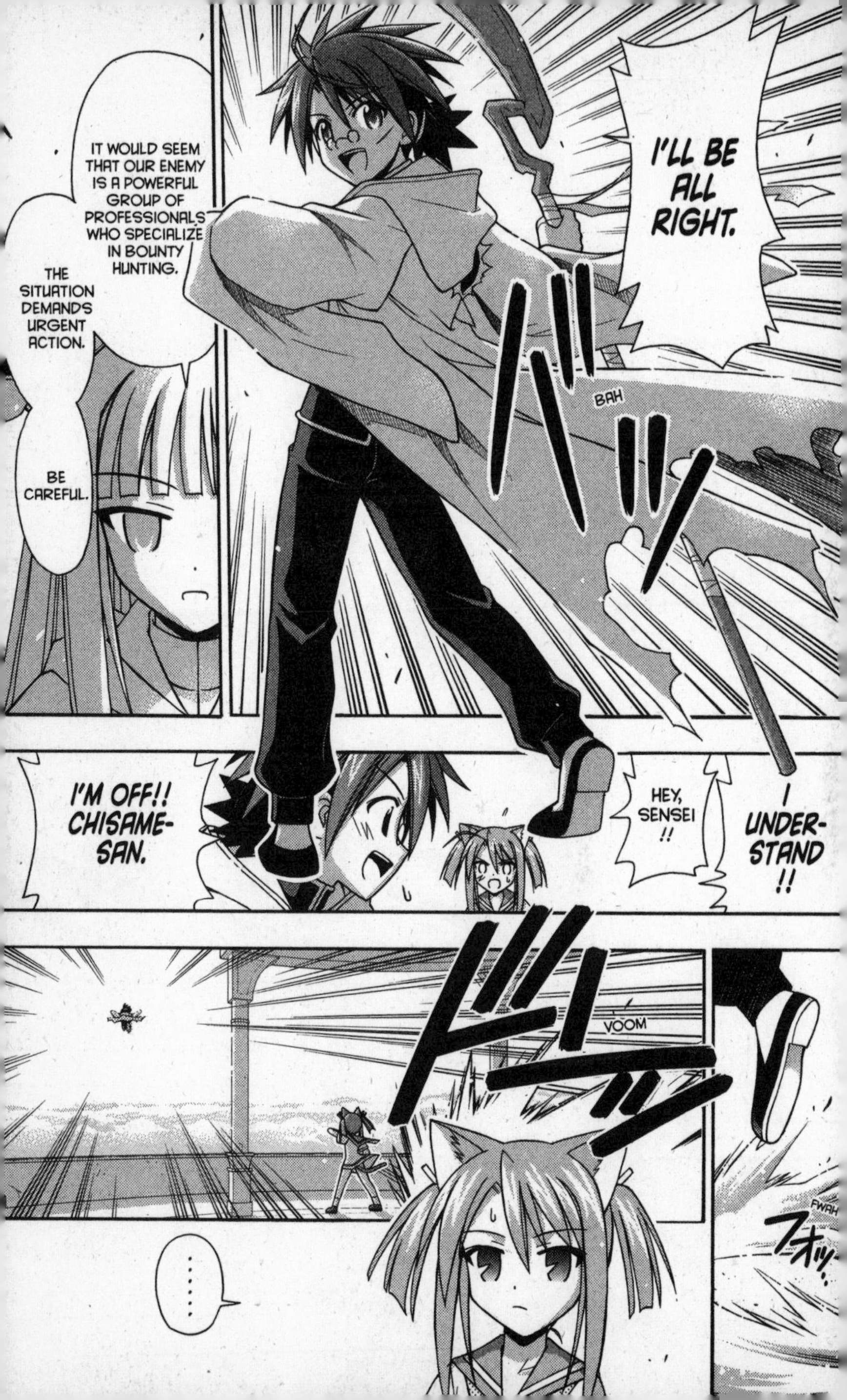
I'LL BE ALL RIGHT.
BAH
IT WOULD SEEM THAT OUR ENEMY IS A POWERFUL GROUP OF PROFESSIONALS WHO SPECIALIZE IN BOUNTY HUNTING.
THE SITUATION DEMANDS URGENT ACTION.
BE CAREFUL.
I UNDERSTAND!!
HEY, SENSEI!!
I'M OFF!! CHISAME-SAN.
VOOM
FWAH
......

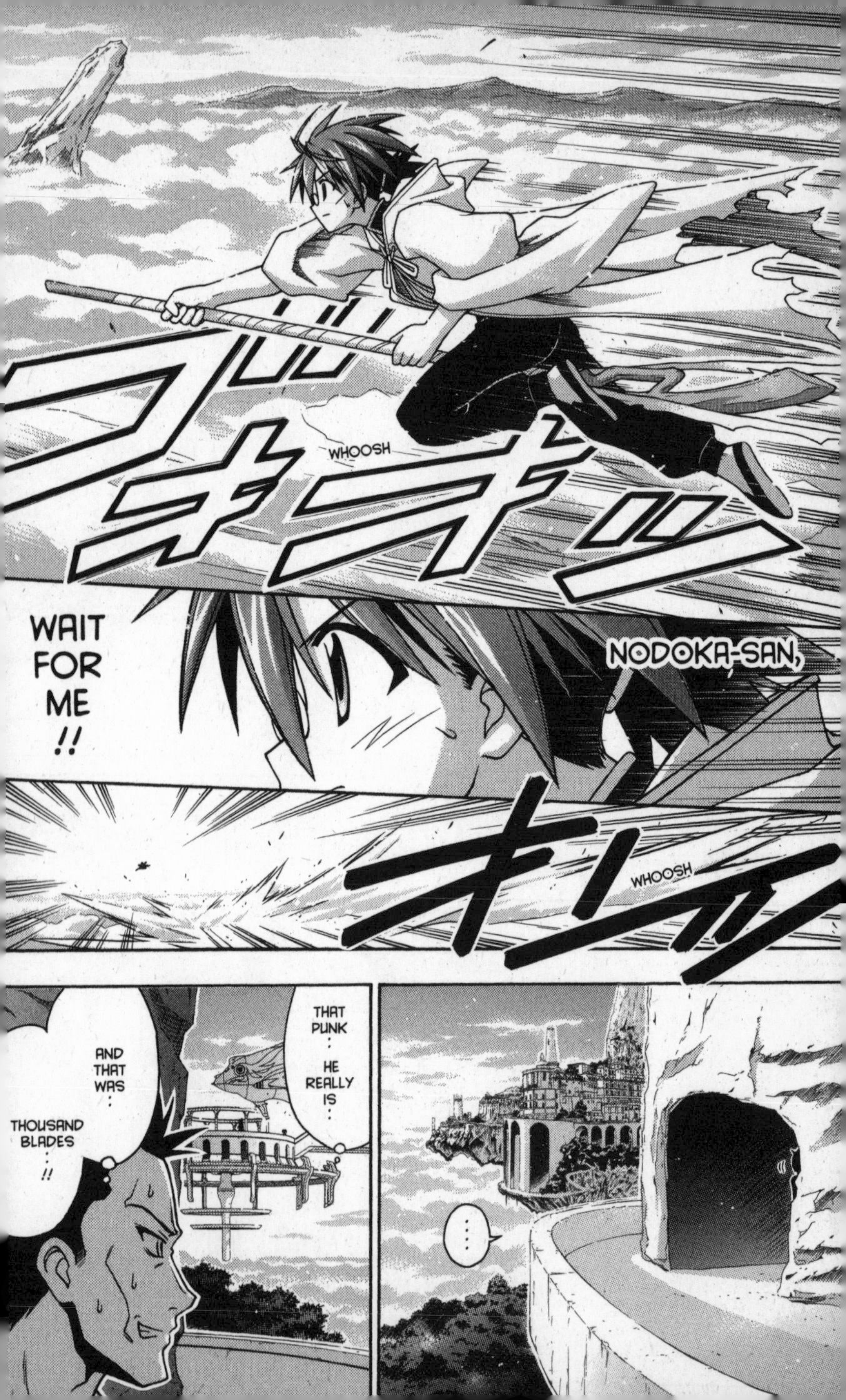
WHOOSH
NODOKA-SAN,
WAIT FOR ME!!
WHOOSH
....
THAT PUNK... HE REALLY IS...
AND THAT WAS... THOUSAND BLADES...!!

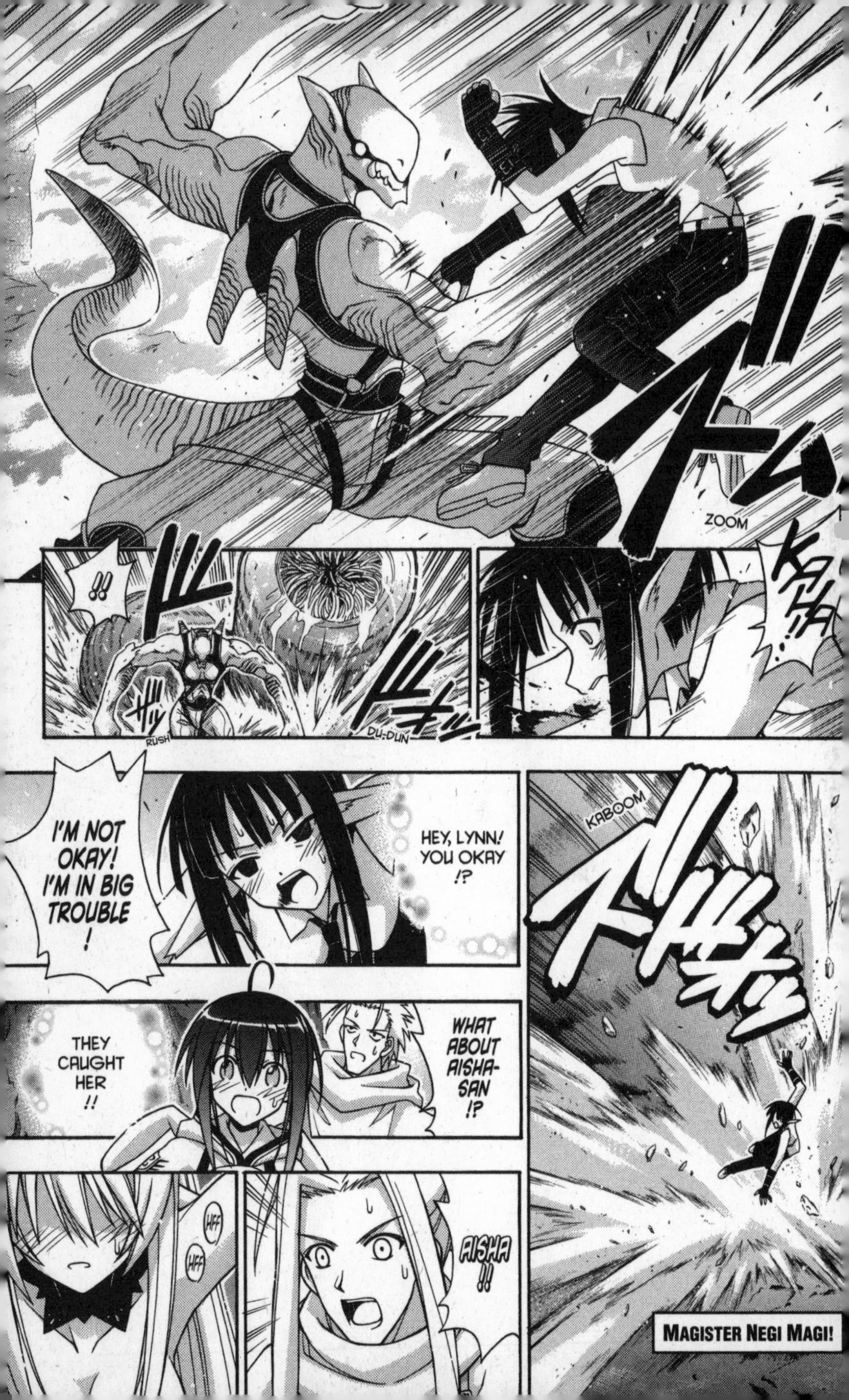
ZOOM
KAHA!!
!!
RUSH
DU-DUN
KABOOM
MAGISTER NEGI MAGI!
HEY, LYNN! YOU OKAY !?
I'M NOT OKAY! I'M IN BIG TROUBLE !
WHAT ABOUT AISHA-SAN !?
THEY CAUGHT HER !!
AISHA !!
HFF
HFF

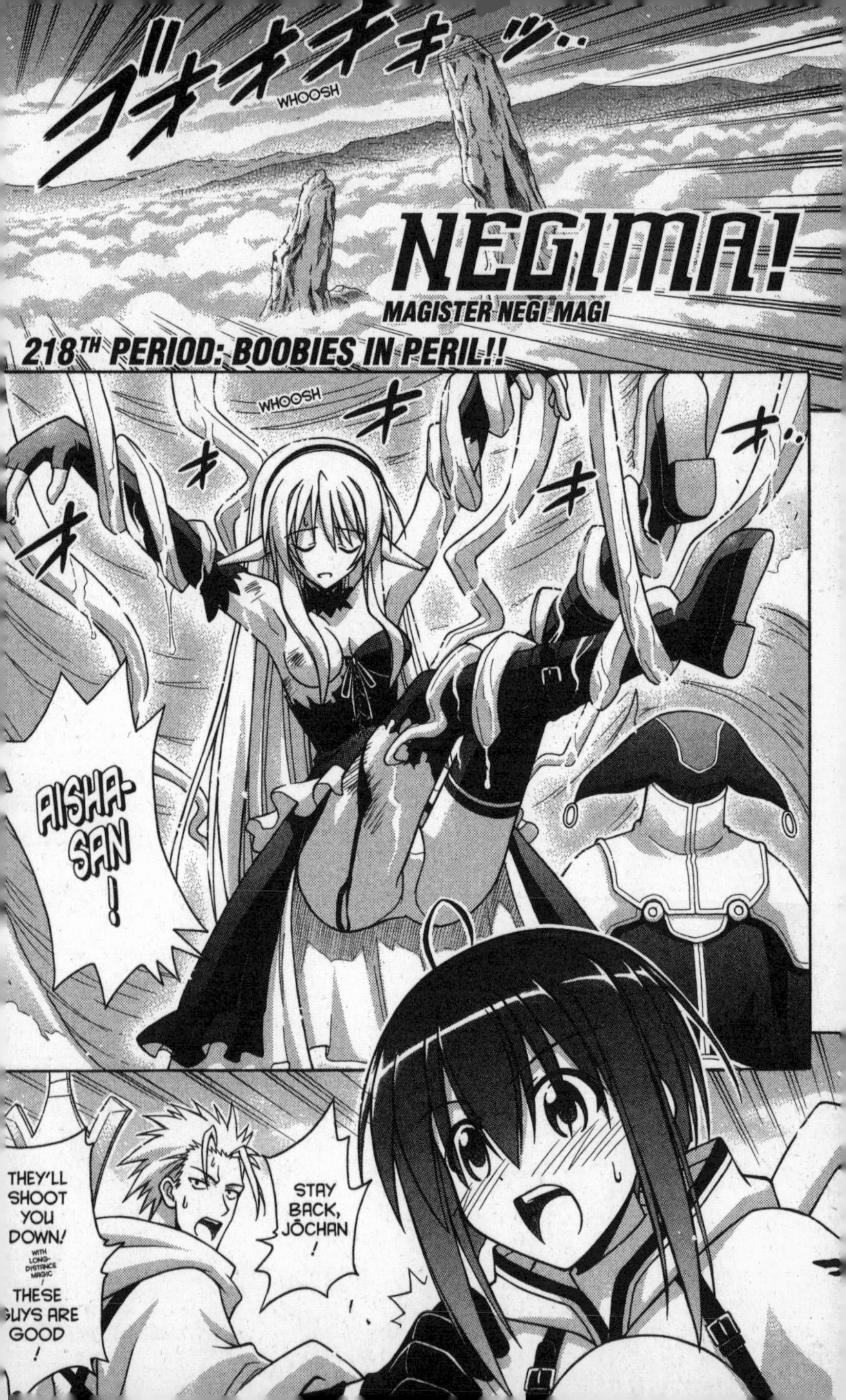
WHOOSH
NEGIMA!
MAGISTER NEGI MAGI
218TH PERIOD: BOOBIES IN PERIL!!
WHOOSH
AISHA-SAN!
STAY BACK, JŌCHAN!
THEY'LL SHOOT YOU DOWN!
WITH LONG-DISTANCE MAGIC!
THESE GUYS ARE GOOD!

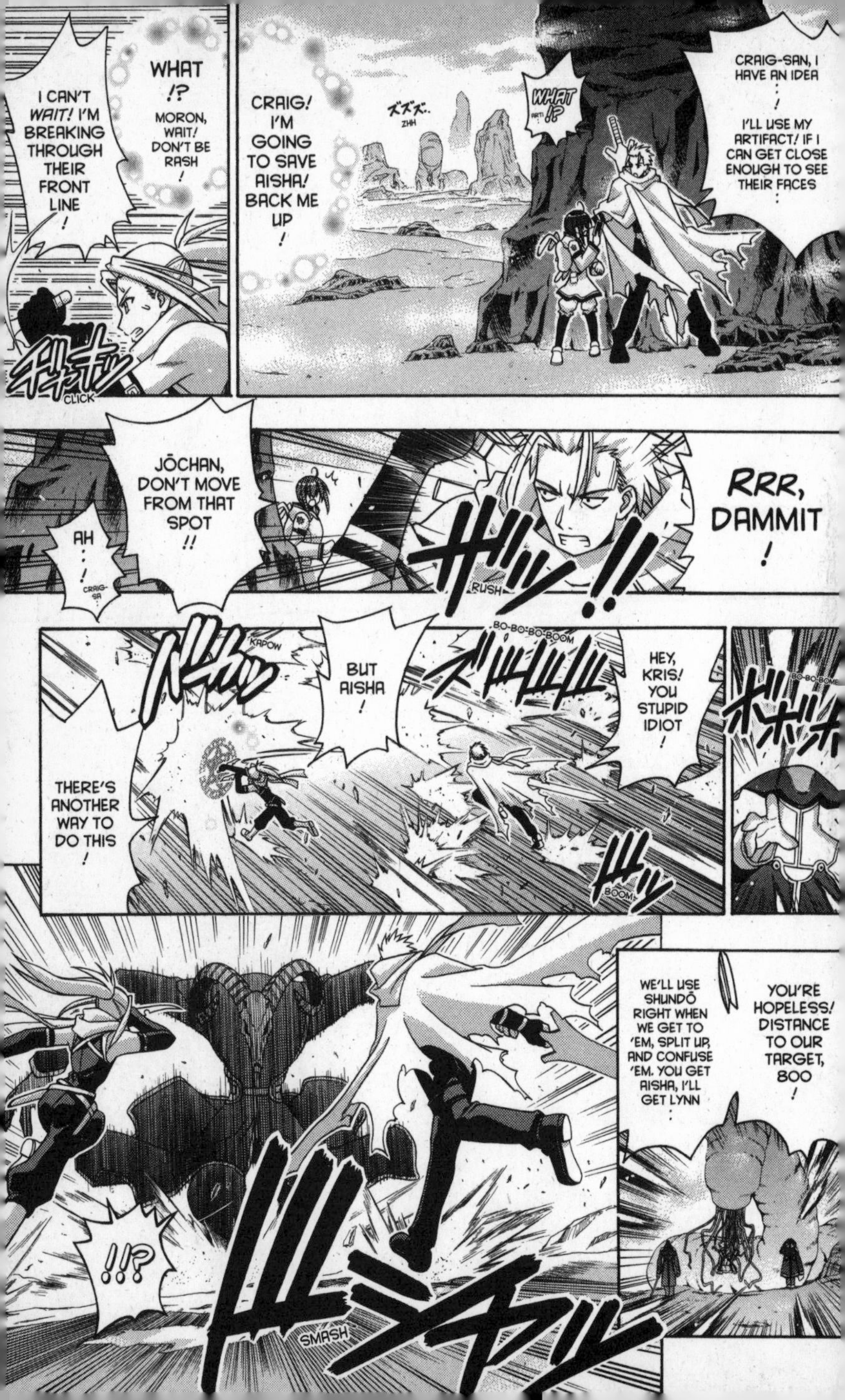
CRAIG-SAN, I HAVE AN IDEA...!
I'LL USE MY ARTIFACT! IF I CAN GET CLOSE ENOUGH TO SEE THEIR FACES...
WHAT!?
ARTI!
ズズズ..
ZHH
CRAIG! I'M GOING TO SAVE AISHA! BACK ME UP!
WHAT!? MORON, WAIT! DON'T BE RASH!
I CAN'T WAIT! I'M BREAKING THROUGH THEIR FRONT LINE!
CLICK
RRR, DAMMIT!
RUSH
JŌCHAN, DON'T MOVE FROM THAT SPOT!!
AH...!
CRAIG-SA
BO-BO-BOMB
HEY, KRIS! YOU STUPID IDIOT!
BO-BO-BO-BOOM
BOOM
BUT AISHA!
KAPOW
THERE'S ANOTHER WAY TO DO THIS!
YOU'RE HOPELESS! DISTANCE TO OUR TARGET, 800!
WE'LL USE SHUNDŌ RIGHT WHEN WE GET TO 'EM, SPLIT UP, AND CONFUSE 'EM. YOU GET AISHA, I'LL GET LYNN...
!!?
SMASH

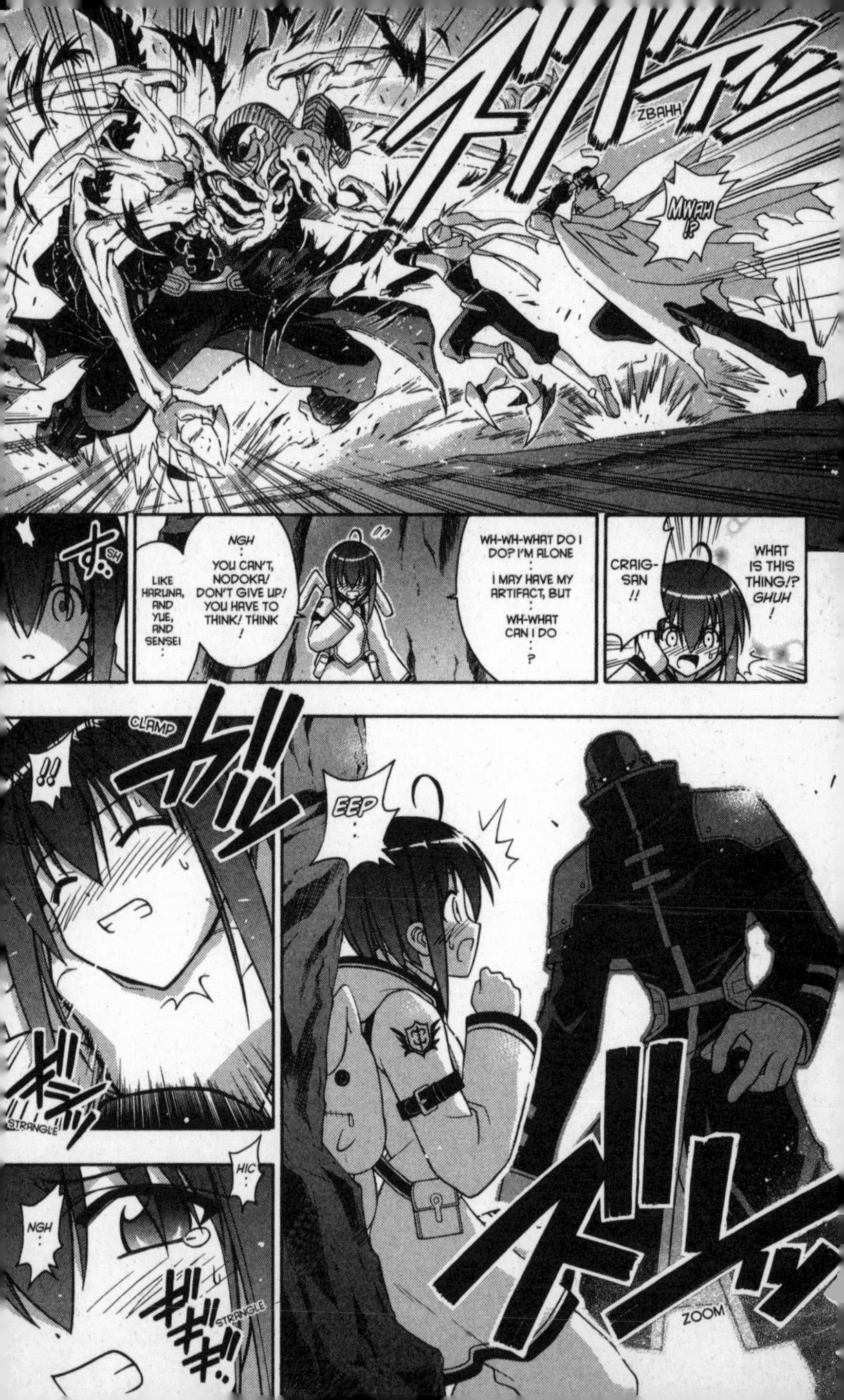
ZBAHH
MWAH !?
WHAT IS THIS THING!? GHUH !
CRAIG-SAN !!
WH-WH-WHAT DO I DO? I'M ALONE . . . I MAY HAVE MY ARTIFACT, BUT . . . WH-WHAT CAN I DO . . . ?
NGH . . . YOU CAN'T, NODOKA! DON'T GIVE UP! YOU HAVE TO THINK! THINK !
LIKE HARUNA, AND YUE, AND SENSEI . . .
SH
ZOOM
EEP . . .
CLAMP
!!
STRANGLE
HIC . . .
NGH . . .
STRANGLE

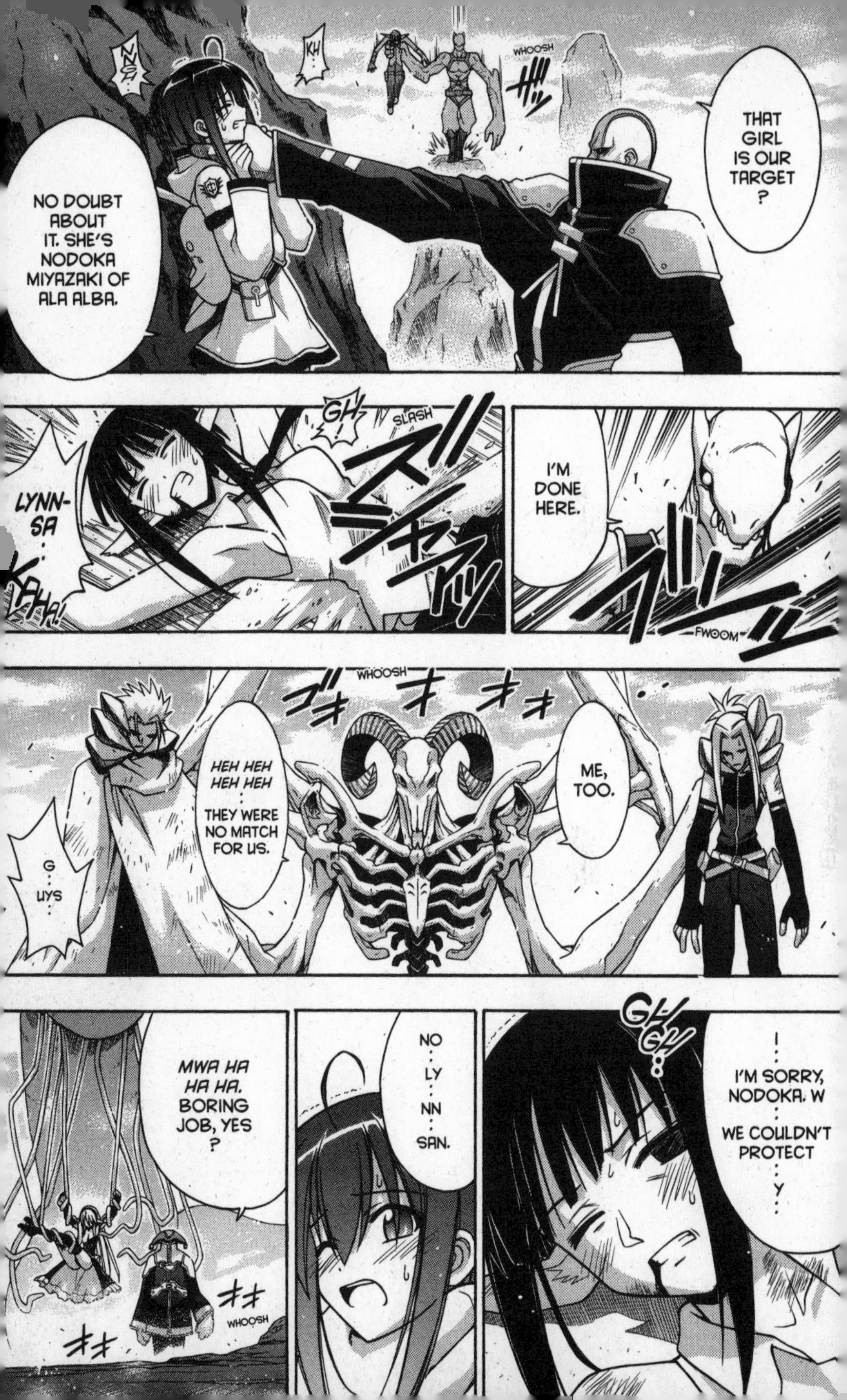
THAT GIRL IS OUR TARGET?
WHOOSH
KH
NNGH...
NO DOUBT ABOUT IT. SHE'S NODOKA MIYAZAKI OF ALA ALBA.
I'M DONE HERE.
FWOOM
SLASH
GH!
LYNN-SA...
KAHA!
ME, TOO.
WHOOSH
HEH HEH HEH HEH... THEY WERE NO MATCH FOR US.
G... UYS...
GH-GH!
I... I'M SORRY, NODOKA. W... WE COULDN'T PROTECT... Y...
NO... LY... NN... SAN.
MWA HA HA HA. BORING JOB, YES?
WHOOSH

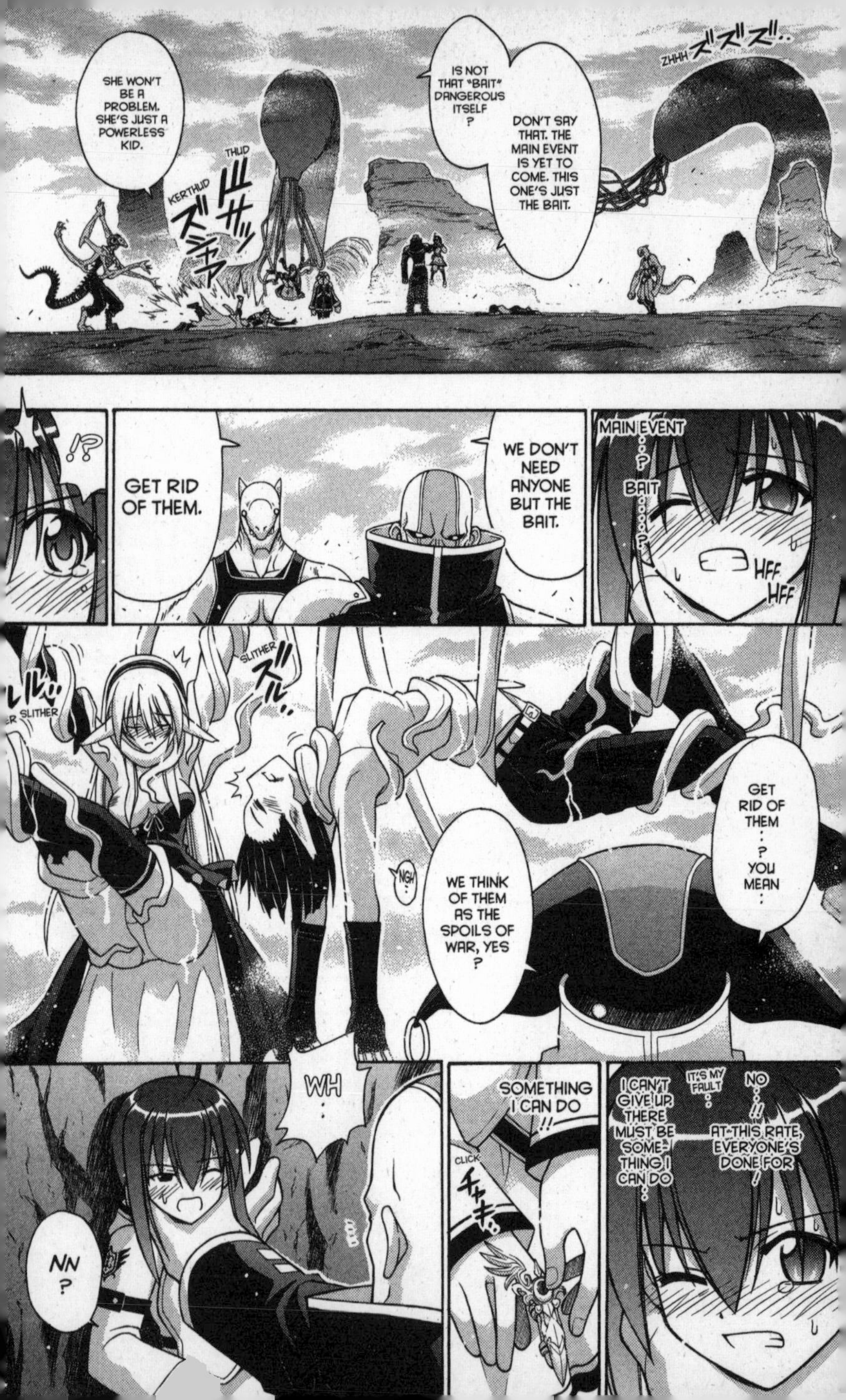
ZHHH ズズズ..
IS NOT THAT "BAIT" DANGEROUS ITSELF?
DON'T SAY THAT. THE MAIN EVENT IS YET TO COME. THIS ONE'S JUST THE BAIT.
SHE WON'T BE A PROBLEM. SHE'S JUST A POWERLESS KID.
THUD
KERTHUD
MAIN EVENT...?
BAIT...?
HFF HFF
WE DON'T NEED ANYONE BUT THE BAIT.
GET RID OF THEM.
!?
GET RID OF THEM...? YOU MEAN...
WE THINK OF THEM AS THE SPOILS OF WAR, YES?
NGH...
SLITHER
SLITHER
NO...!!
AT THIS RATE, EVERYONE'S DONE FOR!
IT'S MY FAULT...
I CAN'T GIVE UP. THERE MUST BE SOMETHING I CAN DO...
SOMETHING I CAN DO!!
CLICK
WH...
NN?

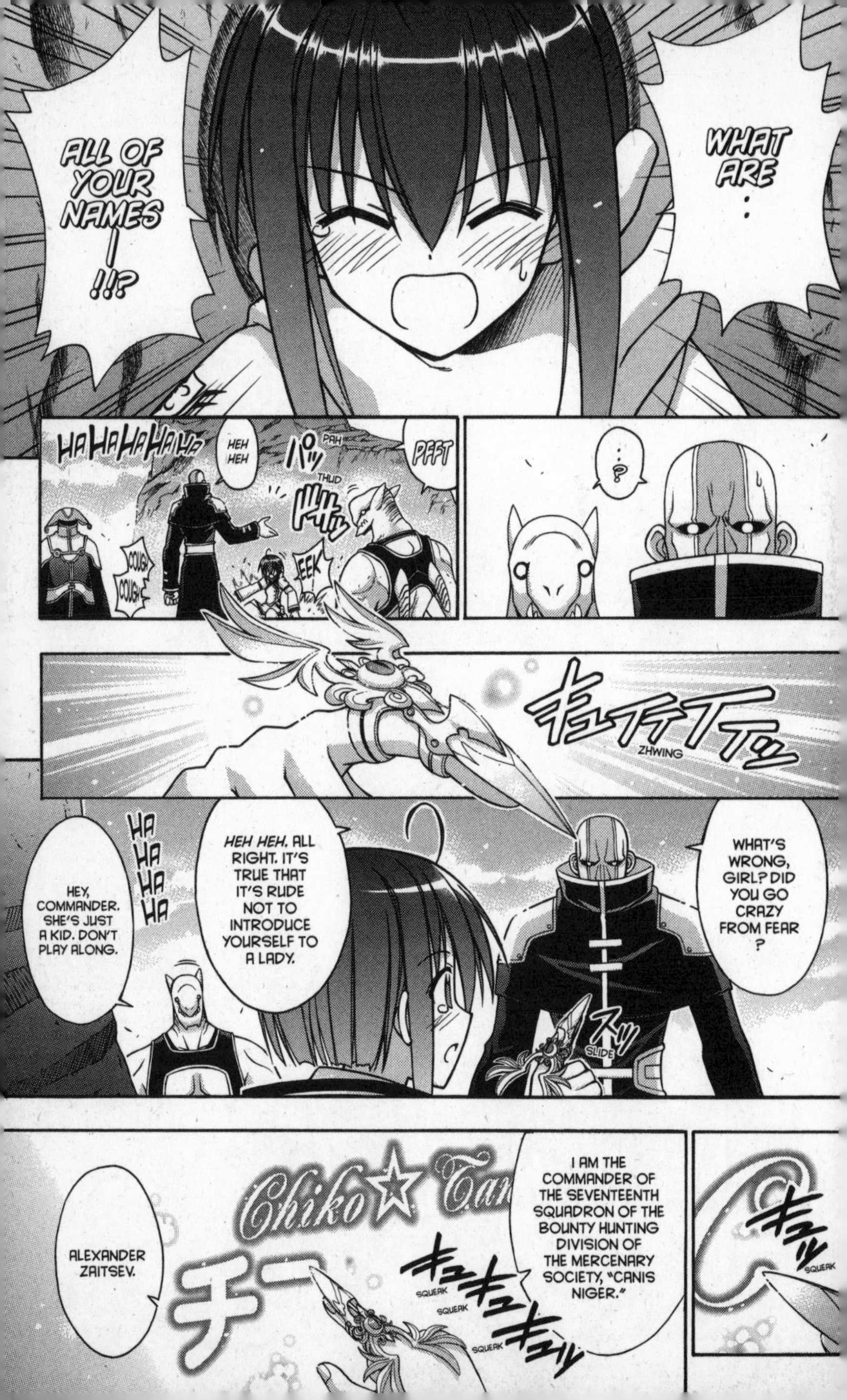
WHAT ARE . . .
ALL OF YOUR NAMES !!?
. . . ?
PFFT
PAH
THUD
HEH HEH
HAHAHAHAHA
EEK
COUGH COUGH
ZHWING
WHAT'S WRONG, GIRL? DID YOU GO CRAZY FROM FEAR ?
HEH HEH. ALL RIGHT. IT'S TRUE THAT IT'S RUDE NOT TO INTRODUCE YOURSELF TO A LADY.
HA HA HA HA
HEY, COMMANDER. SHE'S JUST A KID. DON'T PLAY ALONG.
SLIDE
SQUEAK
I AM THE COMMANDER OF THE SEVENTEENTH SQUADRON OF THE BOUNTY HUNTING DIVISION OF THE MERCENARY SOCIETY, "CANIS NIGER."
SQUEAK SQUEAK SQUEAK
ALEXANDER ZAITSEV.

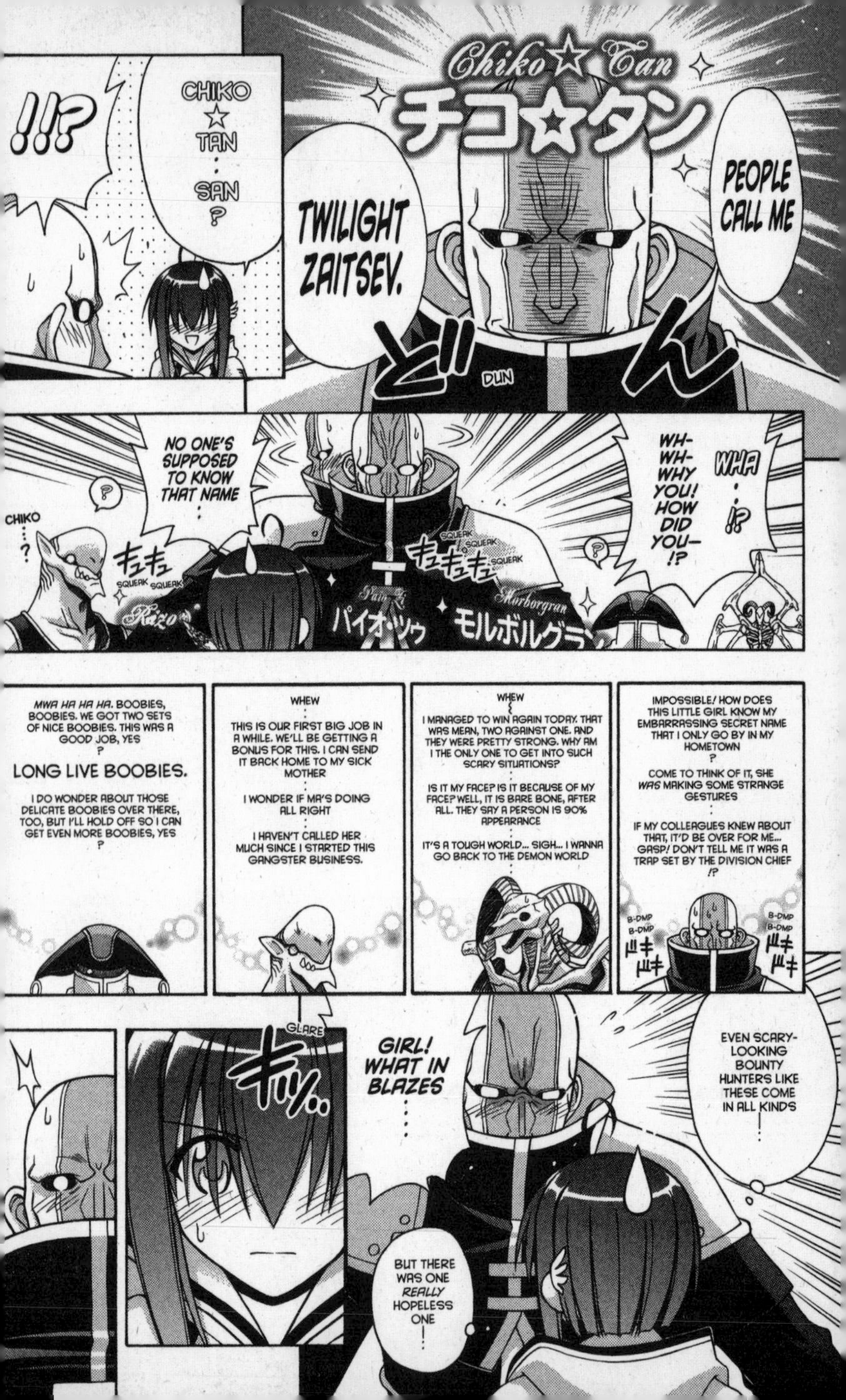
PEOPLE CALL ME
Chiko☆Tan
チコ☆タン
TWILIGHT ZAITSEV.
どん
DUN
CHIKO ☆ TAN . . SAN ?
!!?
WHA . . !?
WH- WH- WHY YOU! HOW DID YOU— !?
SQUEAK SQUEAK SQUEAK
Morborgran
モルボルグラ
NO ONE'S SUPPOSED TO KNOW THAT NAME . .
パイオ・ツゥ
CHIKO . . . ?
SQUEAK SQUEAK
Razo
IMPOSSIBLE! HOW DOES THIS LITTLE GIRL KNOW MY EMBARRASSING SECRET NAME THAT I ONLY GO BY IN MY HOMETOWN ?
COME TO THINK OF IT, SHE *WAS* MAKING SOME STRANGE GESTURES
IF MY COLLEAGUES KNEW ABOUT THAT, IT'D BE OVER FOR ME... GASP! DON'T TELL ME IT WAS A TRAP SET BY THE DIVISION CHIEF !?
B-DMP B-DMP
B-DMP B-DMP
WHEW
I MANAGED TO WIN AGAIN TODAY. THAT WAS MEAN, TWO AGAINST ONE. AND THEY WERE PRETTY STRONG. WHY AM I THE ONLY ONE TO GET INTO SUCH SCARY SITUATIONS?
IS IT MY FACE? IS IT BECAUSE OF MY FACE? WELL, IT IS BARE BONE, AFTER ALL. THEY SAY A PERSON IS 90% APPEARANCE
IT'S A TOUGH WORLD... SIGH... I WANNA GO BACK TO THE DEMON WORLD
WHEW
THIS IS OUR FIRST BIG JOB IN A WHILE. WE'LL BE GETTING A BONUS FOR THIS. I CAN SEND IT BACK HOME TO MY SICK MOTHER
I WONDER IF MA'S DOING ALL RIGHT
I HAVEN'T CALLED HER MUCH SINCE I STARTED THIS GANGSTER BUSINESS.
MWA HA HA HA. BOOBIES, BOOBIES. WE GOT TWO SETS OF NICE BOOBIES. THIS WAS A GOOD JOB, YES ?
LONG LIVE BOOBIES.
I DO WONDER ABOUT THOSE DELICATE BOOBIES OVER THERE, TOO, BUT I'LL HOLD OFF SO I CAN GET EVEN MORE BOOBIES, YES ?
EVEN SCARY-LOOKING BOUNTY HUNTERS LIKE THESE COME IN ALL KINDS !
GIRL! WHAT IN BLAZES . . .
BUT THERE WAS ONE *REALLY* HOPELESS ONE !
GLARE
キッ

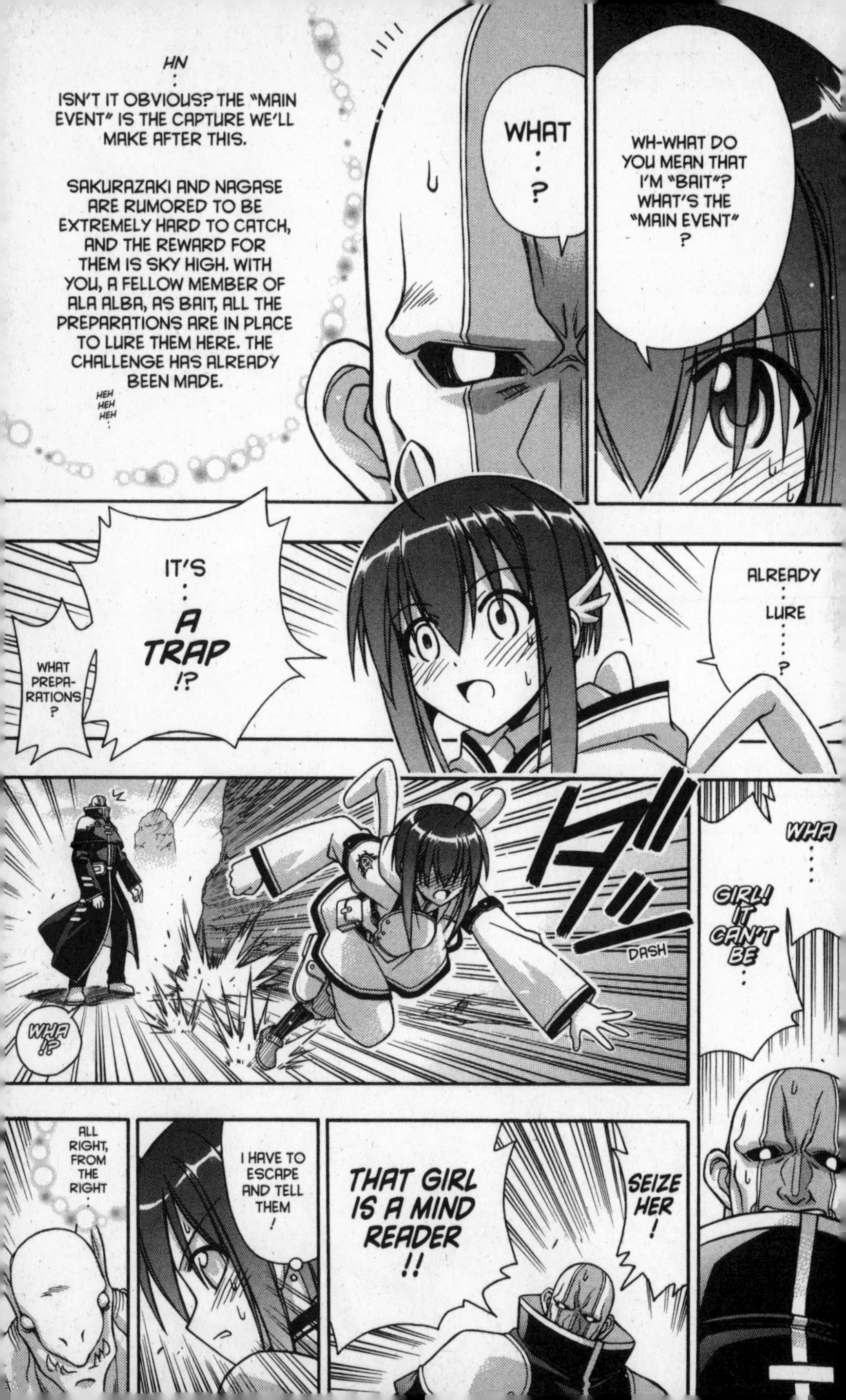
WH-WHAT DO YOU MEAN THAT I'M "BAIT"? WHAT'S THE "MAIN EVENT"?
WHAT...?
HN:
ISN'T IT OBVIOUS? THE "MAIN EVENT" IS THE CAPTURE WE'LL MAKE AFTER THIS.
SAKURAZAKI AND NAGASE ARE RUMORED TO BE EXTREMELY HARD TO CATCH, AND THE REWARD FOR THEM IS SKY HIGH. WITH YOU, A FELLOW MEMBER OF ALA ALBA, AS BAIT, ALL THE PREPARATIONS ARE IN PLACE TO LURE THEM HERE. THE CHALLENGE HAS ALREADY BEEN MADE.
HEH HEH HEH:
ALREADY... LURE...?
IT'S... A TRAP!?
WHAT PREPARATIONS?
WHA...
GIRL! IT CAN'T BE...
DASH
WHA!?
SEIZE HER!
THAT GIRL IS A MIND READER!!
I HAVE TO ESCAPE AND TELL THEM!
ALL RIGHT, FROM THE RIGHT...

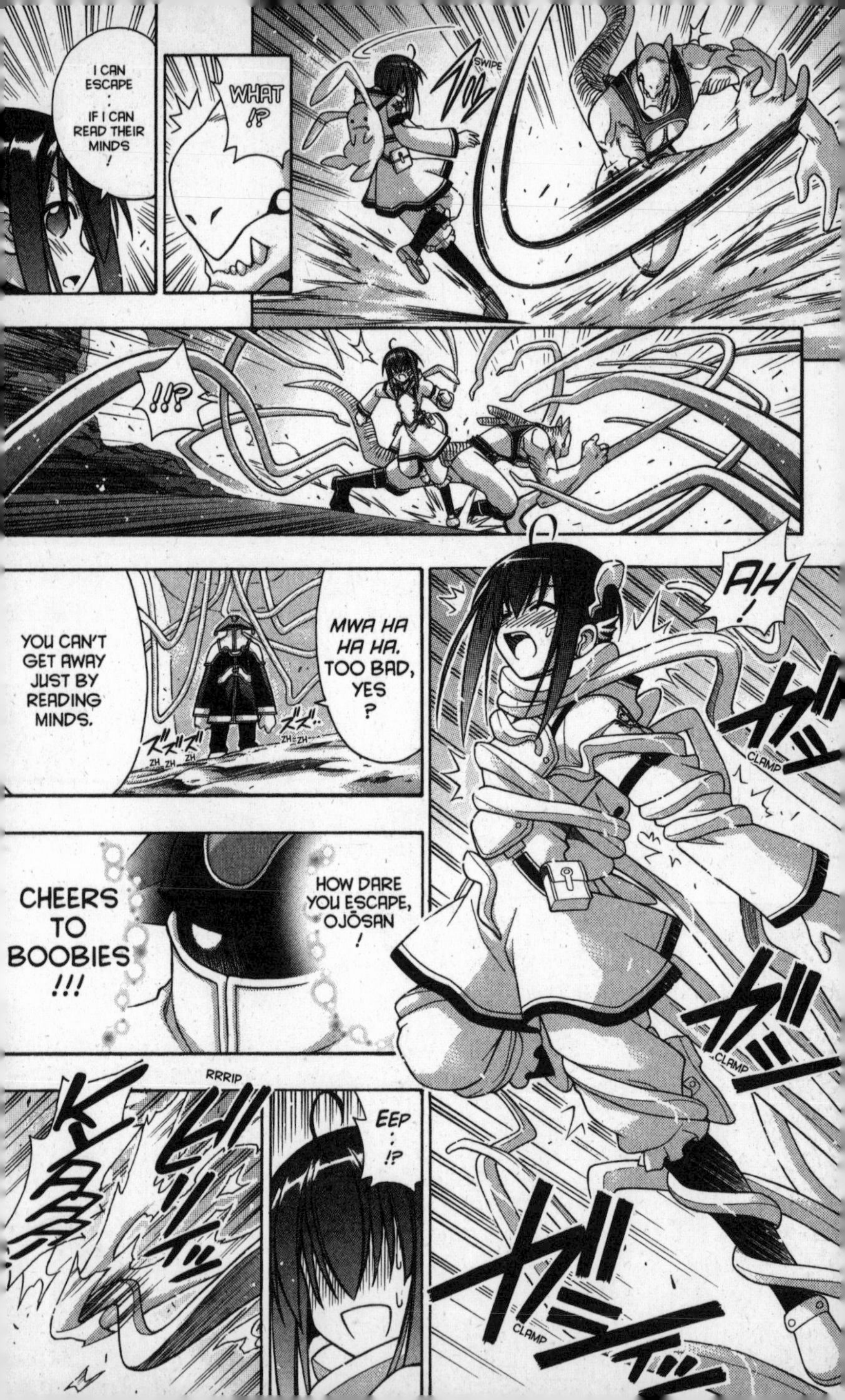
SWIPE
WHAT !?
I CAN ESCAPE
IF I CAN READ THEIR MINDS !
!!?
AH !
CLAMP
CLAMP
CLAMP
MWA HA HA HA. TOO BAD, YES ?
YOU CAN'T GET AWAY JUST BY READING MINDS.
ZH ZH
ZH ZH ZH
HOW DARE YOU ESCAPE, OJŌSAN !
CHEERS TO BOOBIES !!!
EEP ... !?
RRRIP

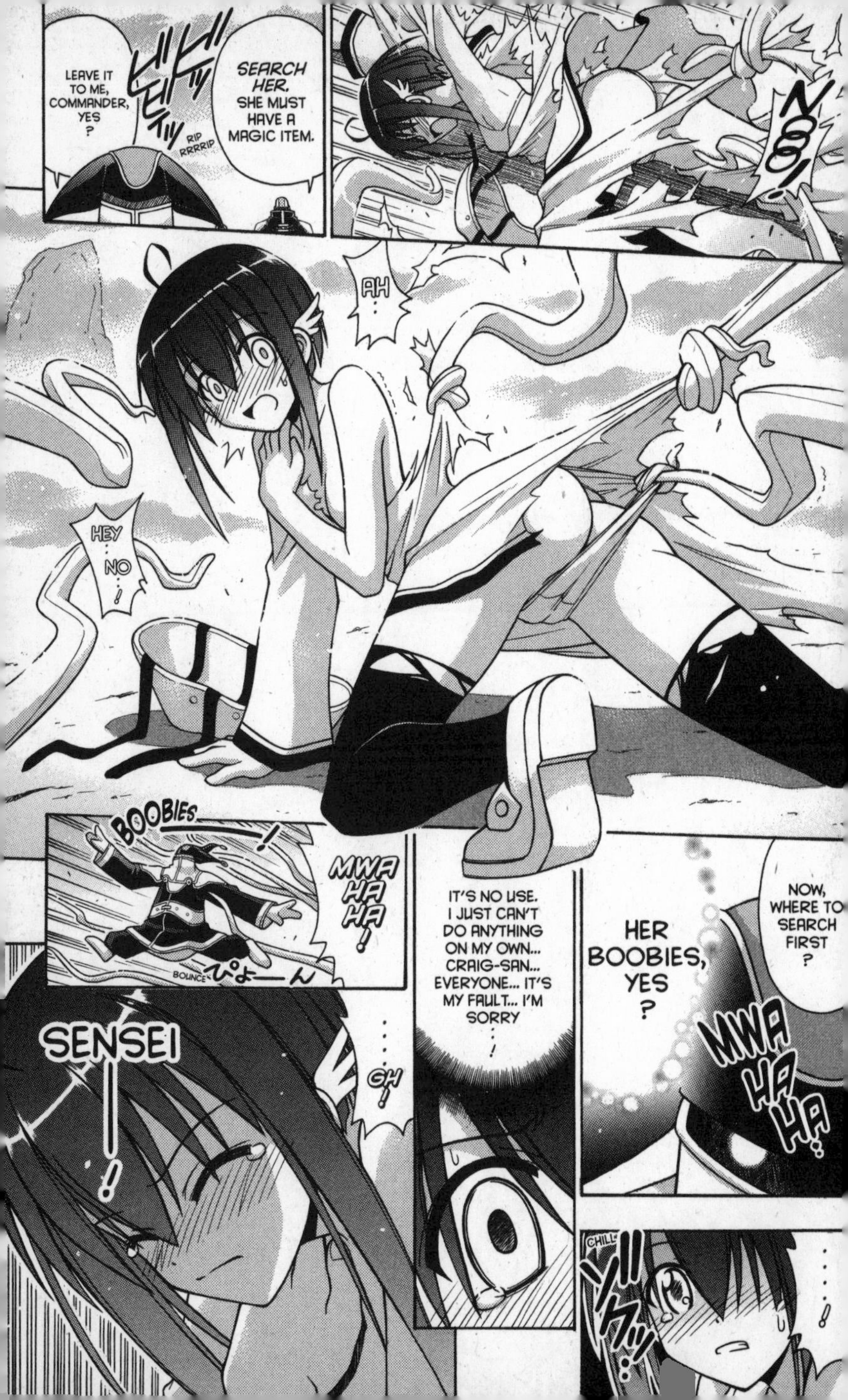
NOOO!
SEARCH HER. SHE MUST HAVE A MAGIC ITEM.
RIP RRRRIP
LEAVE IT TO ME, COMMANDER, YES?
AH...!
HEY... NO...!
NOW, WHERE TO SEARCH FIRST?
HER BOOBIES, YES?
MWA HA HA HA!
...!
CHILL
IT'S NO USE. I JUST CAN'T DO ANYTHING ON MY OWN... CRAIG-SAN... EVERYONE... IT'S MY FAULT... I'M SORRY...!
...GH!
BOOBIES—!
MWA HA HA!
BOUNCE ぴょーん
SENSEI—!

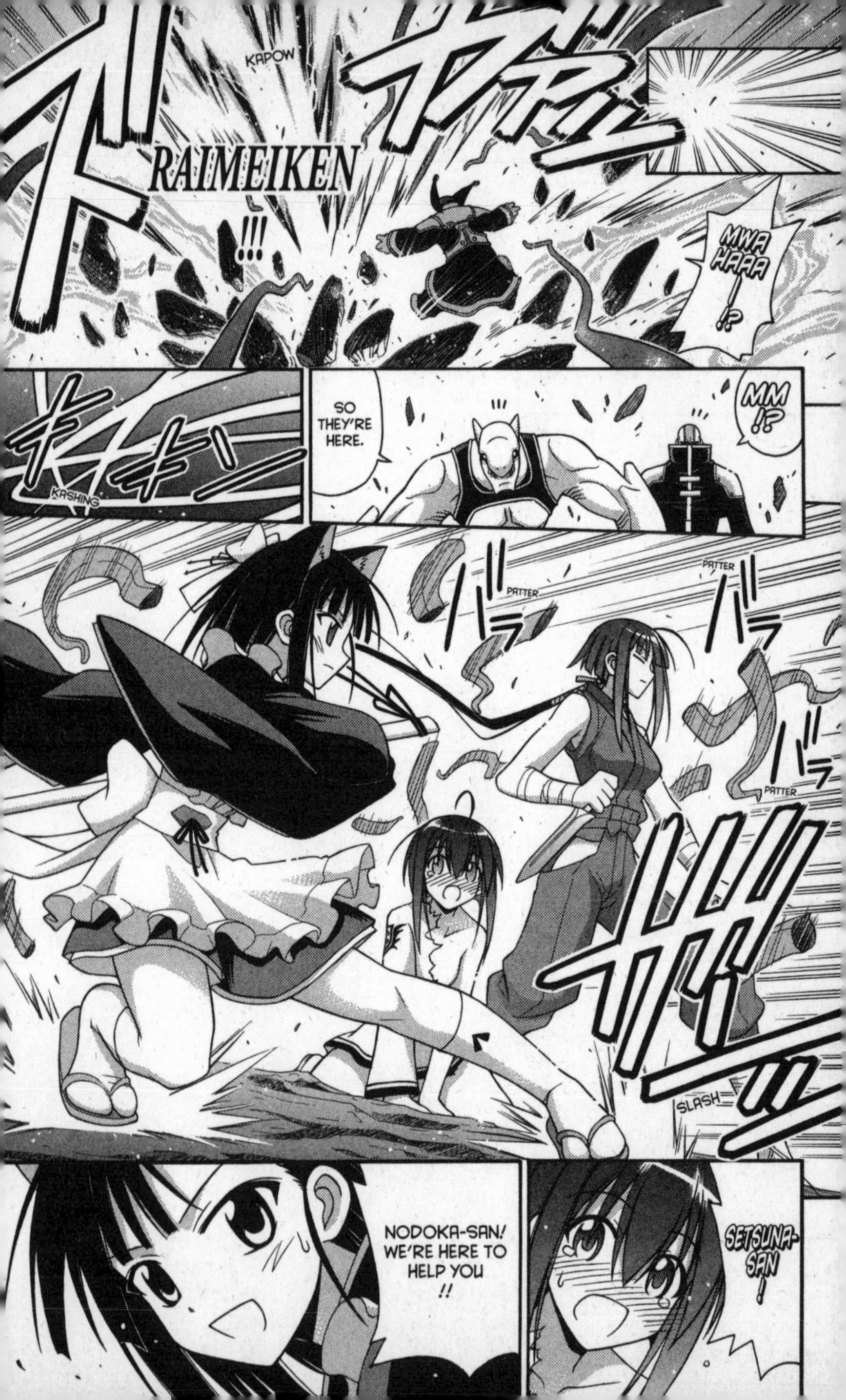
MWA HAAA!!?
KAPOW
RAIMEIKEN
!!!
MM!?
SO THEY'RE HERE.
KASHING
PATTER
PATTER
PATTER
SLASH
SETSUNA-SAN!
NODOKA-SAN! WE'RE HERE TO HELP YOU!!

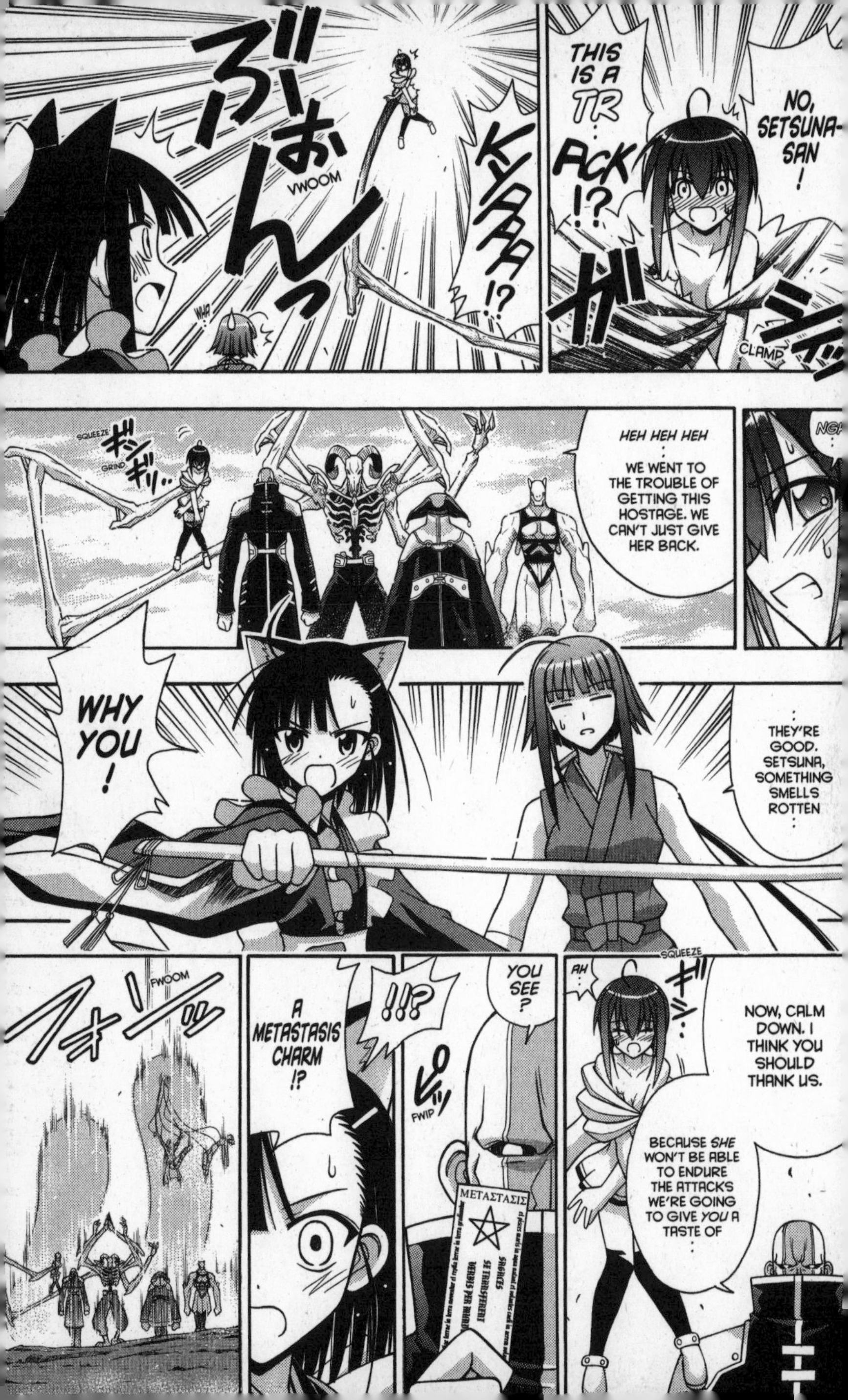
NO, SETSUNA-SAN!
THIS IS A TR... ACK!?
CLAMP
KYAAA!?
VWOOM
WHA
NGH
HEH HEH HEH... WE WENT TO THE TROUBLE OF GETTING THIS HOSTAGE. WE CAN'T JUST GIVE HER BACK.
SQUEEZE
GRIND
...THEY'RE GOOD. SETSUNA, SOMETHING SMELLS ROTTEN...
WHY YOU!
SQUEEZE
AH
NOW, CALM DOWN. I THINK YOU SHOULD THANK US.
BECAUSE SHE WON'T BE ABLE TO ENDURE THE ATTACKS WE'RE GOING TO GIVE YOU A TASTE OF...
YOU SEE?
FWIP
METAΣTAΣIΣ
!!?
A METASTASIS CHARM!?
FWOOM

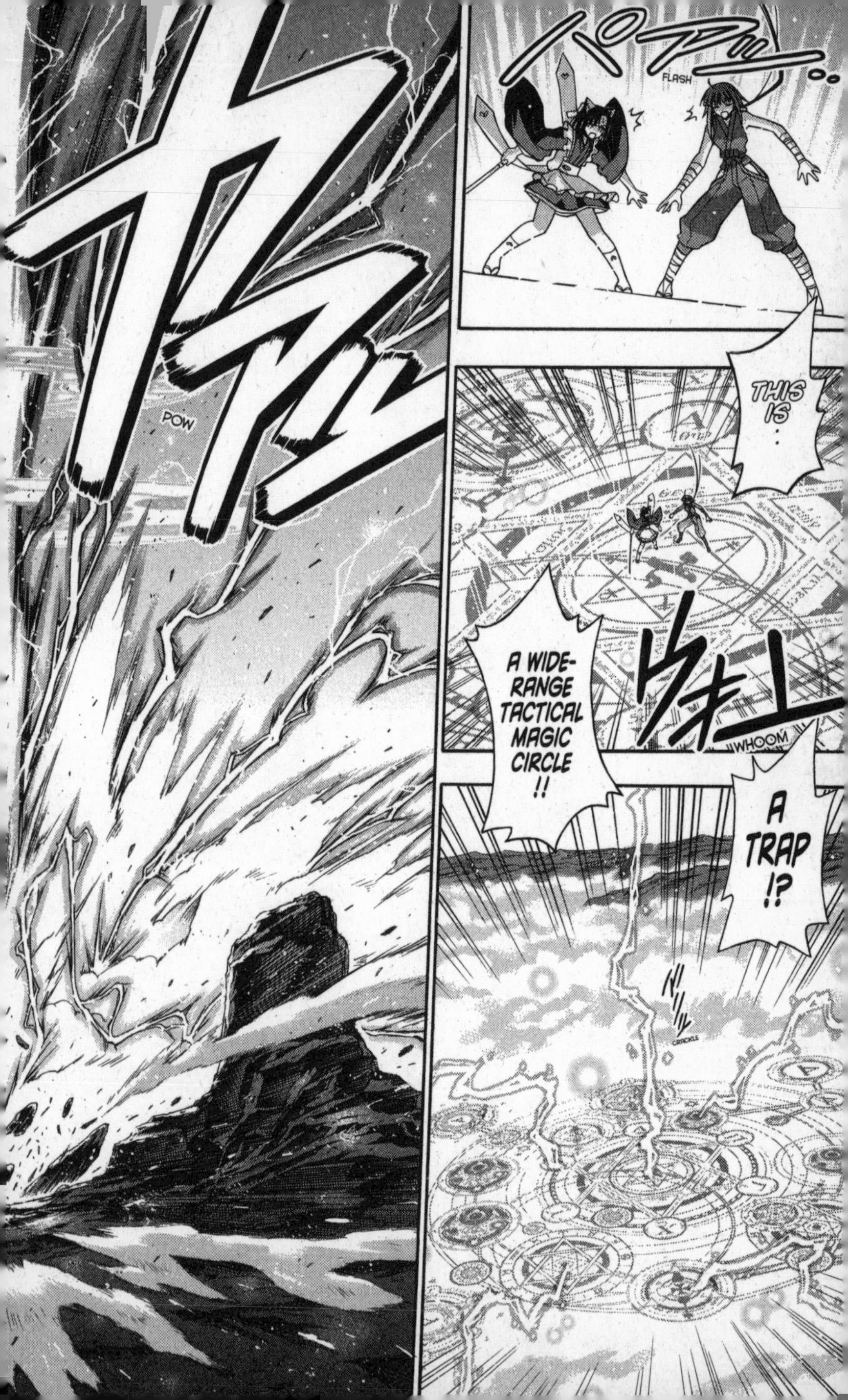
FLASH
THIS IS...
A WIDE-RANGE TACTICAL MAGIC CIRCLE!!
WHOOM
A TRAP!?
CRACKLE
POW

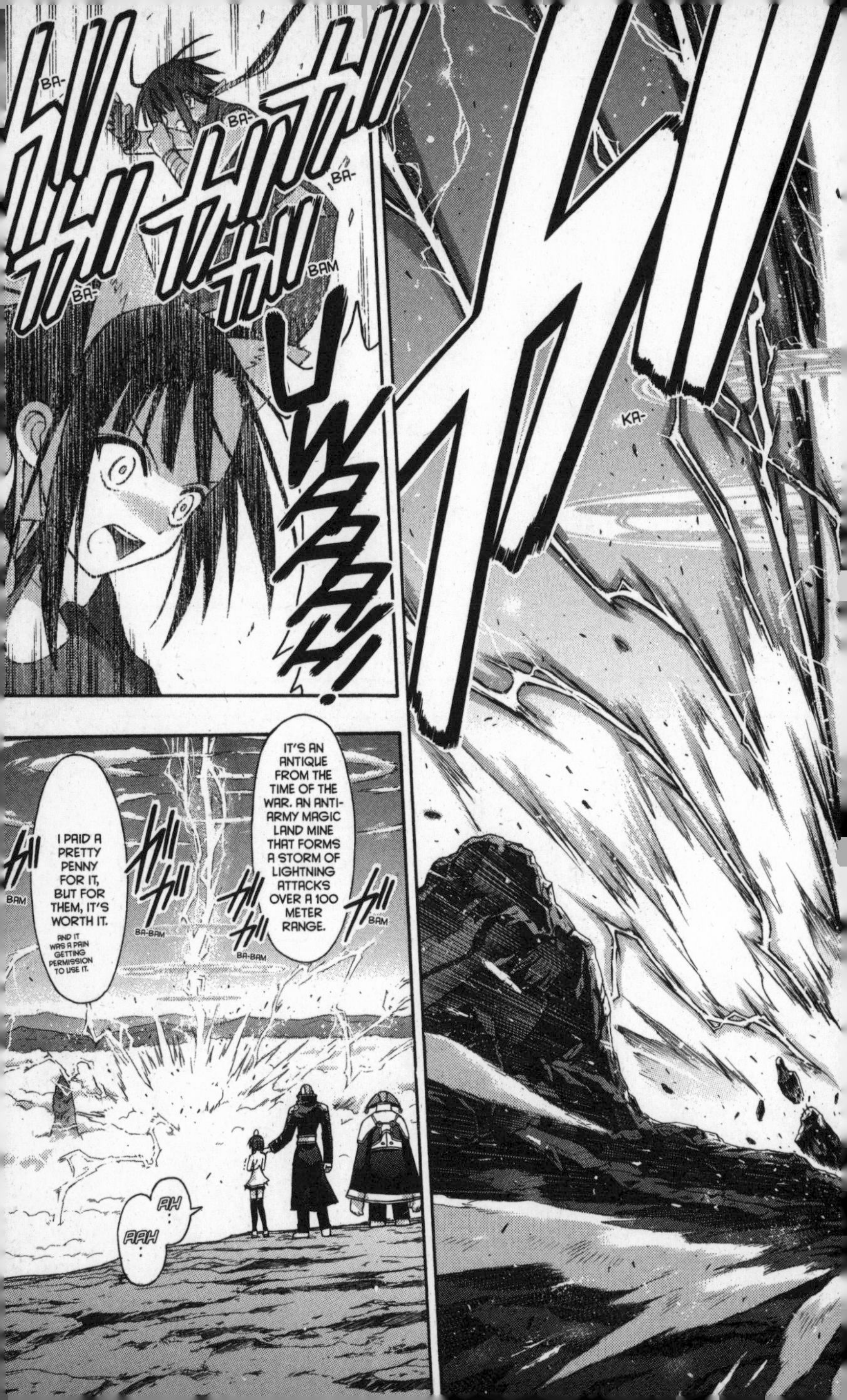
KA-
BA-
BA-
BA-
BA-
BAM
BAM
IT'S AN ANTIQUE FROM THE TIME OF THE WAR. AN ANTI-ARMY MAGIC LAND MINE THAT FORMS A STORM OF LIGHTNING ATTACKS OVER A 100 METER RANGE.
BA-BAM
BA-BAM
I PAID A PRETTY PENNY FOR IT, BUT FOR THEM, IT'S WORTH IT.
AND IT WAS A PAIN GETTING PERMISSION TO USE IT.
BAM
AH
AAH...

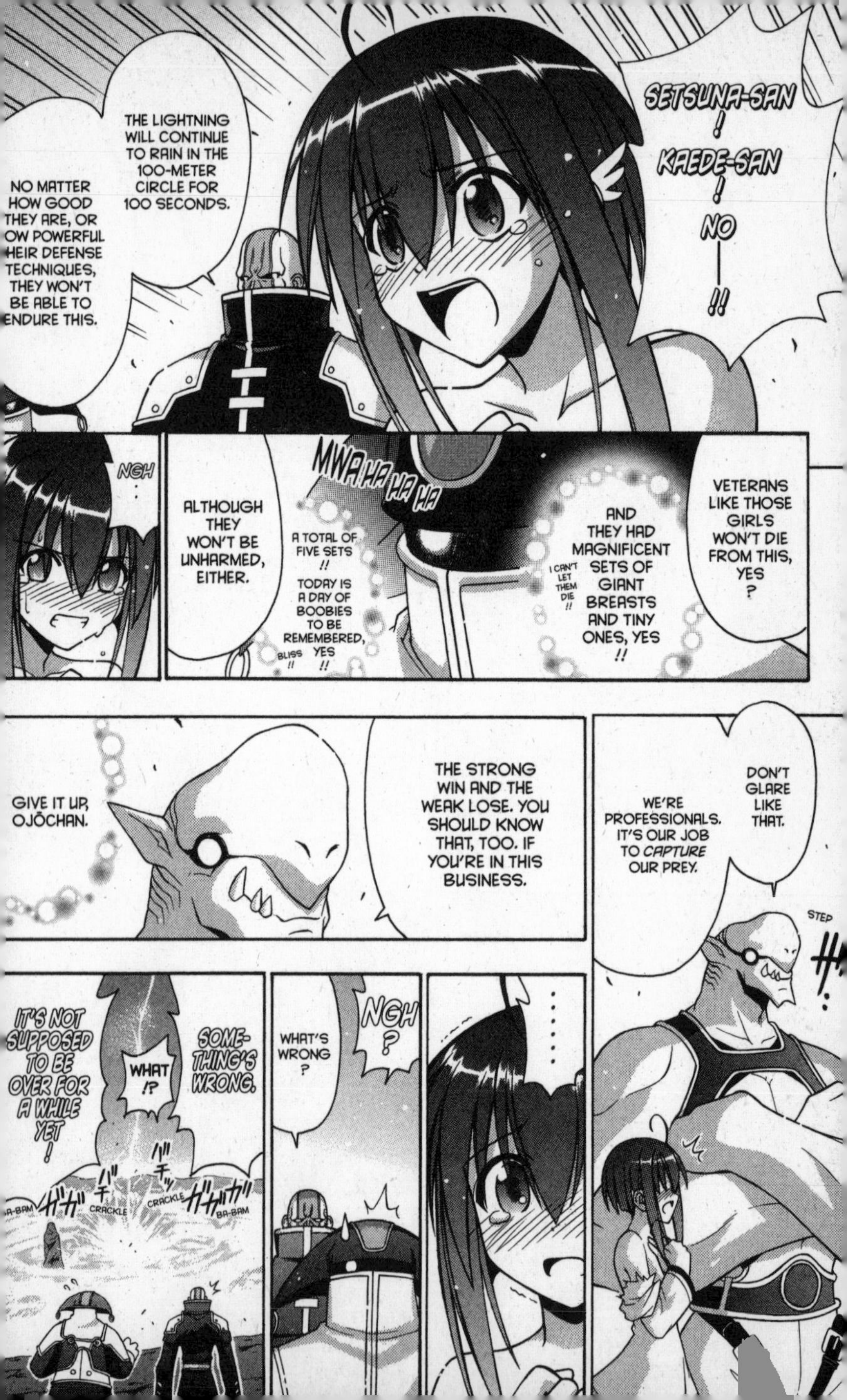
SETSUNA-SAN! KAEDE-SAN! NO—!!
THE LIGHTNING WILL CONTINUE TO RAIN IN THE 100-METER CIRCLE FOR 100 SECONDS.
NO MATTER HOW GOOD THEY ARE, OR OW POWERFUL HEIR DEFENSE TECHNIQUES, THEY WON'T BE ABLE TO ENDURE THIS.
VETERANS LIKE THOSE GIRLS WON'T DIE FROM THIS, YES?
AND THEY HAD MAGNIFICENT SETS OF GIANT BREASTS AND TINY ONES, YES!!
I CAN'T LET THEM DIE!!
MWAHAHAHAHA
A TOTAL OF FIVE SETS!!
TODAY IS A DAY OF BOOBIES TO BE REMEMBERED, YES!!
BLISS!!
ALTHOUGH THEY WON'T BE UNHARMED, EITHER.
NGH...
DON'T GLARE LIKE THAT.
WE'RE PROFESSIONALS. IT'S OUR JOB TO *CAPTURE* OUR PREY.
STEP
THE STRONG WIN AND THE WEAK LOSE. YOU SHOULD KNOW THAT, TOO. IF YOU'RE IN THIS BUSINESS.
GIVE IT UP, OJŌCHAN.
......
NGH?
WHAT'S WRONG?
SOMETHING'S WRONG.
WHAT!?
IT'S NOT SUPPOSED TO BE OVER FOR A WHILE YET!
BA-BAM
CRACKLE
CRACKLE
A-BAM

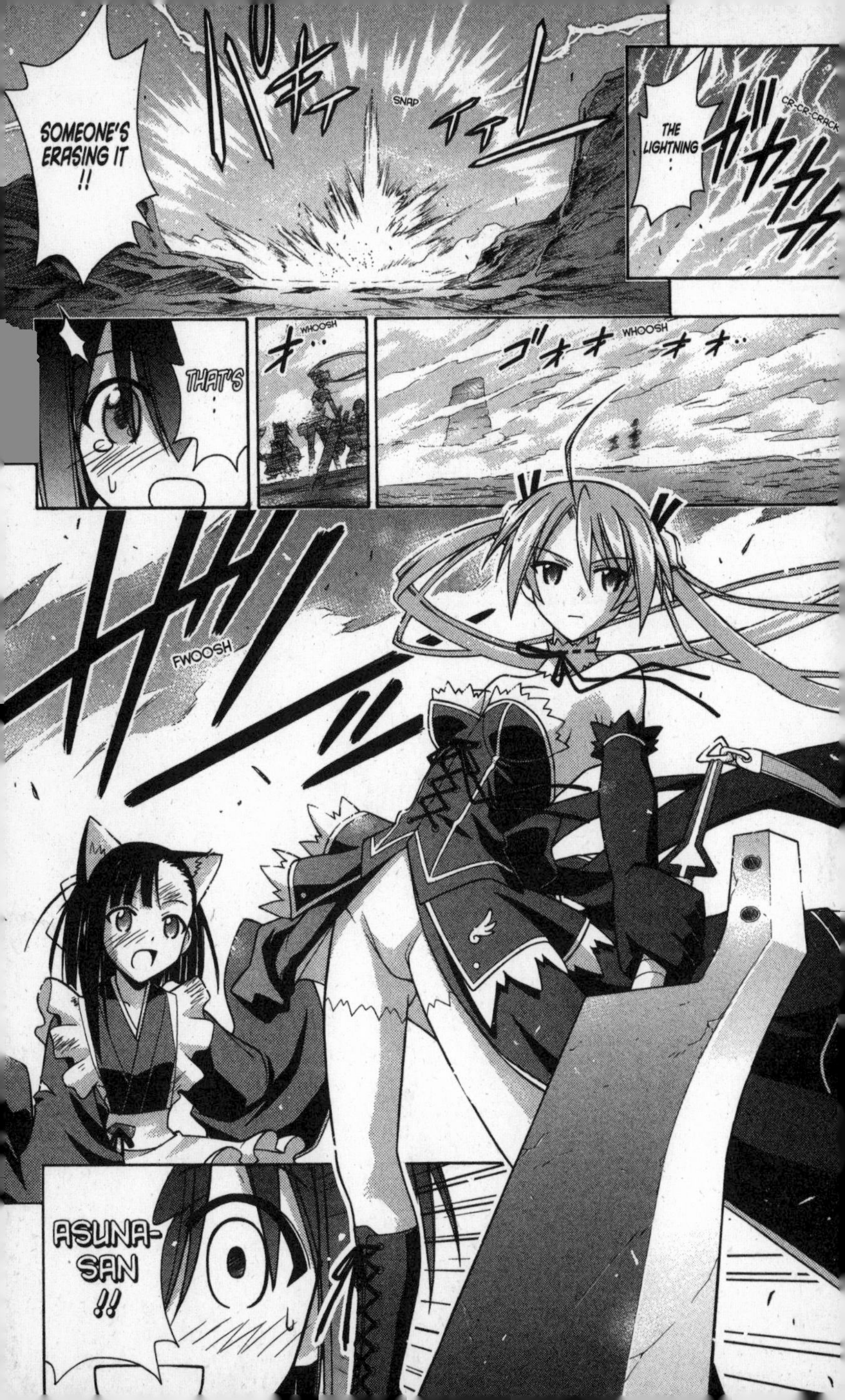
CR-CR-CRACK
THE LIGHTNING :
SNAP
SOMEONE'S ERASING IT !!
WHOOSH
WHOOSH
THAT'S :
FWOOSH
ASUNA-SAN !!

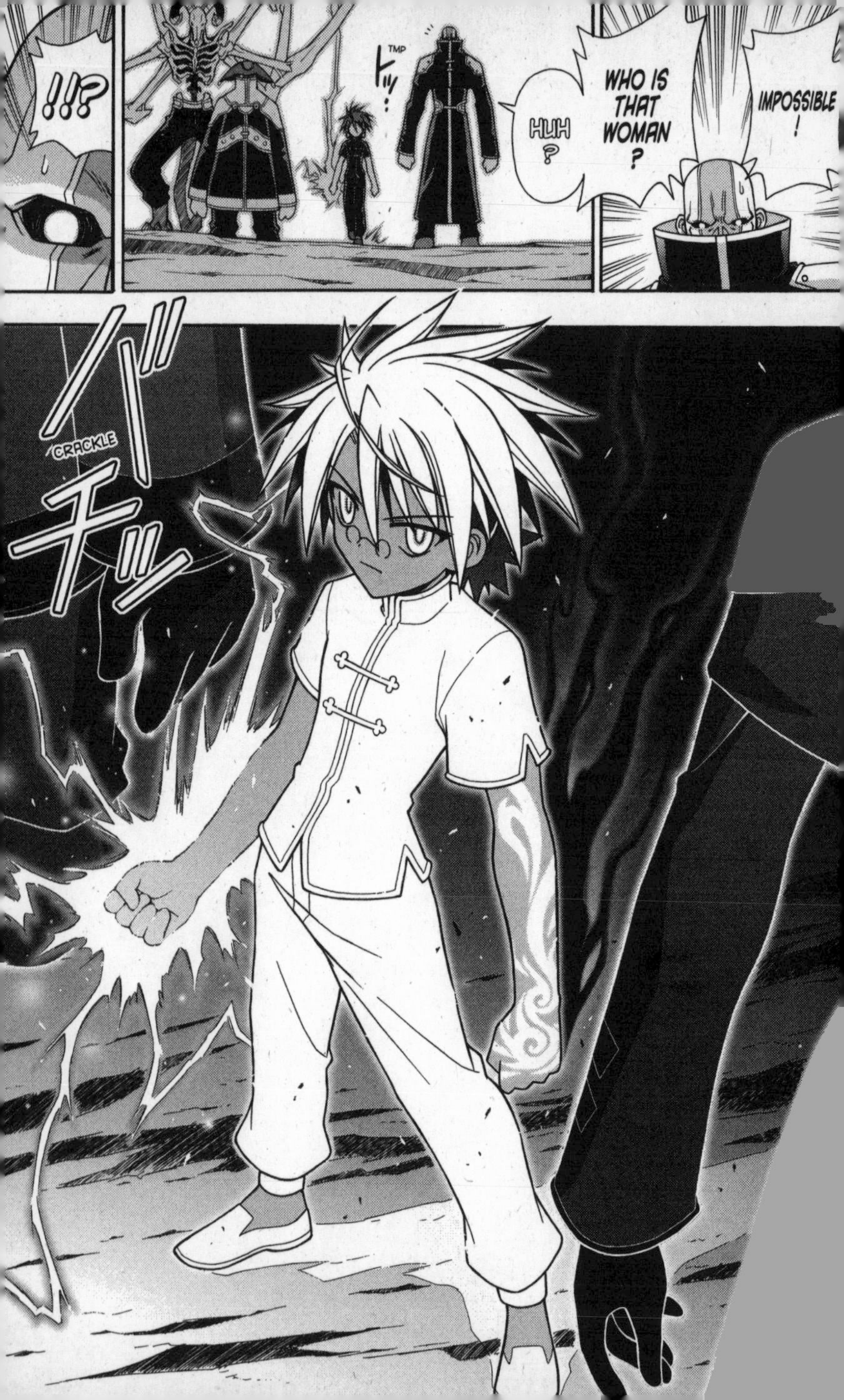
IMPOSSIBLE!
WHO IS THAT WOMAN?
HUH?
ドッ
TMP
!!?
バチッ
CRACKLE

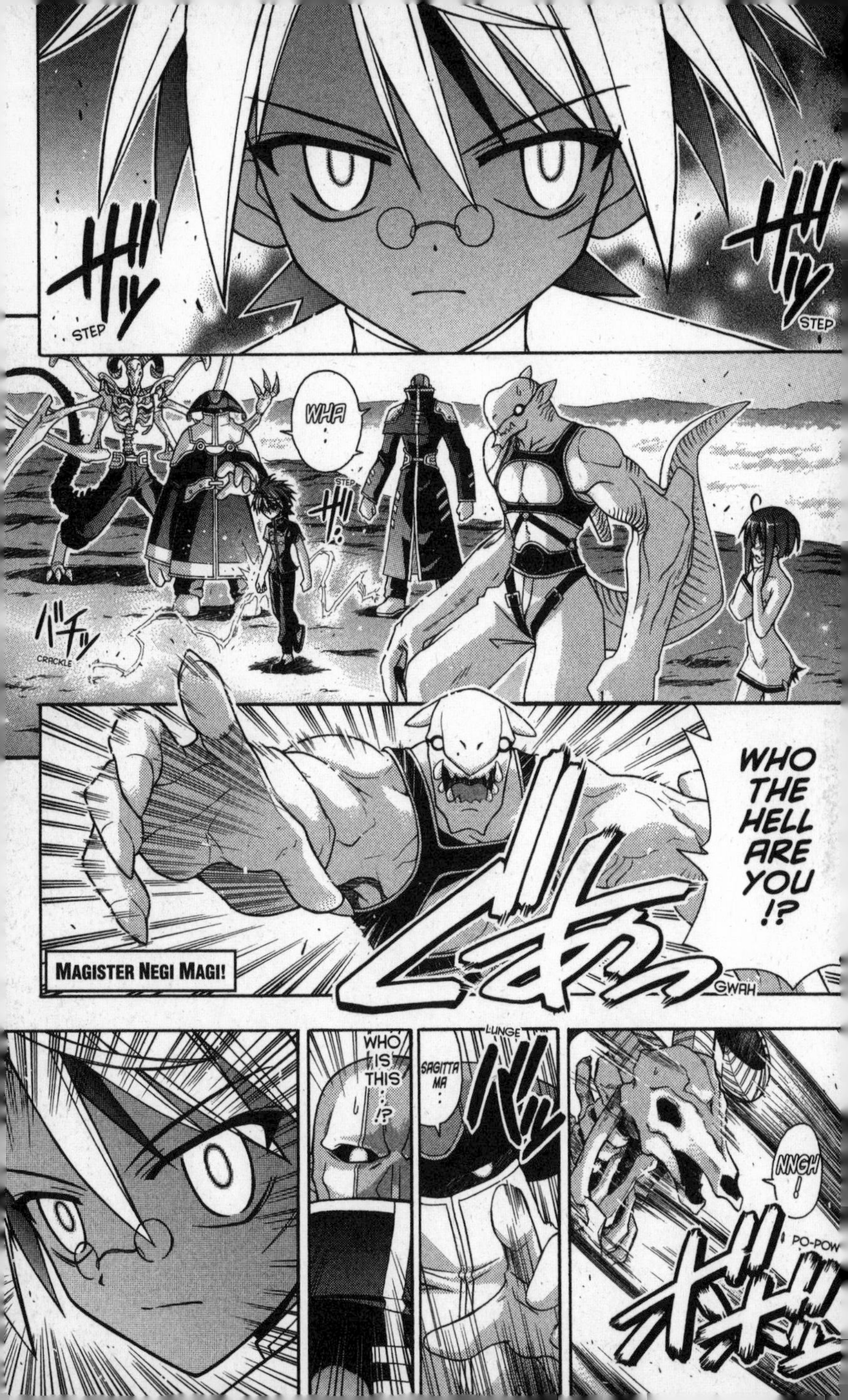
STEP
STEP
WHA...
STEP
CRACKLE
WHO THE HELL ARE YOU!?
GWAH
MAGISTER NEGI MAGI!
NNGH!
PO-POW
LUNGE
SAGITTA MA...
WHO IS THIS...!?

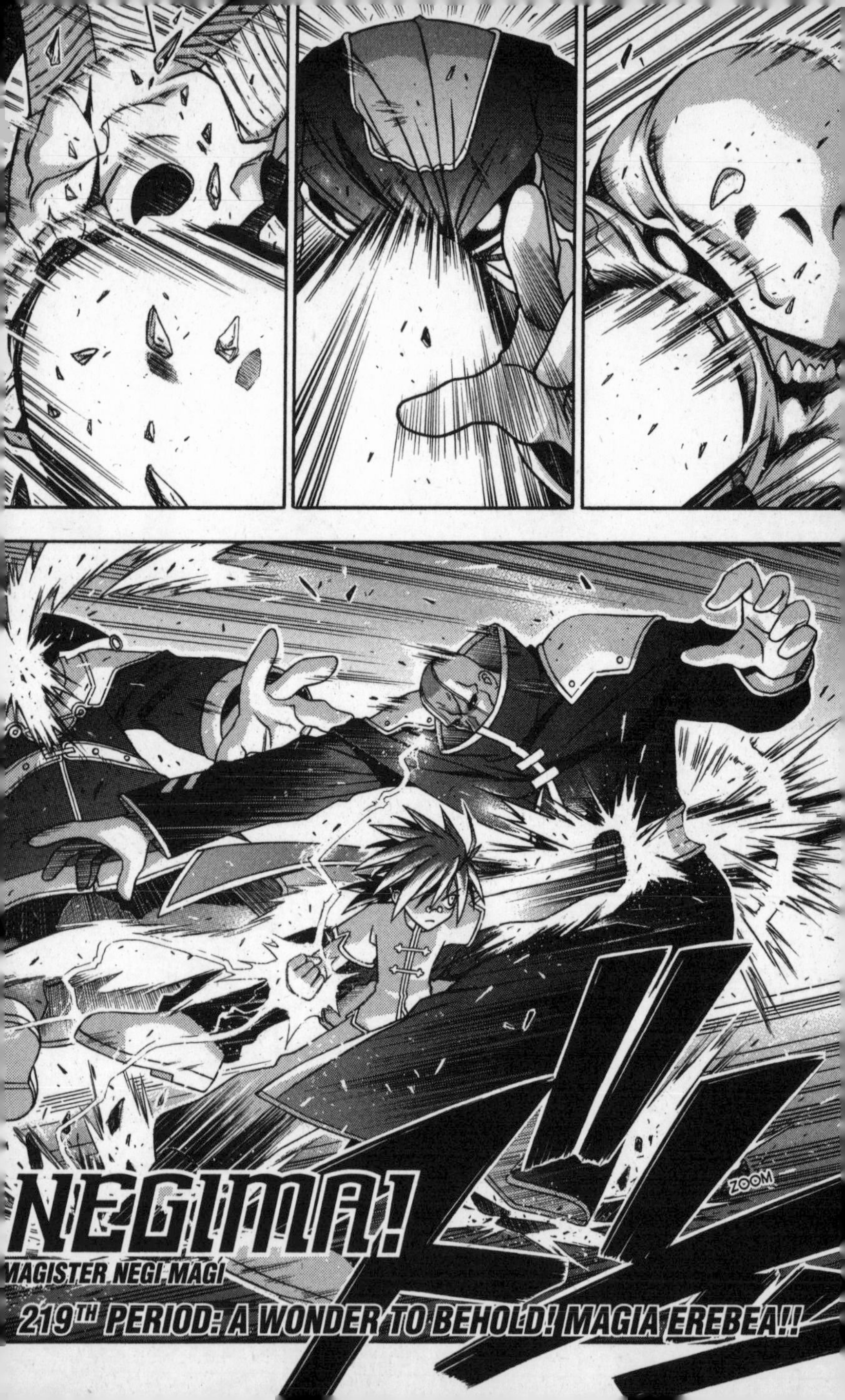
ZOOM
NEGIMA!
MAGISTER NEGI MAGI
219TH PERIOD: A WONDER TO BEHOLD! MAGIA EREBEA!!

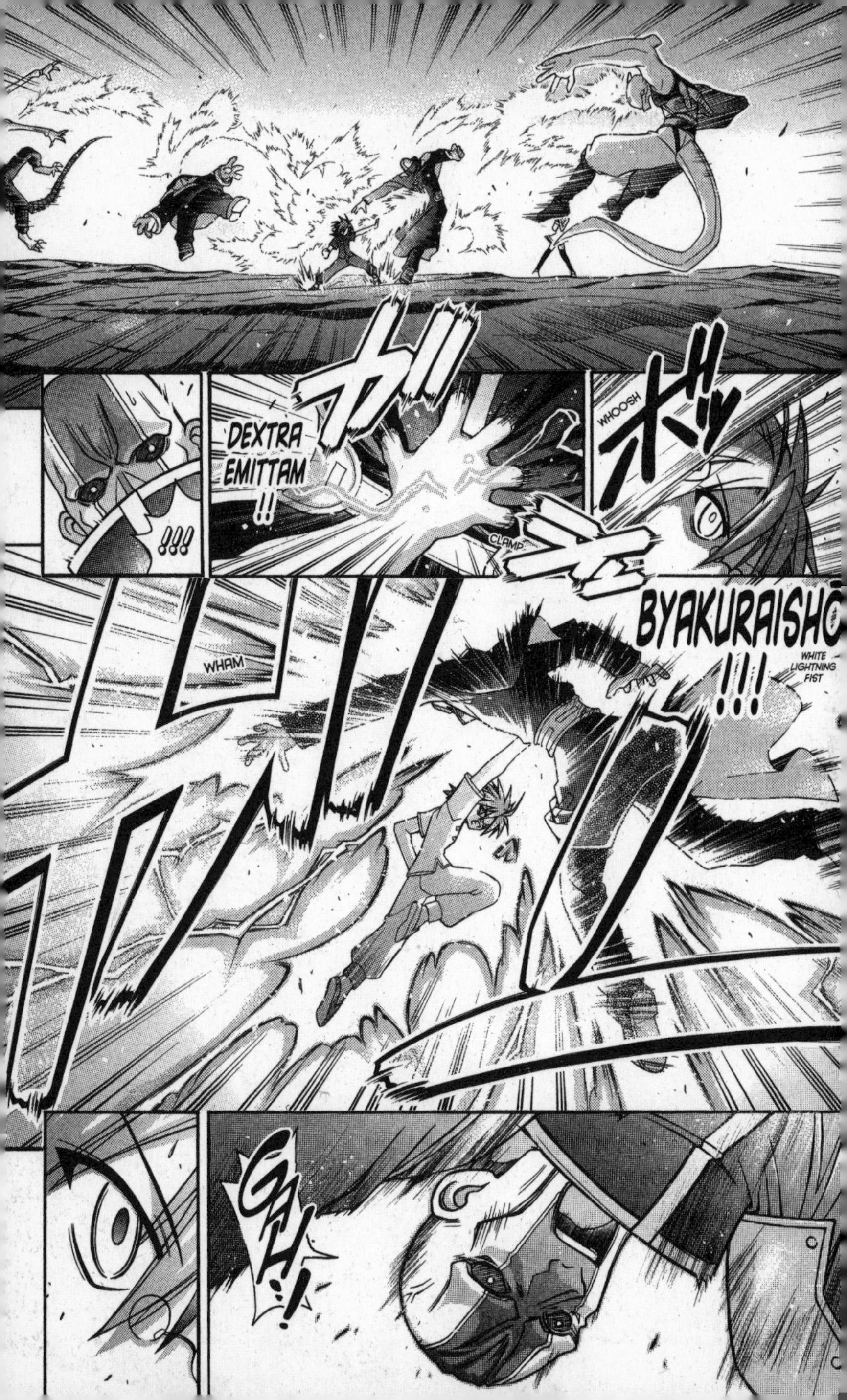
WHOOSH
DEXTRA EMITTAM !!
CLAMP
!!!
BYAKURAISHŌ !!!
WHITE LIGHTNING FIST
WHAM
GAH!

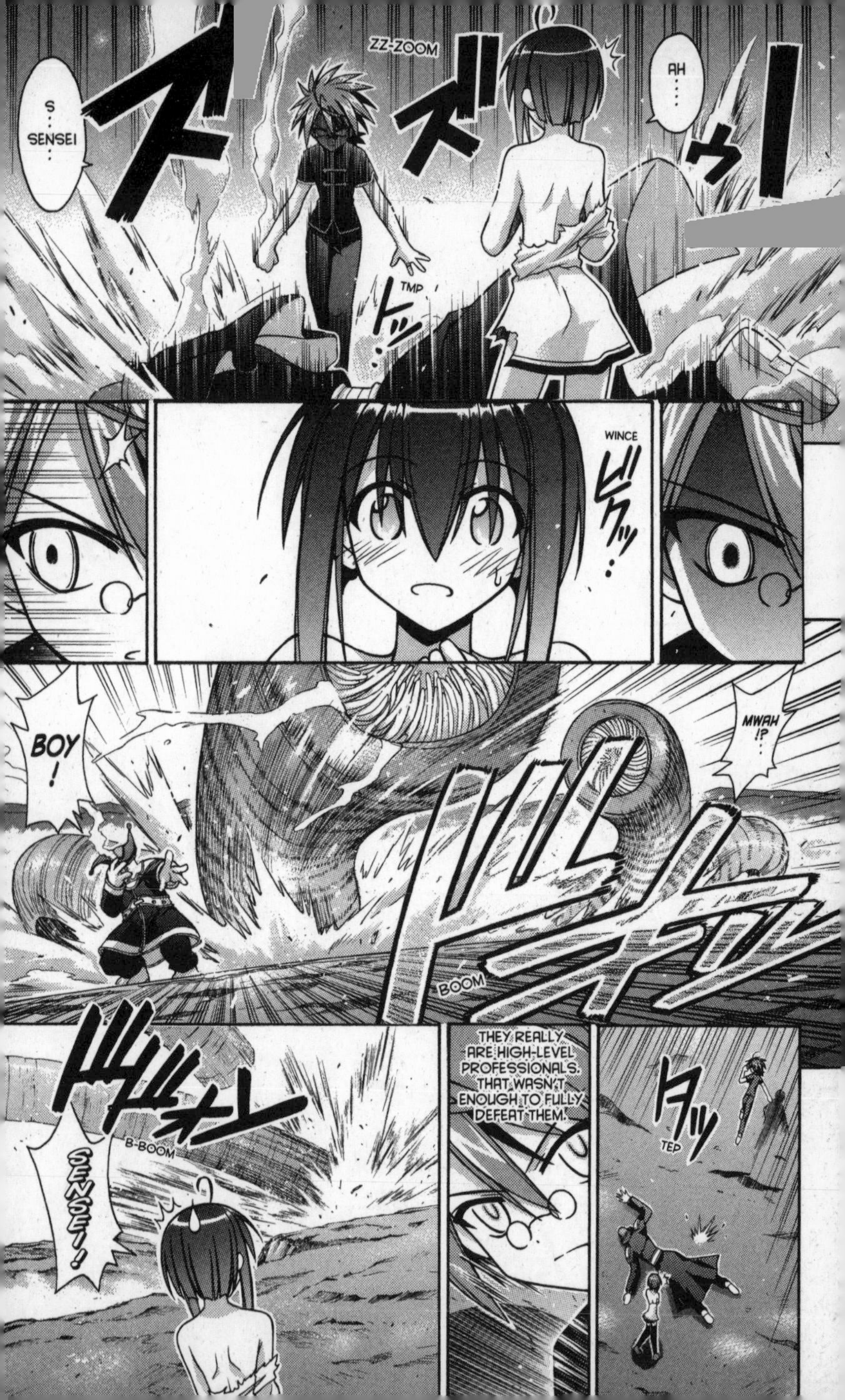
AH......
ZZ-ZOOM
S... SENSEI...
TMP
WINCE
MWAH !?
BOY !
BOOM
TEP
THEY REALLY ARE HIGH-LEVEL PROFESSIONALS. THAT WASN'T ENOUGH TO FULLY DEFEAT THEM.
B-BOOM
SENSEI!!

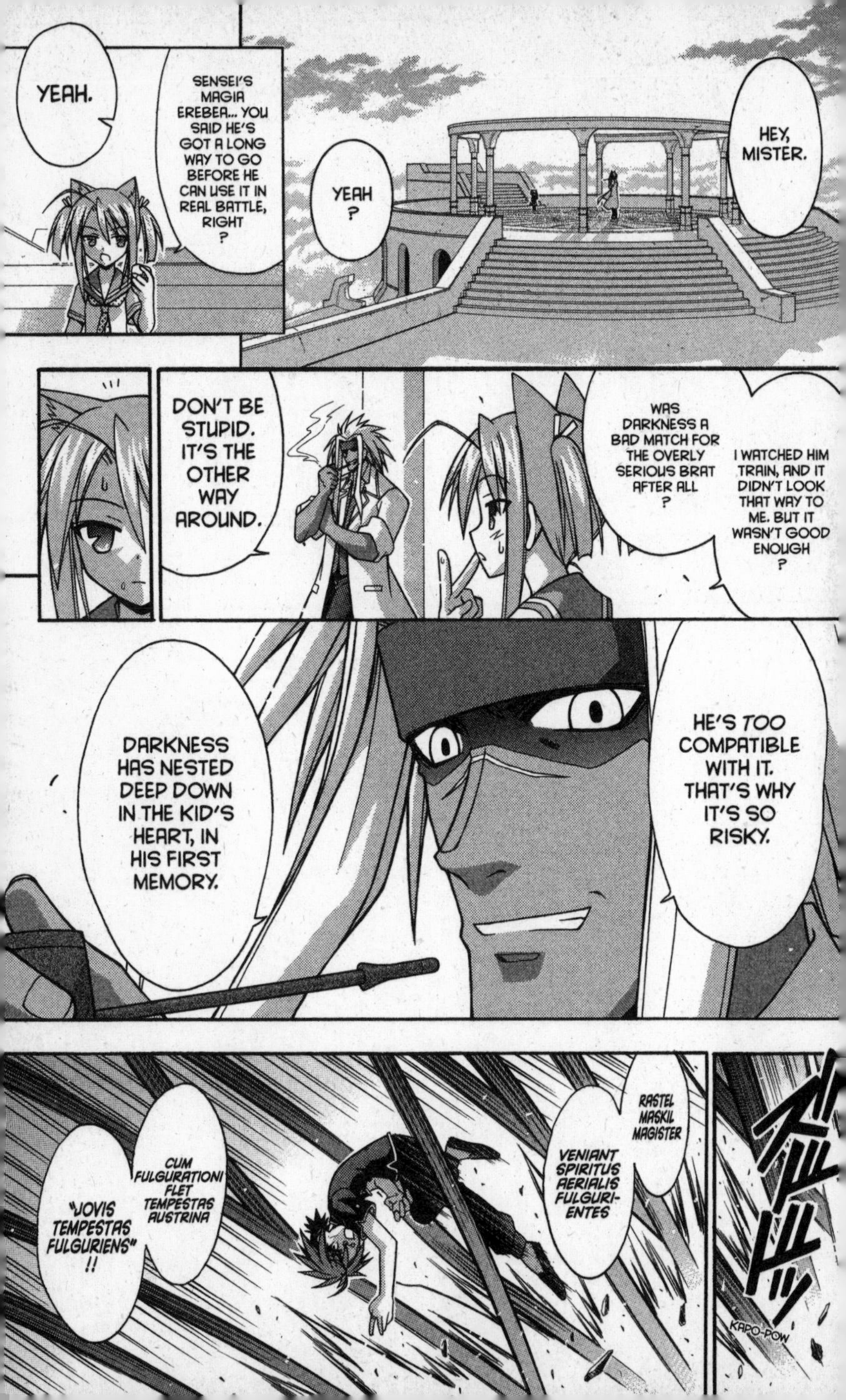
HEY, MISTER.
YEAH?
SENSEI'S MAGIA EREBEA... YOU SAID HE'S GOT A LONG WAY TO GO BEFORE HE CAN USE IT IN REAL BATTLE, RIGHT?
YEAH.
I WATCHED HIM TRAIN, AND IT DIDN'T LOOK THAT WAY TO ME. BUT IT WASN'T GOOD ENOUGH?
WAS DARKNESS A BAD MATCH FOR THE OVERLY SERIOUS BRAT AFTER ALL?
DON'T BE STUPID. IT'S THE OTHER WAY AROUND.
HE'S *TOO* COMPATIBLE WITH IT. THAT'S WHY IT'S SO RISKY.
DARKNESS HAS NESTED DEEP DOWN IN THE KID'S HEART, IN HIS FIRST MEMORY.
KAPO-POW
RASTEL MASKIL MAGISTER
VENIANT SPIRITUS AERIALIS FULGURIENTES
CUM FULGURATIONI FLET TEMPESTAS AUSTRINA
"JOVIS TEMPESTAS FULGURIENS"!!

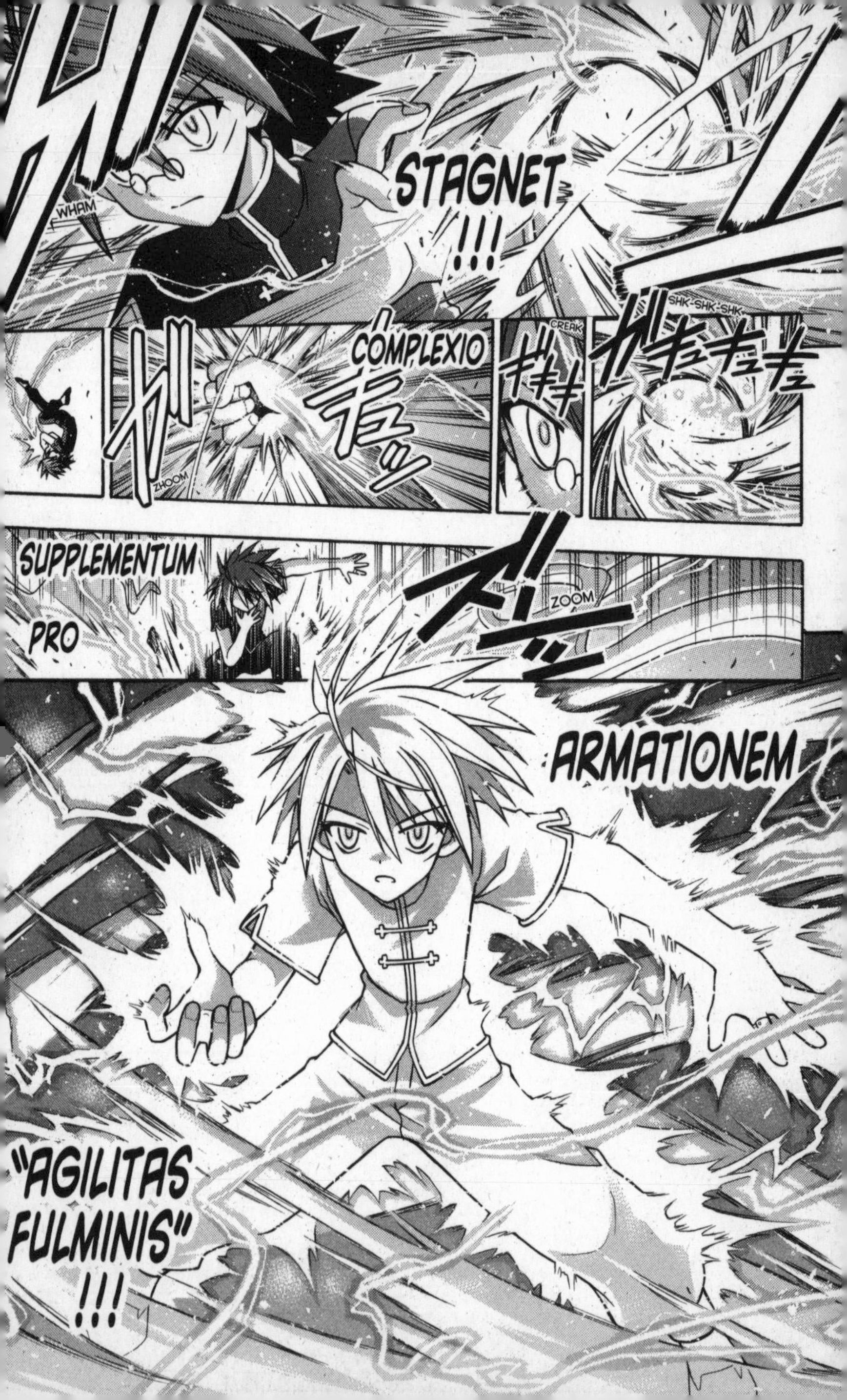
STAGNET !!!
WHAM
SHK-SHK-SHK
CREAK
COMPLEXIO
ZHOOM
ZOOM
SUPPLEMENTUM PRO
ARMATIONEM
"AGILITAS FULMINIS" !!!

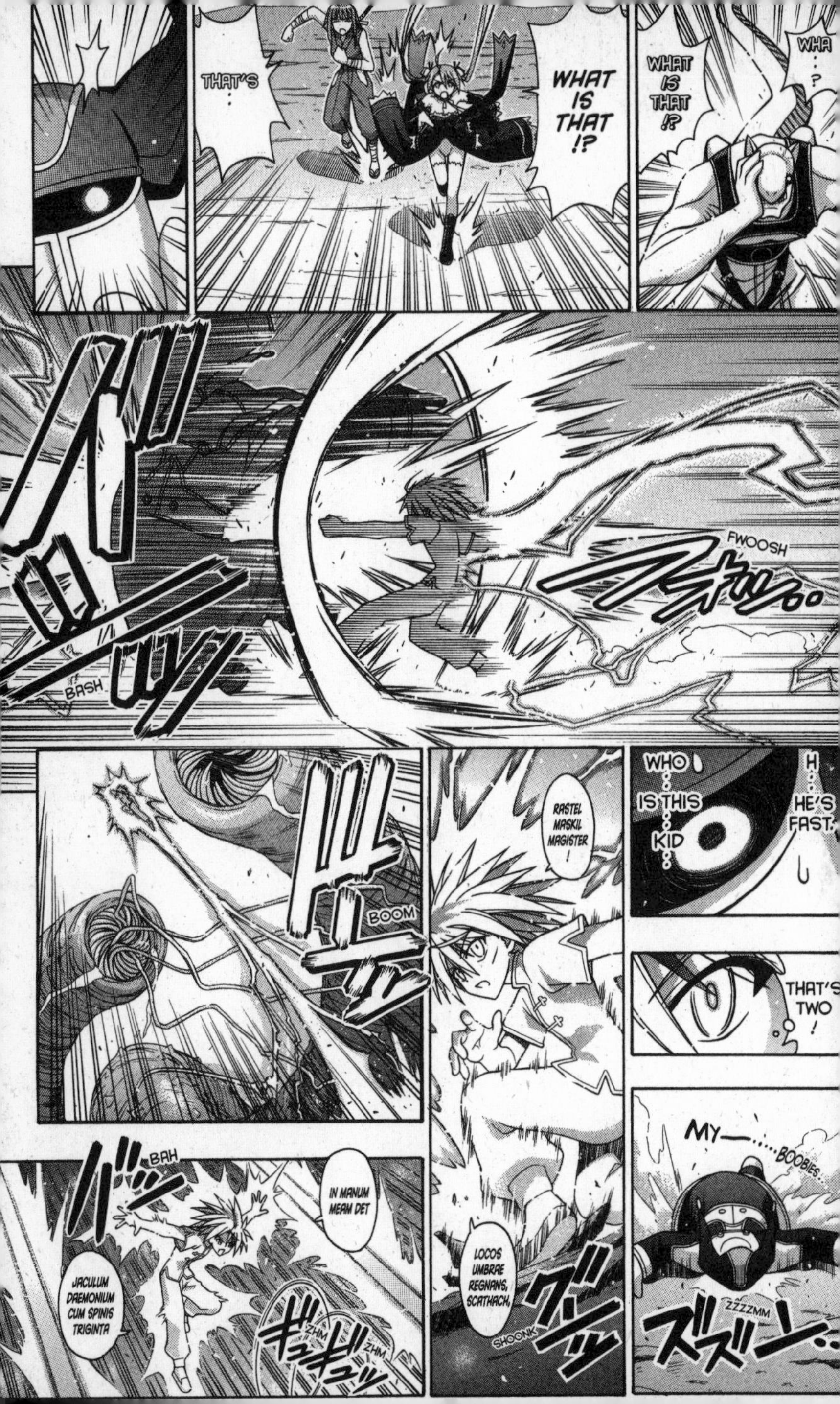
WHA...?
WHAT IS THAT!?
WHAT IS THAT!?
THAT'S...
FWOOSH
BASH
H... HE'S FAST.
WHO... IS THIS KID...
THAT'S TWO!
MY—......BOOBIES...
ZZZZMM
RASTEL MASKIL MAGISTER!
LOCOS UMBRAE REGNANS, SCATHACH,
SHOONK
BOOM
IN MANUM MEAM DET
BAH
JACULUM DAEMONIUM CUM SPINIS TRIGINTA
ZHM
ZHM

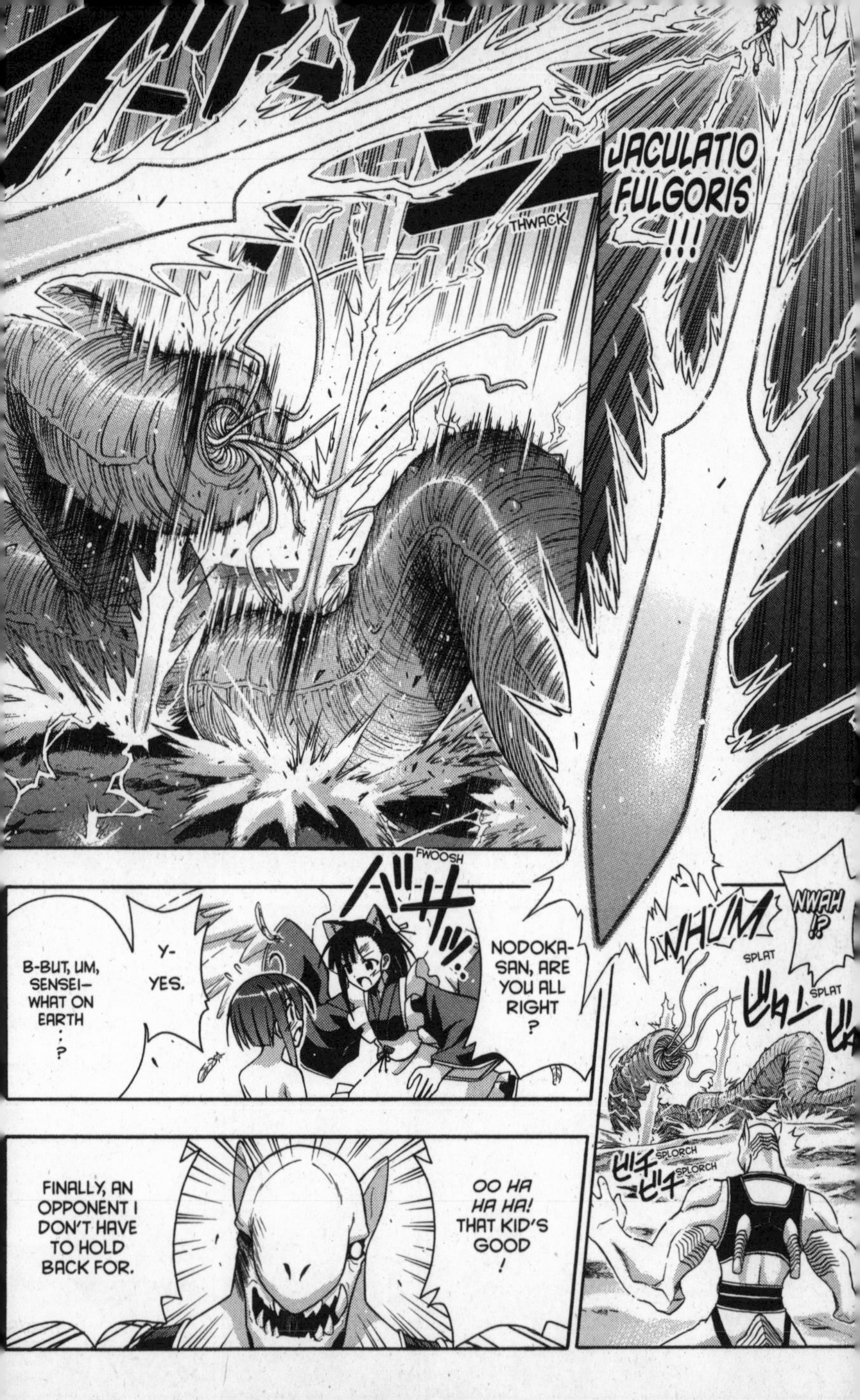

JACULATIO FULGORIS!!!
THWACK
WHUM
NWAH!?
SPLAT
SPLAT
SPLORCH
SPLORCH
FWOOSH
NODOKA-SAN, ARE YOU ALL RIGHT?
Y-YES.
B-BUT, UM, SENSEI— WHAT ON EARTH...?
OO HA HA HA! THAT KID'S GOOD!
FINALLY, AN OPPONENT I DON'T HAVE TO HOLD BACK FOR.

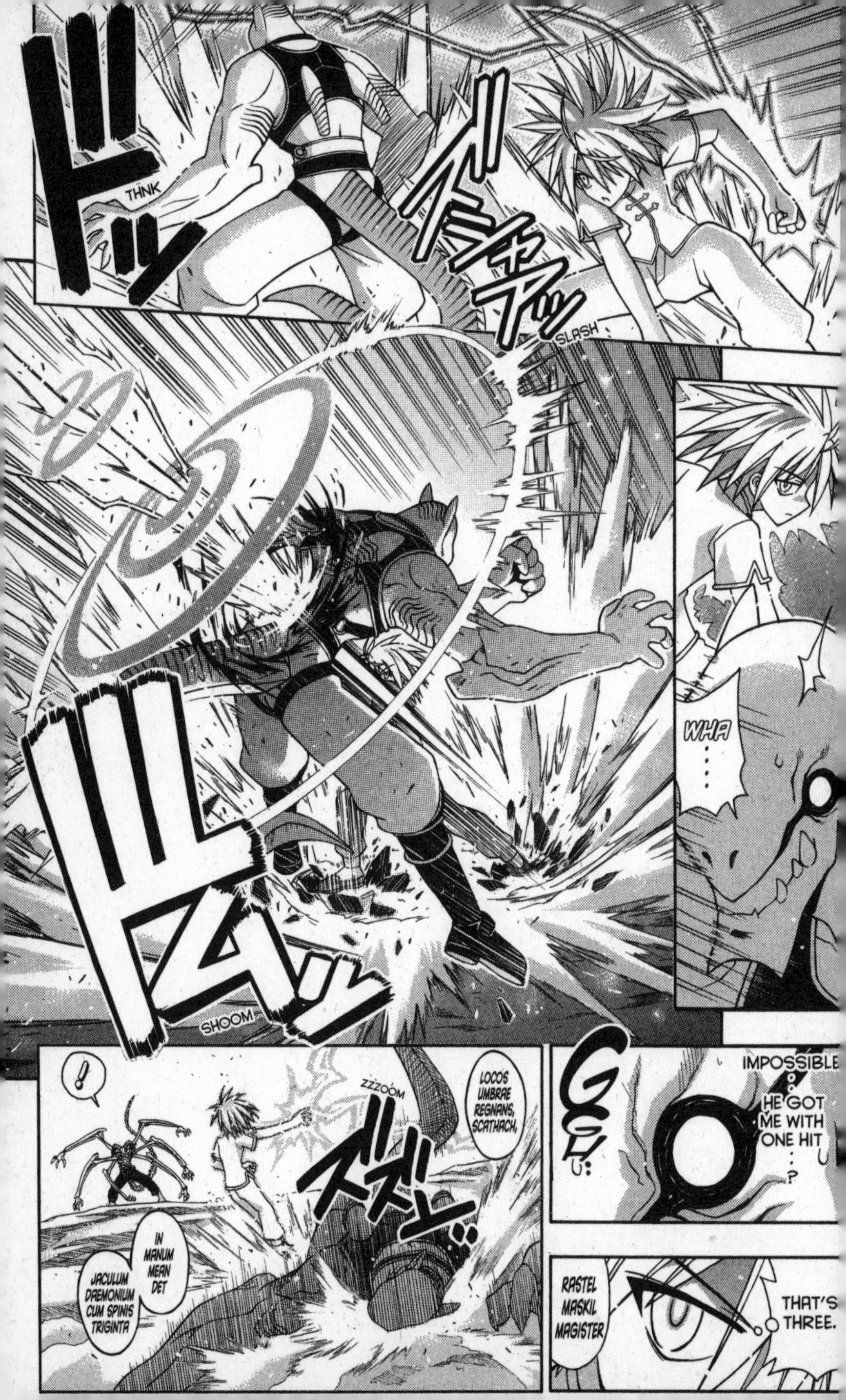
THNK
SLASH
SHOOM
WHA ...
IMPOSSIBLE ...
HE GOT ME WITH ONE HIT ...?
THAT'S THREE.
RASTEL MASKIL MAGISTER
LOCOS UMBRAE REGNANS, SCATHACH,
ZZZOOM
IN MANUM MEAN DET
JACULUM DAEMONIUM CUM SPINIS TRIGINTA
!

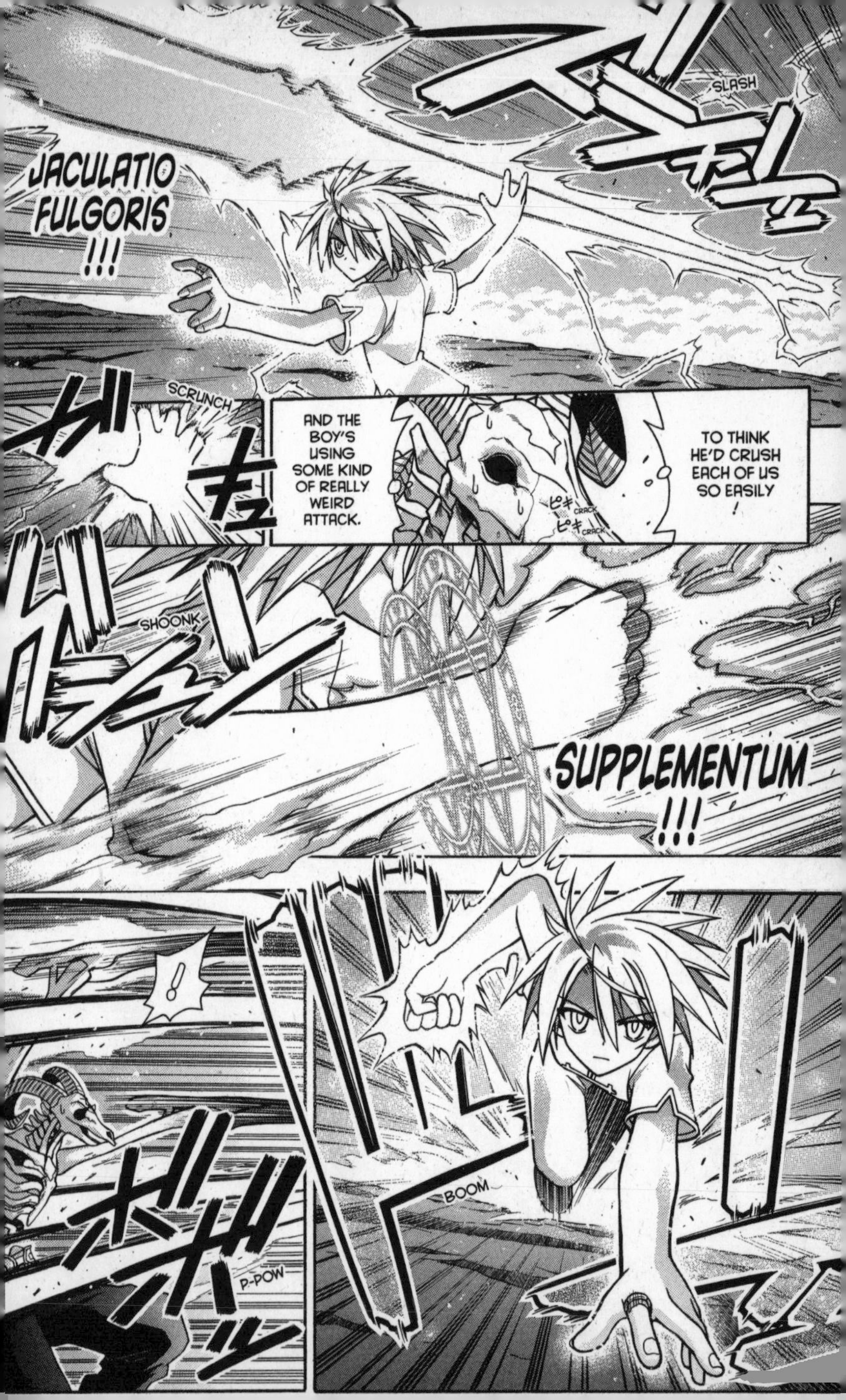
SLASH
JACULATIO FULGORIS !!!
TO THINK HE'D CRUSH EACH OF US SO EASILY !
ピキ CRACK
ピキ CRACK
AND THE BOY'S USING SOME KIND OF REALLY WEIRD ATTACK.
SCRUNCH
SHOONK
SUPPLEMENTUM !!!
BOOM
!
P-POW

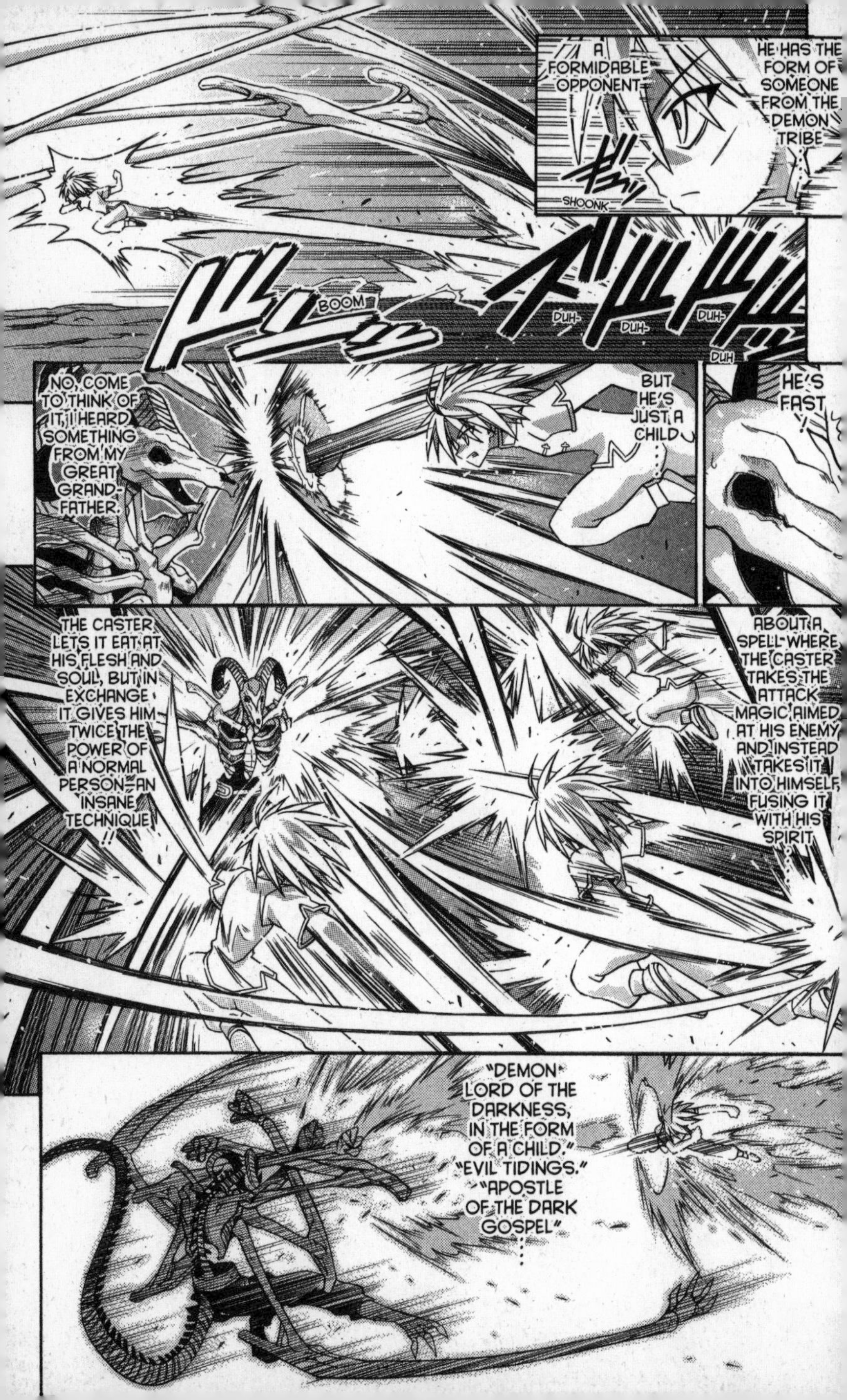
HE HAS THE FORM OF SOMEONE FROM THE DEMON TRIBE
A FORMIDABLE OPPONENT
SHOONK
DUH-DUH-DUH-DUH
BOOM
HE'S FAST!
BUT HE'S JUST A CHILD
NO, COME TO THINK OF IT, I HEARD SOMETHING FROM MY GREAT GRAND-FATHER.
ABOUT A SPELL WHERE THE CASTER TAKES THE ATTACK MAGIC AIMED AT HIS ENEMY AND INSTEAD TAKES IT INTO HIMSELF, FUSING IT WITH HIS SPIRIT...
THE CASTER LETS IT EAT AT HIS FLESH AND SOUL, BUT IN EXCHANGE IT GIVES HIM TWICE THE POWER OF A NORMAL PERSON—AN INSANE TECHNIQUE!!
"DEMON LORD OF THE DARKNESS, IN THE FORM OF A CHILD." "EVIL TIDINGS." "APOSTLE OF THE DARK GOSPEL"...

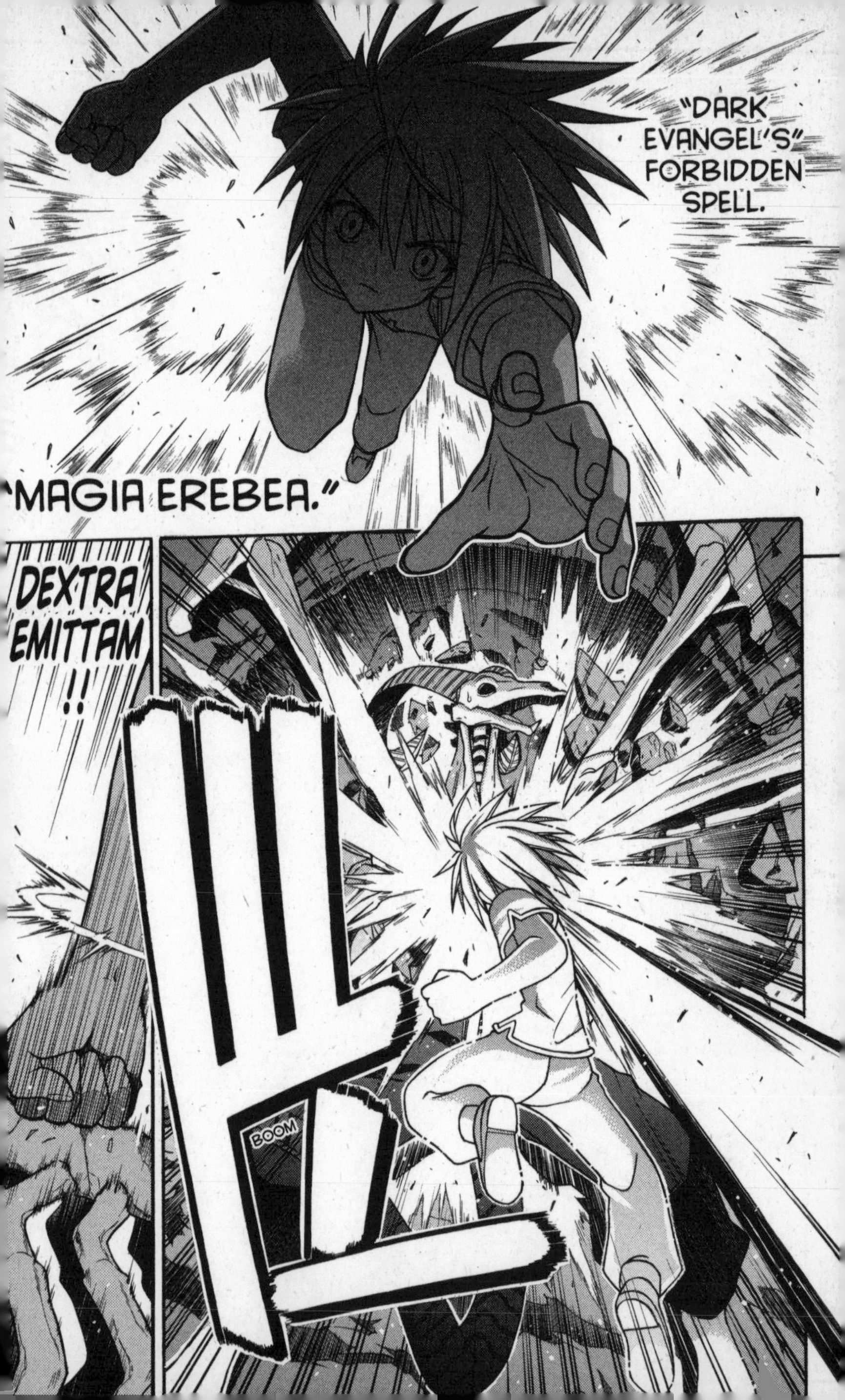
"DARK EVANGEL'S" FORBIDDEN SPELL.
"MAGIA EREBEA."
DEXTRA EMITTAM !!
BOOM

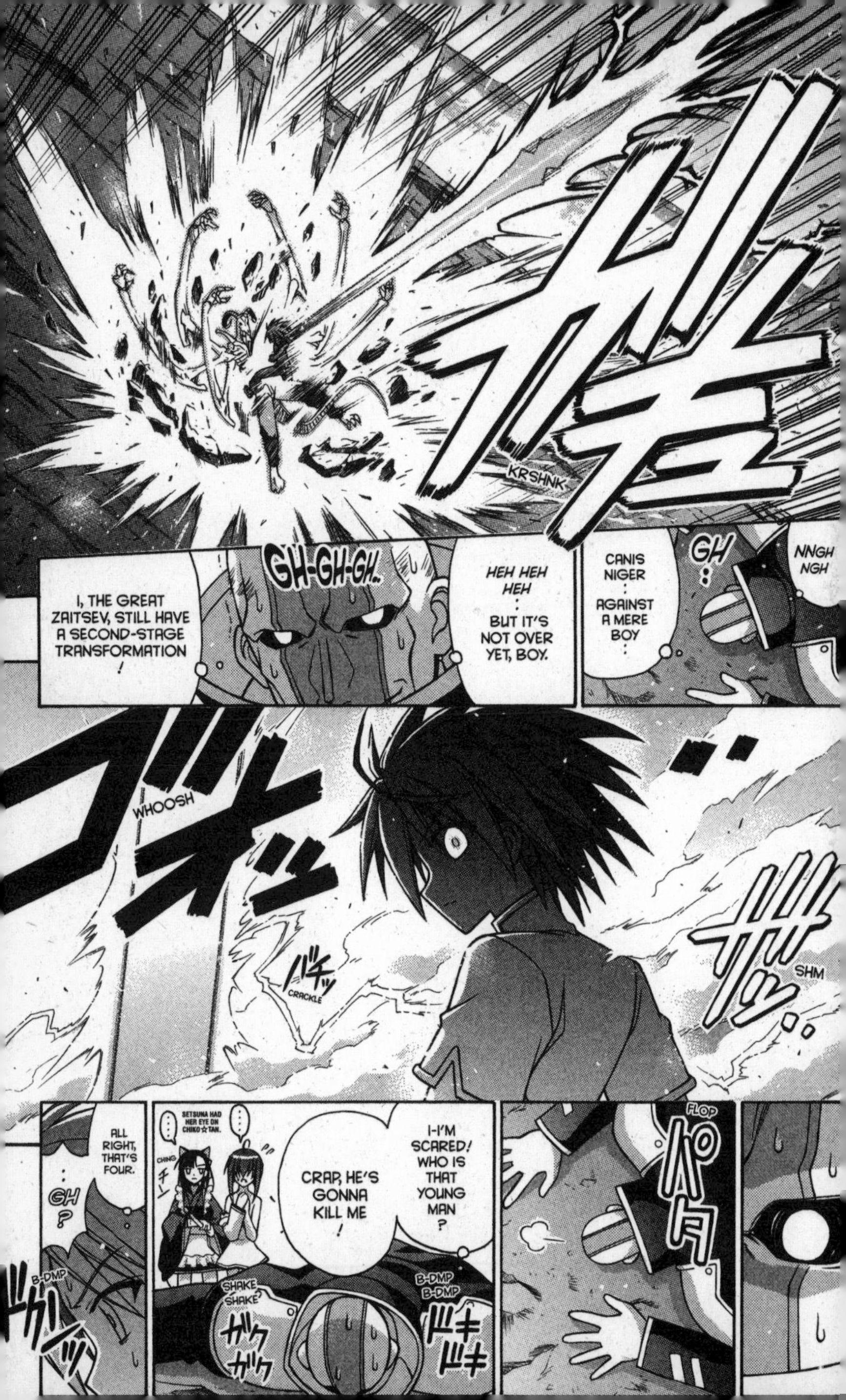

KRSHNK
NNGH NGH
GH :
CANIS NIGER : AGAINST A MERE BOY :
HEH HEH HEH : BUT IT'S NOT OVER YET, BOY.
GH-GH-GH..
I, THE GREAT ZAITSEV, STILL HAVE A SECOND-STAGE TRANSFORMATION !
SHM
CRACKLE
WHOOSH
FLOP
I-I'M SCARED! WHO IS THAT YOUNG MAN ?
B-DMP B-DMP
CRAP, HE'S GONNA KILL ME !
SETSUNA HAD HER EYE ON CHIKO☆TAN.
...
...
CHING
SHAKE SHAKE
ALL RIGHT, THAT'S FOUR.
: GH ?
B-DMP

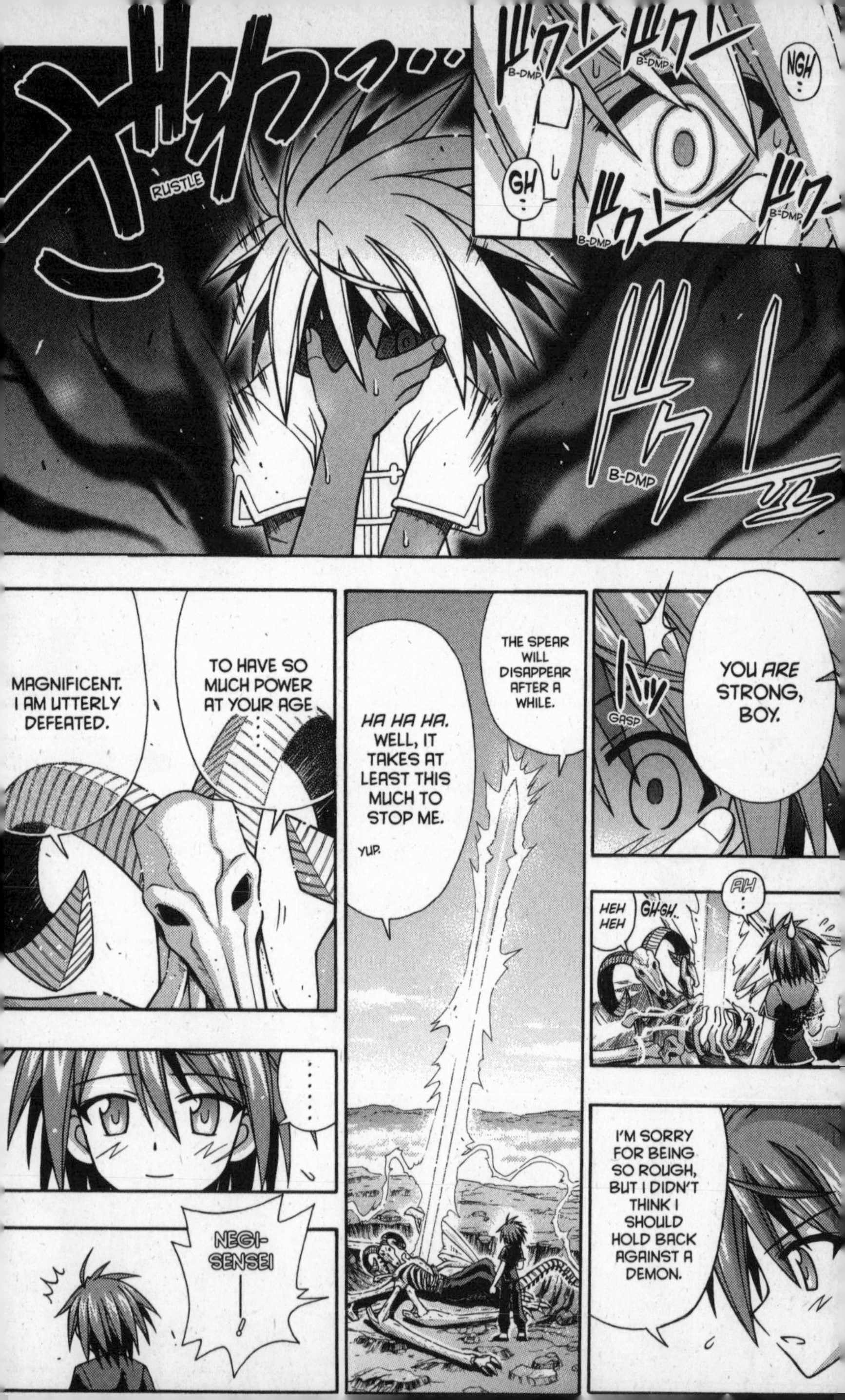
B-DMP
B-DMP
NGH
...
GH
...
B-DMP
B-DMP
RUSTLE
B-DMP
YOU ARE STRONG, BOY.
GASP
AH
...
HEH HEH
GH-GH..
I'M SORRY FOR BEING SO ROUGH, BUT I DIDN'T THINK I SHOULD HOLD BACK AGAINST A DEMON.
THE SPEAR WILL DISAPPEAR AFTER A WHILE.
HA HA HA. WELL, IT TAKES AT LEAST THIS MUCH TO STOP ME.
YUP.
TO HAVE SO MUCH POWER AT YOUR AGE
...
MAGNIFICENT. I AM UTTERLY DEFEATED.
......
NEGI-SENSEI
—!

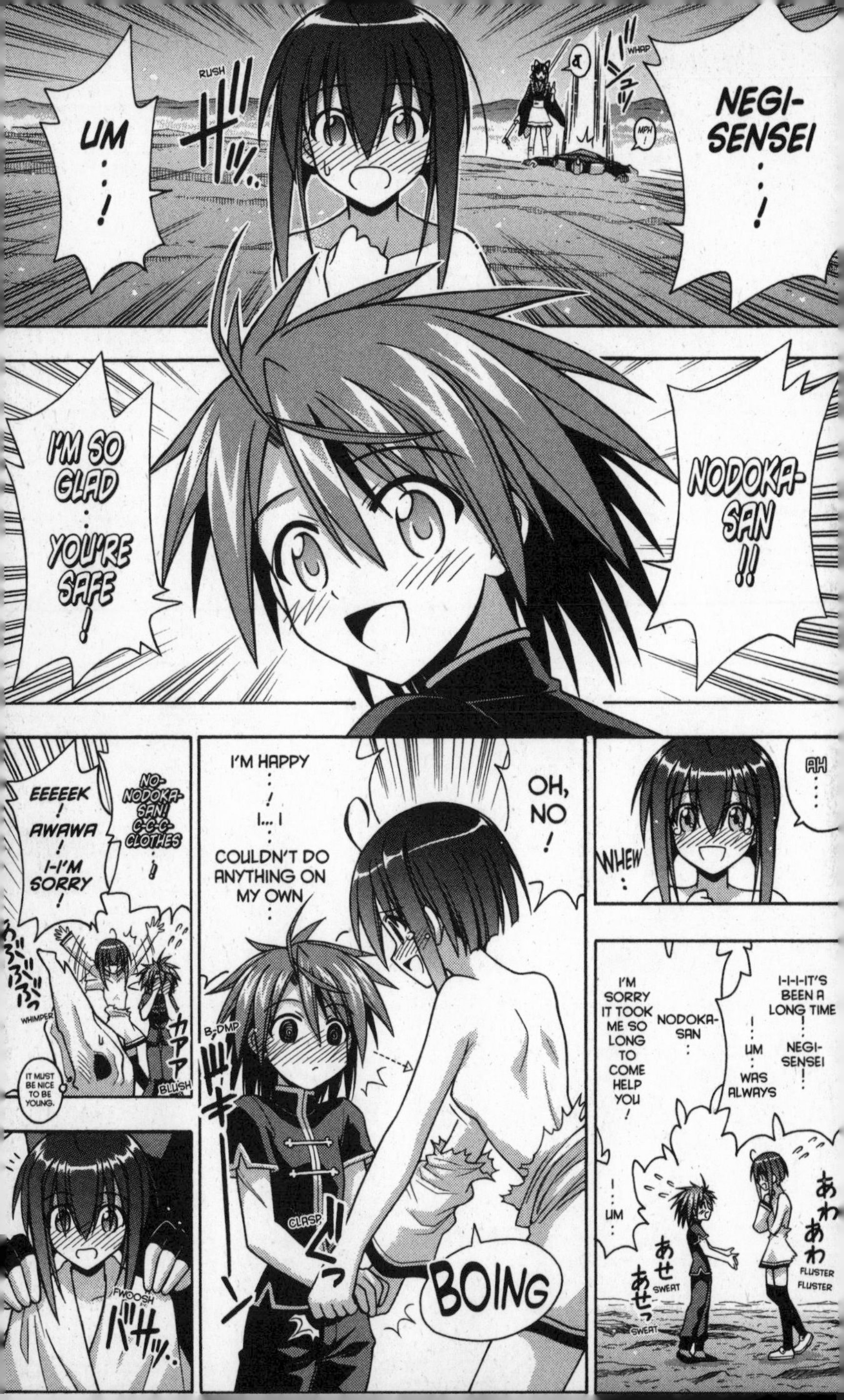
NEGI-SENSEI...!
WHAP
MPH!
RUSH
UM...!
NODOKA-SAN!!
I'M SO GLAD... YOU'RE SAFE!
AH...
WHEW...
I-I-I-IT'S BEEN A LONG TIME... NEGI-SENSEI!
...UM... WAS ALWAYS
NODOKA-SAN...
I'M SORRY IT TOOK ME SO LONG TO COME HELP YOU!
...UM...
FLUSTER FLUSTER
SWEAT
SWEAT
OH, NO!
I'M HAPPY...! I... I... COULDN'T DO ANYTHING ON MY OWN...
B-DMP
CLASP
BOING
NO-NODOKA-SAN! C-C-C-CLOTHES...!
EEEEEK! AWAWA! I-I'M SORRY!
WHIMPER
BLUSH
IT MUST BE NICE TO BE YOUNG.
FWOOSH

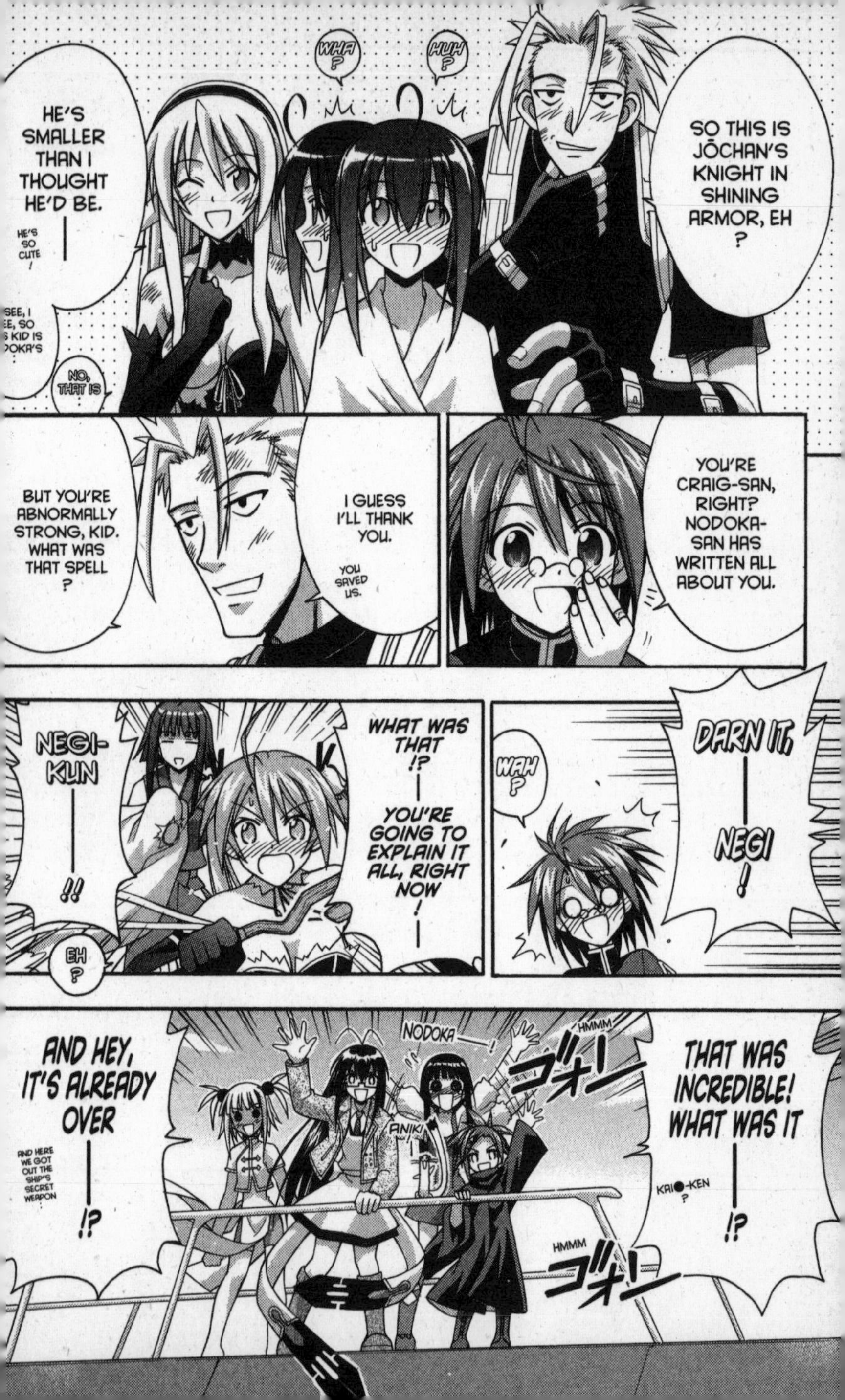
SO THIS IS JŌCHAN'S KNIGHT IN SHINING ARMOR, EH?
HUH?
WHA?
HE'S SMALLER THAN I THOUGHT HE'D BE. —
HE'S SO CUTE!
SEE, I EE, SO S KID IS DOKA'S
NO, THAT IS
YOU'RE CRAIG-SAN, RIGHT? NODOKA-SAN HAS WRITTEN ALL ABOUT YOU.
I GUESS I'LL THANK YOU.
YOU SAVED US.
BUT YOU'RE ABNORMALLY STRONG, KID. WHAT WAS THAT SPELL?
DARN IT, — NEGI!
WAH?
WHAT WAS THAT!? — YOU'RE GOING TO EXPLAIN IT ALL, RIGHT NOW! —
NEGI-KUN —!!
EH?
THAT WAS INCREDIBLE! WHAT WAS IT —!?
KAI●-KEN?
HMMM
ゴォー
HMMM
ゴォー
NODOKA—!
ANIKI!
AND HEY, IT'S ALREADY OVER —!?
AND HERE WE GOT OUT THE SHIP'S SECRET WEAPON

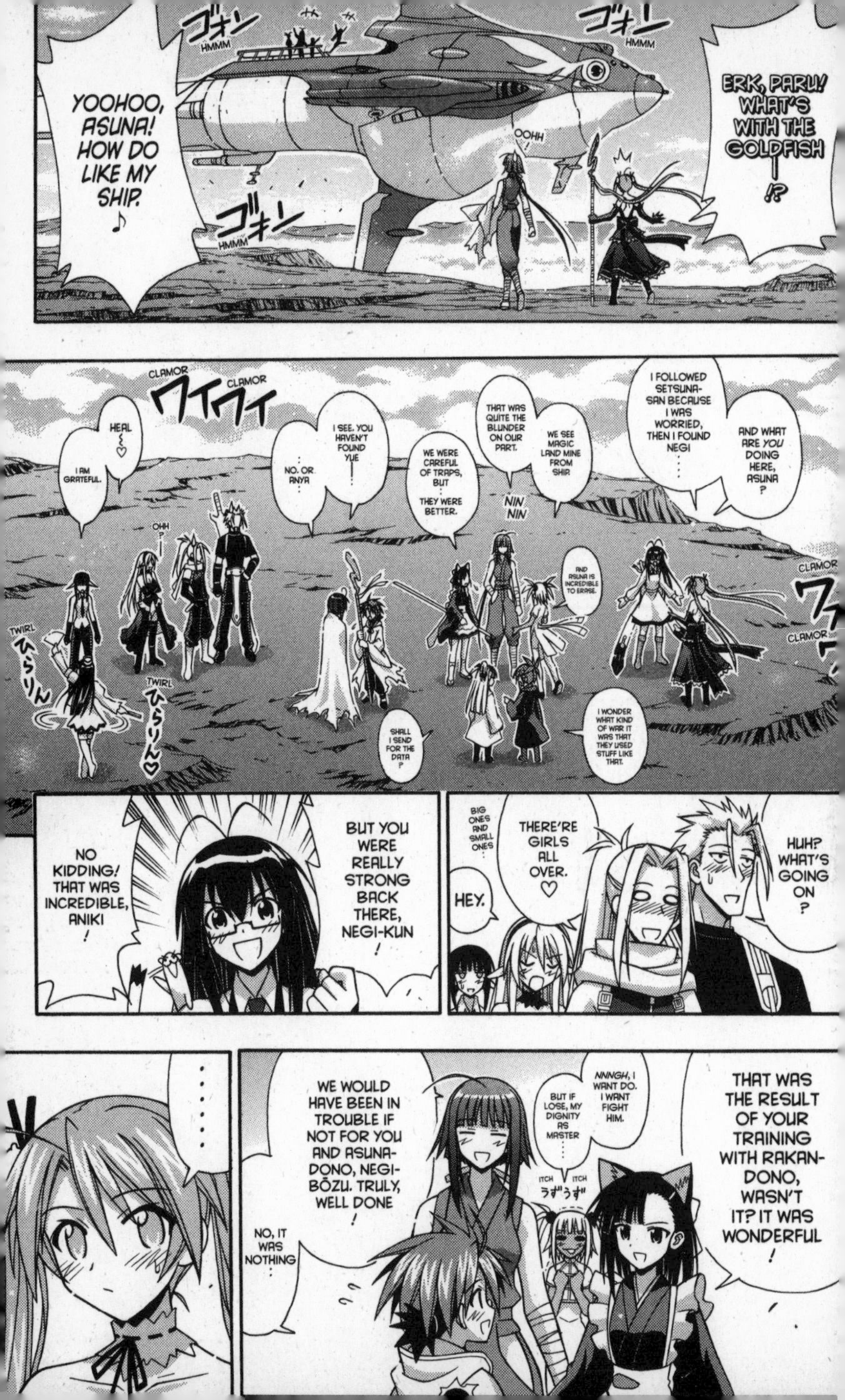

ERK, PARU! WHAT'S WITH THE GOLDFISH !?
ゴオン HMMM
OOHH!
YOOHOO, ASUNA! HOW DO LIKE MY SHIP. ♪
ゴオン HMMM
ゴオン HMMM
AND WHAT ARE *YOU* DOING HERE, ASUNA?
I FOLLOWED SETSUNA-SAN BECAUSE I WAS WORRIED, THEN I FOUND NEGI...
CLAMOR ワイ CLAMOR
WE SEE MAGIC LAND MINE FROM SHIP.
NIN NIN
THAT WAS QUITE THE BLUNDER ON OUR PART.
AND ASUNA IS INCREDIBLE TO ERASE.
WE WERE CAREFUL OF TRAPS, BUT... THEY WERE BETTER.
I SEE. YOU HAVEN'T FOUND YUE!
...NO. OR ANYA...
I WONDER WHAT KIND OF WAR IT WAS THAT THEY USED STUFF LIKE THAT.
SHALL I SEND FOR THE DATA?
HEAL~♡
I AM GRATEFUL.
OHH?
CLAMOR ワイワイ CLAMOR
TWIRL ひらりん
TWIRL ひらりん♡
HUH? WHAT'S GOING ON?
THERE'RE GIRLS ALL OVER. ♡
BIG ONES AND SMALL ONES...
HEY.
BUT YOU WERE REALLY STRONG BACK THERE, NEGI-KUN!
NO KIDDING! THAT WAS INCREDIBLE, ANIKI!
THAT WAS THE RESULT OF YOUR TRAINING WITH RAKAN-DONO, WASN'T IT? IT WAS WONDERFUL!
NNNGH, I WANT DO. I WANT FIGHT HIM.
BUT IF LOSE, MY DIGNITY AS MASTER...
ITCH うずうず ITCH
WE WOULD HAVE BEEN IN TROUBLE IF NOT FOR YOU AND ASUNA-DONO, NEGI-BŌZU. TRULY, WELL DONE!
NO, IT WAS NOTHING...
......

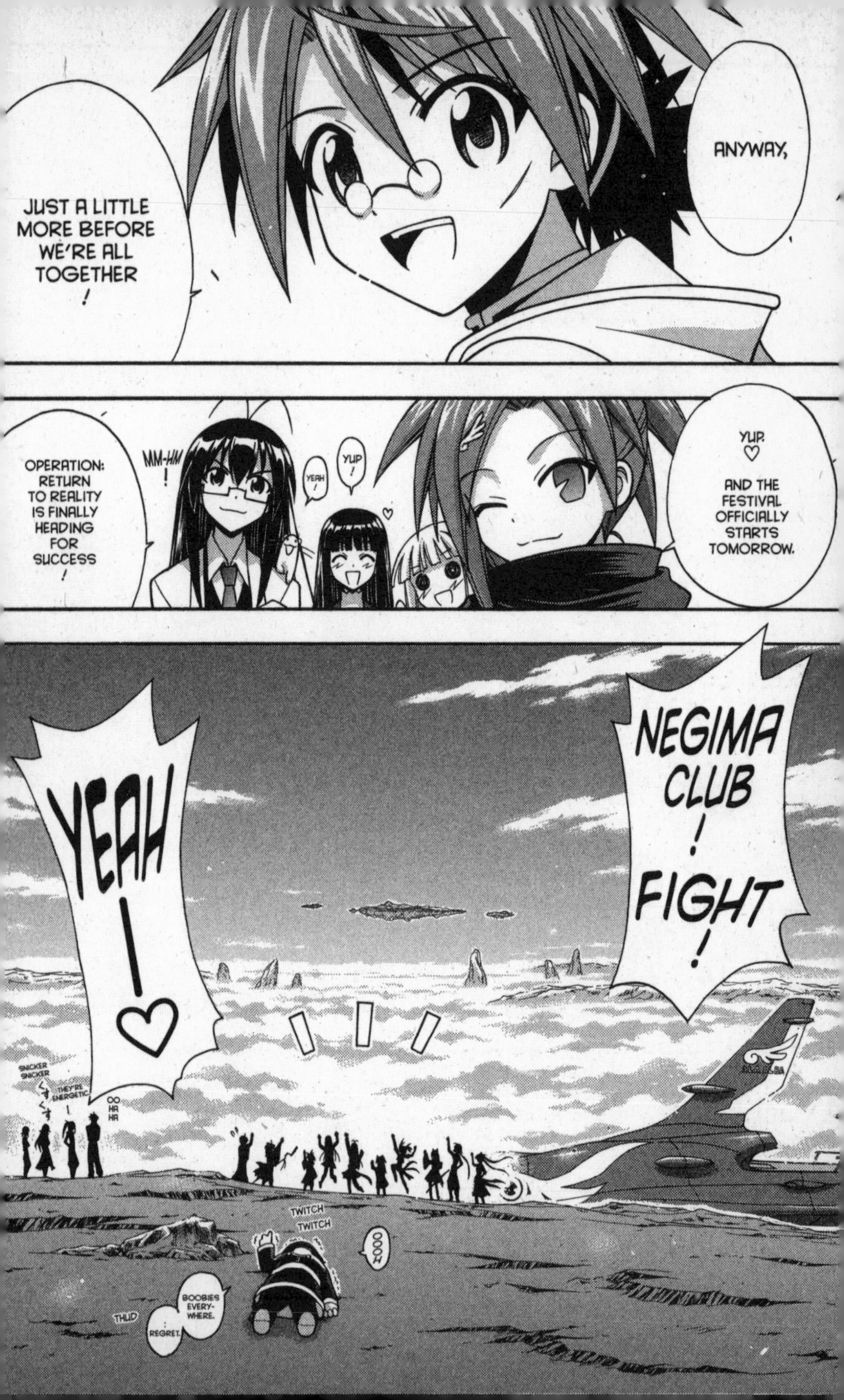
ANYWAY,
JUST A LITTLE MORE BEFORE WE'RE ALL TOGETHER!
YUP. ♡ AND THE FESTIVAL OFFICIALLY STARTS TOMORROW.
YUP!
YEAH!
MM-HM!
OPERATION: RETURN TO REALITY IS FINALLY HEADING FOR SUCCESS!
NEGIMA CLUB! FIGHT!
YEAH! ♡
OOOH
TWITCH TWITCH
OO HA HA
THEY'RE ENERGETIC!
SNICKER SNICKER
くすくす
BOOBIES EVERYWHERE.
: REGRET.
THUD

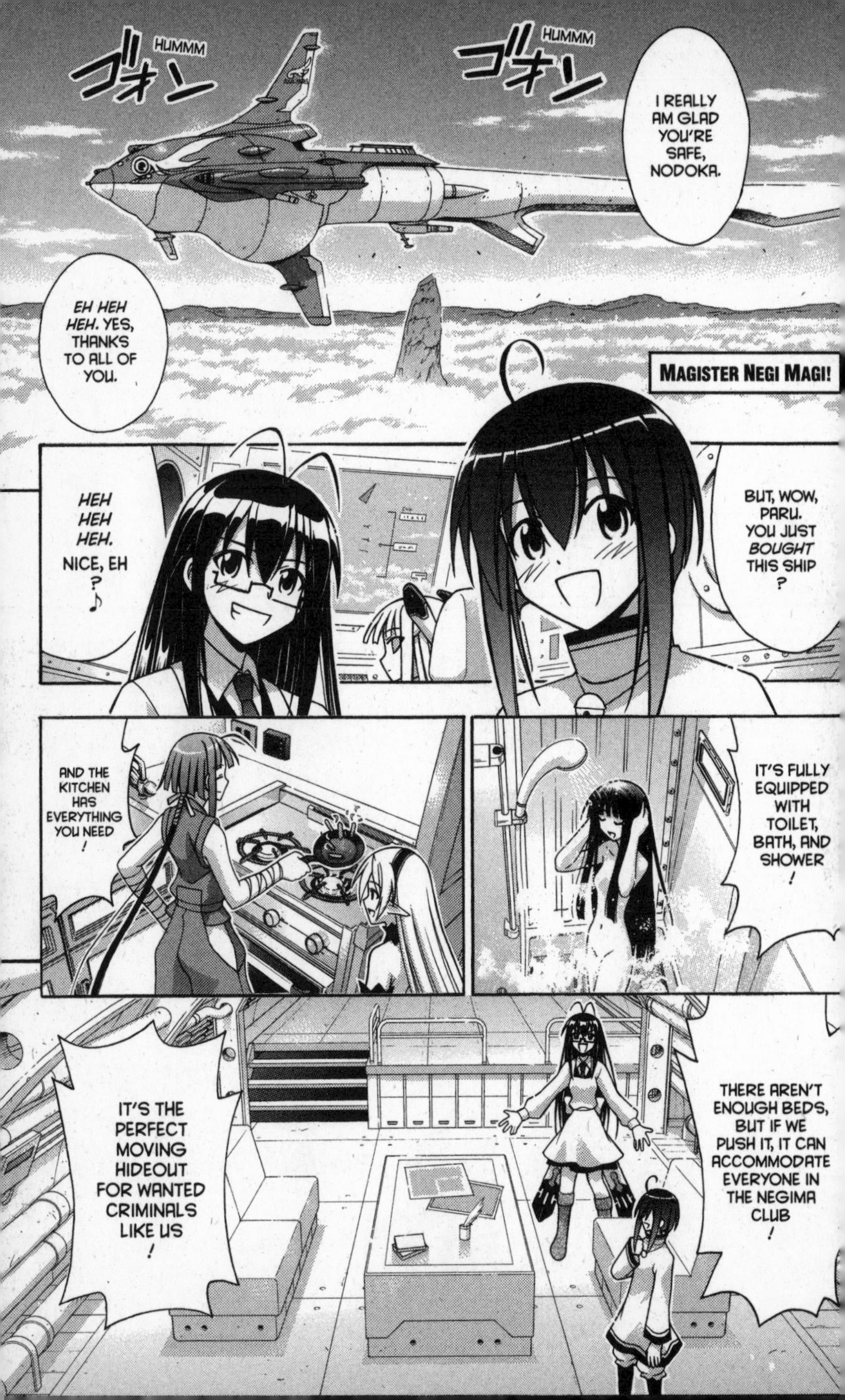

ゴオン
HUMMM
I REALLY AM GLAD YOU'RE SAFE, NODOKA.
ゴオン
HUMMM
EH HEH HEH. YES, THANKS TO ALL OF YOU.
MAGISTER NEGI MAGI!
BUT, WOW, PARU. YOU JUST *BOUGHT* THIS SHIP?
HEH HEH HEH. NICE, EH?♪
IT'S FULLY EQUIPPED WITH TOILET, BATH, AND SHOWER!
AND THE KITCHEN HAS EVERYTHING YOU NEED!
THERE AREN'T ENOUGH BEDS, BUT IF WE PUSH IT, IT CAN ACCOMMODATE EVERYONE IN THE NEGIMA CLUB!
IT'S THE PERFECT MOVING HIDEOUT FOR WANTED CRIMINALS LIKE US!

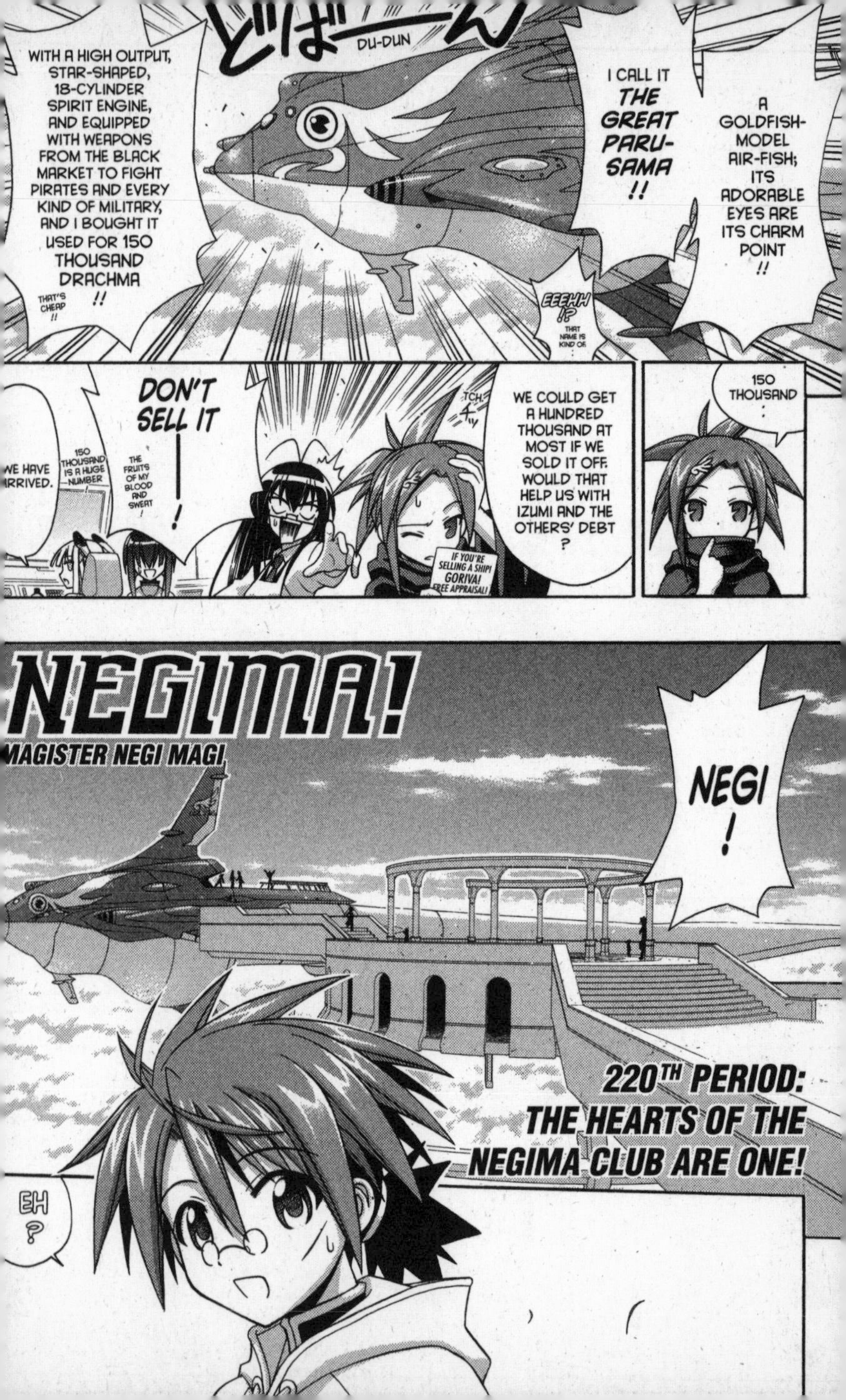

A GOLDFISH-MODEL AIR-FISH; ITS ADORABLE EYES ARE ITS CHARM POINT!!
I CALL IT THE GREAT PARU-SAMA!!
EEEHH!?
THAT NAME IS KIND OF...
DU-DUN
WITH A HIGH OUTPUT, STAR-SHAPED, 18-CYLINDER SPIRIT ENGINE, AND EQUIPPED WITH WEAPONS FROM THE BLACK MARKET TO FIGHT PIRATES AND EVERY KIND OF MILITARY, AND I BOUGHT IT USED FOR 150 THOUSAND DRACHMA!!
THAT'S CHEAP!!
150 THOUSAND...
WE COULD GET A HUNDRED THOUSAND AT MOST IF WE SOLD IT OFF. WOULD THAT HELP US WITH IZUMI AND THE OTHERS' DEBT?
TCH
IF YOU'RE SELLING A SHIP! GORIVA! FREE APPRAISAL!
DON'T SELL IT!
THE FRUITS OF MY BLOOD AND SWEAT!
150 THOUSAND IS A HUGE NUMBER!
WE HAVE RRIVED.
NEGIMA!
MAGISTER NEGI MAGI
NEGI!
220TH PERIOD: THE HEARTS OF THE NEGIMA CLUB ARE ONE!
EH?

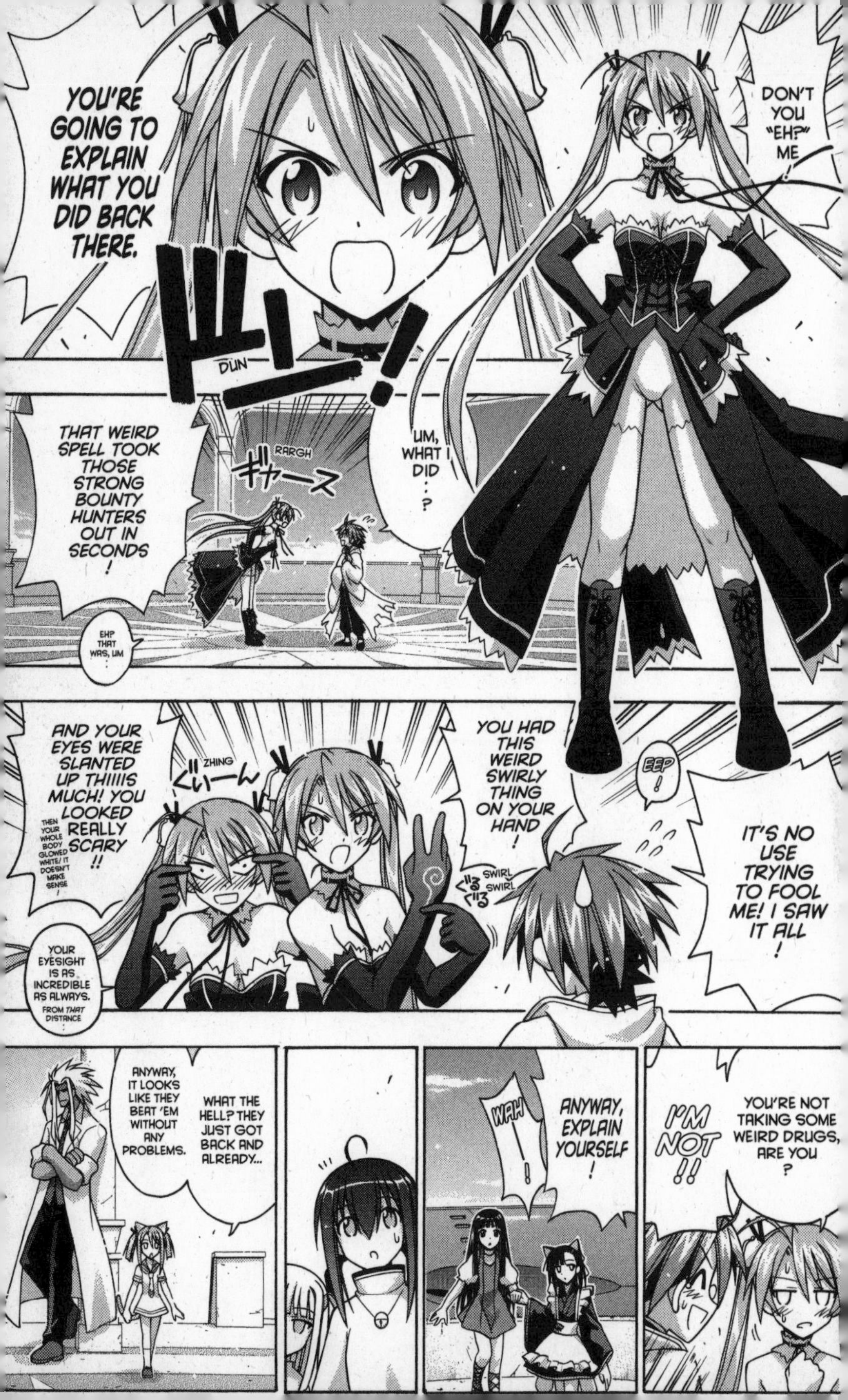
DON'T YOU "EH?" ME!
YOU'RE GOING TO EXPLAIN WHAT YOU DID BACK THERE.
ドーン!
DUN
UM, WHAT I DID...?
ギャース
RARGH
THAT WEIRD SPELL TOOK THOSE STRONG BOUNTY HUNTERS OUT IN SECONDS!
EH? THAT WAS, UM...
IT'S NO USE TRYING TO FOOL ME! I SAW IT ALL!
EEP!
YOU HAD THIS WEIRD SWIRLY THING ON YOUR HAND!
ぐるぐる
SWIRL SWIRL
AND YOUR EYES WERE SLANTED UP THIIIIS MUCH! YOU LOOKED REALLY SCARY!!
ぐいーん
ZHING
THEN YOUR WHOLE BODY GLOWED WHITE/ IT DOESN'T MAKE SENSE!
YOUR EYESIGHT IS AS INCREDIBLE AS ALWAYS.
FROM *THAT* DISTANCE
YOU'RE NOT TAKING SOME WEIRD DRUGS, ARE YOU?
I'M NOT!!
ANYWAY, EXPLAIN YOURSELF!
WAH!
WHAT THE HELL? THEY JUST GOT BACK AND ALREADY...
ANYWAY, IT LOOKS LIKE THEY BEAT 'EM WITHOUT ANY PROBLEMS.

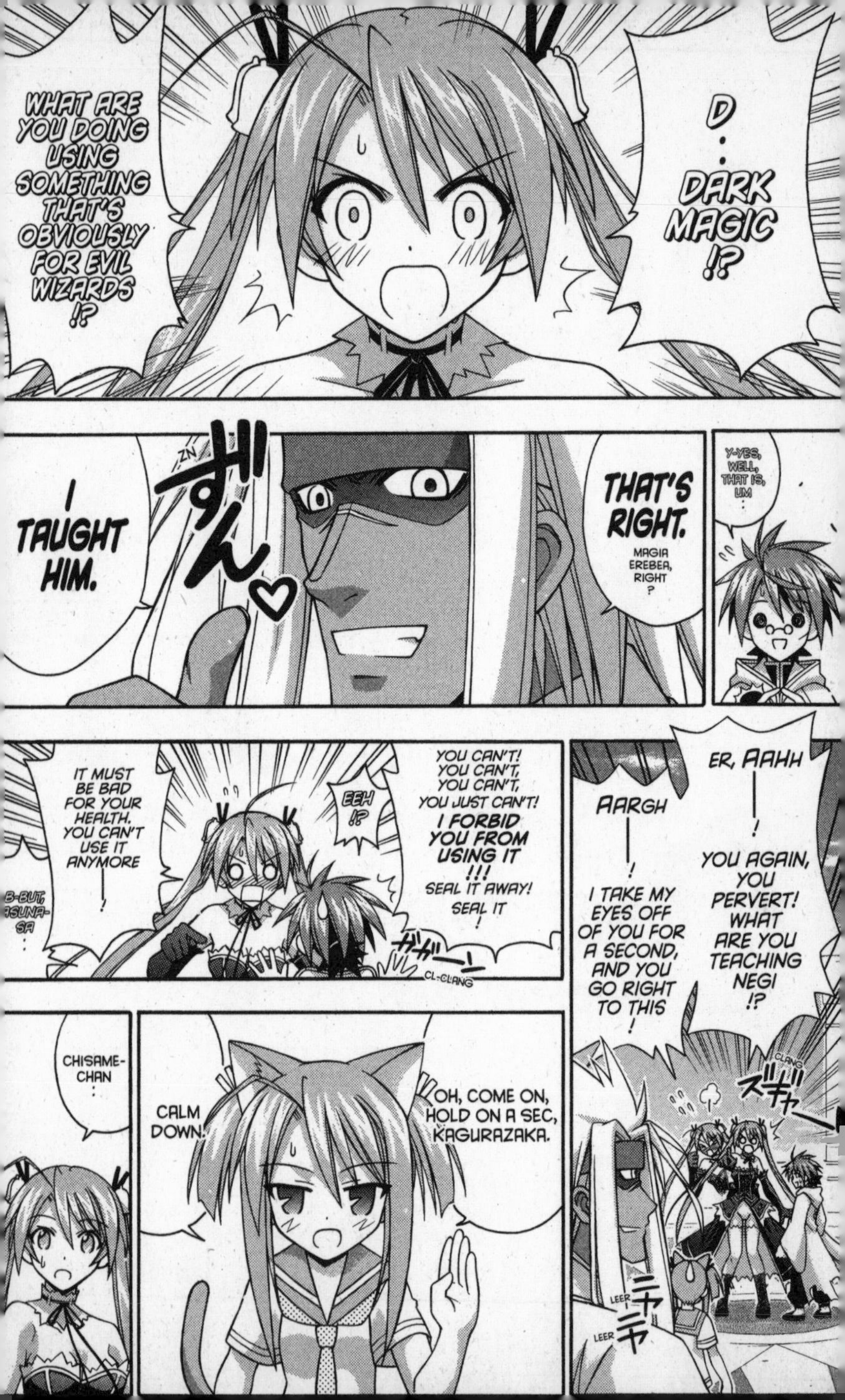

D... DARK MAGIC!?
WHAT ARE YOU DOING USING SOMETHING THAT'S OBVIOUSLY FOR EVIL WIZARDS!?
Y-YES, WELL, THAT IS, UM...
THAT'S RIGHT.
MAGIA EREBEA, RIGHT?
ZN
I TAUGHT HIM.
ER, AAHH—!
YOU AGAIN, YOU PERVERT! WHAT ARE YOU TEACHING NEGI!?
AARGH—!
I TAKE MY EYES OFF OF YOU FOR A SECOND, AND YOU GO RIGHT TO THIS!
CLANG
LEER
LEER
YOU CAN'T! YOU CAN'T, YOU CAN'T, YOU JUST CAN'T! I FORBID YOU FROM USING IT!!! SEAL IT AWAY! SEAL IT!
EEH!?
IT MUST BE BAD FOR YOUR HEALTH. YOU CAN'T USE IT ANYMORE—!
B-BUT, ASUNA-SA...
CL-CLANG
OH, COME ON, HOLD ON A SEC, KAGURAZAKA.
CALM DOWN.
CHISAME-CHAN...

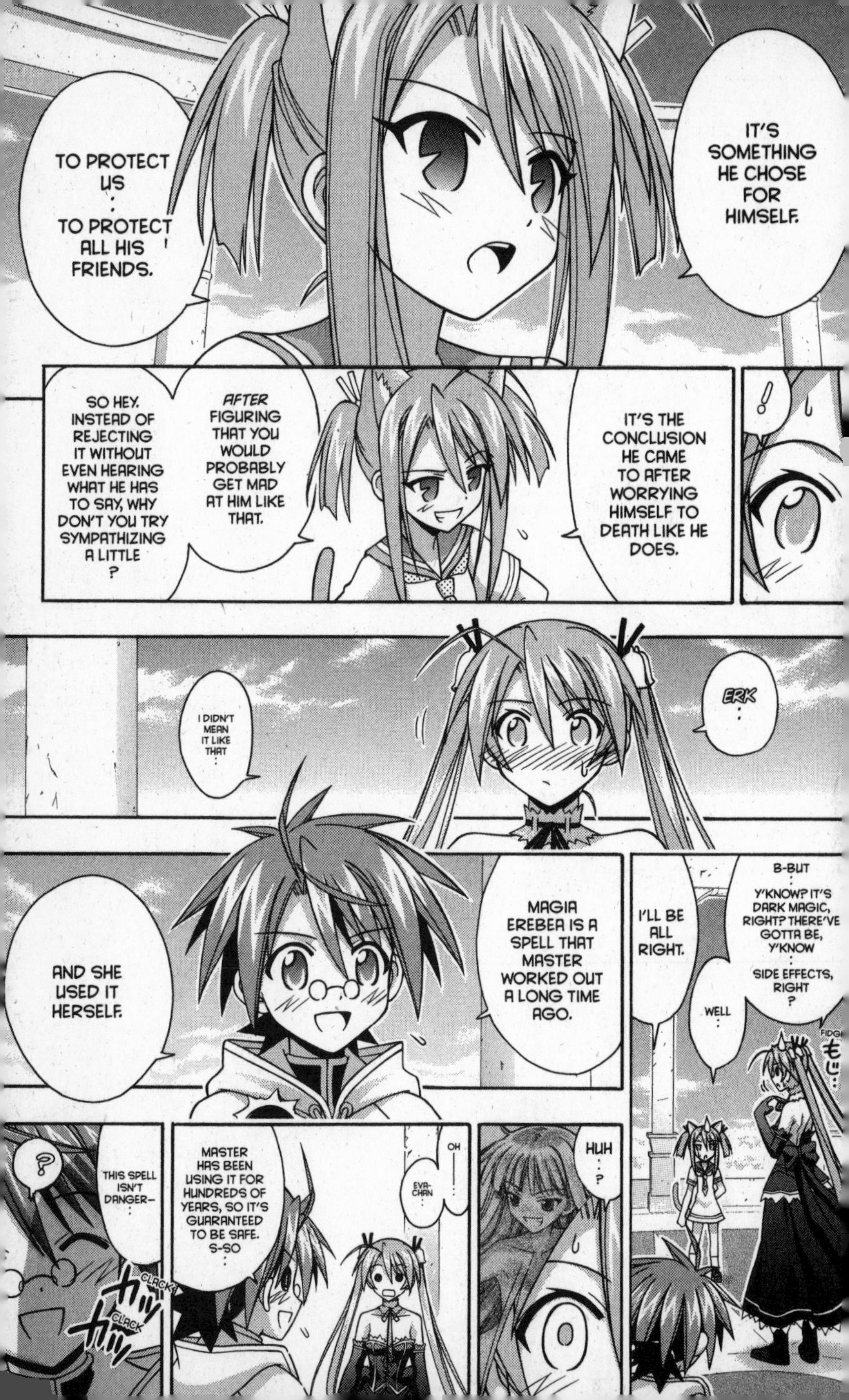
IT'S SOMETHING HE CHOSE FOR HIMSELF.
TO PROTECT US... TO PROTECT ALL HIS FRIENDS.
!
IT'S THE CONCLUSION HE CAME TO AFTER WORRYING HIMSELF TO DEATH LIKE HE DOES.
AFTER FIGURING THAT YOU WOULD PROBABLY GET MAD AT HIM LIKE THAT.
SO HEY. INSTEAD OF REJECTING IT WITHOUT EVEN HEARING WHAT HE HAS TO SAY, WHY DON'T YOU TRY SYMPATHIZING A LITTLE?
ERK...
I DIDN'T MEAN IT LIKE THAT...
B-BUT... Y'KNOW? IT'S DARK MAGIC, RIGHT? THERE'VE GOTTA BE, Y'KNOW... SIDE EFFECTS, RIGHT?
WELL...
FIDG
I'LL BE ALL RIGHT.
MAGIA EREBEA IS A SPELL THAT MASTER WORKED OUT A LONG TIME AGO.
AND SHE USED IT HERSELF.
HUH...?
OH... EVA-CHAN...
MASTER HAS BEEN USING IT FOR HUNDREDS OF YEARS, SO IT'S GUARANTEED TO BE SAFE. S-SO...
THIS SPELL ISN'T DANGER-...
?
CLACK
CLACK

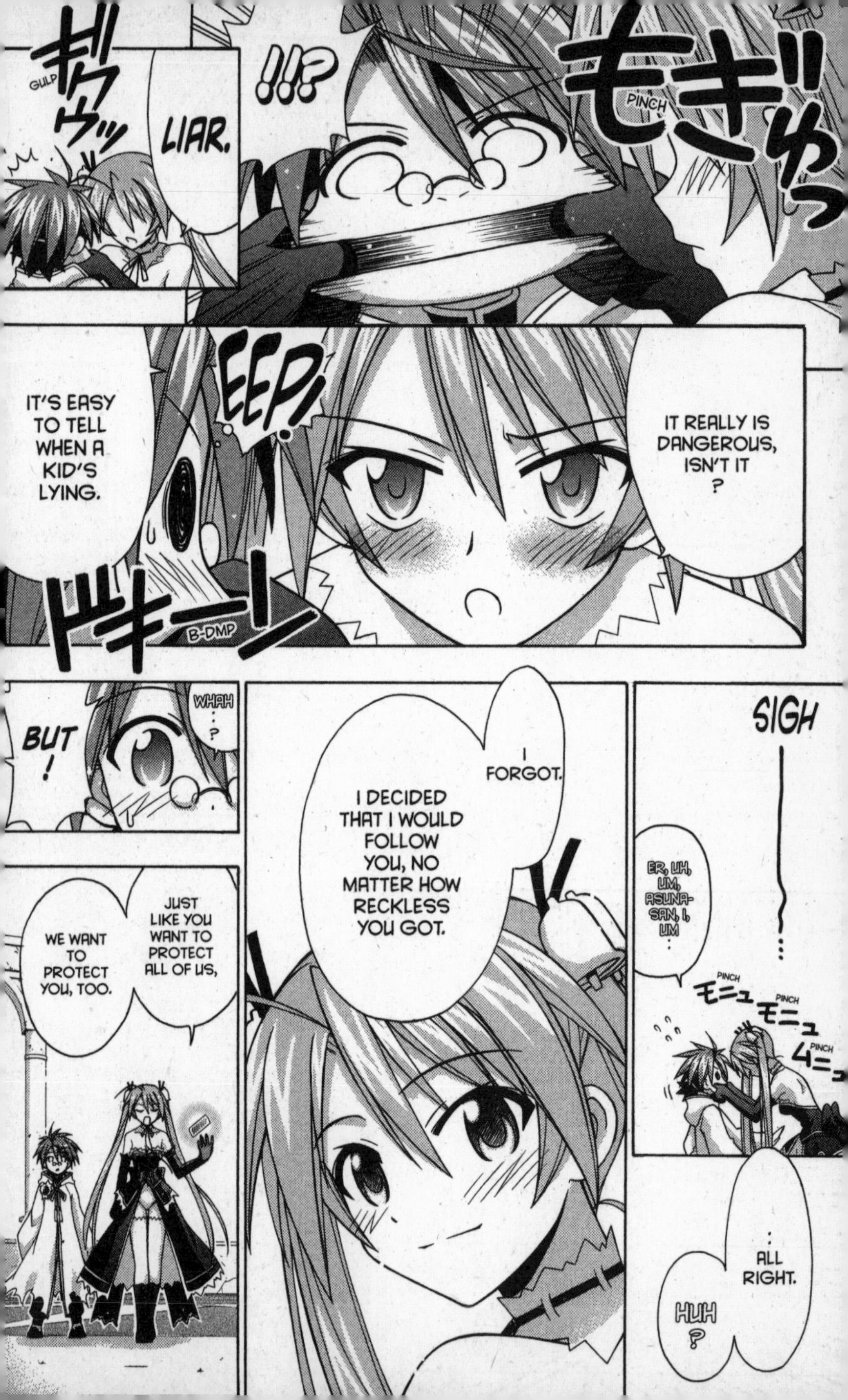

PINCH
!!?
GULP
LIAR.
IT REALLY IS DANGEROUS, ISN'T IT?
EEP!
IT'S EASY TO TELL WHEN A KID'S LYING.
B-DMP
SIGH...
ER, UH, UM, ASUNA-SAN, I, UM...
PINCH
PINCH
PINCH
...ALL RIGHT.
HUH?
I FORGOT.
I DECIDED THAT I WOULD FOLLOW YOU, NO MATTER HOW RECKLESS YOU GOT.
WHAH...?
BUT!
JUST LIKE YOU WANT TO PROTECT ALL OF US,
WE WANT TO PROTECT YOU, TOO.

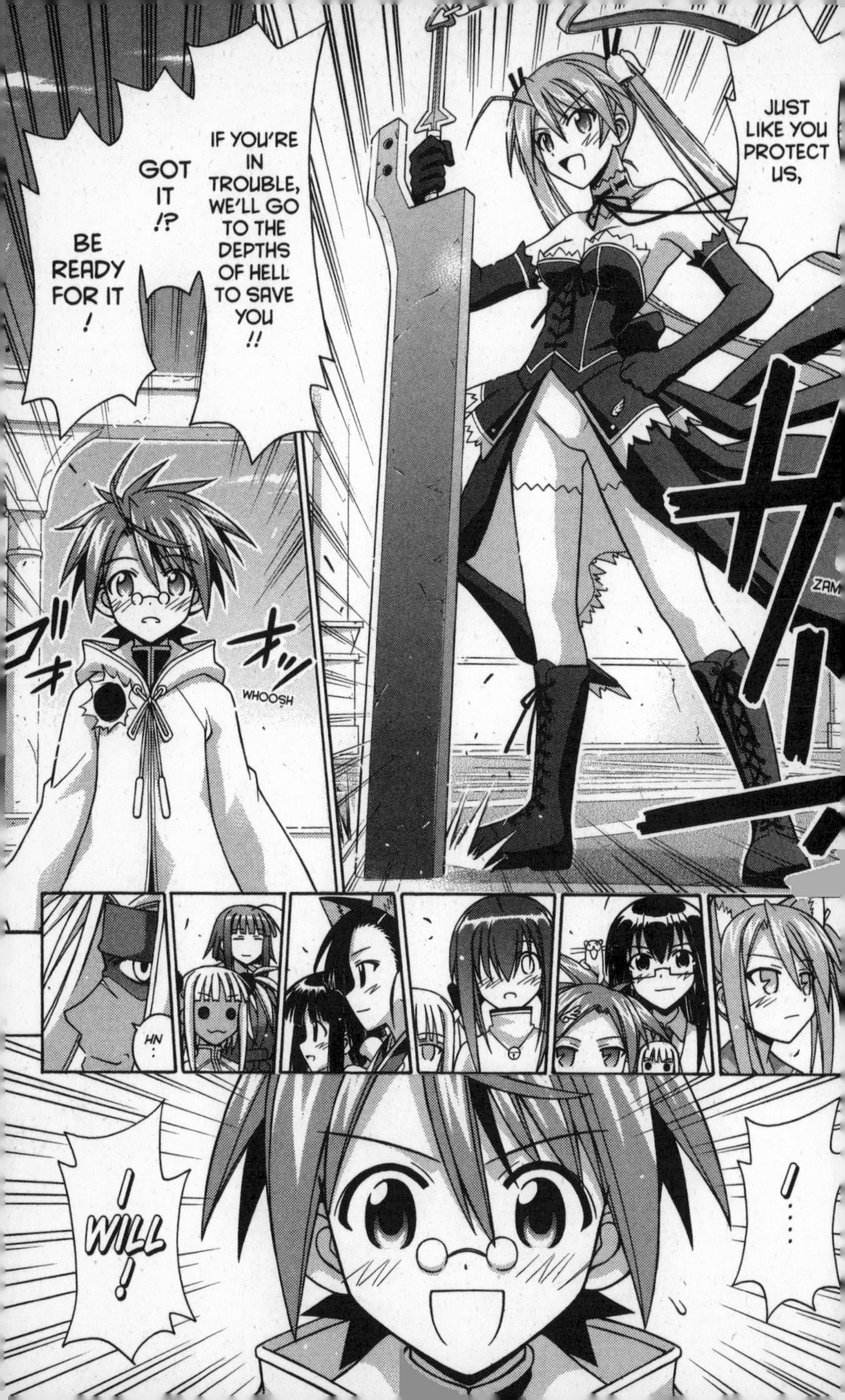
JUST LIKE YOU PROTECT US,
IF YOU'RE IN TROUBLE, WE'LL GO TO THE DEPTHS OF HELL TO SAVE YOU!!
GOT IT!?
BE READY FOR IT!
ZAM
WHOOSH
HN...
I......
I WILL!

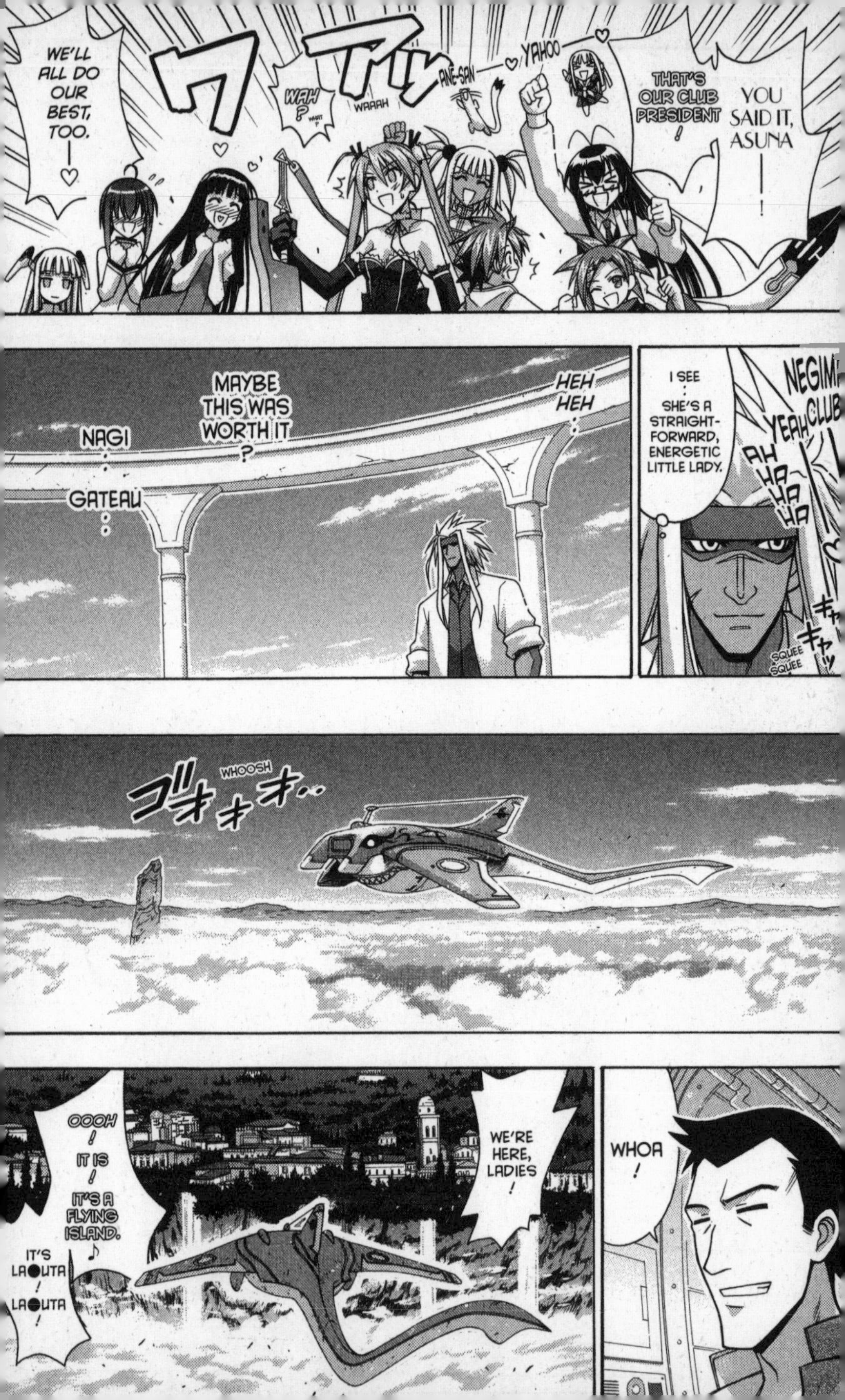
YOU SAID IT, ASUNA!
THAT'S OUR CLUB PRESIDENT!
YAHOO ♡
ANE-SAN ♡
WAAAH
WAH? WHAT?
WE'LL ALL DO OUR BEST, TOO. ♡
CLUB
YEAH
AH HA HA HA HA
I SEE... SHE'S A STRAIGHT-FORWARD, ENERGETIC LITTLE LADY.
SQUEE SQUEE
HEH HEH...
MAYBE THIS WAS WORTH IT?
NAGI...
GATEAU...
WHOOSH
WHOA!
WE'RE HERE, LADIES!
OOOH! IT IS! IT'S A FLYING ISLAND. ♪
IT'S LA●UTA! LA●UTA!

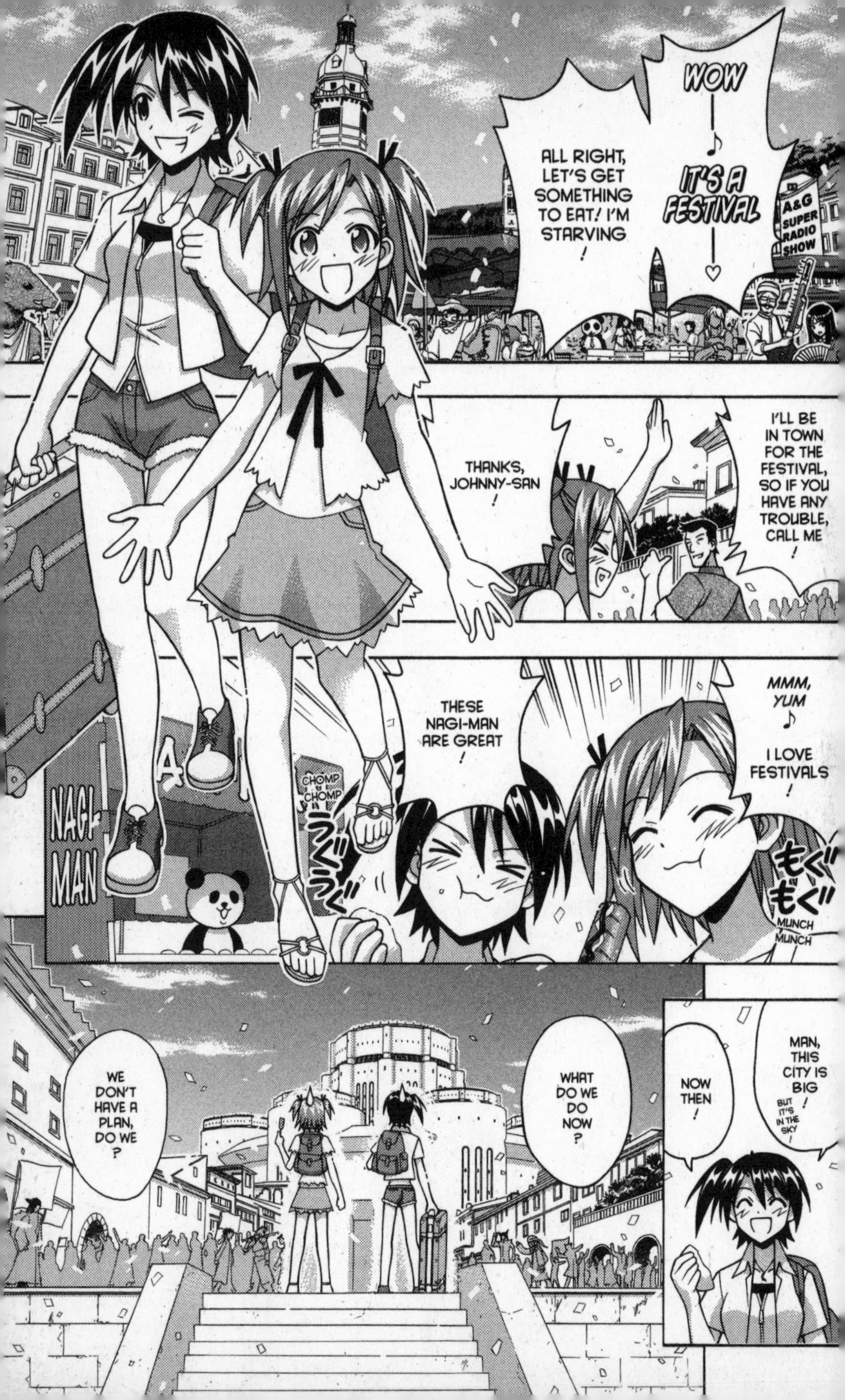
WOW ♪ IT'S A FESTIVAL ♡
A&G SUPER RADIO SHOW
ALL RIGHT, LET'S GET SOMETHING TO EAT! I'M STARVING!
I'LL BE IN TOWN FOR THE FESTIVAL, SO IF YOU HAVE ANY TROUBLE, CALL ME!
THANKS, JOHNNY-SAN!
MMM, YUM ♪ I LOVE FESTIVALS!
もぐ もぐ
MUNCH MUNCH
THESE NAGI-MAN ARE GREAT!
うぐうぐ
CHOMP CHOMP
NAGI-MAN
MAN, THIS CITY IS BIG!
BUT IT'S IN THE SKY
NOW THEN!
WHAT DO WE DO NOW?
WE DON'T HAVE A PLAN, DO WE?

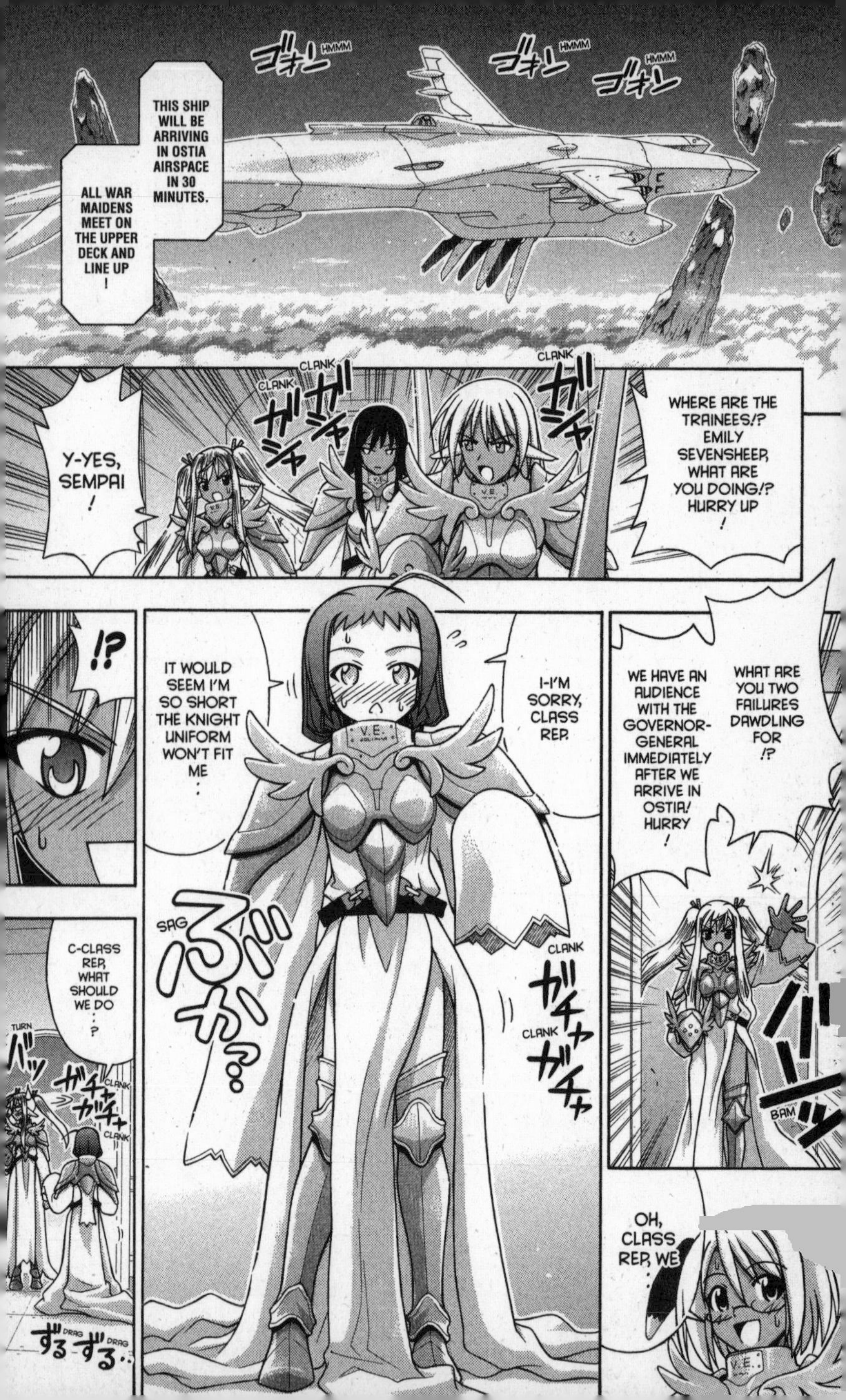

HMMM
HMMM
HMMM
THIS SHIP WILL BE ARRIVING IN OSTIA AIRSPACE IN 30 MINUTES.
ALL WAR MAIDENS MEET ON THE UPPER DECK AND LINE UP!
WHERE ARE THE TRAINEES!? EMILY SEVENSHEEP, WHAT ARE YOU DOING!? HURRY UP!
CLANK
CLANK
Y-YES, SEMPAI!
WHAT ARE YOU TWO FAILURES DAWDLING FOR!?
WE HAVE AN AUDIENCE WITH THE GOVERNOR-GENERAL IMMEDIATELY AFTER WE ARRIVE IN OSTIA! HURRY!
BAM
OH, CLASS REP, WE...
I-I'M SORRY, CLASS REP.
IT WOULD SEEM I'M SO SHORT THE KNIGHT UNIFORM WON'T FIT ME...
SAG
CLANK
CLANK
!?
C-CLASS REP, WHAT SHOULD WE DO...?
TURN
CLANK
CLANK
DRAG
DRAG

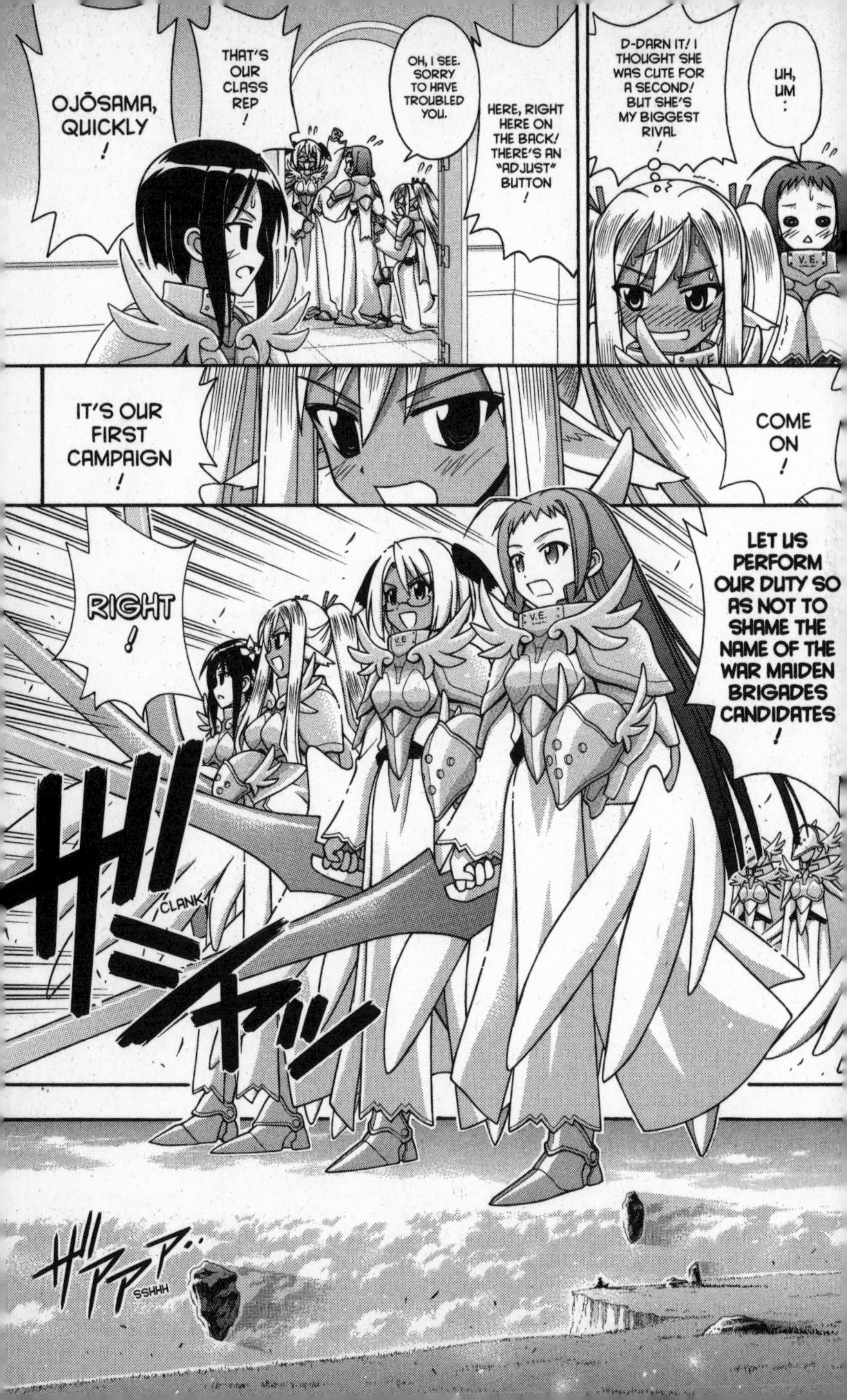
UH, UM…
D-DARN IT! I THOUGHT SHE WAS CUTE FOR A SECOND! BUT SHE'S MY BIGGEST RIVAL!
HERE, RIGHT HERE ON THE BACK! THERE'S AN "ADJUST" BUTTON!
OH, I SEE. SORRY TO HAVE TROUBLED YOU.
THAT'S OUR CLASS REP!
OJŌSAMA, QUICKLY!
COME ON!
IT'S OUR FIRST CAMPAIGN!
LET US PERFORM OUR DUTY SO AS NOT TO SHAME THE NAME OF THE WAR MAIDEN BRIGADES CANDIDATES!
RIGHT!
CLANK
SSHHH

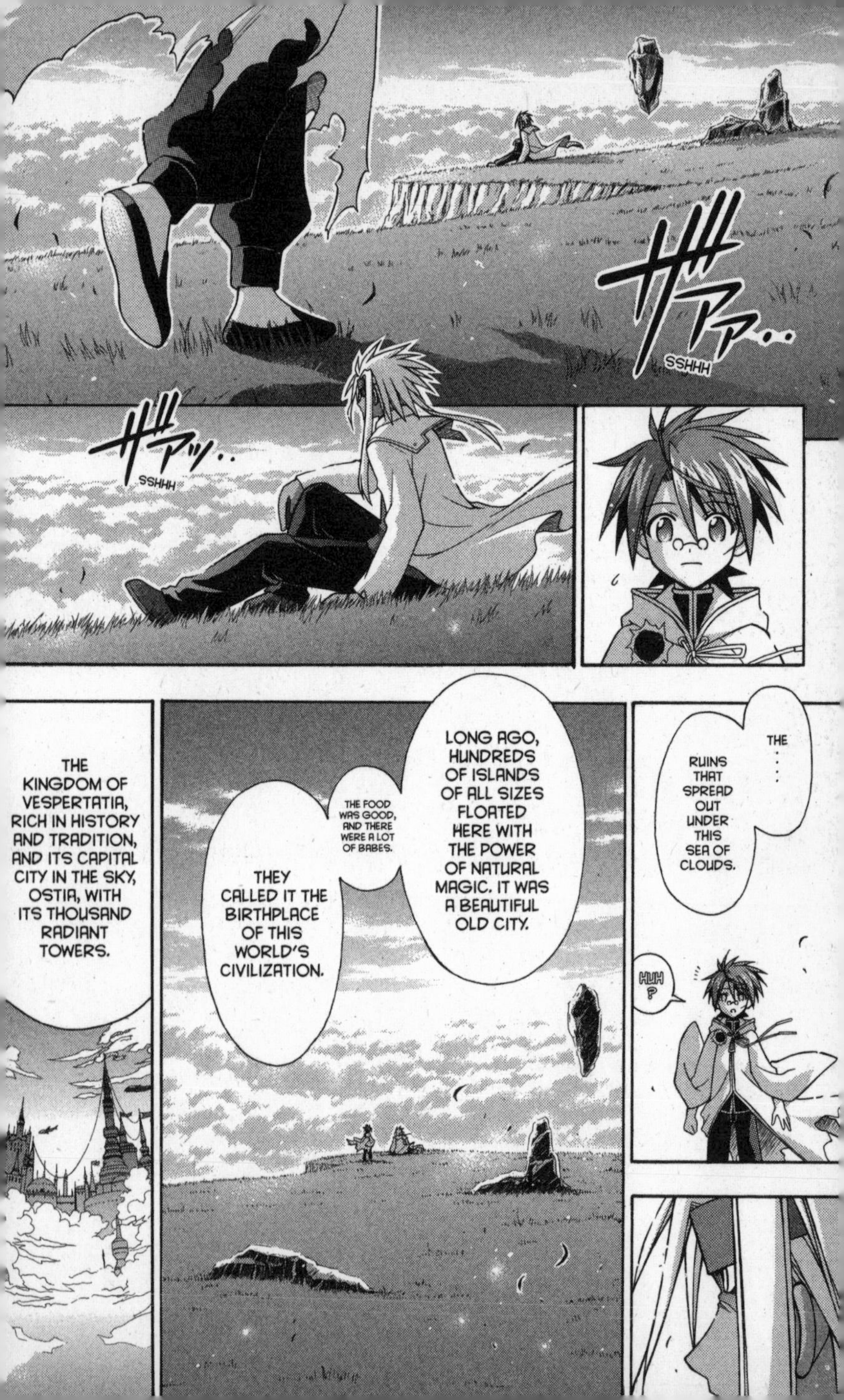
ザァァ..
SSHHH
ザアッ..
SSHHH
THE . . .
RUINS THAT SPREAD OUT UNDER THIS SEA OF CLOUDS.
HUH ?
LONG AGO, HUNDREDS OF ISLANDS OF ALL SIZES FLOATED HERE WITH THE POWER OF NATURAL MAGIC. IT WAS A BEAUTIFUL OLD CITY.
THE FOOD WAS GOOD, AND THERE WERE A LOT OF BABES.
THEY CALLED IT THE BIRTHPLACE OF THIS WORLD'S CIVILIZATION.
THE KINGDOM OF VESPERTATIA, RICH IN HISTORY AND TRADITION, AND ITS CAPITAL CITY IN THE SKY, OSTIA, WITH ITS THOUSAND RADIANT TOWERS.

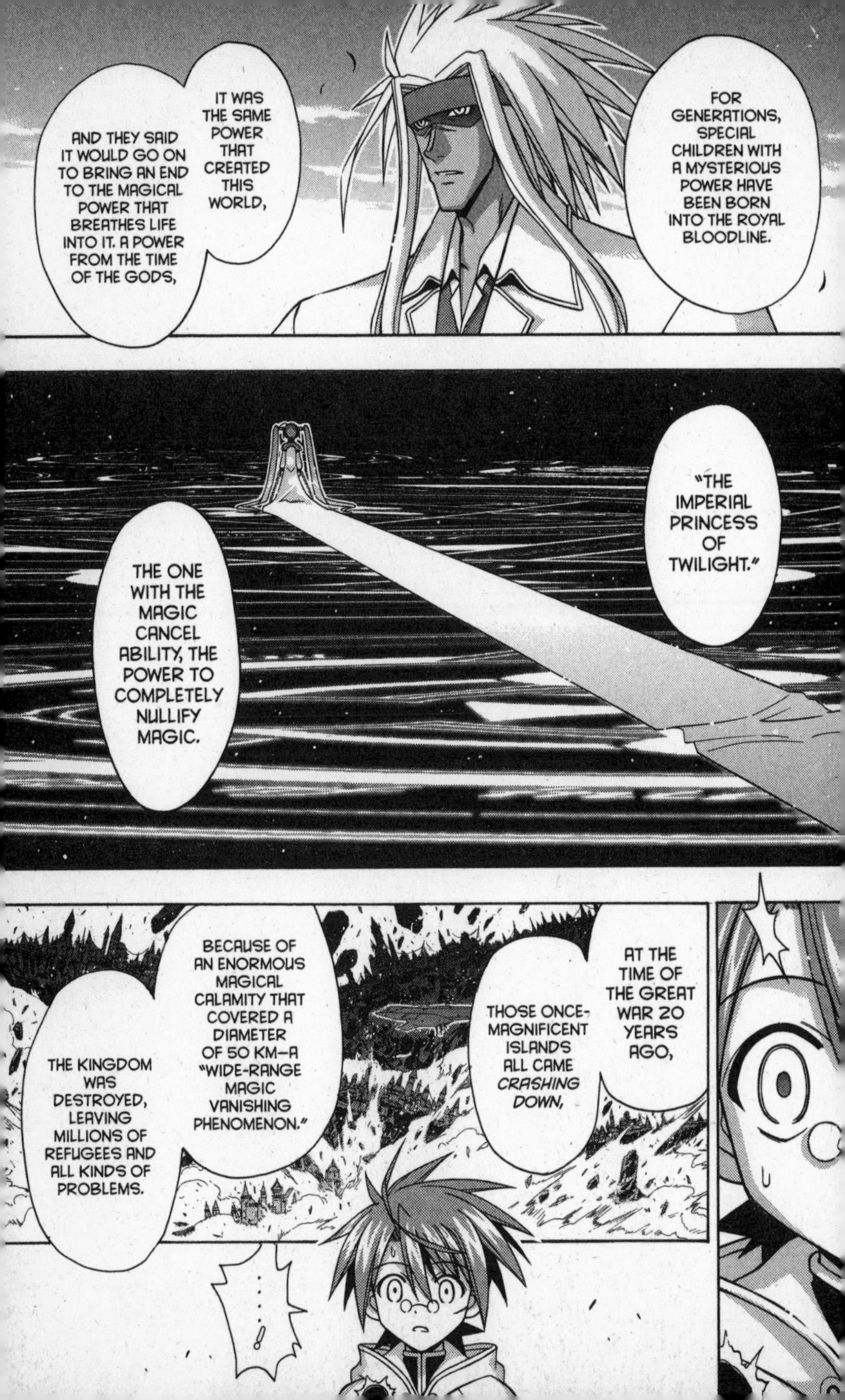

FOR GENERATIONS, SPECIAL CHILDREN WITH A MYSTERIOUS POWER HAVE BEEN BORN INTO THE ROYAL BLOODLINE.
IT WAS THE SAME POWER THAT CREATED THIS WORLD,
AND THEY SAID IT WOULD GO ON TO BRING AN END TO THE MAGICAL POWER THAT BREATHES LIFE INTO IT. A POWER FROM THE TIME OF THE GODS,
"THE IMPERIAL PRINCESS OF TWILIGHT."
THE ONE WITH THE MAGIC CANCEL ABILITY, THE POWER TO COMPLETELY NULLIFY MAGIC.
AT THE TIME OF THE GREAT WAR 20 YEARS AGO,
THOSE ONCE-MAGNIFICENT ISLANDS ALL CAME *CRASHING DOWN*,
BECAUSE OF AN ENORMOUS MAGICAL CALAMITY THAT COVERED A DIAMETER OF 50 KM—A "WIDE-RANGE MAGIC VANISHING PHENOMENON."
THE KINGDOM WAS DESTROYED, LEAVING MILLIONS OF REFUGEES AND ALL KINDS OF PROBLEMS.
...!

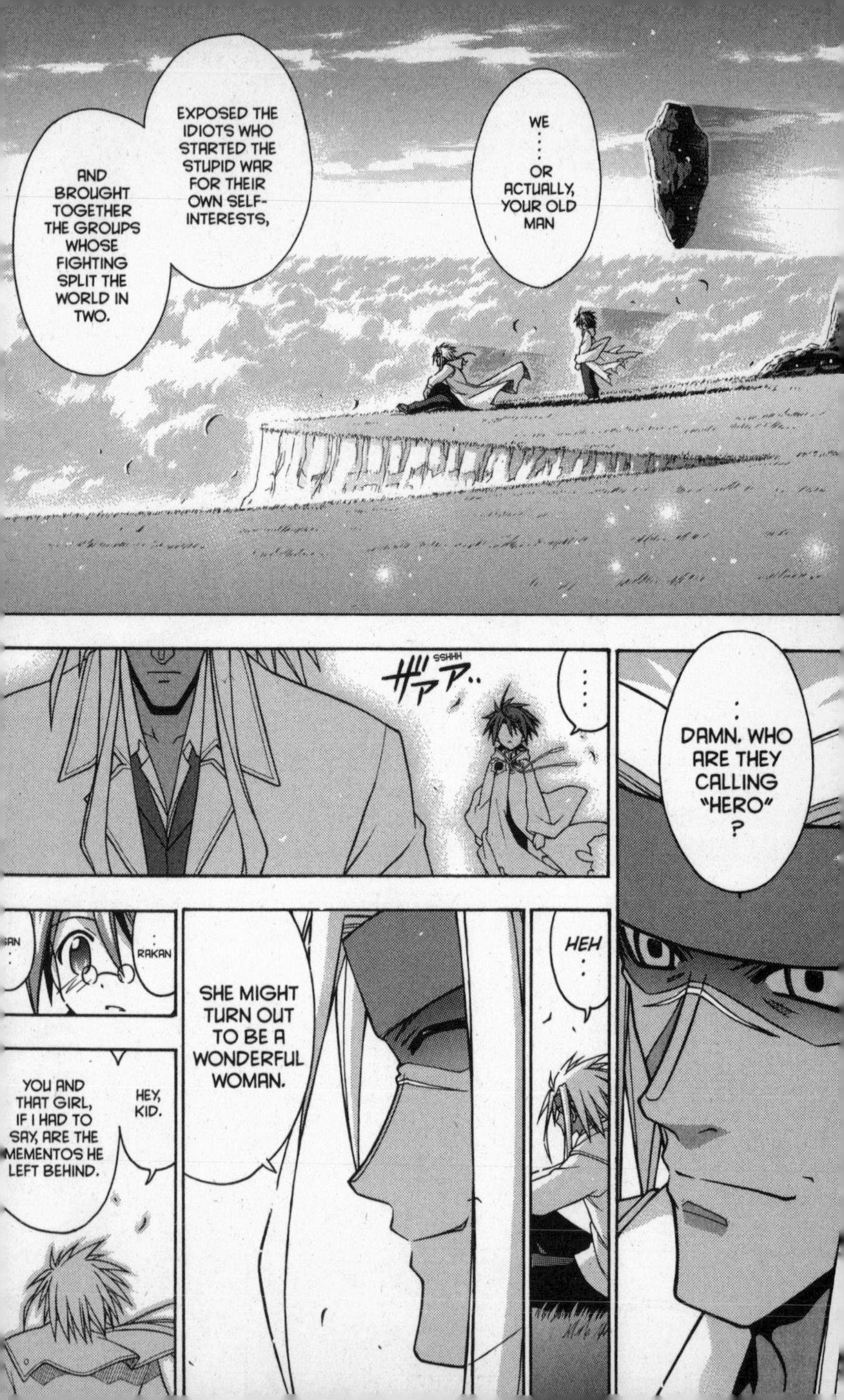
WE . . . OR ACTUALLY, YOUR OLD MAN
EXPOSED THE IDIOTS WHO STARTED THE STUPID WAR FOR THEIR OWN SELF-INTERESTS,
AND BROUGHT TOGETHER THE GROUPS WHOSE FIGHTING SPLIT THE WORLD IN TWO.
. . . DAMN. WHO ARE THEY CALLING "HERO"?
ザァア.. SSHHH
. . . .
HEH . . .
SHE MIGHT TURN OUT TO BE A WONDERFUL WOMAN.
. . . RAKAN
HEY, KID.
YOU AND THAT GIRL, IF I HAD TO SAY, ARE THE MEMENTOS HE LEFT BEHIND.

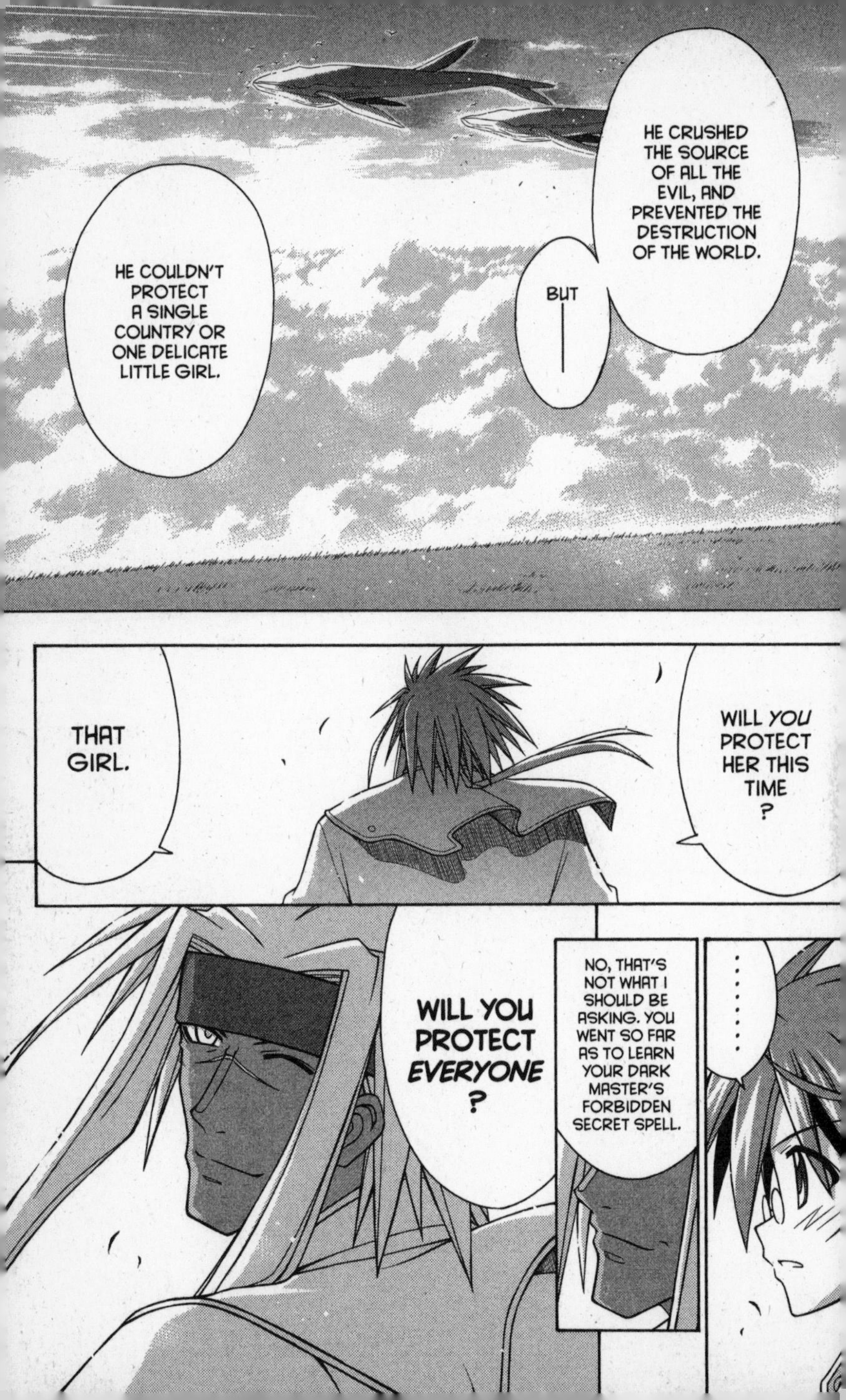
HE CRUSHED THE SOURCE OF ALL THE EVIL, AND PREVENTED THE DESTRUCTION OF THE WORLD.
BUT —
HE COULDN'T PROTECT A SINGLE COUNTRY OR ONE DELICATE LITTLE GIRL.
WILL *YOU* PROTECT HER THIS TIME?
THAT GIRL.
......
NO, THAT'S NOT WHAT I SHOULD BE ASKING. YOU WENT SO FAR AS TO LEARN YOUR DARK MASTER'S FORBIDDEN SECRET SPELL.
WILL YOU PROTECT *EVERYONE*?

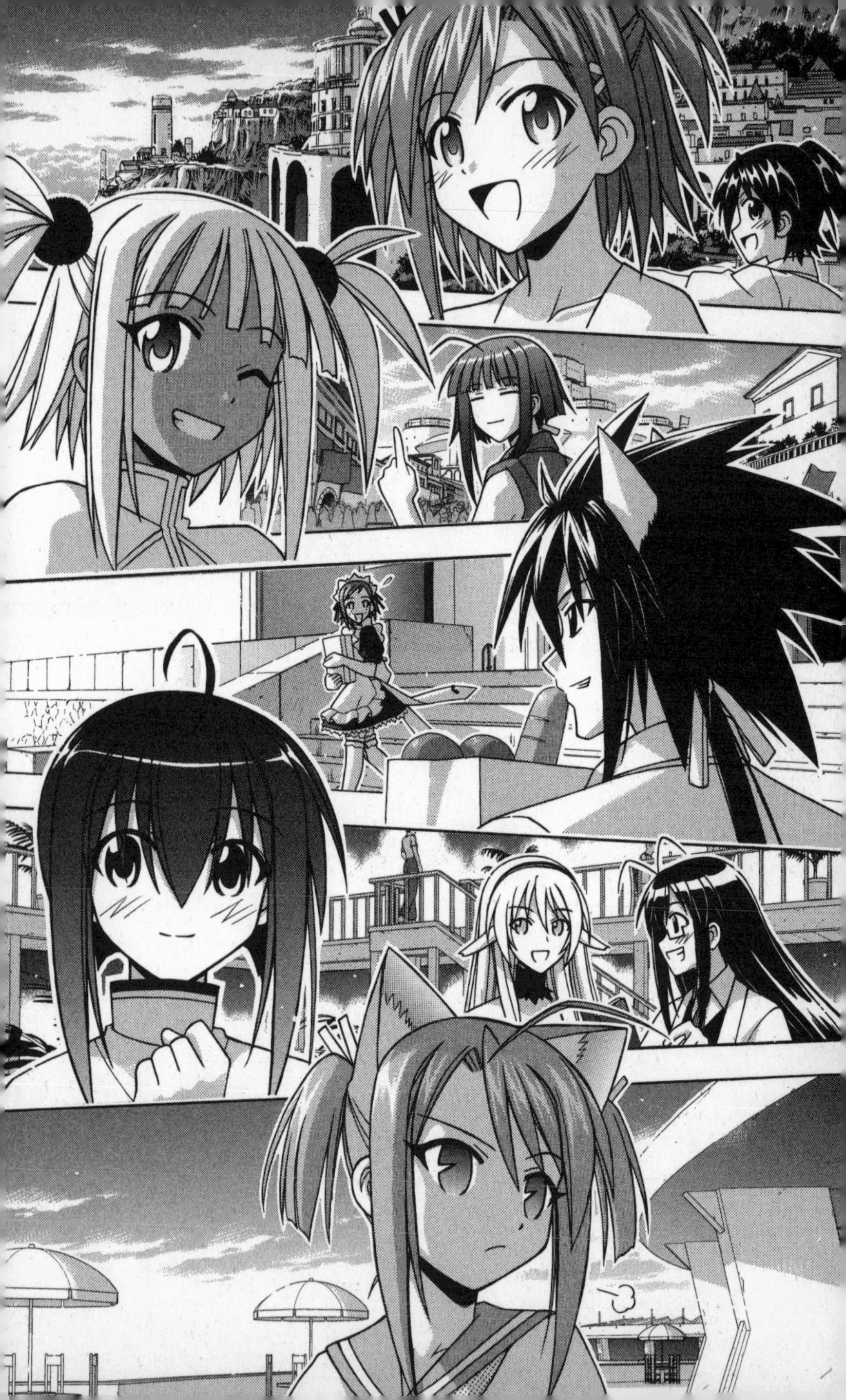

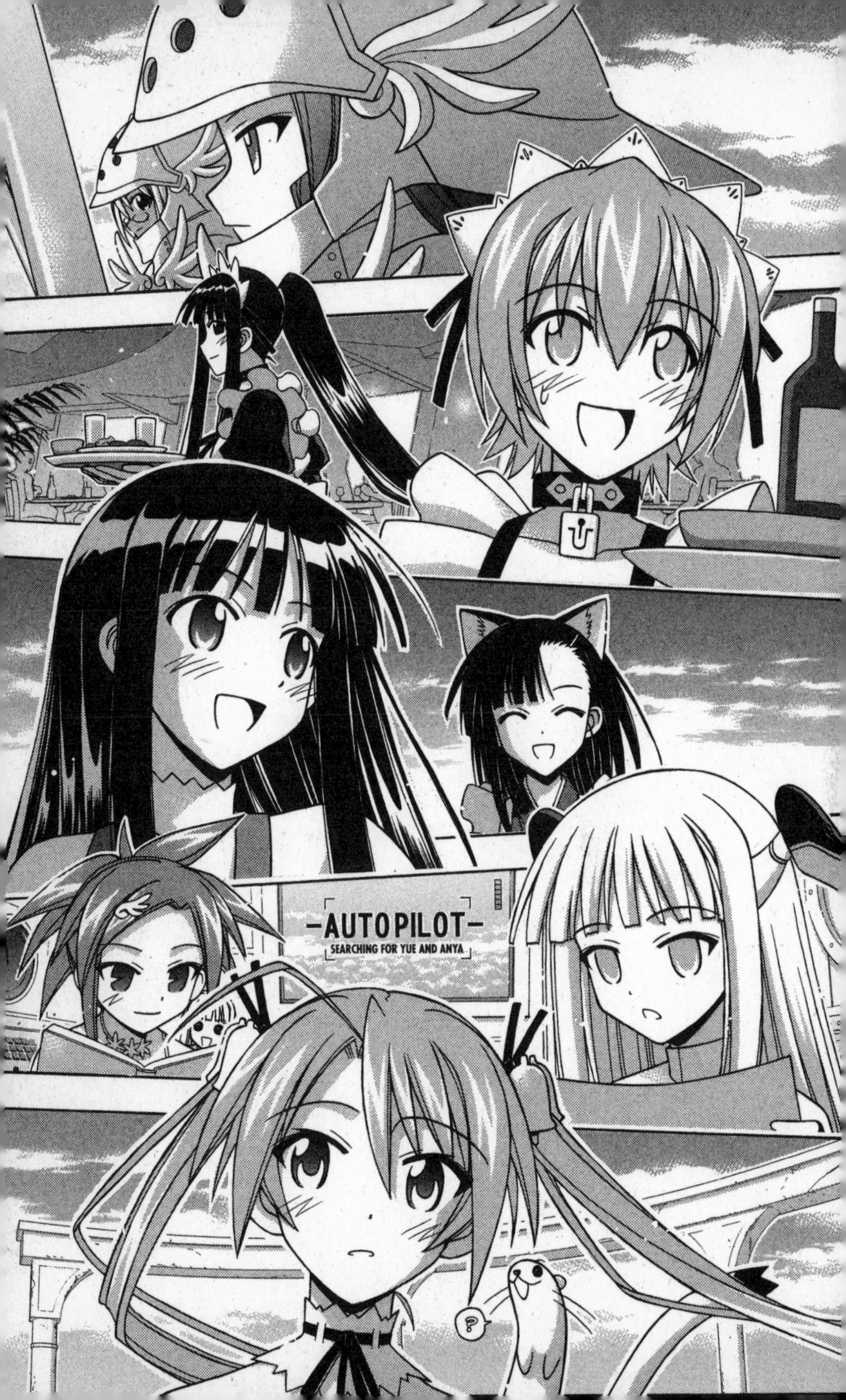
-AUTOPILOT-
SEARCHING FOR YUE AND ANYA
?

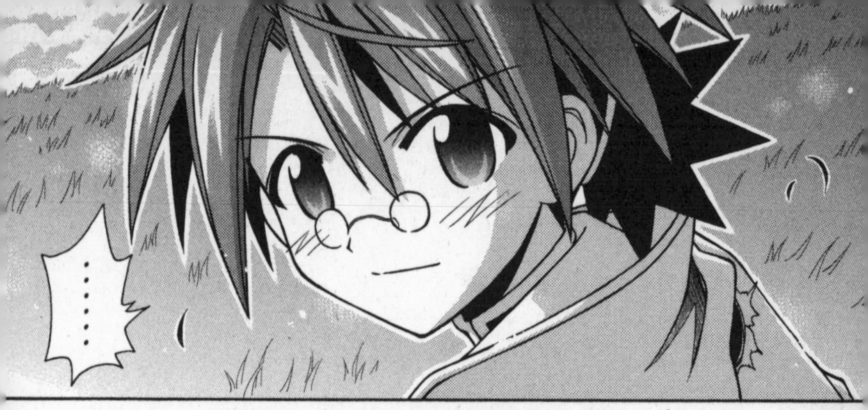
......

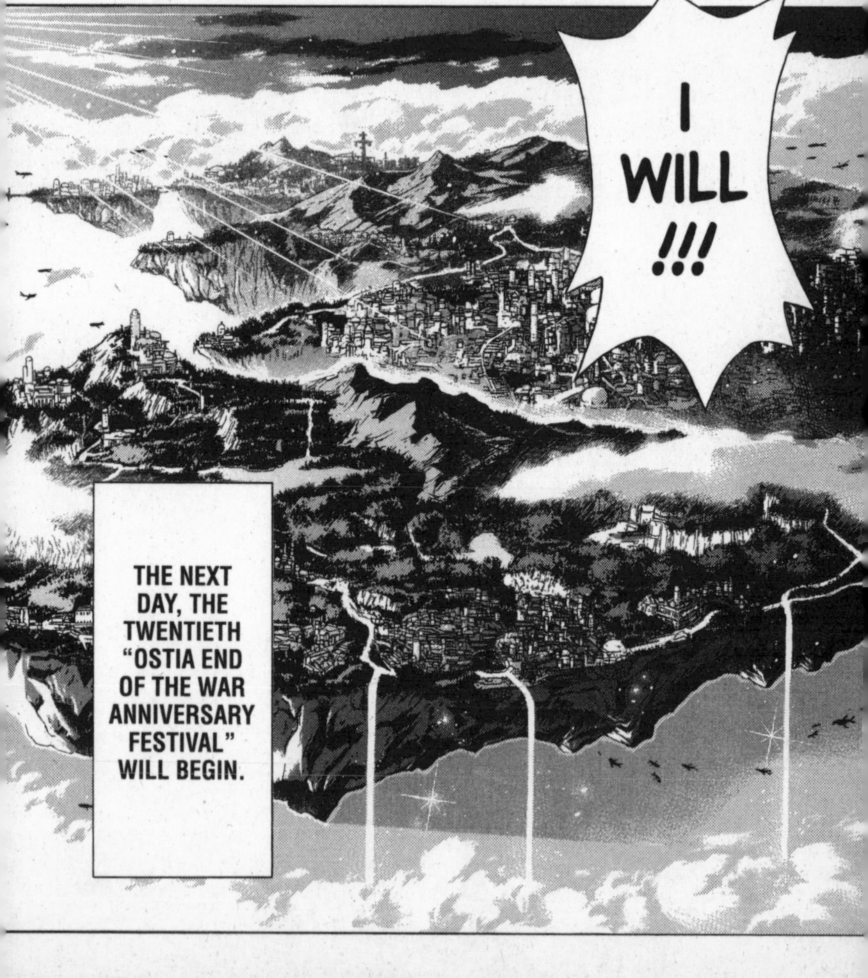
I WILL !!!
THE NEXT DAY, THE TWENTIETH "OSTIA END OF THE WAR ANNIVERSARY FESTIVAL" WILL BEGIN.

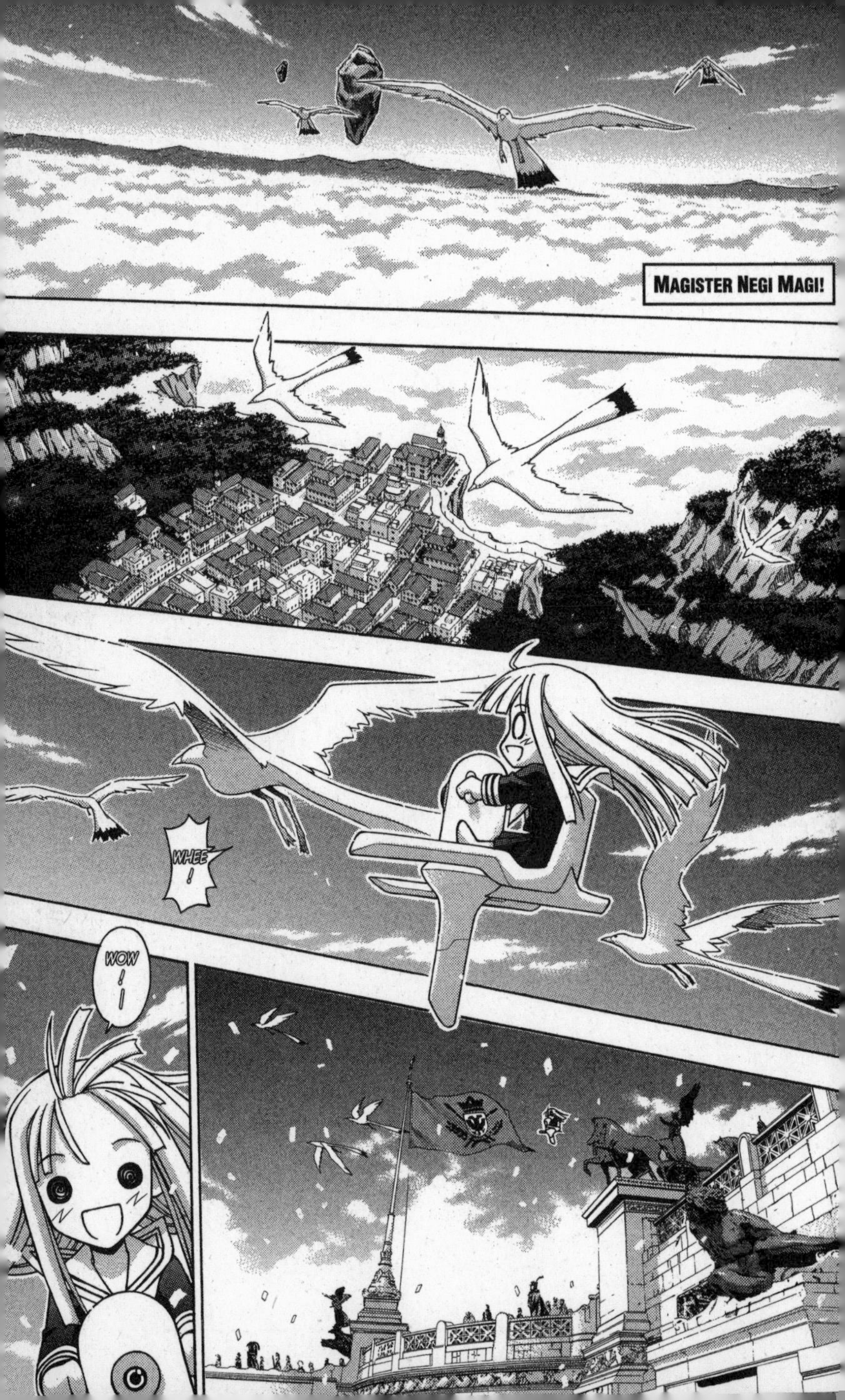
MAGISTER NEGI MAGI!
WHEE!
WOW!!

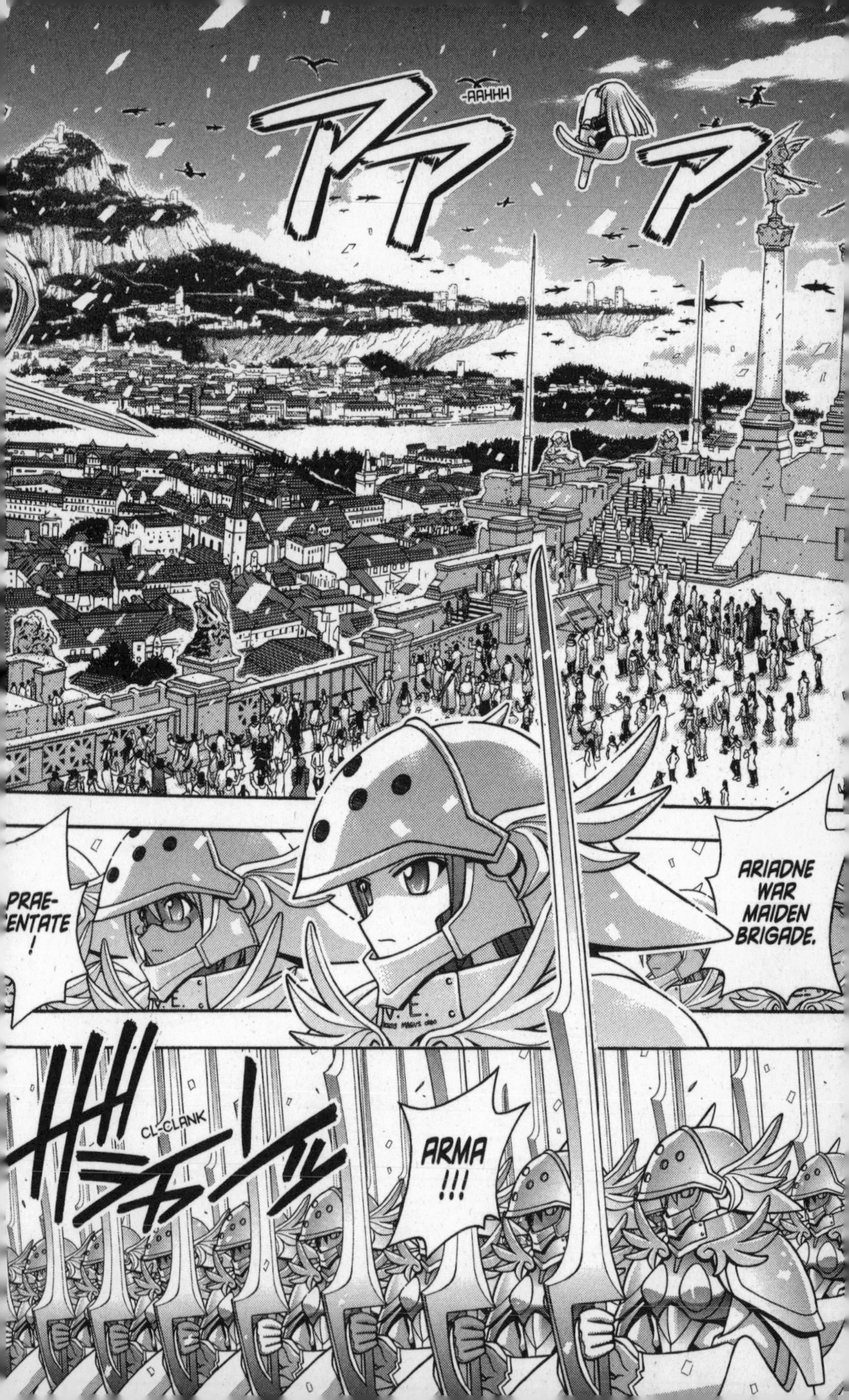
-AAHHH
ARIADNE WAR MAIDEN BRIGADE.
PRAE- ENTATE !
ARMA !!!
CL-CLANK

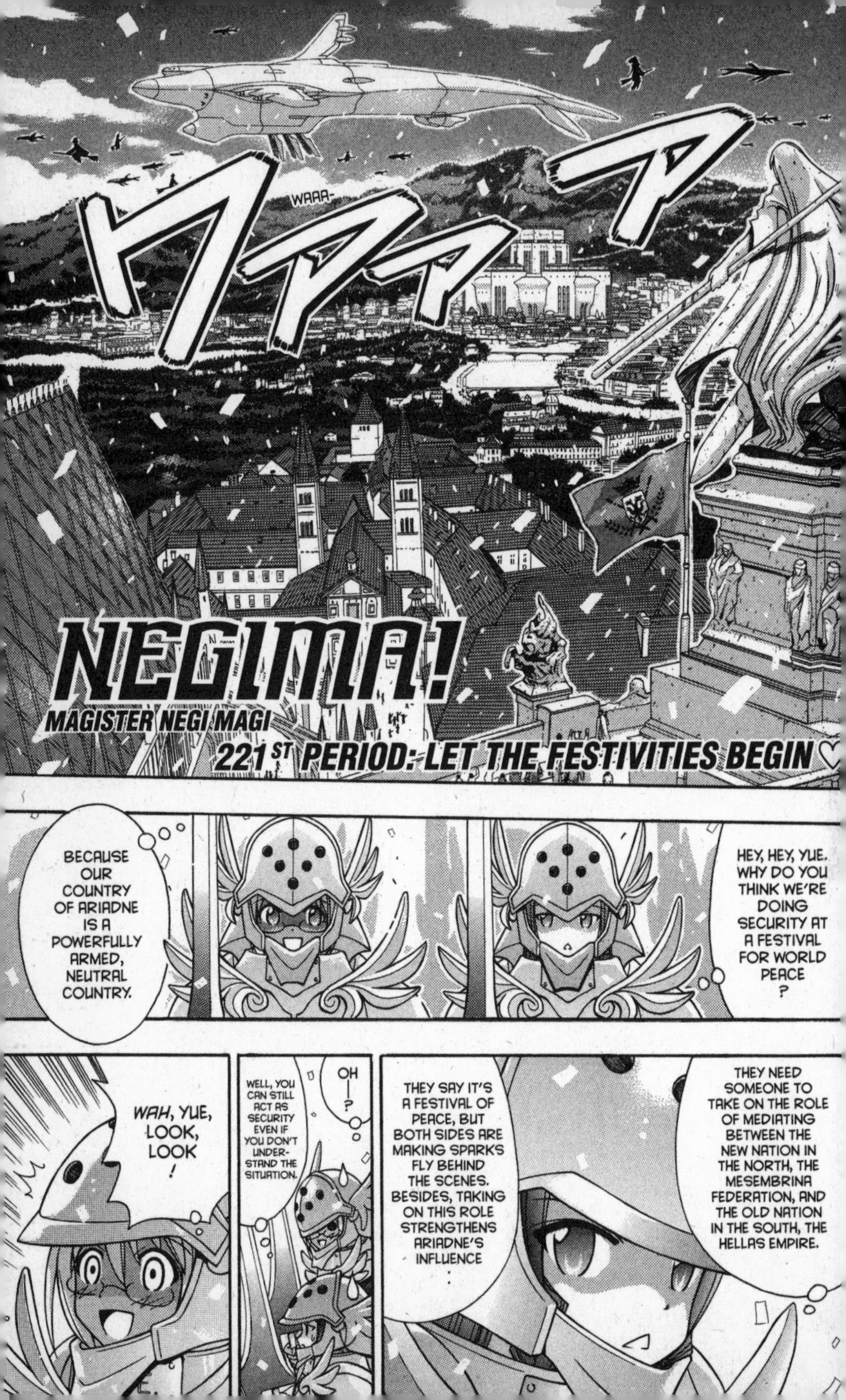
WAAA-
NEGIMA!
MAGISTER NEGI MAGI
221ST PERIOD: LET THE FESTIVITIES BEGIN ♡
HEY, HEY, YUE. WHY DO YOU THINK WE'RE DOING SECURITY AT A FESTIVAL FOR WORLD PEACE?
BECAUSE OUR COUNTRY OF ARIADNE IS A POWERFULLY ARMED, NEUTRAL COUNTRY.
THEY NEED SOMEONE TO TAKE ON THE ROLE OF MEDIATING BETWEEN THE NEW NATION IN THE NORTH, THE MESEMBRINA FEDERATION, AND THE OLD NATION IN THE SOUTH, THE HELLAS EMPIRE.
THEY SAY IT'S A FESTIVAL OF PEACE, BUT BOTH SIDES ARE MAKING SPARKS FLY BEHIND THE SCENES. BESIDES, TAKING ON THIS ROLE STRENGTHENS ARIADNE'S INFLUENCE
OH—?
WELL, YOU CAN STILL ACT AS SECURITY EVEN IF YOU DON'T UNDER-STAND THE SITUATION.
WAH, YUE, LOOK, LOOK!

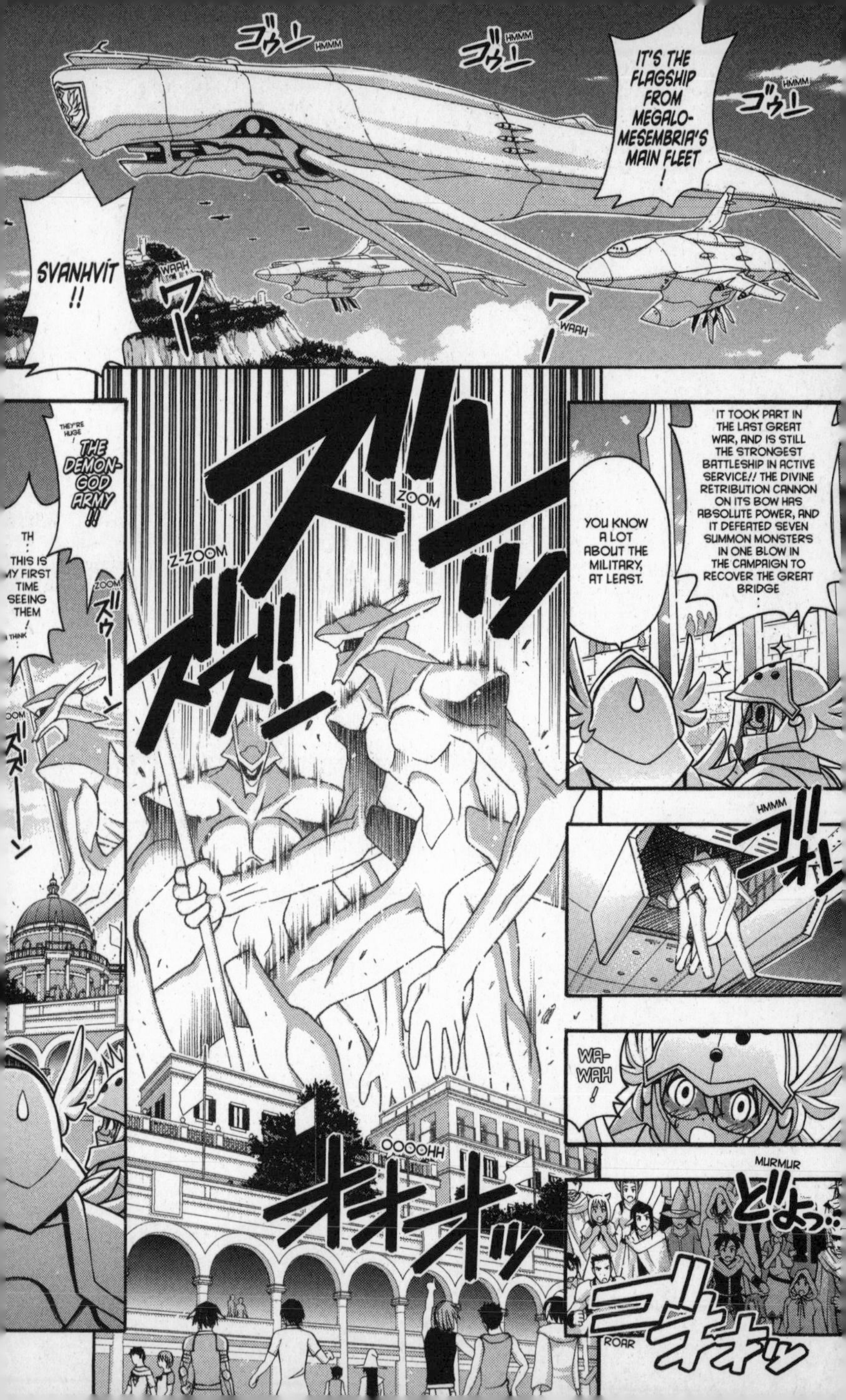
HMMM
IT'S THE FLAGSHIP FROM MEGALO-MESEMBRIA'S MAIN FLEET!
HMMM
HMMM
SVANHVÍT!!
WAAH
WAAH
IT TOOK PART IN THE LAST GREAT WAR, AND IS STILL THE STRONGEST BATTLESHIP IN ACTIVE SERVICE!! THE DIVINE RETRIBUTION CANNON ON ITS BOW HAS ABSOLUTE POWER, AND IT DEFEATED SEVEN SUMMON MONSTERS IN ONE BLOW IN THE CAMPAIGN TO RECOVER THE GREAT BRIDGE...
YOU KNOW A LOT ABOUT THE MILITARY, AT LEAST.
HMMM
WA-WAH!
MURMUR
ROAR
ZOOM
Z-ZOOM
OOOOHH
THEY'RE HUGE
THE DEMON-GOD ARMY!!
TH... THIS IS MY FIRST TIME SEEING THEM! I THINK
ZOOM

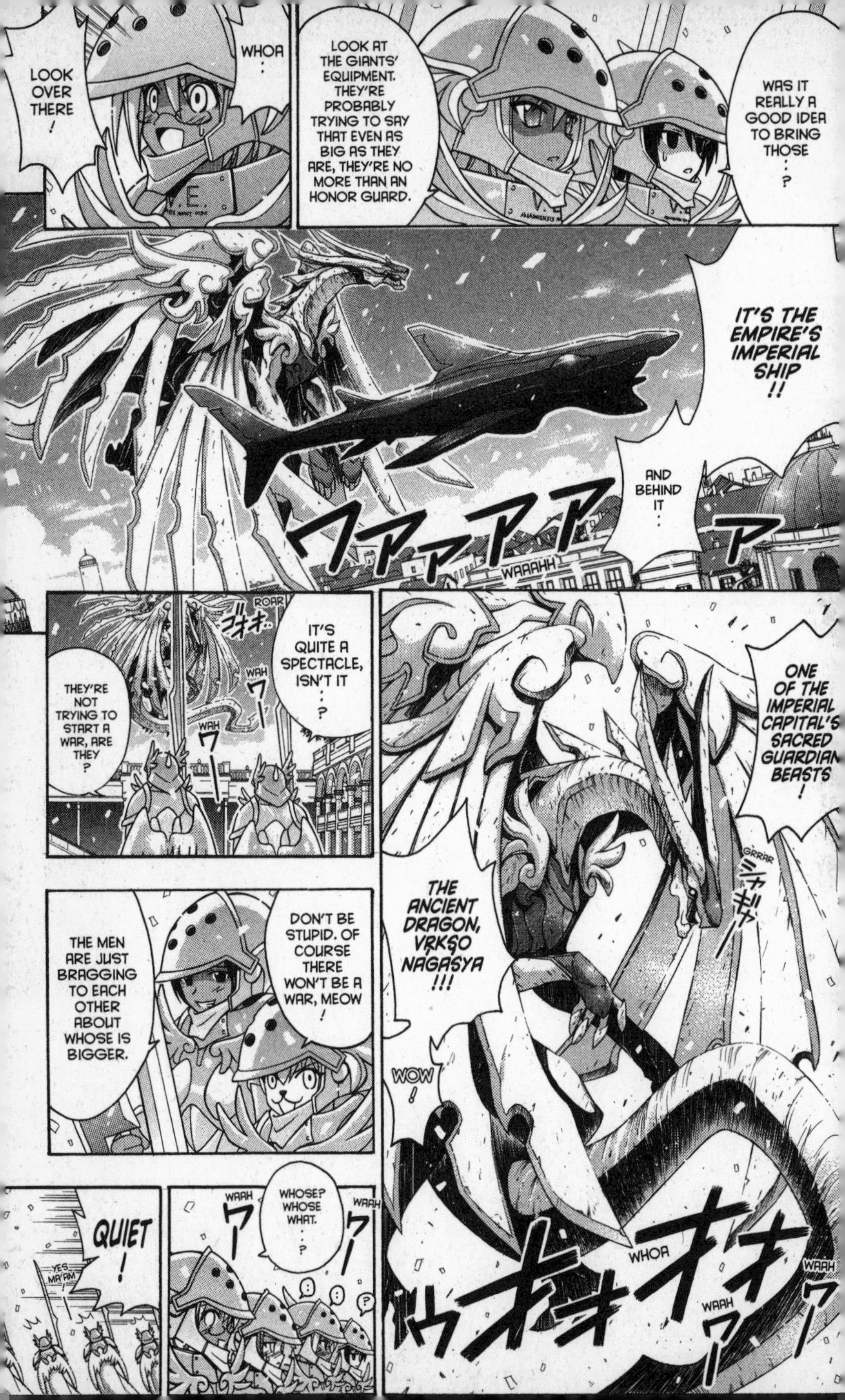
LOOK AT THE GIANTS' EQUIPMENT. THEY'RE PROBABLY TRYING TO SAY THAT EVEN AS BIG AS THEY ARE, THEY'RE NO MORE THAN AN HONOR GUARD.
WAS IT REALLY A GOOD IDEA TO BRING THOSE...?
LOOK OVER THERE!
WHOA...
IT'S THE EMPIRE'S IMPERIAL SHIP!!
AND BEHIND IT...
ワァァァァ
WAAAHH
ONE OF THE IMPERIAL CAPITAL'S SACRED GUARDIAN BEASTS!
GRRRAR
THE ANCIENT DRAGON, VRKSO NAGASYA!!!
WOW!
WHOA
WAAH
WAAH
IT'S QUITE A SPECTACLE, ISN'T IT...?
ROAR
ゴオォ
THEY'RE NOT TRYING TO START A WAR, ARE THEY?
WAH
ワー
WAH
ワー
DON'T BE STUPID. OF COURSE THERE WON'T BE A WAR, MEOW!
THE MEN ARE JUST BRAGGING TO EACH OTHER ABOUT WHOSE IS BIGGER.
WAAH
ワー
WHOSE? WHOSE WHAT...?
WAAH
ワー
QUIET!
YES MA'AM!

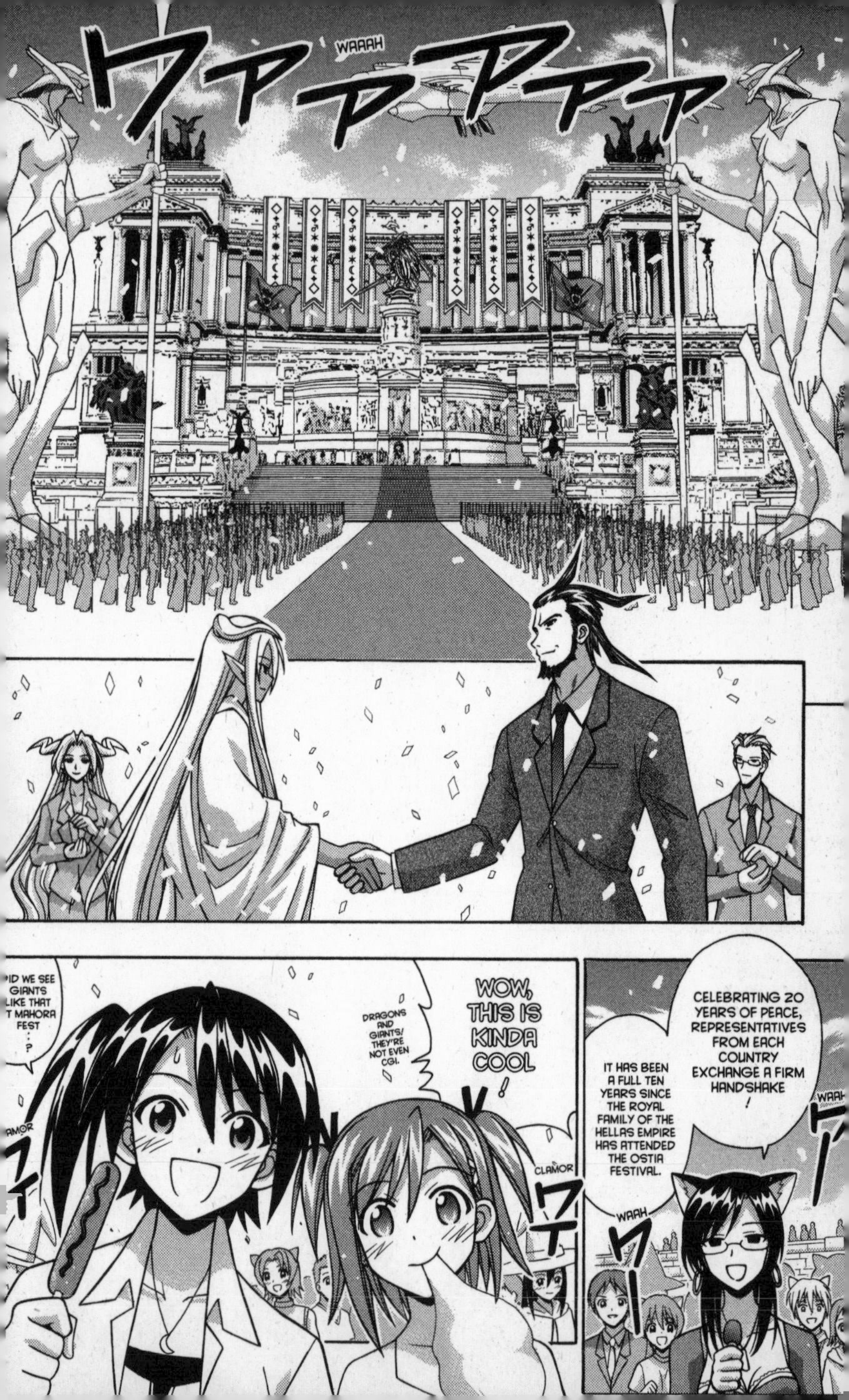

WAAAH
CELEBRATING 20 YEARS OF PEACE, REPRESENTATIVES FROM EACH COUNTRY EXCHANGE A FIRM HANDSHAKE!
WAAH
IT HAS BEEN A FULL TEN YEARS SINCE THE ROYAL FAMILY OF THE HELLAS EMPIRE HAS ATTENDED THE OSTIA FESTIVAL.
WAAH
WOW, THIS IS KINDA COOL!
CLAMOR
DRAGONS AND GIANTS! THEY'RE NOT EVEN CGI.
ID WE SEE GIANTS LIKE THAT T MAHORA FEST . . . ?
AMOR

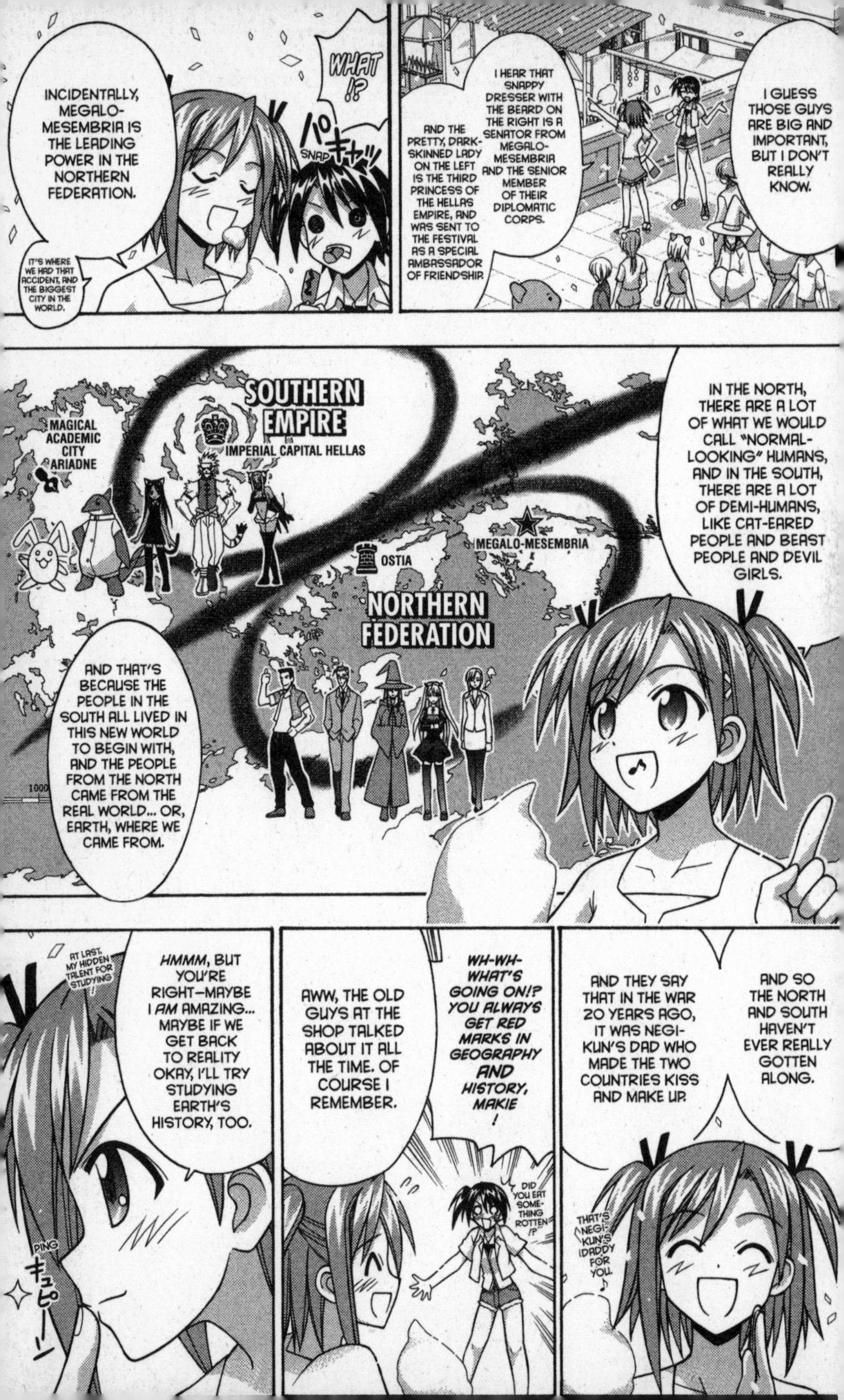
I GUESS THOSE GUYS ARE BIG AND IMPORTANT, BUT I DON'T REALLY KNOW.
I HEAR THAT SNAPPY DRESSER WITH THE BEARD ON THE RIGHT IS A SENATOR FROM MEGALO-MESEMBRIA AND THE SENIOR MEMBER OF THEIR DIPLOMATIC CORPS.
AND THE PRETTY, DARK-SKINNED LADY ON THE LEFT IS THE THIRD PRINCESS OF THE HELLAS EMPIRE, AND WAS SENT TO THE FESTIVAL AS A SPECIAL AMBASSADOR OF FRIENDSHIP.
WHAT!?
SNAP
INCIDENTALLY, MEGALO-MESEMBRIA IS THE LEADING POWER IN THE NORTHERN FEDERATION.
IT'S WHERE WE HAD THAT ACCIDENT, AND THE BIGGEST CITY IN THE WORLD.
IN THE NORTH, THERE ARE A LOT OF WHAT WE WOULD CALL "NORMAL-LOOKING" HUMANS, AND IN THE SOUTH, THERE ARE A LOT OF DEMI-HUMANS, LIKE CAT-EARED PEOPLE AND BEAST PEOPLE AND DEVIL GIRLS.
SOUTHERN EMPIRE
MAGICAL ACADEMIC CITY ARIADNE
IMPERIAL CAPITAL HELLAS
MEGALO-MESEMBRIA
OSTIA
NORTHERN FEDERATION
1000
AND THAT'S BECAUSE THE PEOPLE IN THE SOUTH ALL LIVED IN THIS NEW WORLD TO BEGIN WITH, AND THE PEOPLE FROM THE NORTH CAME FROM THE REAL WORLD... OR, EARTH, WHERE WE CAME FROM.
AND SO THE NORTH AND SOUTH HAVEN'T EVER REALLY GOTTEN ALONG.
AND THEY SAY THAT IN THE WAR 20 YEARS AGO, IT WAS NEGI-KUN'S DAD WHO MADE THE TWO COUNTRIES KISS AND MAKE UP.
THAT'S NEGI-KUN'S DADDY FOR YOU. ♪
WH-WH-WHAT'S GOING ON!? YOU ALWAYS GET RED MARKS IN GEOGRAPHY AND HISTORY, MAKIE!
AWW, THE OLD GUYS AT THE SHOP TALKED ABOUT IT ALL THE TIME. OF COURSE I REMEMBER.
DID YOU EAT SOMETHING ROTTEN!?
HMMM, BUT YOU'RE RIGHT—MAYBE I AM AMAZING... MAYBE IF WE GET BACK TO REALITY OKAY, I'LL TRY STUDYING EARTH'S HISTORY, TOO.
AT LAST, MY HIDDEN TALENT FOR STUDYING!
PING

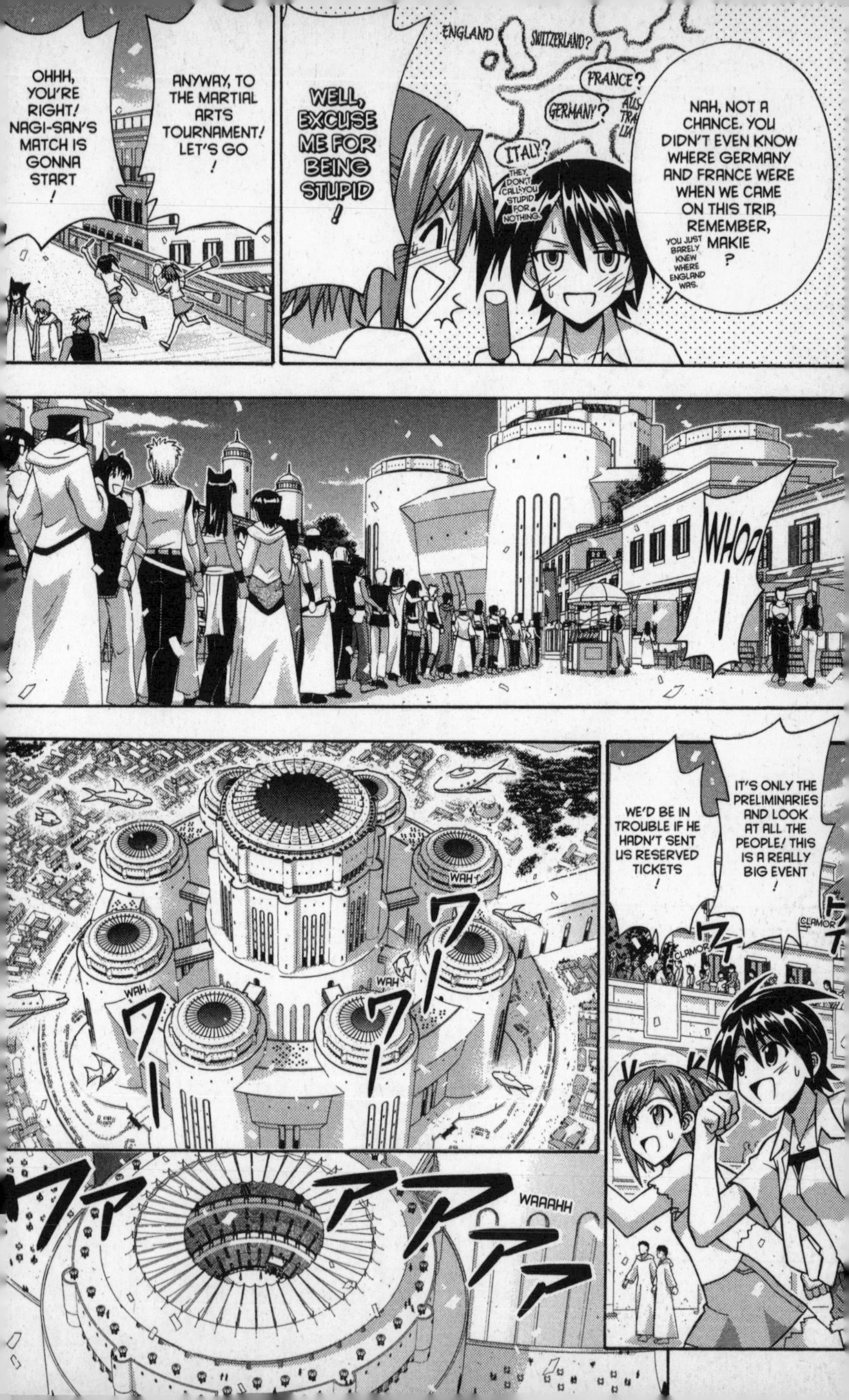

ENGLAND
SWITZERLAND?
FRANCE?
GERMANY?
ITALY?
NAH, NOT A CHANCE. YOU DIDN'T EVEN KNOW WHERE GERMANY AND FRANCE WERE WHEN WE CAME ON THIS TRIP, REMEMBER, MAKIE?
YOU JUST BARELY KNEW WHERE ENGLAND WAS.
THEY DON'T CALL YOU STUPID FOR NOTHING.
WELL, EXCUSE ME FOR BEING STUPID!
ANYWAY, TO THE MARTIAL ARTS TOURNAMENT! LET'S GO!
OHHH, YOU'RE RIGHT! NAGI-SAN'S MATCH IS GONNA START!
WHOA!
IT'S ONLY THE PRELIMINARIES AND LOOK AT ALL THE PEOPLE! THIS IS A REALLY BIG EVENT!
WE'D BE IN TROUBLE IF HE HADN'T SENT US RESERVED TICKETS!
CLAMOR
CLAMOR
WAH
WAH
WAH
WAAAHH

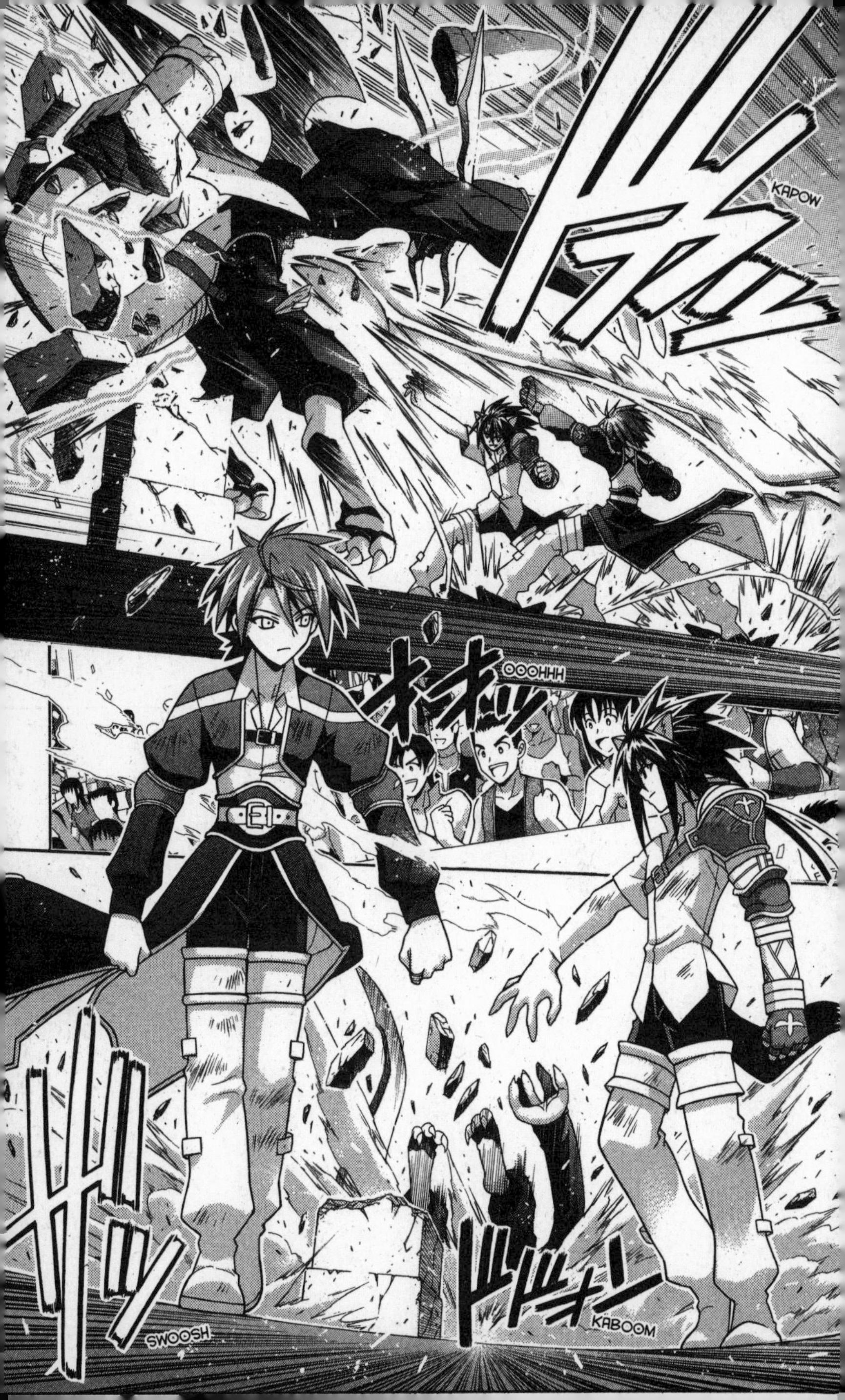
KAPOW
OOOHHH
KABOOM
SWOOSH

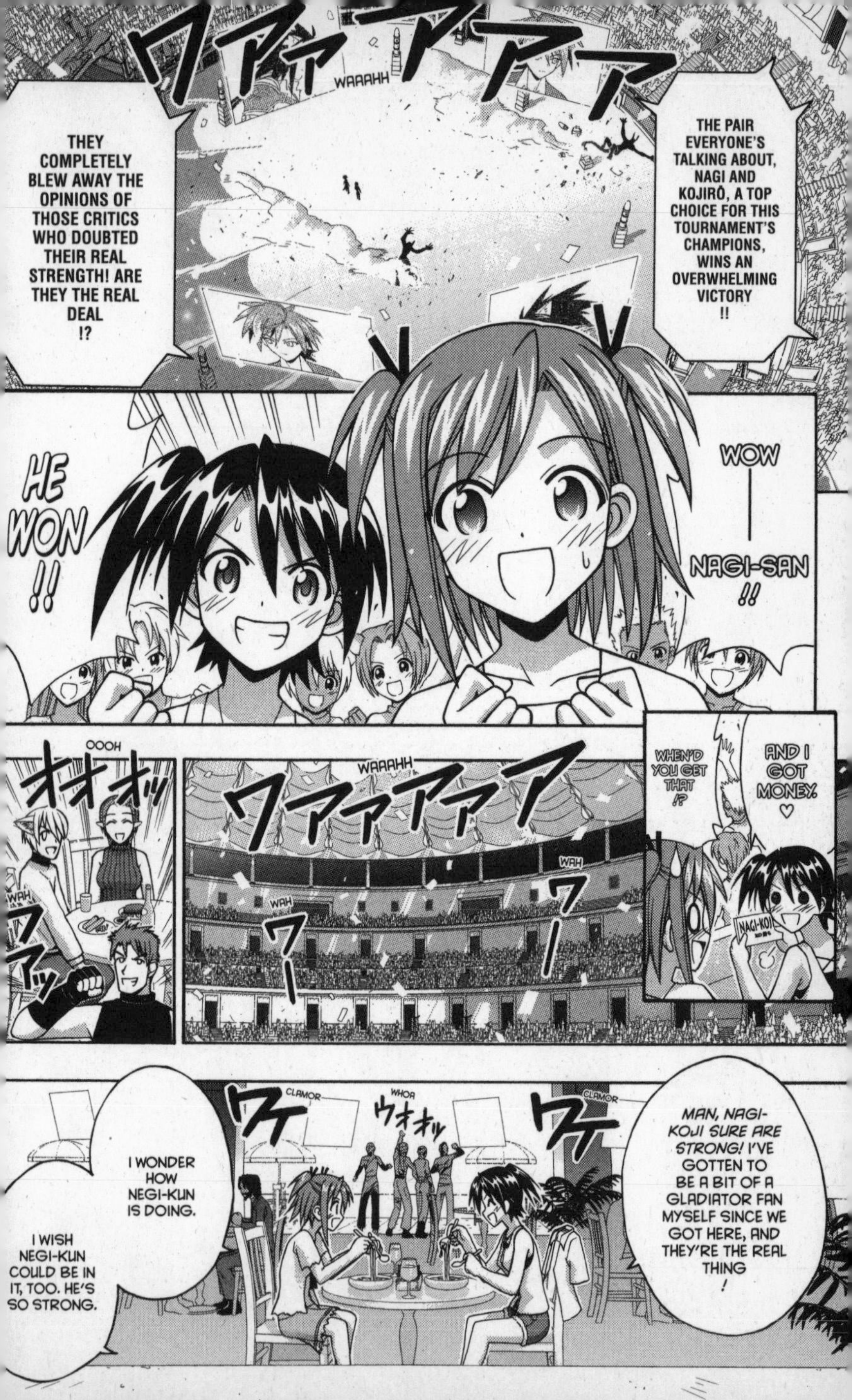

ワァァーアアア
WAAAHH
THE PAIR EVERYONE'S TALKING ABOUT, NAGI AND KOJIRŌ, A TOP CHOICE FOR THIS TOURNAMENT'S CHAMPIONS, WINS AN OVERWHELMING VICTORY !!
THEY COMPLETELY BLEW AWAY THE OPINIONS OF THOSE CRITICS WHO DOUBTED THEIR REAL STRENGTH! ARE THEY THE REAL DEAL !?
WOW — NAGI-SAN !!
HE WON !!
AND I GOT MONEY. ♥
WHEN'D YOU GET THAT !?
NAGI-KOJI
ワァァアァア
WAAAHH
ワー
WAH
ワー
WAH
オオオッ
OOOH
ワァッ
WAH
MAN, NAGI-KOJI SURE ARE STRONG! I'VE GOTTEN TO BE A BIT OF A GLADIATOR FAN MYSELF SINCE WE GOT HERE, AND THEY'RE THE REAL THING !
ワイ
CLAMOR
ウオオッ
WHOA
ワイ
CLAMOR
I WONDER HOW NEGI-KUN IS DOING.
I WISH NEGI-KUN COULD BE IN IT, TOO. HE'S SO STRONG.

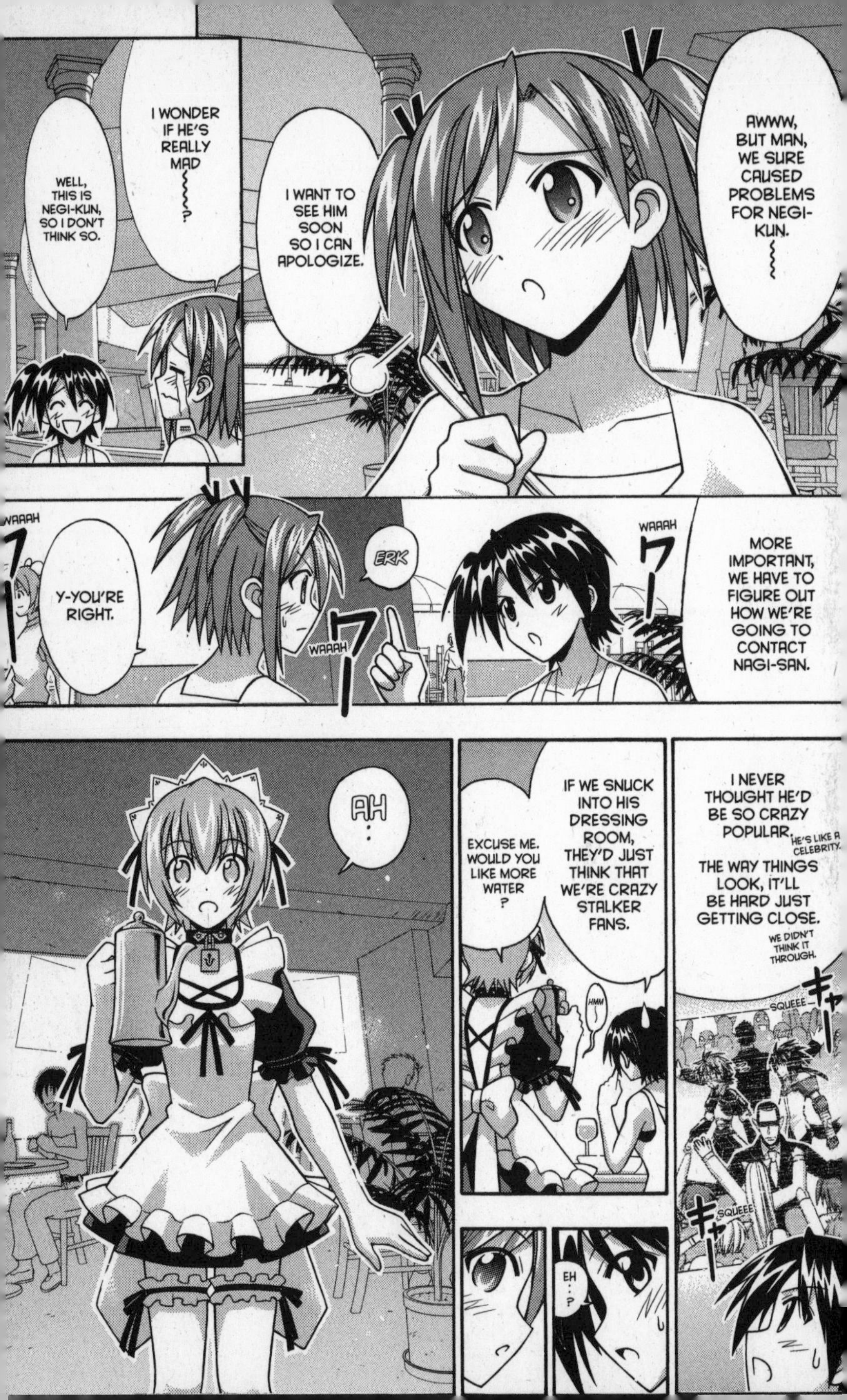
AWWW, BUT MAN, WE SURE CAUSED PROBLEMS FOR NEGI-KUN.
I WANT TO SEE HIM SOON SO I CAN APOLOGIZE.
I WONDER IF HE'S REALLY MAD?
WELL, THIS IS NEGI-KUN, SO I DON'T THINK SO.
MORE IMPORTANT, WE HAVE TO FIGURE OUT HOW WE'RE GOING TO CONTACT NAGI-SAN.
WAAAH
ERK
WAAAH
Y-YOU'RE RIGHT.
WAAAH
I NEVER THOUGHT HE'D BE SO CRAZY POPULAR.
HE'S LIKE A CELEBRITY.
THE WAY THINGS LOOK, IT'LL BE HARD JUST GETTING CLOSE.
WE DIDN'T THINK IT THROUGH.
SQUEEE
SQUEEE
IF WE SNUCK INTO HIS DRESSING ROOM, THEY'D JUST THINK THAT WE'RE CRAZY STALKER FANS.
EXCUSE ME. WOULD YOU LIKE MORE WATER?
HMM
EH...?
AH...

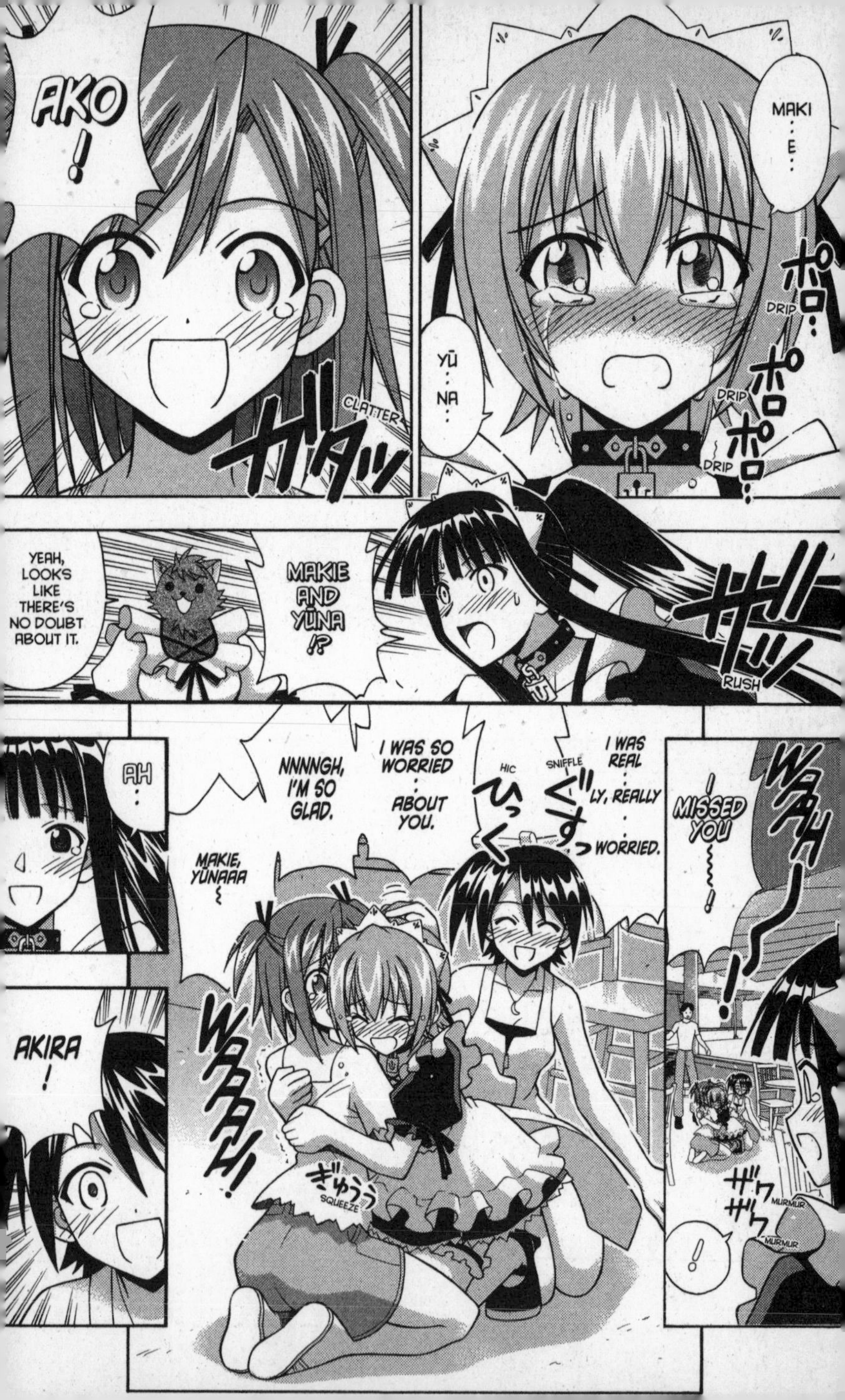
MAKI...E...
YŪ...NA...
ポロ DRIP
ポロ DRIP
ポロ DRIP
AKO!
ガタッ CLATTER
ザザッ RUSH
MAKIE AND YŪNA!?
YEAH, LOOKS LIKE THERE'S NO DOUBT ABOUT IT.
WAAAH~!
I MISSED YOU~!
I WAS REAL...LY, REALLY...WORRIED.
ぐすっ SNIFFLE
ひっく HIC
I WAS SO WORRIED...ABOUT YOU.
NNNNGH, I'M SO GLAD.
MAKIE, YŪNAAA~
WAAAH!
ぎゅうう SQUEEZE
ザワ MURMUR
ザワ MURMUR
!
AH...
AKIRA!

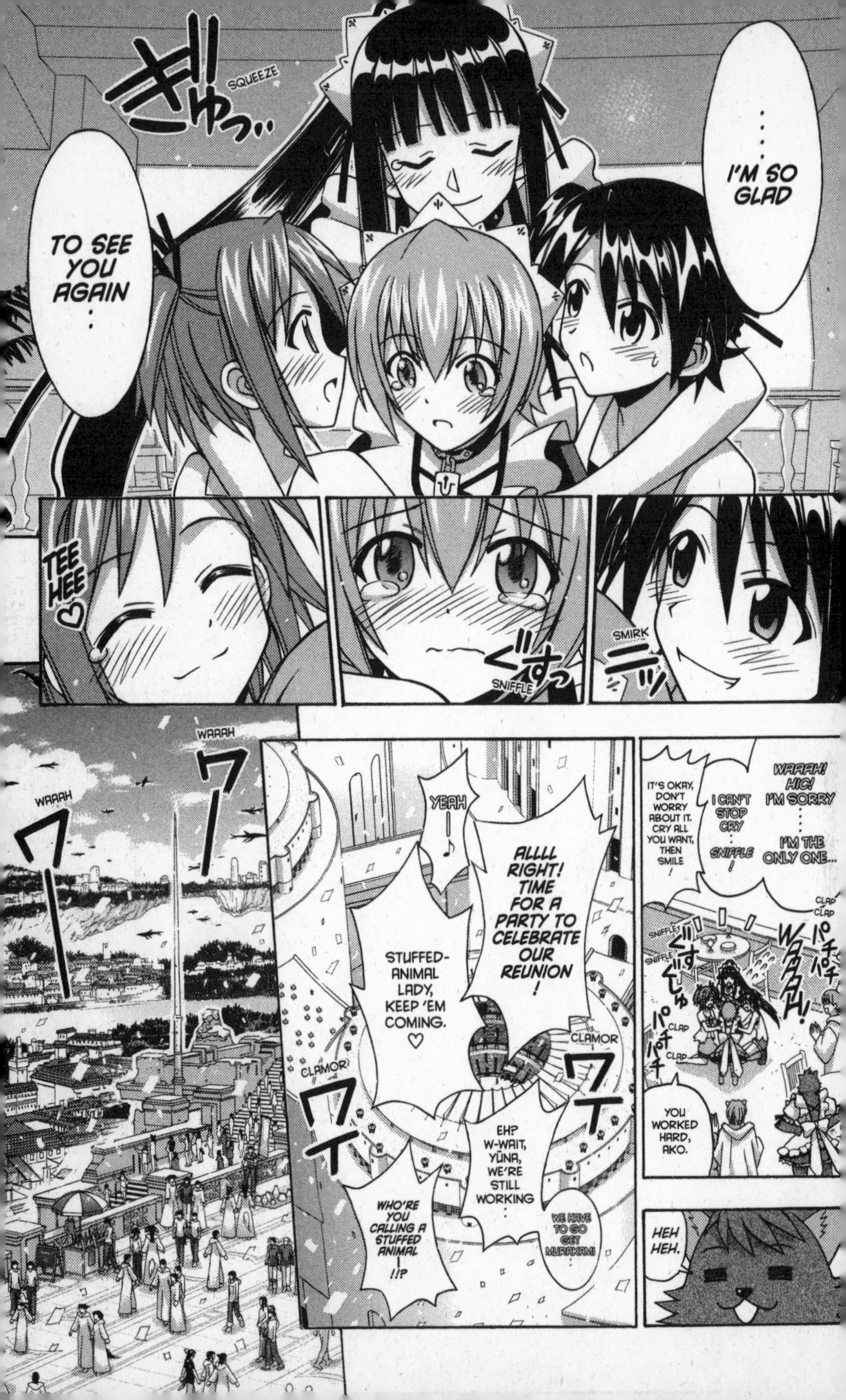

...I'M SO GLAD
SQUEEZE
TO SEE YOU AGAIN...
SMIRK
SNIFFLE
TEE HEE ♡
WAAAH! HIC! I'M SORRY... I'M THE ONLY ONE...
I CAN'T STOP CRY... SNIFFLE!
IT'S OKAY, DON'T WORRY ABOUT IT. CRY ALL YOU WANT, THEN SMILE!
CLAP CLAP
WAAAAH!
SNIFFLE
SNIFFLE
CLAP CLAP
YOU WORKED HARD, AKO.
HEH HEH.
YEAH! ♪
ALLLL RIGHT! TIME FOR A PARTY TO CELEBRATE OUR REUNION!
STUFFED-ANIMAL LADY, KEEP 'EM COMING. ♡
CLAMOR
CLAMOR
EH? W-WAIT, YŪNA, WE'RE STILL WORKING...
WE HAVE TO GO GET MURAKAMI
WHO'RE YOU CALLING A STUFFED ANIMAL!!?
WAAAH
WAAAH

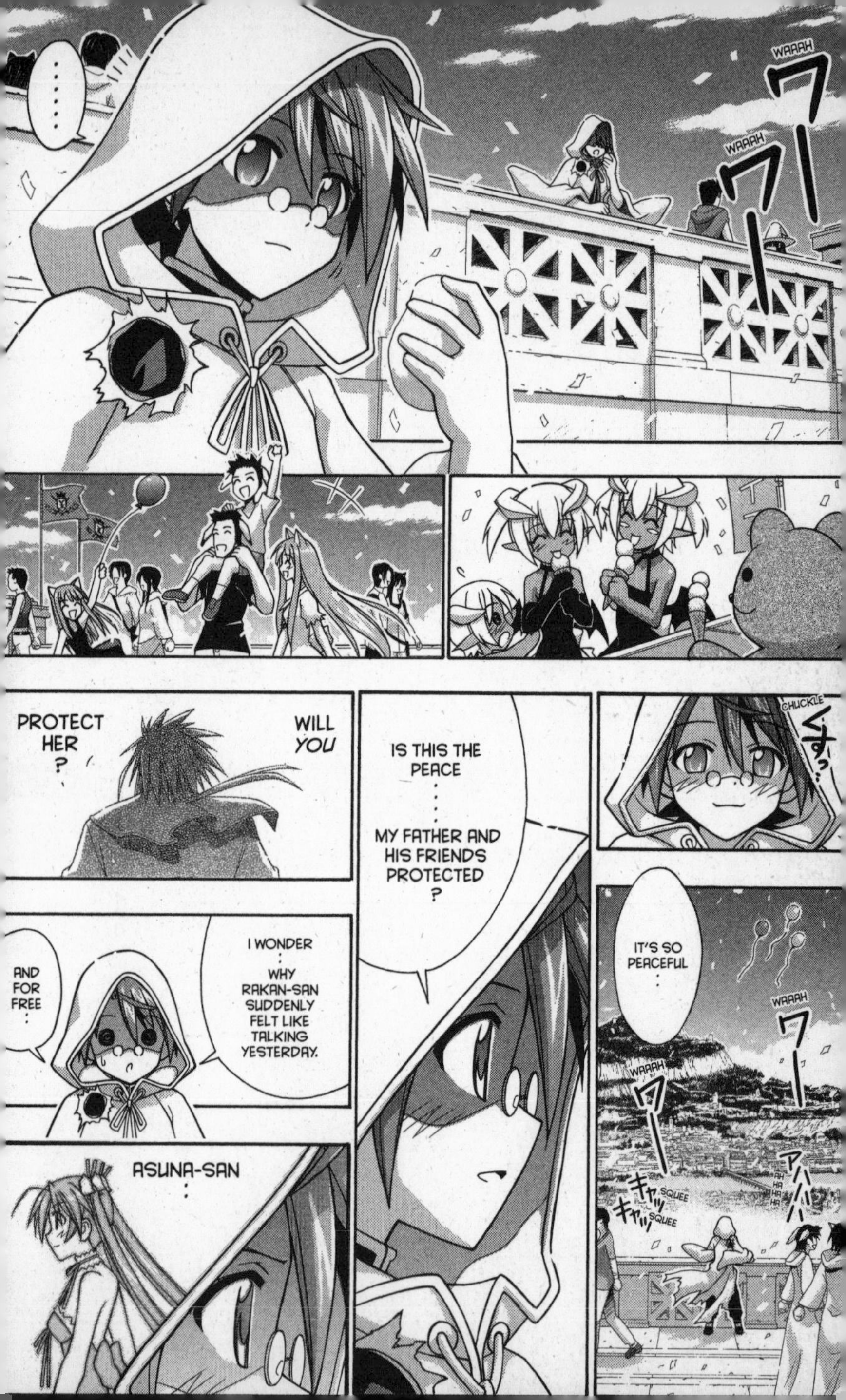
WAAAH
ワー
WAAAH
ワー
......
CHUCKLE
くすっ
IT'S SO PEACEFUL
:
WAAAH
ワー
WAAAH
ワー
AH HA HA HA
アハハ
SQUEE
キャッ
SQUEE
キャッ
IS THIS THE PEACE
...
MY FATHER AND HIS FRIENDS PROTECTED
?
WILL YOU
PROTECT HER
?
I WONDER
:
WHY RAKAN-SAN SUDDENLY FELT LIKE TALKING YESTERDAY.
AND FOR FREE
:
ASUNA-SAN
:

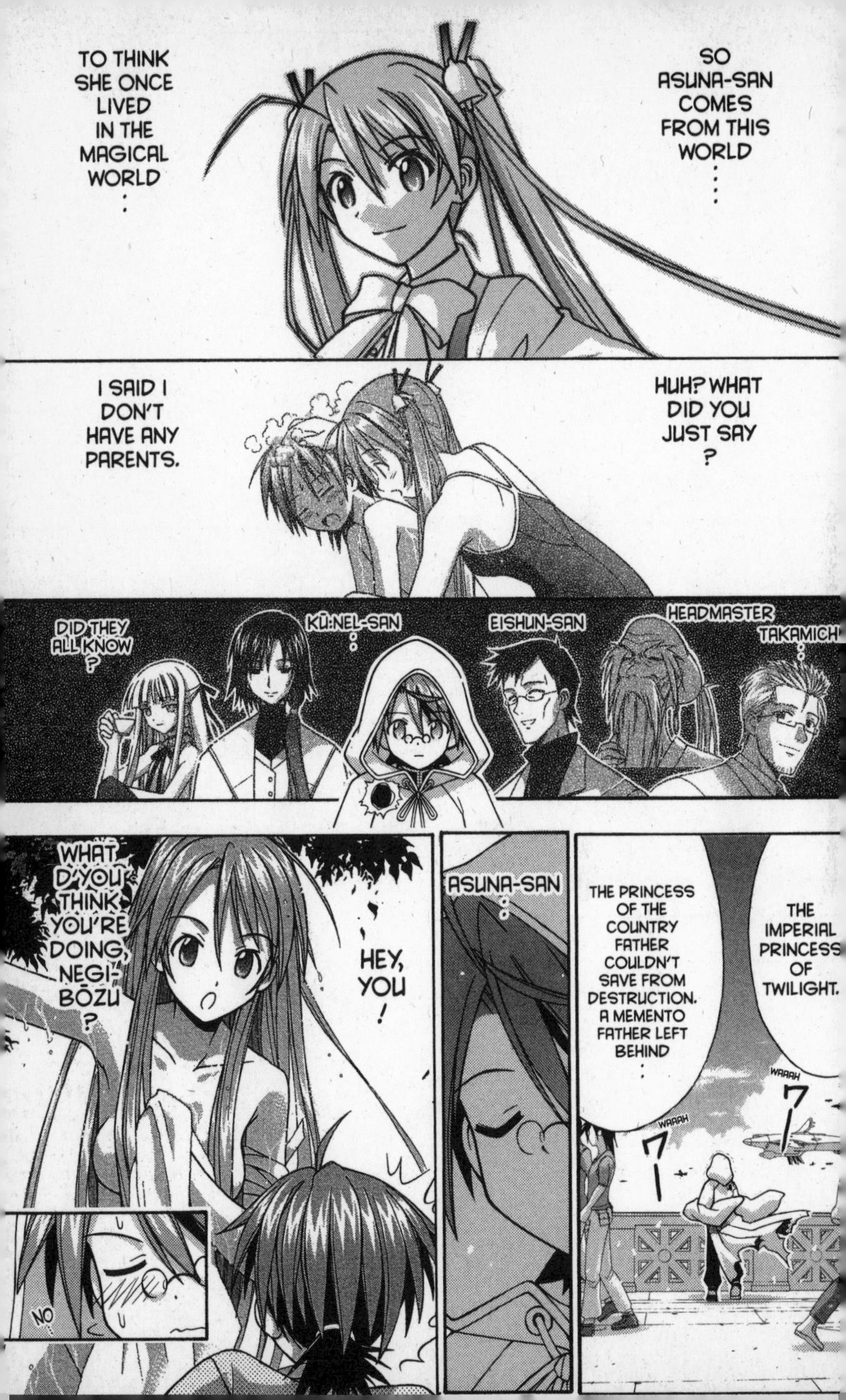
SO ASUNA-SAN COMES FROM THIS WORLD...
TO THINK SHE ONCE LIVED IN THE MAGICAL WORLD...
HUH? WHAT DID YOU JUST SAY?
I SAID I DON'T HAVE ANY PARENTS.
TAKAMICH...
HEADMASTER
EISHUN-SAN
KŪ:NEL-SAN...
DID THEY ALL KNOW?
THE IMPERIAL PRINCESS OF TWILIGHT.
THE PRINCESS OF THE COUNTRY FATHER COULDN'T SAVE FROM DESTRUCTION. A MEMENTO FATHER LEFT BEHIND...
WAAAH
WAAAH
ASUNA-SAN...
HEY, YOU!
WHAT D'YOU THINK YOU'RE DOING, NEGI-BŌZU?
NO

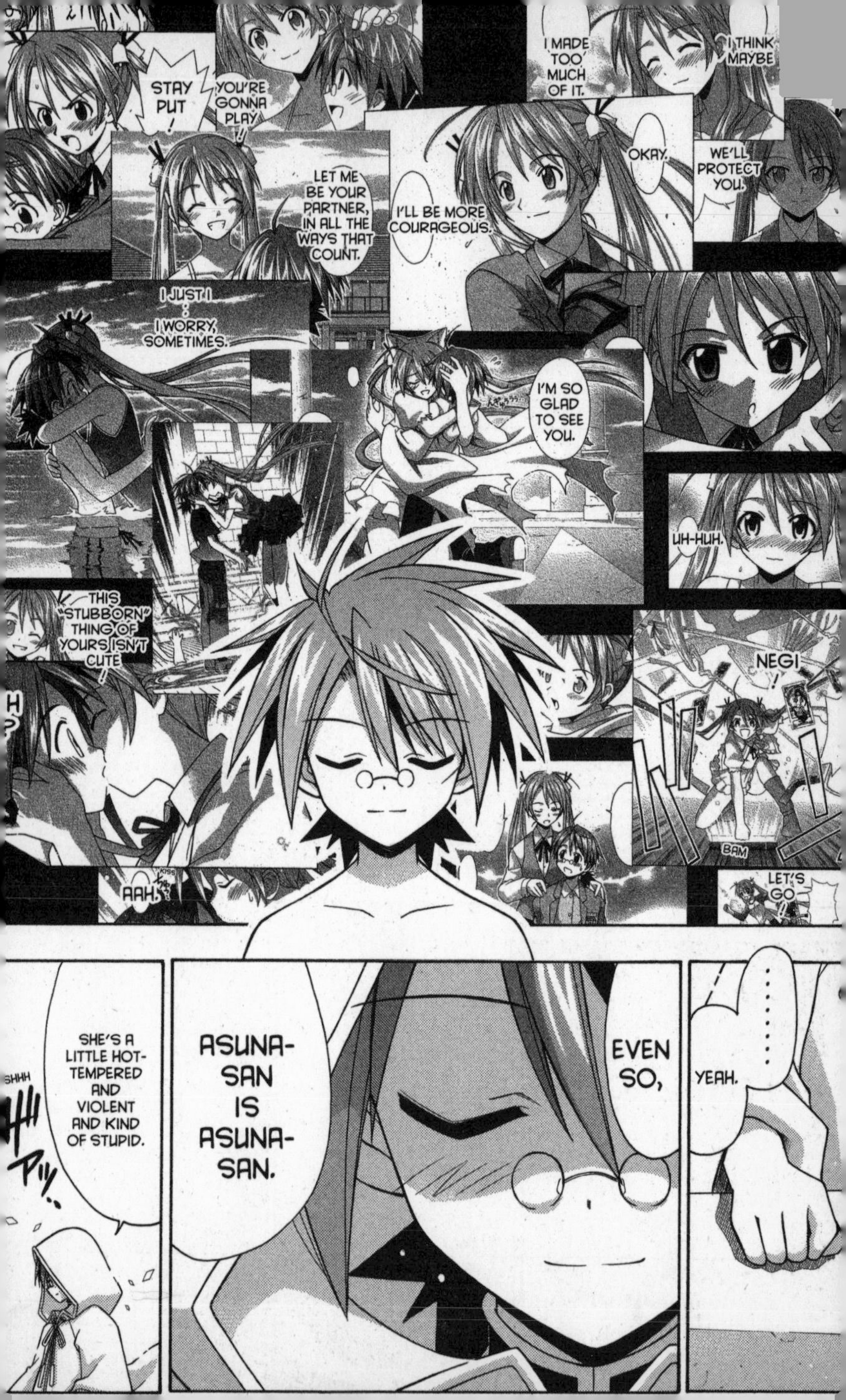
I THINK MAYBE
I MADE TOO MUCH OF IT.
YOU'RE GONNA PLAY!!
STAY PUT!
WE'LL PROTECT YOU.
OKAY.
I'LL BE MORE COURAGEOUS.
LET ME BE YOUR PARTNER, IN ALL THE WAYS THAT COUNT.
I'M SO GLAD TO SEE YOU.
I JUST I... I WORRY, SOMETIMES.
UH-HUH.
NEGI!
BAM
THIS "STUBBORN" THING OF YOURS ISN'T CUTE!
LET'S GO!
KISS
AAH.
......
YEAH.
EVEN SO,
ASUNA-SAN IS ASUNA-SAN.
SHE'S A LITTLE HOT-TEMPERED AND VIOLENT AND KIND OF STUPID.
SHHH

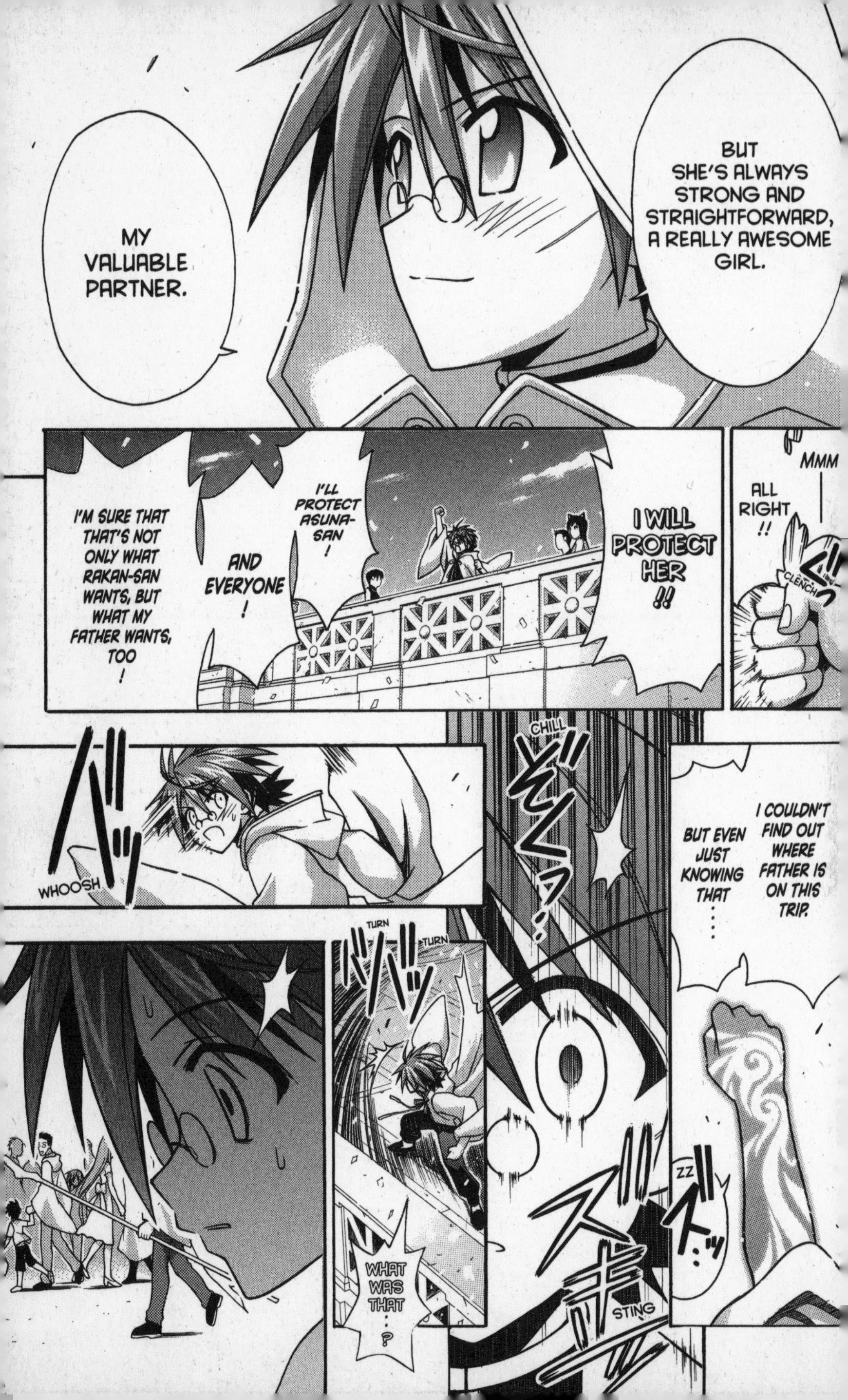
BUT SHE'S ALWAYS STRONG AND STRAIGHTFORWARD, A REALLY AWESOME GIRL.
MY VALUABLE PARTNER.
MMM
ALL RIGHT!!
CLENCH
I WILL PROTECT HER!!
I'LL PROTECT ASUNA-SAN!
AND EVERYONE!
I'M SURE THAT THAT'S NOT ONLY WHAT RAKAN-SAN WANTS, BUT WHAT MY FATHER WANTS, TOO!
I COULDN'T FIND OUT WHERE FATHER IS ON THIS TRIP.
BUT EVEN JUST KNOWING THAT...
ZZ
STING
CHILL
WHOOSH
TURN
TURN
WHAT WAS THAT...?

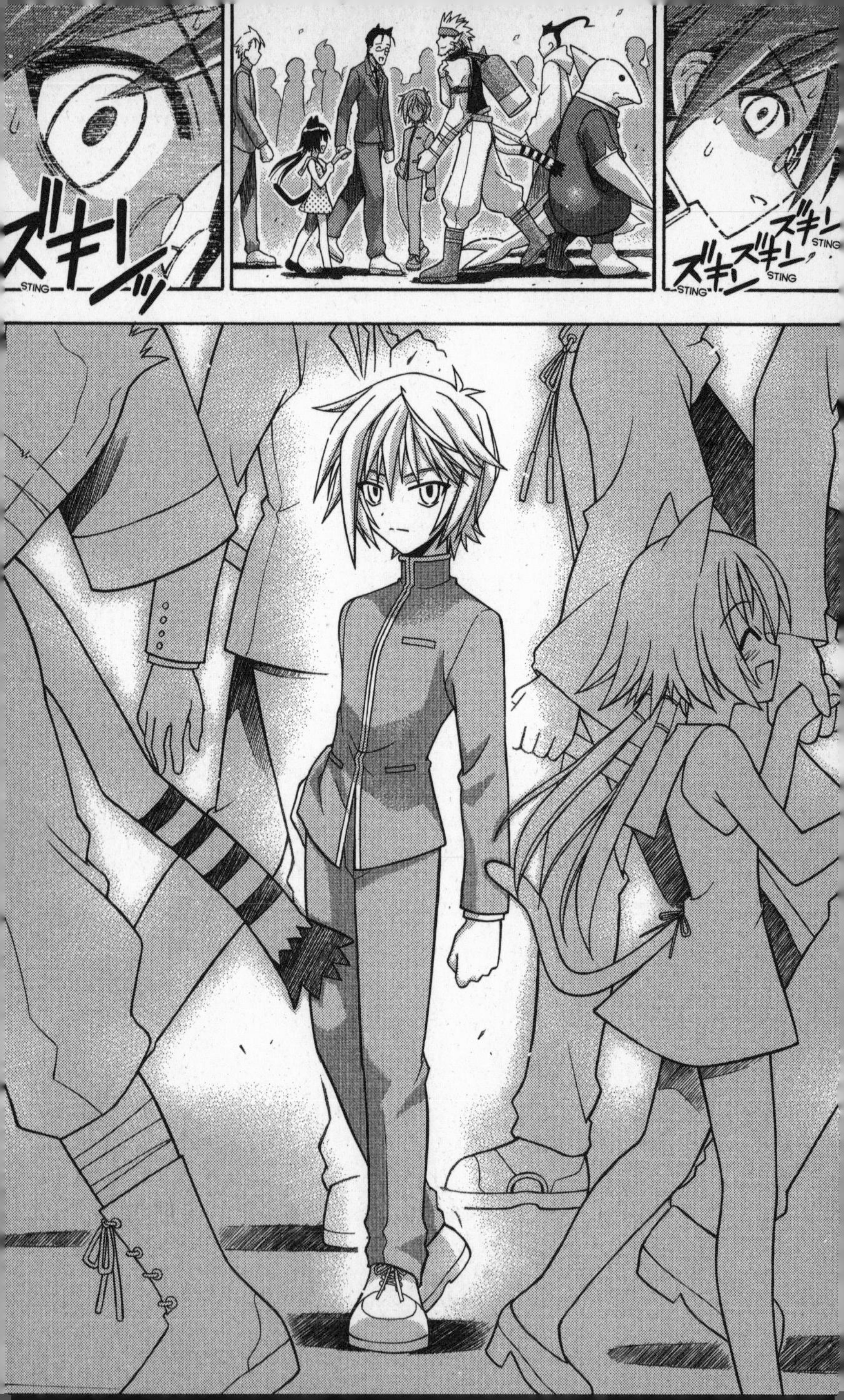
ズキン
STING
ズキン
STING
ズキン
STING
ズキーンッ
STING

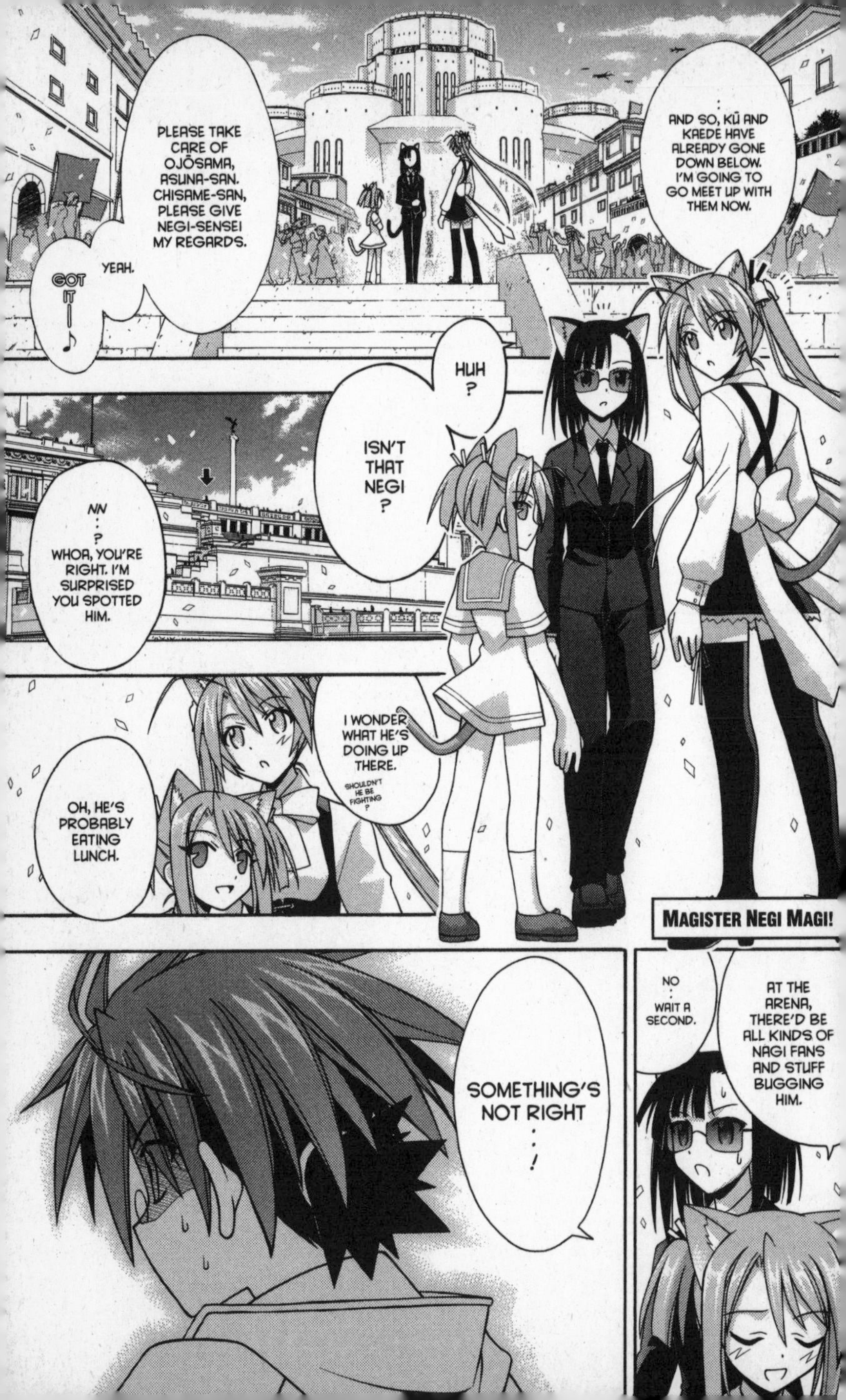
AND SO, KŪ AND KAEDE HAVE ALREADY GONE DOWN BELOW. I'M GOING TO GO MEET UP WITH THEM NOW.
PLEASE TAKE CARE OF OJŌSAMA, ASUNA-SAN. CHISAME-SAN, PLEASE GIVE NEGI-SENSEI MY REGARDS.
YEAH.
GOT IT ♪
HUH?
ISN'T THAT NEGI?
NN...? WHOA, YOU'RE RIGHT. I'M SURPRISED YOU SPOTTED HIM.
I WONDER WHAT HE'S DOING UP THERE.
SHOULDN'T HE BE FIGHTING?
OH, HE'S PROBABLY EATING LUNCH.
MAGISTER NEGI MAGI!
NO... WAIT A SECOND.
AT THE ARENA, THERE'D BE ALL KINDS OF NAGI FANS AND STUFF BUGGING HIM.
SOMETHING'S NOT RIGHT...!

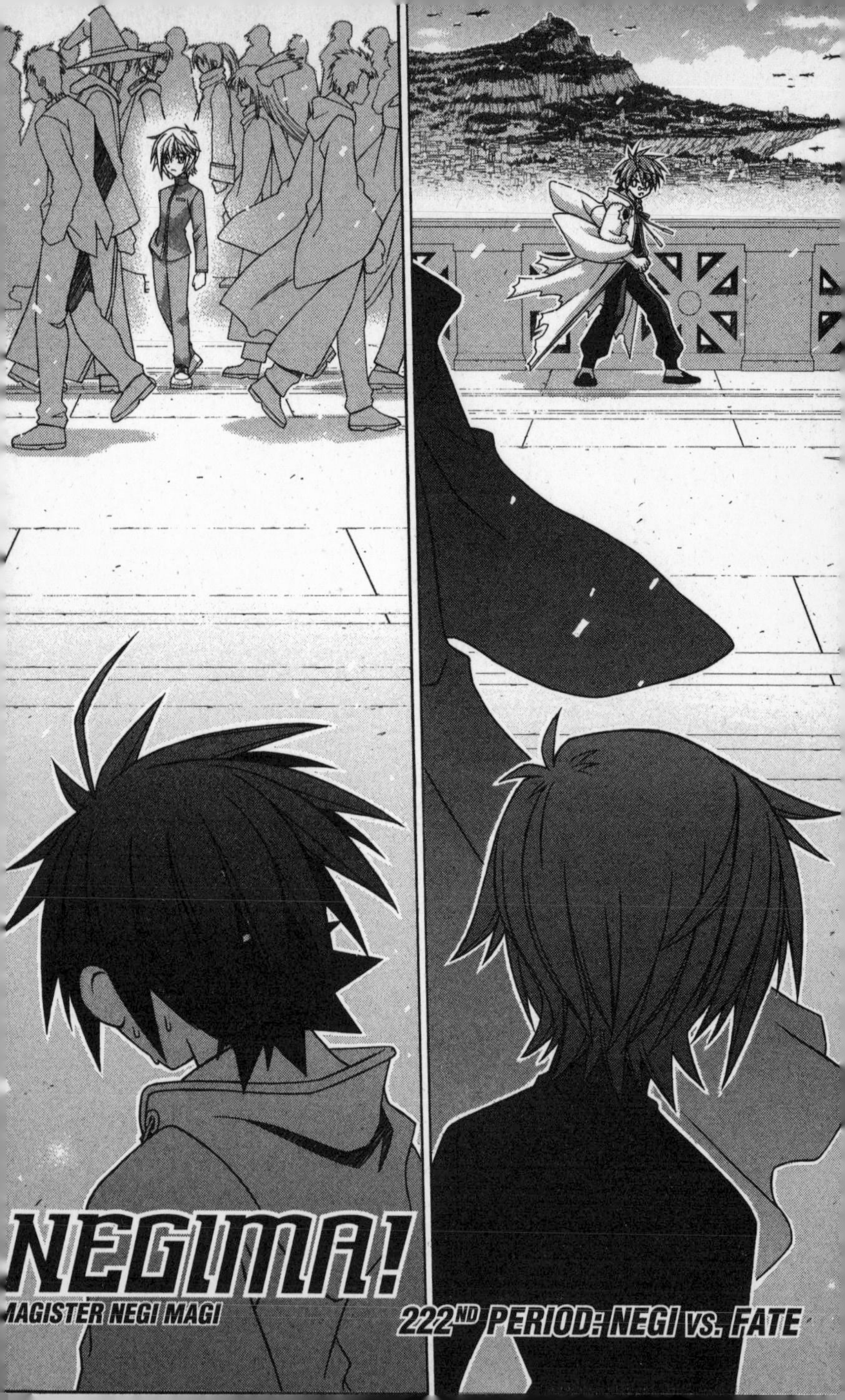
NEGIMA!
MAGISTER NEGI MAGI
222ND PERIOD: NEGI vs. FATE

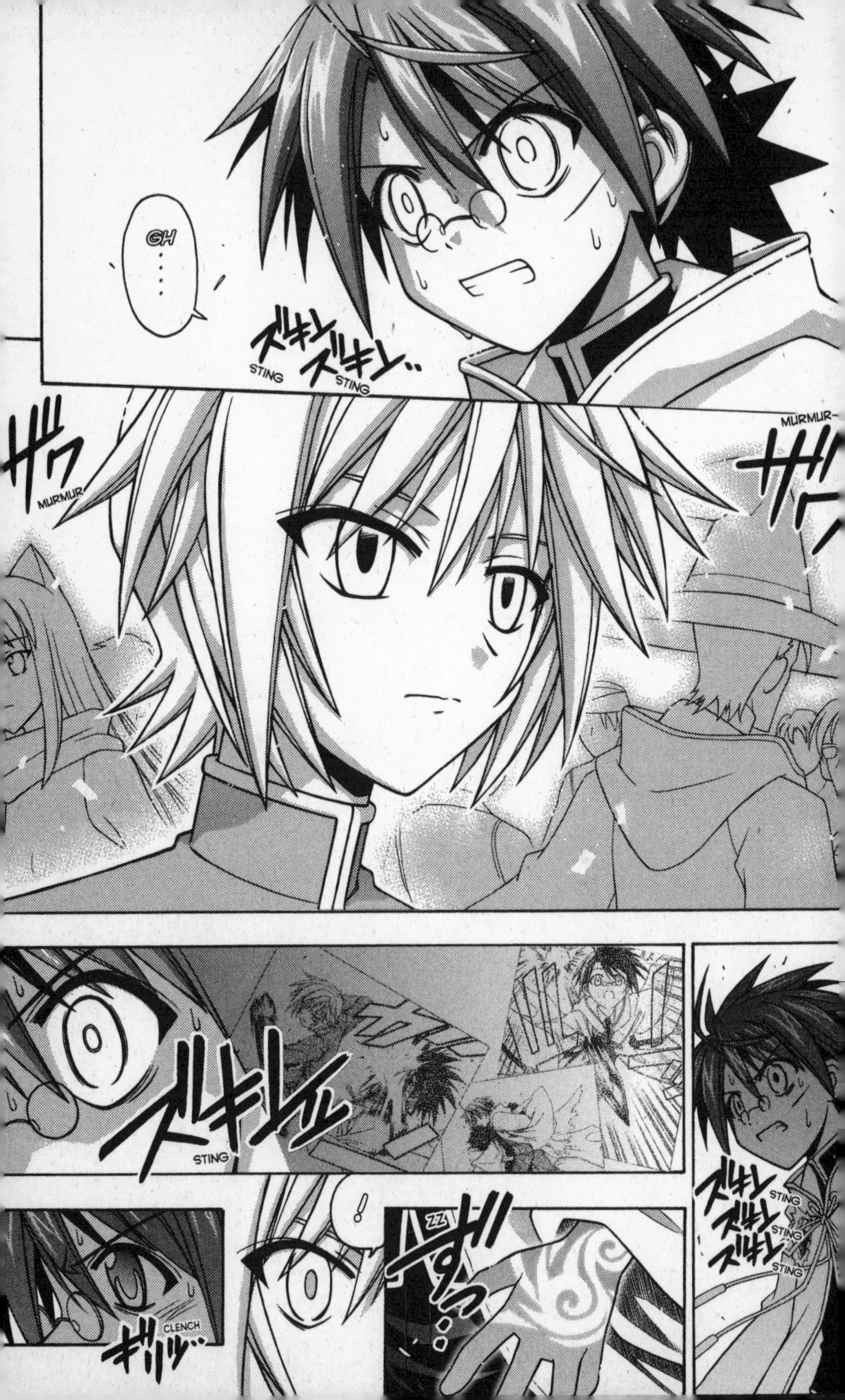
GH .....
ズキンズキン
STING
STING
MURMUR
ザワ
ザワ
MURMUR
ズキンズキンズキン
STING
STING
STING
ズキン
STING
ZZ
!
CLENCH
ギリッ

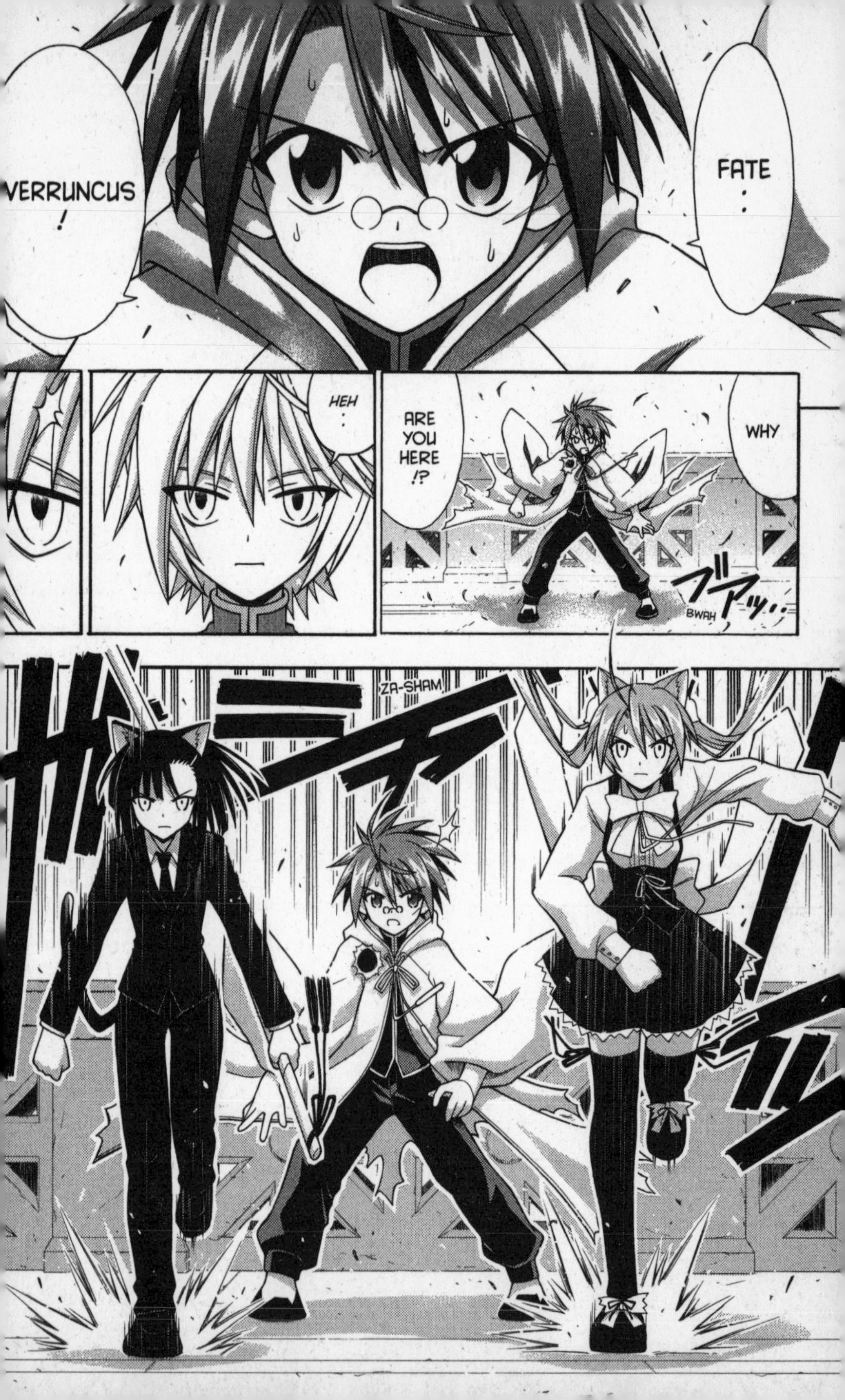

FATE…
VERRUNCUS!
WHY
ARE YOU HERE!?
BWAH
HEH…
ZA-SHAM

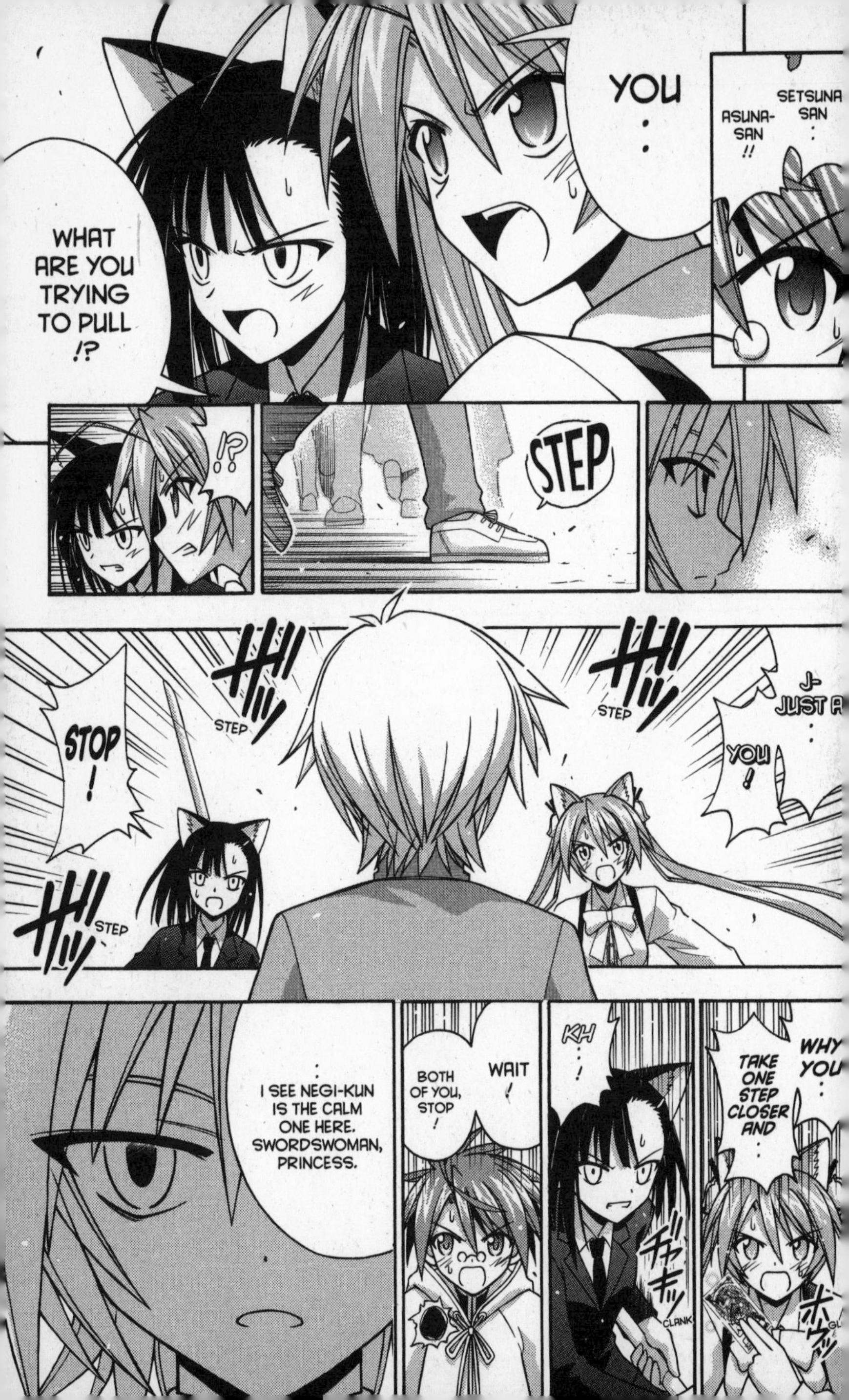
SETSUNA-SAN :
ASUNA-SAN !!
YOU :
WHAT ARE YOU TRYING TO PULL !?
STEP
!?
J- JUST A :
YOU !
STEP
STEP
STOP !
STEP
WHY YOU :
TAKE ONE STEP CLOSER AND :
KH : !
CLANK
WAIT !
BOTH OF YOU, STOP !
: I SEE NEGI-KUN IS THE CALM ONE HERE. SWORDSWOMAN, PRINCESS.

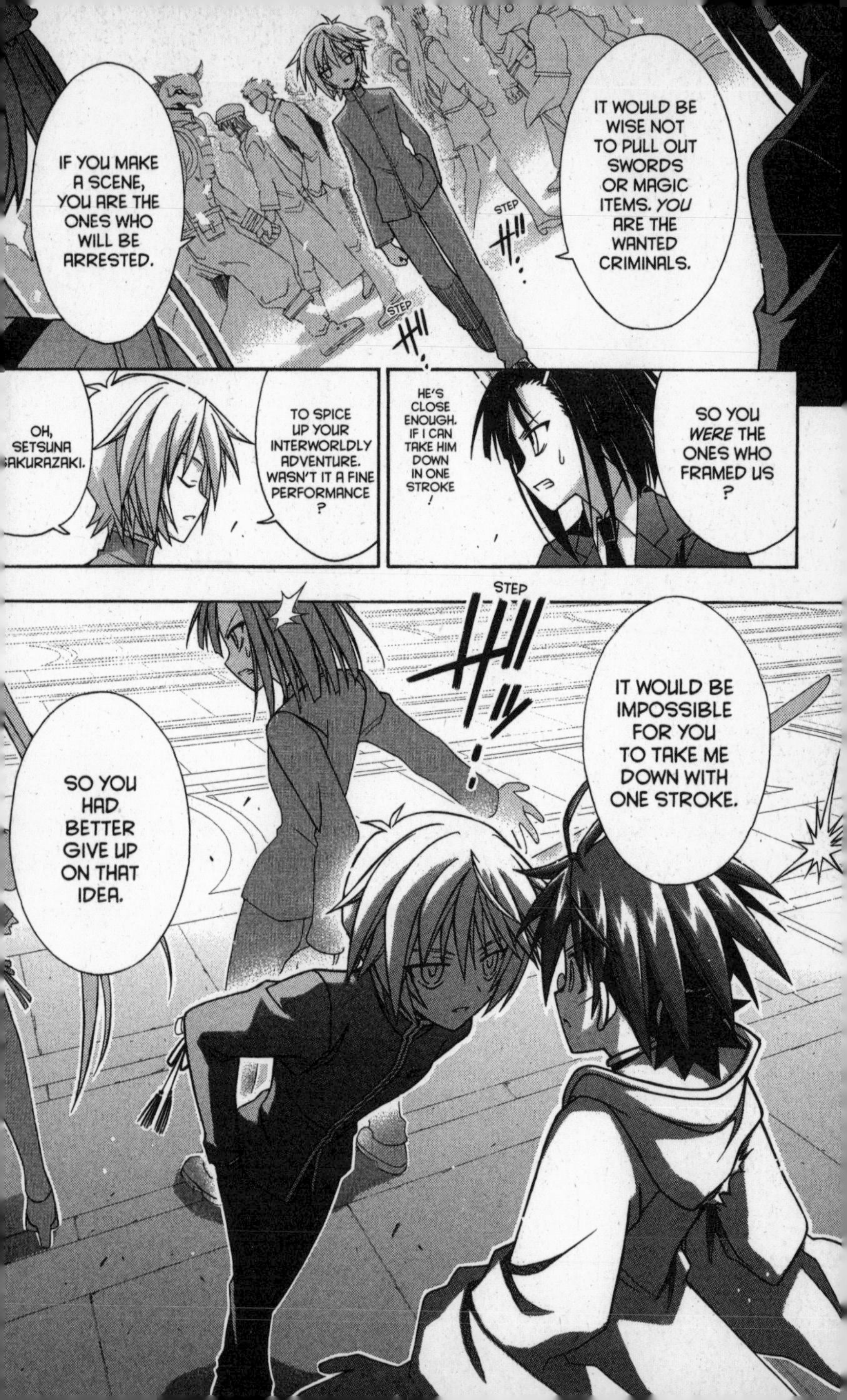
IT WOULD BE WISE NOT TO PULL OUT SWORDS OR MAGIC ITEMS. *YOU* ARE THE WANTED CRIMINALS.
STEP
STEP
IF YOU MAKE A SCENE, YOU ARE THE ONES WHO WILL BE ARRESTED.
SO YOU *WERE* THE ONES WHO FRAMED US?
HE'S CLOSE ENOUGH. IF I CAN TAKE HIM DOWN IN ONE STROKE!
TO SPICE UP YOUR INTERWORLDLY ADVENTURE. WASN'T IT A FINE PERFORMANCE?
OH, SETSUNA SAKURAZAKI.
STEP
IT WOULD BE IMPOSSIBLE FOR YOU TO TAKE ME DOWN WITH ONE STROKE.
SO YOU HAD BETTER GIVE UP ON THAT IDEA.

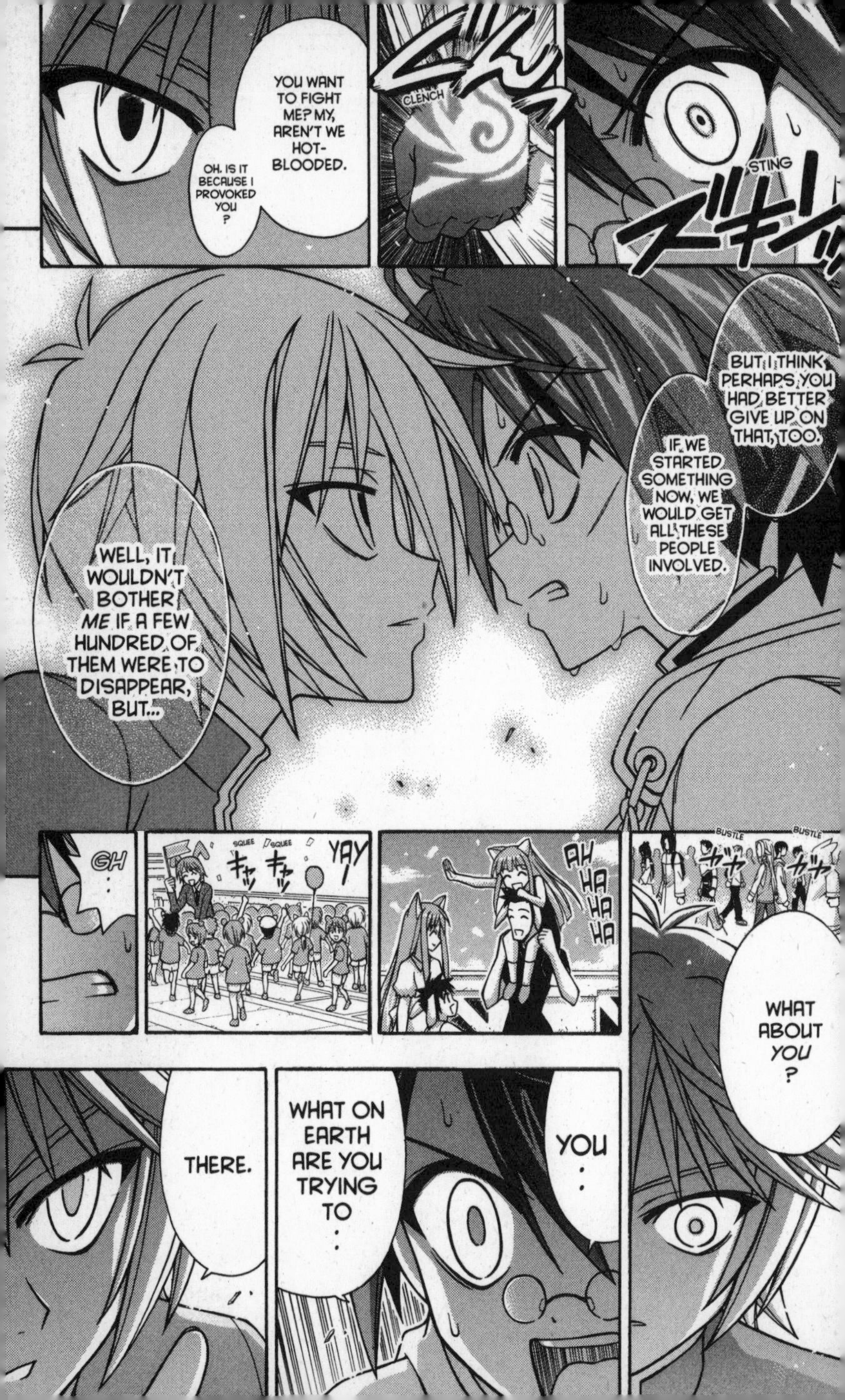
STING
CLENCH
YOU WANT TO FIGHT ME? MY, AREN'T WE HOT-BLOODED.
OH, IS IT BECAUSE I PROVOKED YOU?
BUT I THINK PERHAPS YOU HAD BETTER GIVE UP ON THAT, TOO.
IF WE STARTED SOMETHING NOW, WE WOULD GET ALL THESE PEOPLE INVOLVED.
WELL, IT WOULDN'T BOTHER *ME* IF A FEW HUNDRED OF THEM WERE TO DISAPPEAR, BUT...
BUSTLE
BUSTLE
WHAT ABOUT *YOU*?
AH HA HA HA HA
SQUEE
SQUEE
YAY!
GH...
YOU...
WHAT ON EARTH ARE YOU TRYING TO...
THERE.

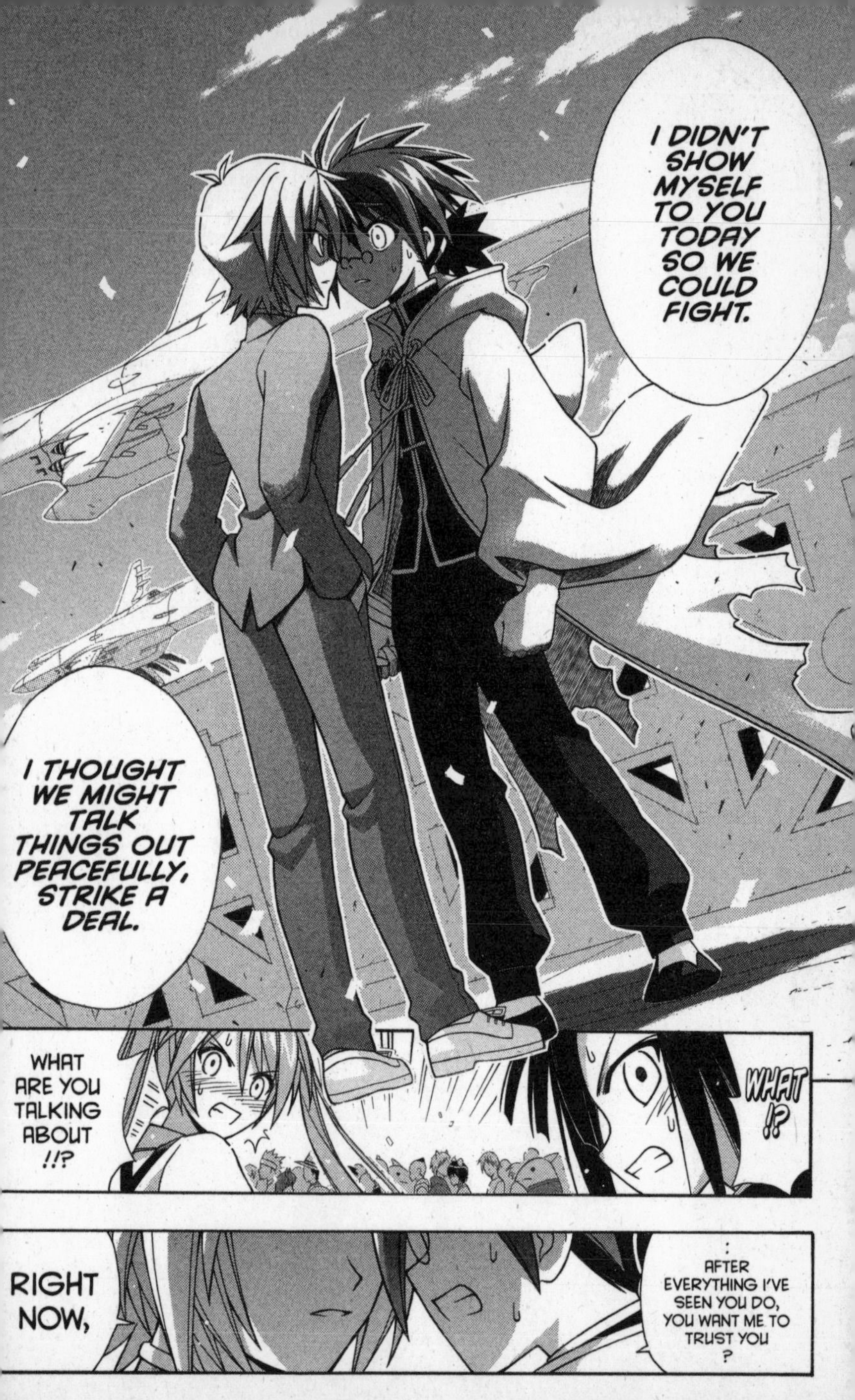
I DIDN'T SHOW MYSELF TO YOU TODAY SO WE COULD FIGHT.
I THOUGHT WE MIGHT TALK THINGS OUT PEACEFULLY, STRIKE A DEAL.
WHAT !?
WHAT ARE YOU TALKING ABOUT !!?
: AFTER EVERYTHING I'VE SEEN YOU DO, YOU WANT ME TO TRUST YOU ?
RIGHT NOW,

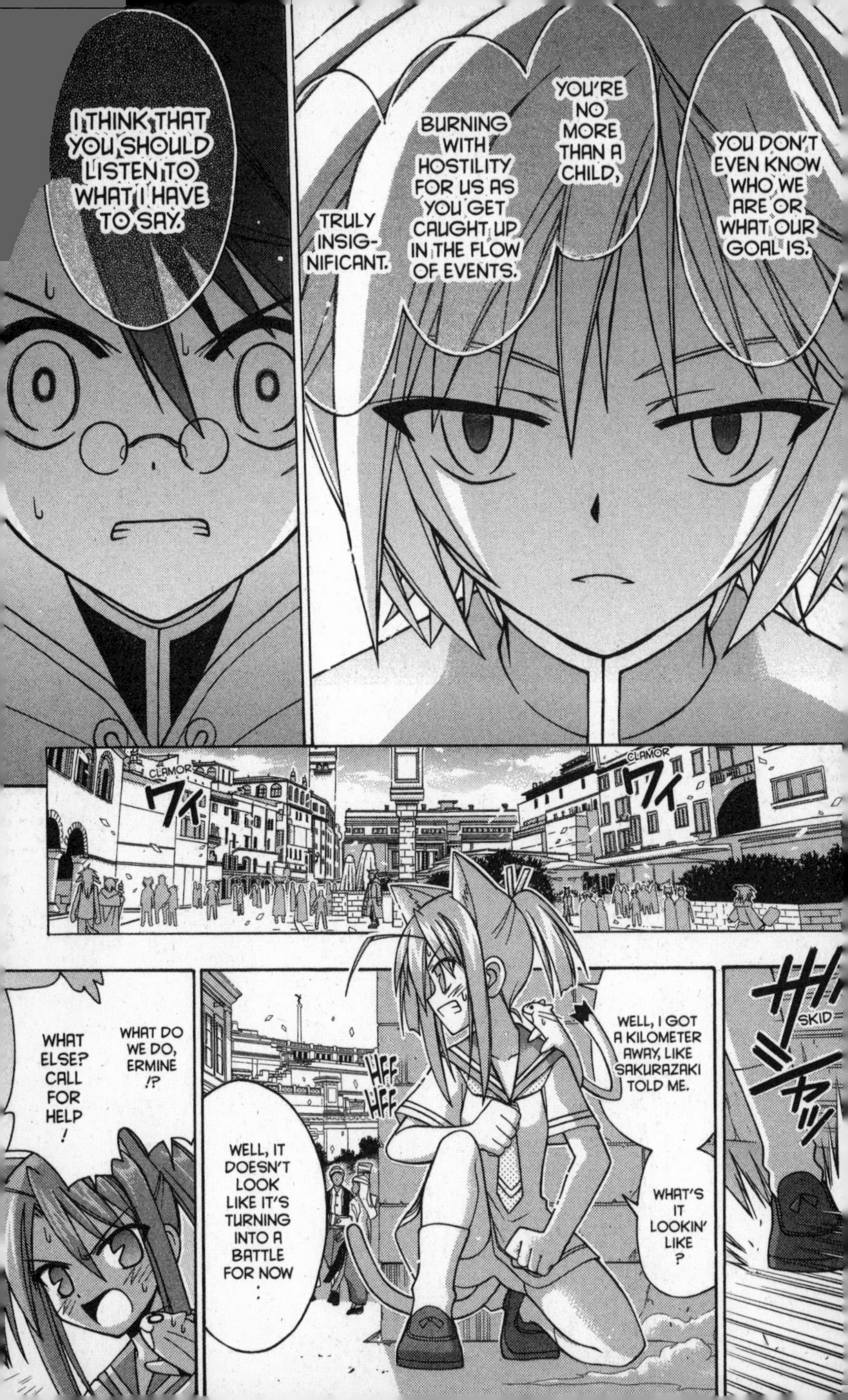
YOU DON'T EVEN KNOW WHO WE ARE OR WHAT OUR GOAL IS.
YOU'RE NO MORE THAN A CHILD,
BURNING WITH HOSTILITY FOR US AS YOU GET CAUGHT UP IN THE FLOW OF EVENTS.
TRULY INSIG-NIFICANT.
I THINK THAT YOU SHOULD LISTEN TO WHAT I HAVE TO SAY.
CLAMOR
ワイ
CLAMOR
ワイ
SKID
ザシャッ
WELL, I GOT A KILOMETER AWAY, LIKE SAKURAZAKI TOLD ME.
WHAT'S IT LOOKIN' LIKE?
HFF HFF
WELL, IT DOESN'T LOOK LIKE IT'S TURNING INTO A BATTLE FOR NOW...
WHAT DO WE DO, ERMINE!?
WHAT ELSE? CALL FOR HELP!

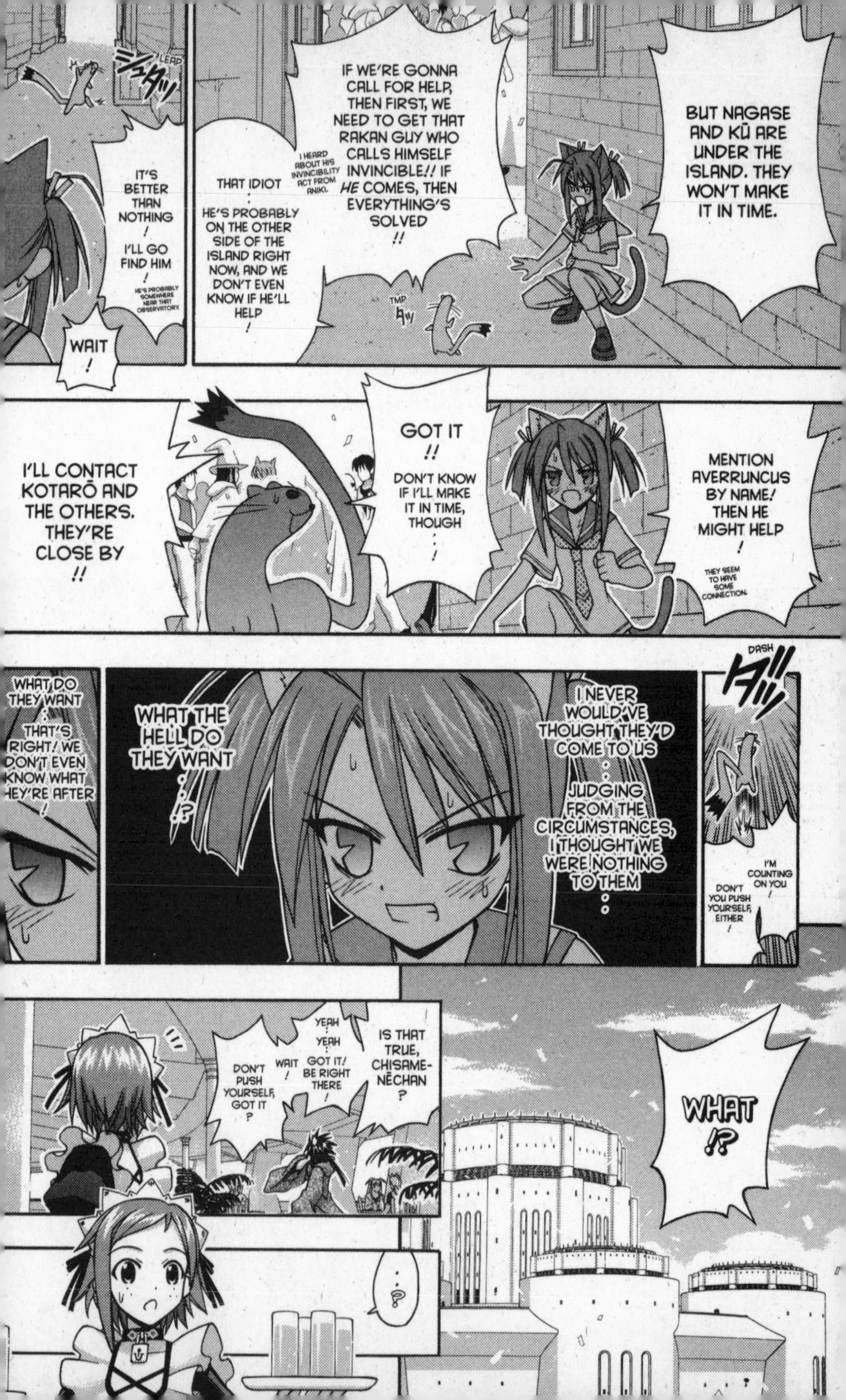
BUT NAGASE AND KŪ ARE UNDER THE ISLAND. THEY WON'T MAKE IT IN TIME.
IF WE'RE GONNA CALL FOR HELP, THEN FIRST, WE NEED TO GET THAT RAKAN GUY WHO CALLS HIMSELF INVINCIBLE!! IF HE COMES, THEN EVERYTHING'S SOLVED!!
I HEARD ABOUT HIS INVINCIBILITY ACT FROM ANIKI.
THAT IDIOT... HE'S PROBABLY ON THE OTHER SIDE OF THE ISLAND RIGHT NOW, AND WE DON'T EVEN KNOW IF HE'LL HELP!
TMP
LEAP
IT'S BETTER THAN NOTHING! I'LL GO FIND HIM!
HE'S PROBABLY SOMEWHERE NEAR THAT OBSERVATORY.
WAIT!
MENTION AVERRUNCUS BY NAME! THEN HE MIGHT HELP!
THEY SEEM TO HAVE SOME CONNECTION.
GOT IT!! DON'T KNOW IF I'LL MAKE IT IN TIME, THOUGH...!
I'LL CONTACT KOTARŌ AND THE OTHERS. THEY'RE CLOSE BY!!
DASH
I'M COUNTING ON YOU!
DON'T YOU PUSH YOURSELF, EITHER!
I NEVER WOULD'VE THOUGHT THEY'D COME TO US... JUDGING FROM THE CIRCUMSTANCES, I THOUGHT WE WERE NOTHING TO THEM...
WHAT THE HELL DO THEY WANT...!?
WHAT DO THEY WANT... THAT'S RIGHT! WE DON'T EVEN KNOW WHAT THEY'RE AFTER!
WHAT!?
IS THAT TRUE, CHISAME-NĒCHAN?
YEAH... YEAH... GOT IT! BE RIGHT THERE!
WAIT!
DON'T PUSH YOURSELF, GOT IT?
...?

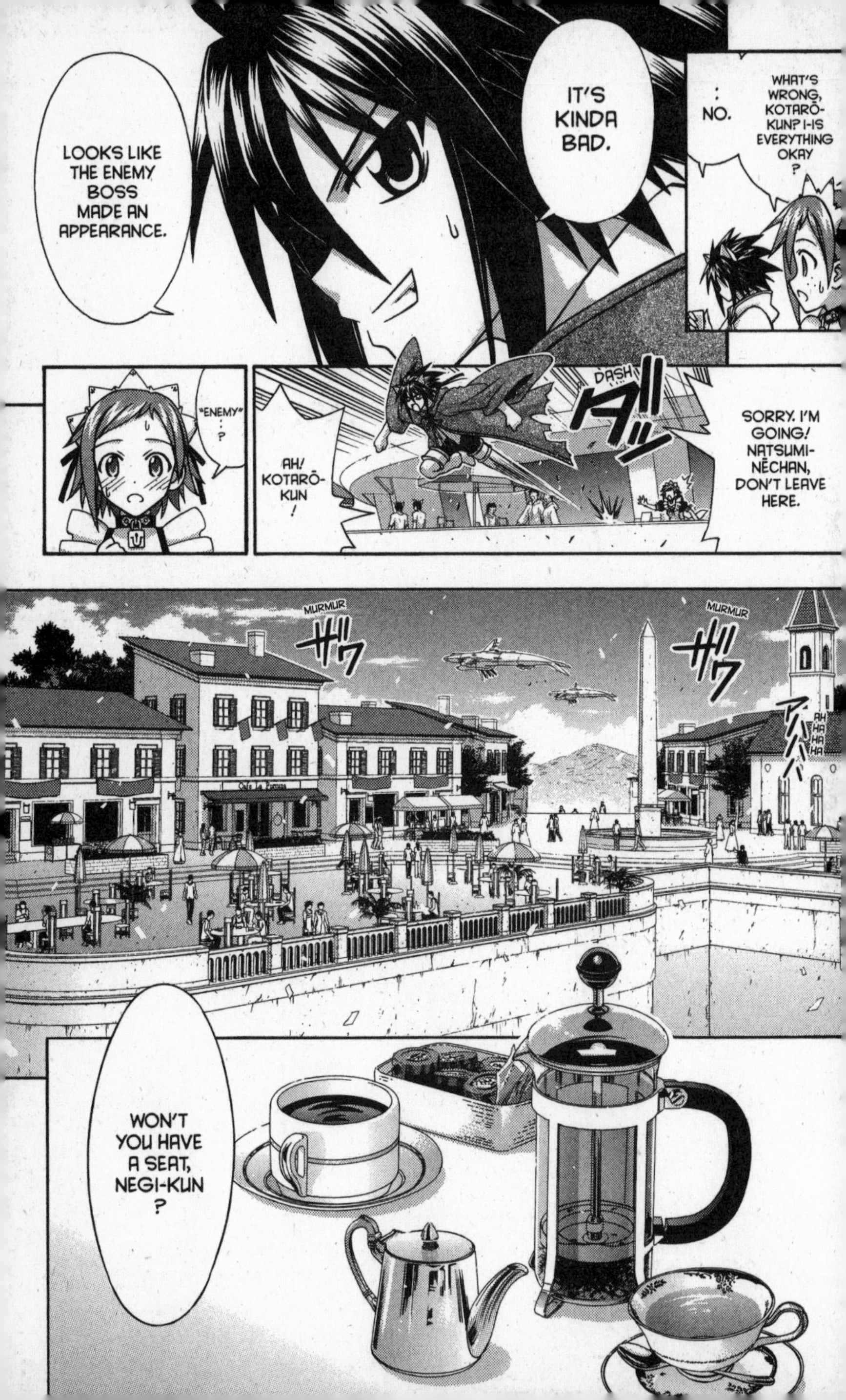
WHAT'S WRONG, KOTARŌ-KUN? I-IS EVERYTHING OKAY?
: NO.
IT'S KINDA BAD.
LOOKS LIKE THE ENEMY BOSS MADE AN APPEARANCE.
SORRY. I'M GOING! NATSUMI-NĒCHAN, DON'T LEAVE HERE.
DASH
AH! KOTARŌ-KUN!
"ENEMY"...?
MURMUR
AH HA HA HA
MURMUR
WON'T YOU HAVE A SEAT, NEGI-KUN?

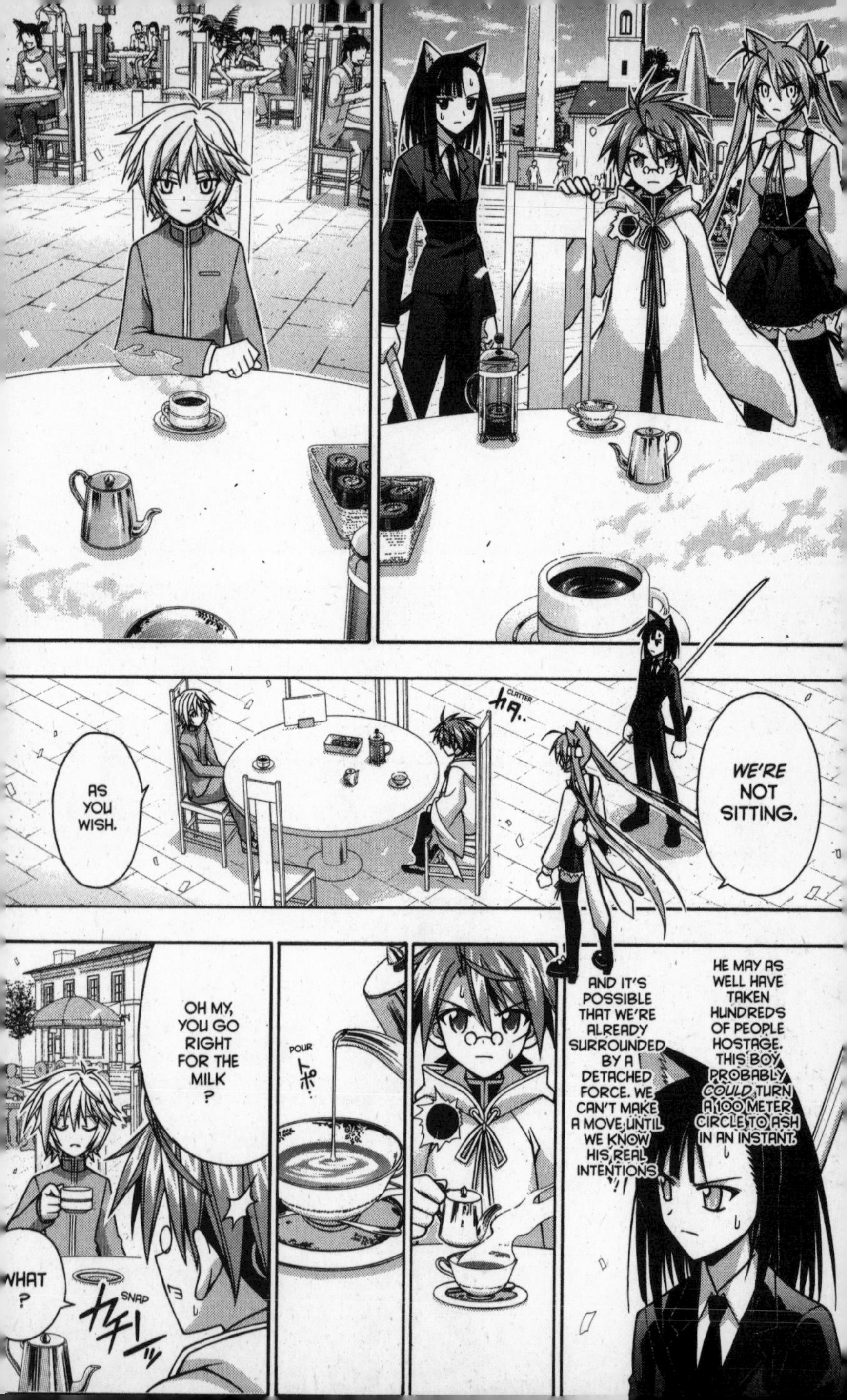
WE'RE NOT SITTING.
CLATTER
カタ..
AS YOU WISH.
HE MAY AS WELL HAVE TAKEN HUNDREDS OF PEOPLE HOSTAGE. THIS BOY PROBABLY COULD TURN A 100 METER CIRCLE TO ASH IN AN INSTANT.
AND IT'S POSSIBLE THAT WE'RE ALREADY SURROUNDED BY A DETACHED FORCE. WE CAN'T MAKE A MOVE UNTIL WE KNOW HIS REAL INTENTIONS
POUR
トポ..
OH MY, YOU GO RIGHT FOR THE MILK ?
WHAT ?
SNAP
カチーッ

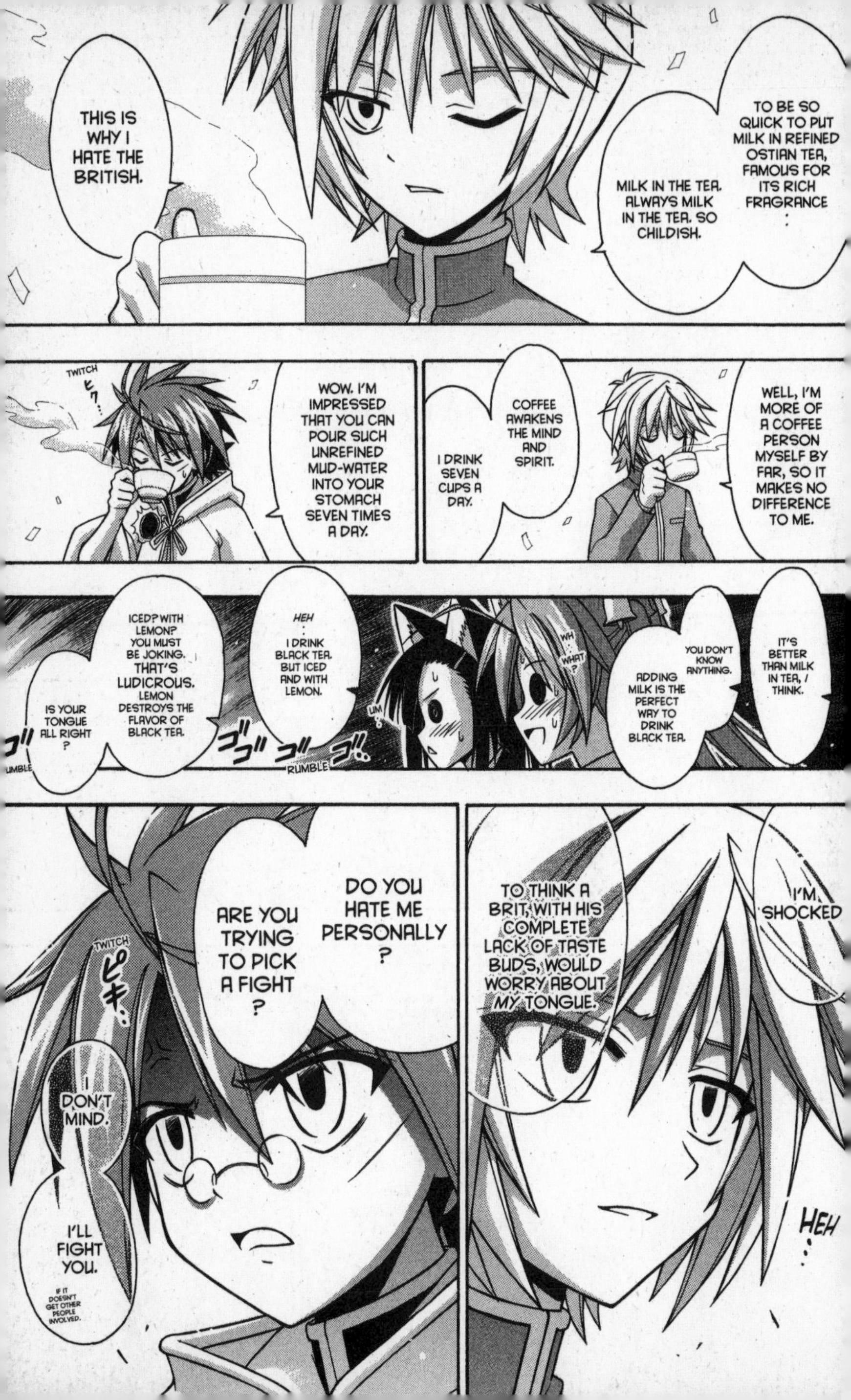
TO BE SO QUICK TO PUT MILK IN REFINED OSTIAN TEA, FAMOUS FOR ITS RICH FRAGRANCE :
MILK IN THE TEA. ALWAYS MILK IN THE TEA. SO CHILDISH.
THIS IS WHY I HATE THE BRITISH.
WELL, I'M MORE OF A COFFEE PERSON MYSELF BY FAR, SO IT MAKES NO DIFFERENCE TO ME.
COFFEE AWAKENS THE MIND AND SPIRIT.
I DRINK SEVEN CUPS A DAY.
WOW. I'M IMPRESSED THAT YOU CAN POUR SUCH UNREFINED MUD-WATER INTO YOUR STOMACH SEVEN TIMES A DAY.
TWITCH ピク…
IT'S BETTER THAN MILK IN TEA, I THINK.
YOU DON'T KNOW ANYTHING.
ADDING MILK IS THE PERFECT WAY TO DRINK BLACK TEA.
WH... WHAT?
UM
HEH : I DRINK BLACK TEA. BUT ICED AND WITH LEMON.
ゴゴゴゴ RUMBLE
ICED? WITH LEMON? YOU MUST BE JOKING. THAT'S LUDICROUS. LEMON DESTROYS THE FLAVOR OF BLACK TEA.
IS YOUR TONGUE ALL RIGHT ?
I'M SHOCKED
TO THINK A BRIT, WITH HIS COMPLETE LACK OF TASTE BUDS, WOULD WORRY ABOUT *MY* TONGUE.
HEH ...
DO YOU HATE ME PERSONALLY ?
ARE YOU TRYING TO PICK A FIGHT ?
TWITCH ピキ…
I DON'T MIND.
I'LL FIGHT YOU.
IF IT DOESN'T GET OTHER PEOPLE INVOLVED.

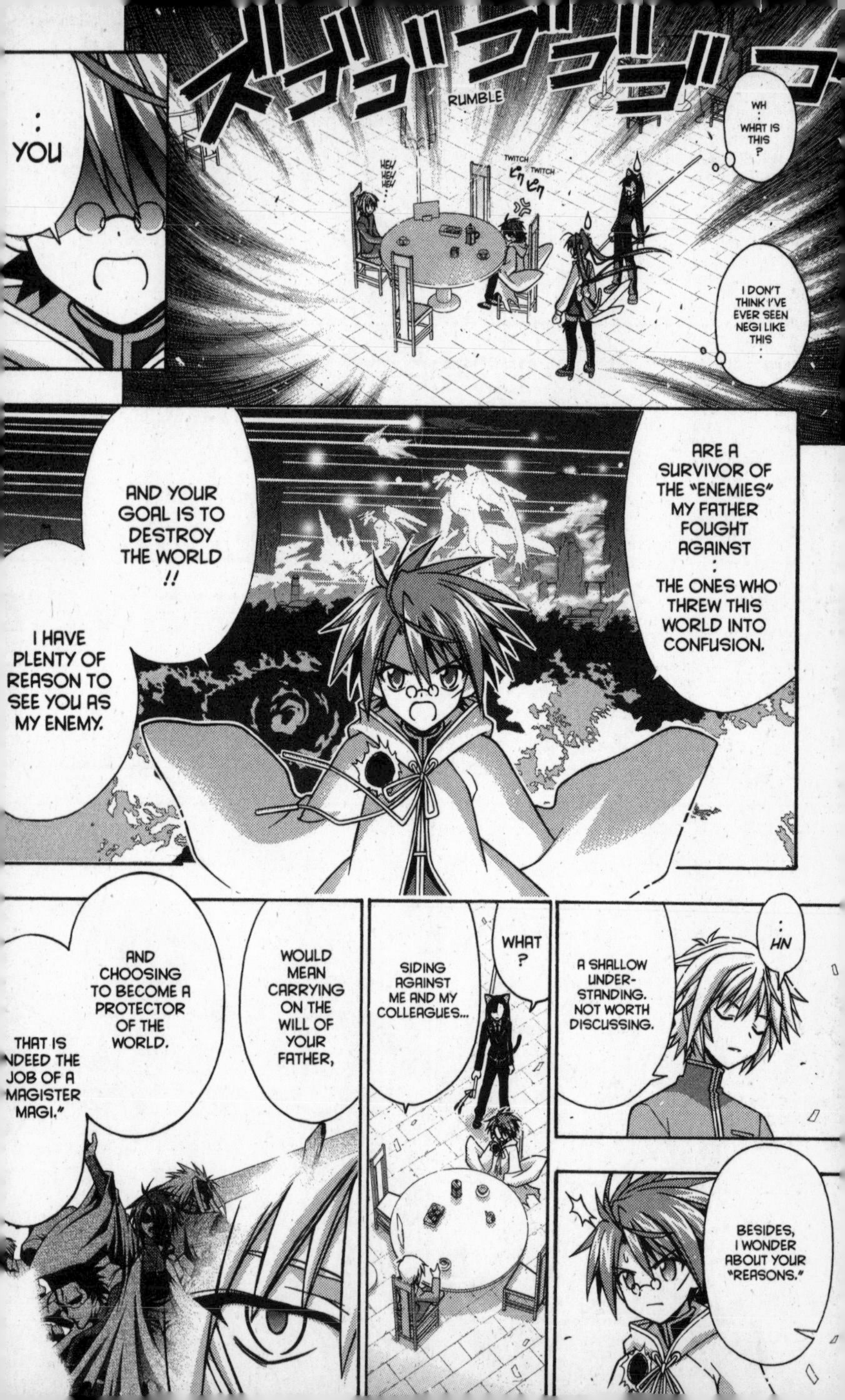
RUMBLE
HEH HEH HEH
TWITCH TWITCH
WH : WHAT IS THIS ?
I DON'T THINK I'VE EVER SEEN NEGI LIKE THIS :
: YOU
ARE A SURVIVOR OF THE "ENEMIES" MY FATHER FOUGHT AGAINST : THE ONES WHO THREW THIS WORLD INTO CONFUSION.
AND YOUR GOAL IS TO DESTROY THE WORLD !!
I HAVE PLENTY OF REASON TO SEE YOU AS MY ENEMY.
: HN
A SHALLOW UNDER-STANDING. NOT WORTH DISCUSSING.
BESIDES, I WONDER ABOUT YOUR "REASONS."
WHAT ?
SIDING AGAINST ME AND MY COLLEAGUES...
WOULD MEAN CARRYING ON THE WILL OF YOUR FATHER,
AND CHOOSING TO BECOME A PROTECTOR OF THE WORLD.
THAT IS NDEED THE JOB OF A MAGISTER MAGI."

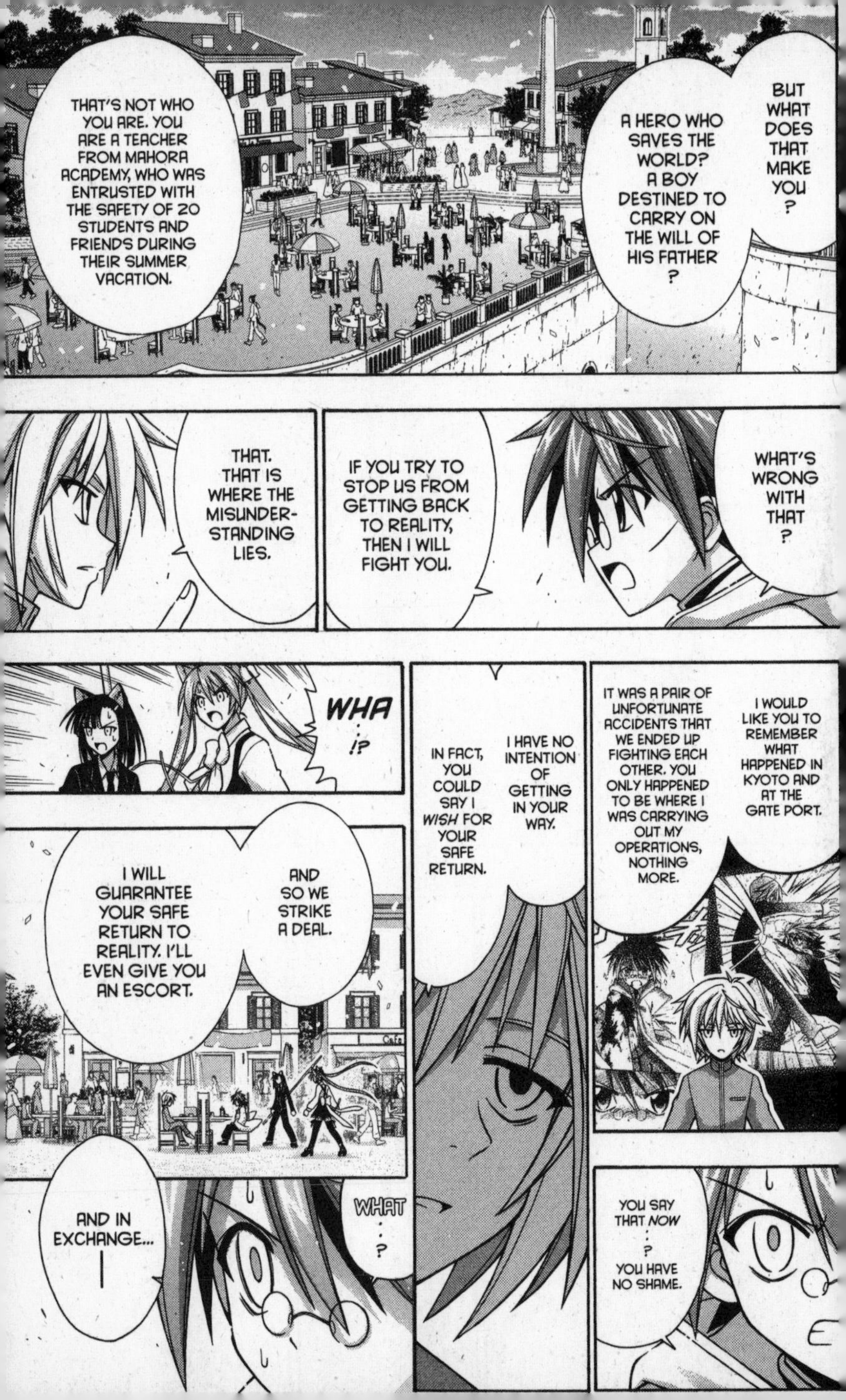
A HERO WHO SAVES THE WORLD? A BOY DESTINED TO CARRY ON THE WILL OF HIS FATHER?
BUT WHAT DOES THAT MAKE YOU?
THAT'S NOT WHO YOU ARE. YOU ARE A TEACHER FROM MAHORA ACADEMY, WHO WAS ENTRUSTED WITH THE SAFETY OF 20 STUDENTS AND FRIENDS DURING THEIR SUMMER VACATION.
WHAT'S WRONG WITH THAT?
IF YOU TRY TO STOP US FROM GETTING BACK TO REALITY, THEN I WILL FIGHT YOU.
THAT. THAT IS WHERE THE MISUNDERSTANDING LIES.
I WOULD LIKE YOU TO REMEMBER WHAT HAPPENED IN KYOTO AND AT THE GATE PORT.
IT WAS A PAIR OF UNFORTUNATE ACCIDENTS THAT WE ENDED UP FIGHTING EACH OTHER. YOU ONLY HAPPENED TO BE WHERE I WAS CARRYING OUT MY OPERATIONS, NOTHING MORE.
YOU SAY THAT *NOW*...? YOU HAVE NO SHAME.
I HAVE NO INTENTION OF GETTING IN YOUR WAY.
IN FACT, YOU COULD SAY I *WISH* FOR YOUR SAFE RETURN.
WHA...!?
AND SO WE STRIKE A DEAL.
I WILL GUARANTEE YOUR SAFE RETURN TO REALITY. I'LL EVEN GIVE YOU AN ESCORT.
WHAT...?
AND IN EXCHANGE...

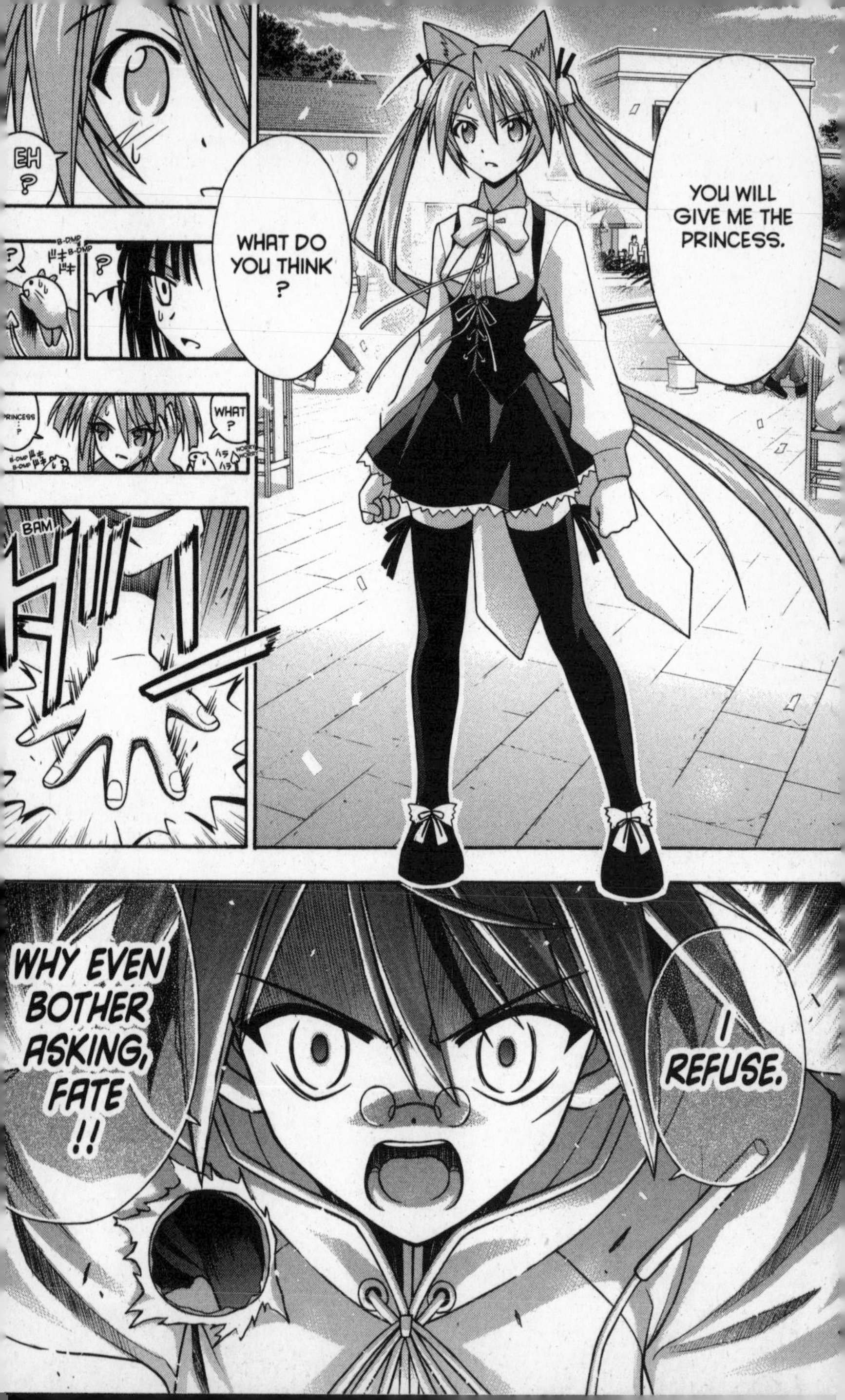
YOU WILL GIVE ME THE PRINCESS.
WHAT DO YOU THINK ?
EH ?
?
?
PRINCESS... ?
WHAT ?
BAM
I REFUSE.
WHY EVEN BOTHER ASKING, FATE !!

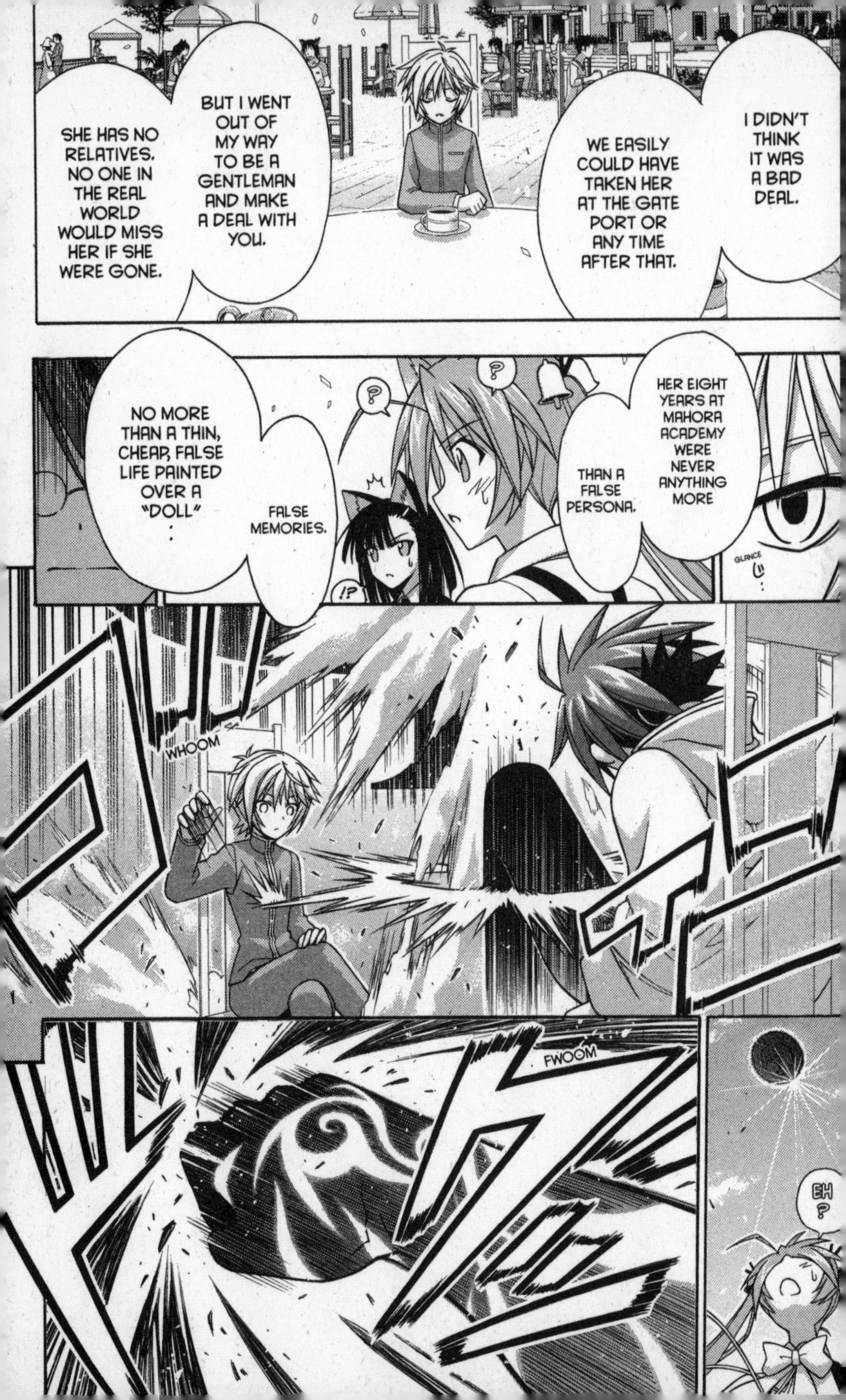
I DIDN'T THINK IT WAS A BAD DEAL.
WE EASILY COULD HAVE TAKEN HER AT THE GATE PORT OR ANY TIME AFTER THAT.
BUT I WENT OUT OF MY WAY TO BE A GENTLEMAN AND MAKE A DEAL WITH YOU.
SHE HAS NO RELATIVES. NO ONE IN THE REAL WORLD WOULD MISS HER IF SHE WERE GONE.
GLANCE
HER EIGHT YEARS AT MAHORA ACADEMY WERE NEVER ANYTHING MORE
THAN A FALSE PERSONA.
?
?
FALSE MEMORIES.
NO MORE THAN A THIN, CHEAP, FALSE LIFE PAINTED OVER A "DOLL"
!?
WHOOM
EH?
FWOOM

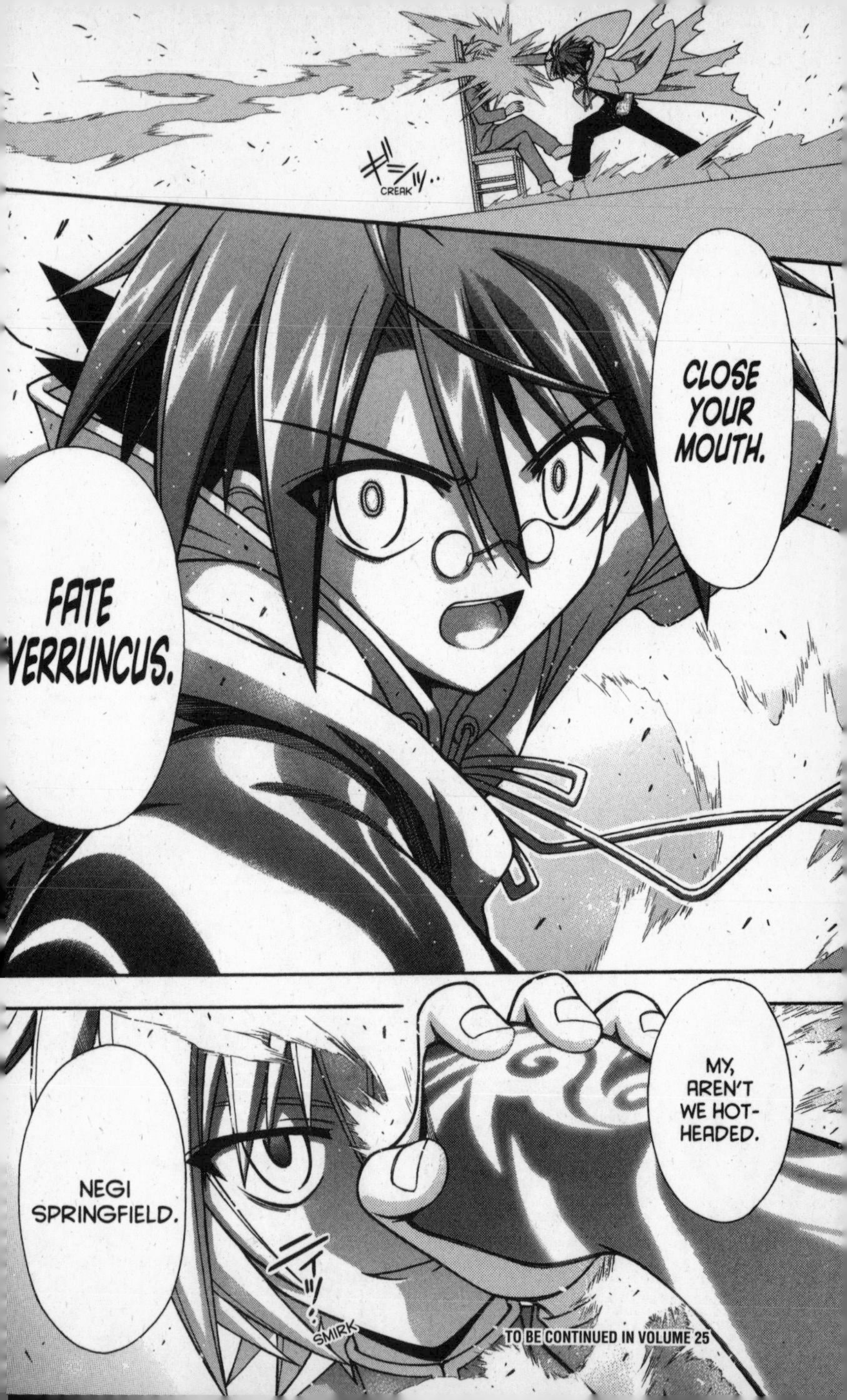
CREAK
CLOSE YOUR MOUTH.
FATE VERRUNCUS.
MY, AREN'T WE HOT-HEADED.
NEGI SPRINGFIELD.
SMIRK
TO BE CONTINUED IN VOLUME 25

-STAFF-

Ken Akamatsu
Takashi Takemoto
Kenichi Nakamura
Masaki Ohyama
Keiichi Yamashita
Tadashi Maki
Tohru Mitsuhashi
Yuichi Yoshida

Thanks to
Ran Ayanaga

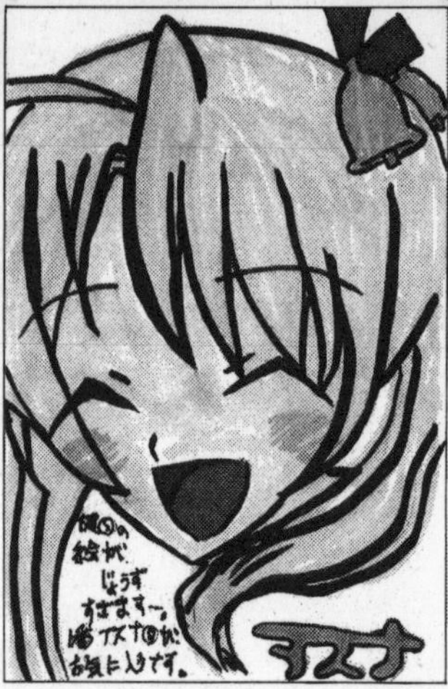

アスナ

HER FULL-FACED SMILE IS SO BRIGHT.

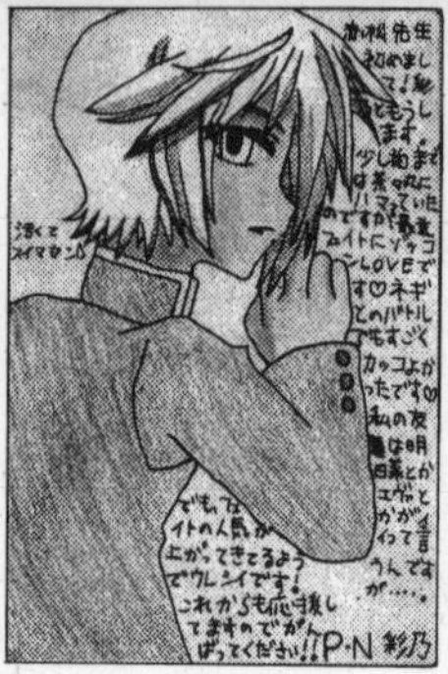

P・N 彩乃

SIDELONG-GLANCING FATE ☆

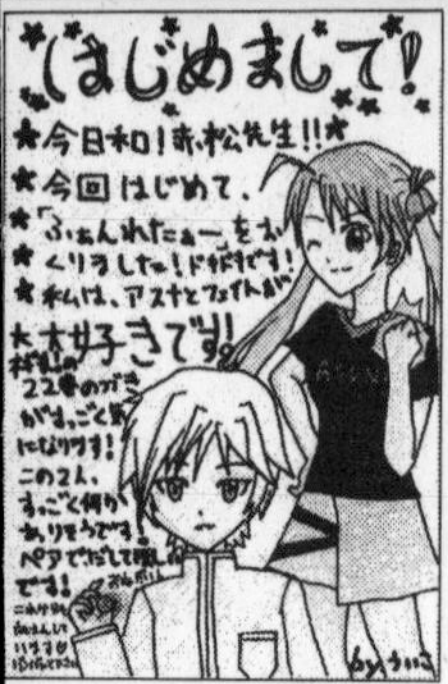

はじめまして!
今日和!赤松先生!!

YOU DON'T SEE THEM TOGETHER OFTEN.

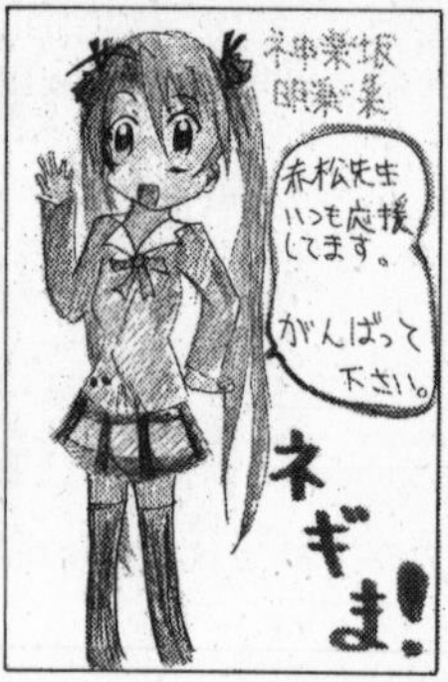

赤松先生 いつも応援してます。
がんばって下さい。
ネギま!

KIND OF BIG-SISTERLY.

NEGIMA! FAN ART CORNER

THIS TREND STARTED A LONG TIME AGO, BUT WE'VE BEEN GETTING MORE AND MORE FAN ART SUBMISSIONS FROM ELEMENTARY AND MIDDLE SCHOOL GIRLS ☆ THANK YOU VERY MUCH! KEEP SENDING 'EM IN ☆

TEXT BY MAX

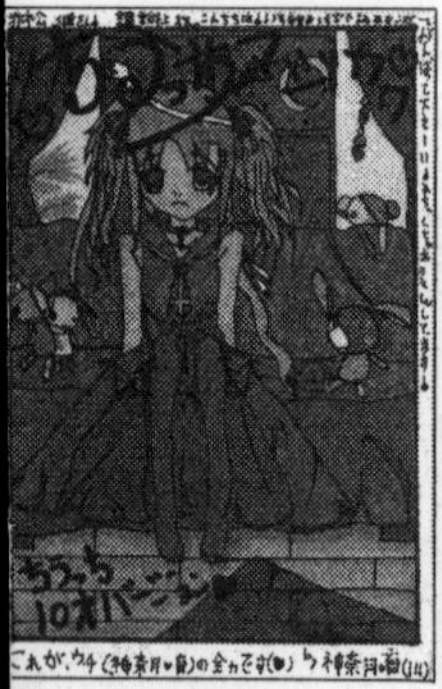

VERY ARTISTIC.

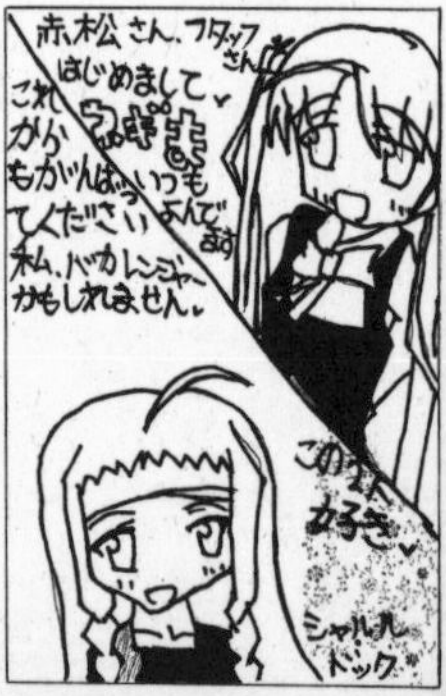

赤松さん、スタッフさん はじめまして

THEY BOTH LOOK SO WELL-BEHAVED.

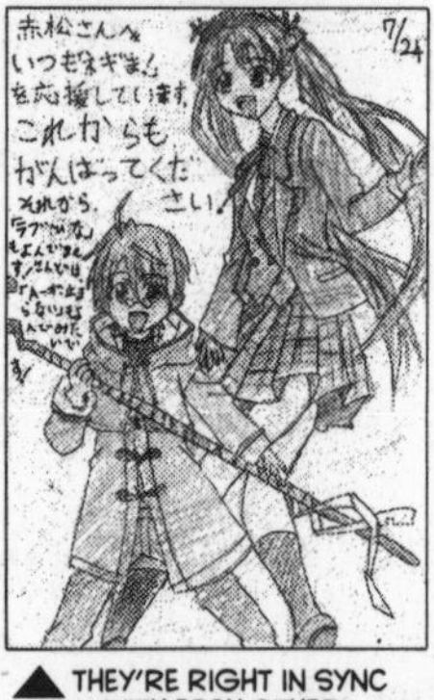

7/24
赤松さんへ いつもネギま!を応援しています これからもがんばってください。

THEY'RE RIGHT IN SYNC WITH EACH OTHER.

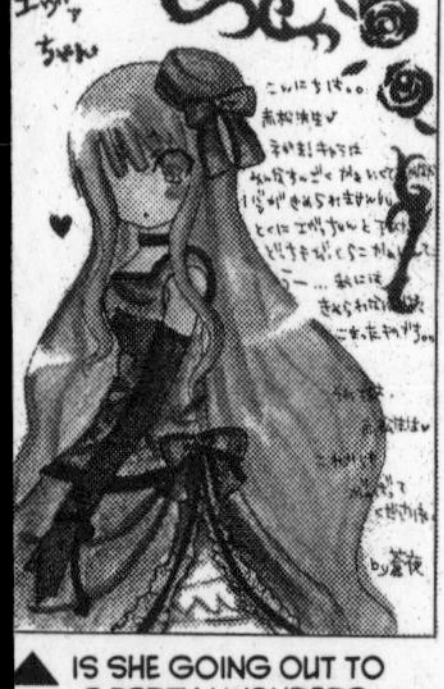

エヴァちゃん

IS SHE GOING OUT TO A PARTY, I WONDER?

NEGI MA!

MAHORA

MAGISTER NEGI MAGI

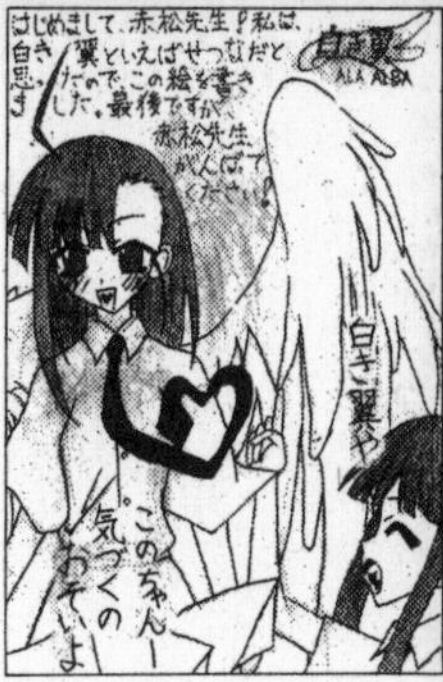

はじめまして、赤松先生！私は、白き翼といえばせつなだと思ったので、この絵を書きました。
このちゃん…気づくのおそいよ

▲ HER NECKTIE MAKES A HEART☆

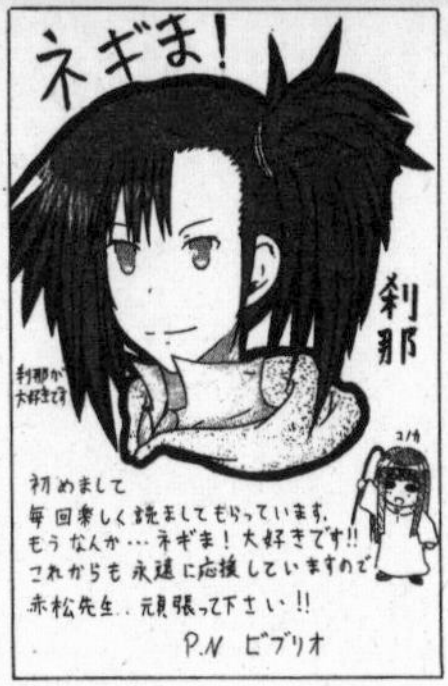

ネギま！
刹那
初めまして
毎回楽しく読ましてもらっています。
もうなんか…ネギま！大好きです!!
これからも永遠に応援していますので
赤松先生、頑張って下さい!!
P.N ビブリオ

▲ SHE'S VERY HANDSOME☆

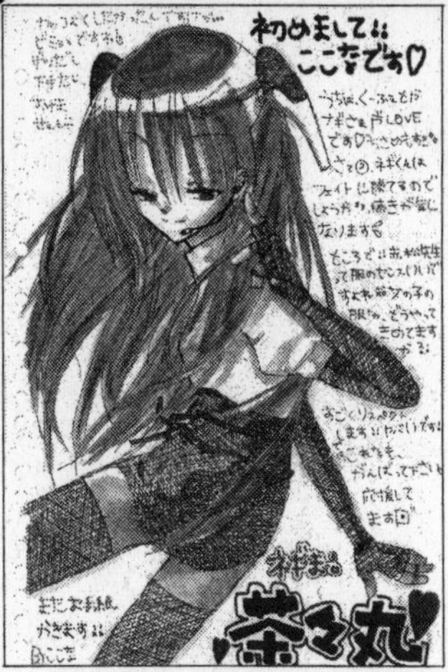

初めまして!!
ここなです♡
茶々丸!

▲ A VERY MATURE CHACHAMARU.

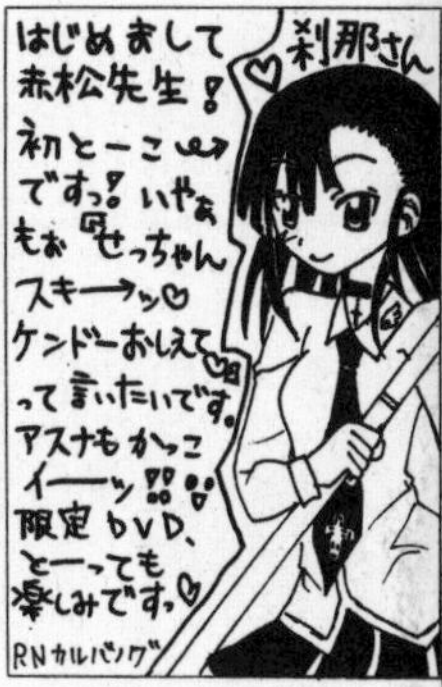

はじめまして
赤松先生！
刹那さん
ケンドーおしえて
って言いたいです。
限定DVD、
と―っても
楽しみです。
RNカルバノグ

▲ YOU *WOULD* WANT TO LEARN KENDO FROM HER, WOULDN'T YOU☆

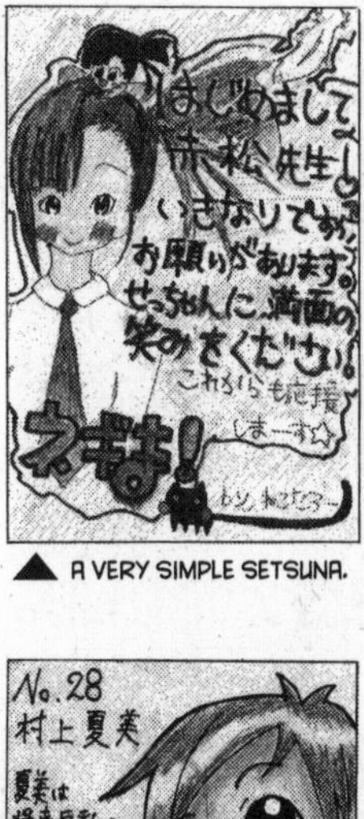

はじめまして
赤松先生
いきなりですが、
お願いがあります。
せっちゃんに満面の
笑みをください！
これからも応援
しまーす☆
ネギま！

▲ A VERY SIMPLE SETSUNA.

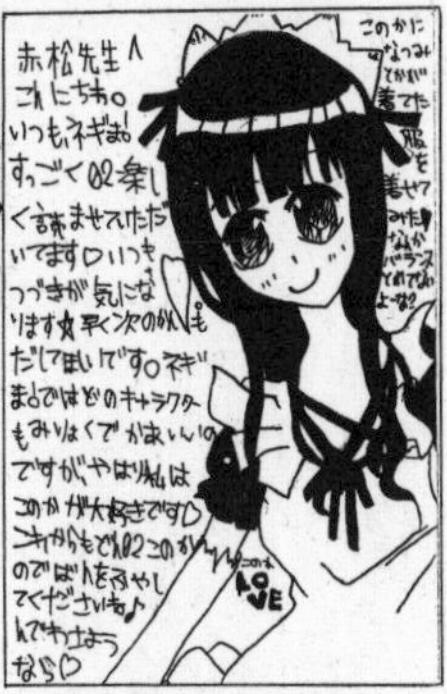

赤松先生へ
こんにちわ。

▲ KONOKA AS A MAID.

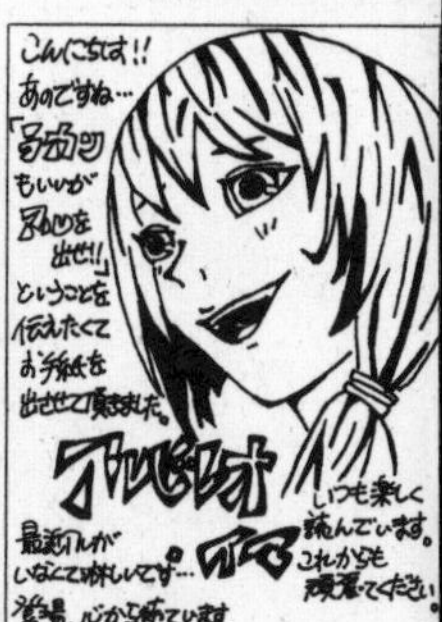

こんにちは!!
あのですね…

▲ AL LOOKS LIKE HE'S HAVING FUN.

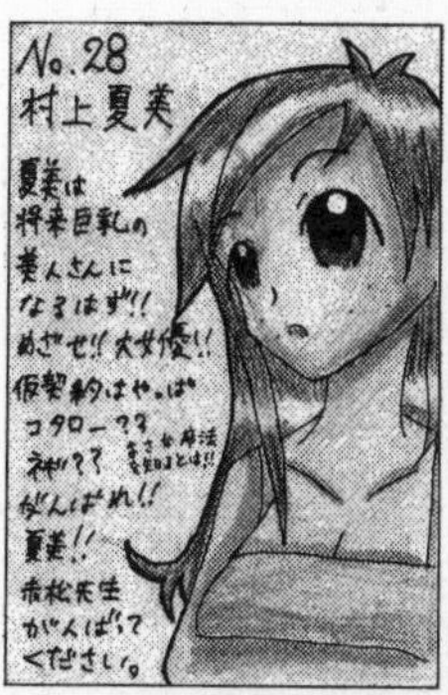

No.28
村上夏美
めざせ!! 大女優!!
赤松先生
がんばってくださいね。

▲ A MATURE-LOOKING NATSUMI COULD BE NICE, TOO.

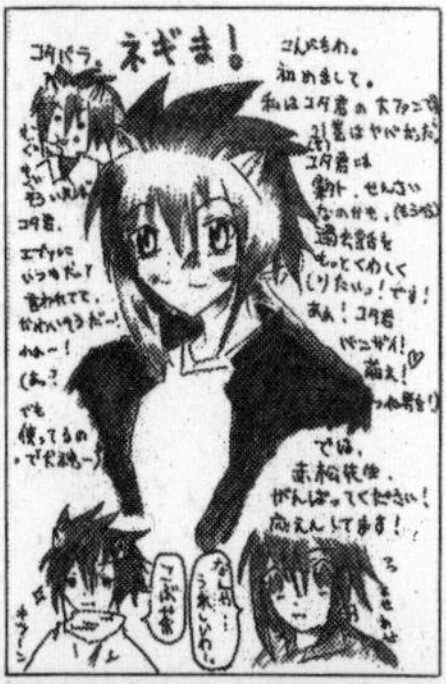

ネギま！
こんにちわ。
初めまして。

▲ I SEE YOU'RE REALLY INTO HIM.

▲ KONO-SETSU...?

DARK

はじめまして赤松先生。友達が読んでいて読んでみたらすべてはまりました。これからも連載楽しみにしています。 by I.Kazuma

▲ HOW DARK.

初めまして赤松先生！私はアスナがネギ大好き♥です。早めにアスナの過去が知りたいです。赤松先生応援しているのでお仕事頑張って下さい。by 音楽青年 ×

▲ THIS IS A NICE ASUNA, TOO.

ネギま！

初投稿！！
ツッコ＆ボケ！
見にこんにゃろきます。
出番が少ないなのに、
最近 18点。行事本
読み返したりしています。
こんにも ネギおもしろ！！
P.S. 赤松先生
体調管理に気をつけて
ガンバって下さい！！
祝OAD!!
by 板路 和正

◀ I MIGHT LIKE THIS DUO.

▲ LOVE-COMEDY MODE.

こんにちは!!
最近 気付きました
でも 私は前髪で目が隠れているキャラが大好きらしい…木乃香ちゃんパーフェクトは合格だ。でも実は
そんな人いたら「前髪、切れパク」て言うんだろうケド～(笑) 難しいトコだ。

◀ HER FOLLOWERS ARE WORKING HARD.

ジャックラカン

▲ SUCH A MANLY PROFILE.

◀ THEY LOOK LIKE MODELS.

ネギま！

はじめまして コンニチワ
ネギまの絵を初めにアクアテラスチームで書いてます。「白き翼バージョン」を手に入れた時は、テンション上がりました。これからもガンバって、テカワイイネカノラを描き続けて下さい！
by レツヤカチ

◀ THE WINGED ONES ☆

▲ 赤松さん、はじめまして

NEGI MA!

THIS VOLUME'S
FEATURED CHARACTER
YUE NAGASE
RANKING

MAGISTER NEGI MAGI

FIRST PLACE

THIS IS A CUTE YUE, ISN'T IT!? YOU SAID "MAYBE IF SHE WERE LOLITA STYLE," BUT I GET THE FEELING IT'S NOT MUCH DIFFERENT... (LAUGH)

ゆえきちゃん
もしもロリだったら
いーなとゆーことで。

SECOND PLACE

ゆえ吉
萌え×2

YUECCHI LOOKS LIKE A PLUSHIE. EVEN MORE SO BECAUSE HER MOUTH IS IN AN X SHAPE (LAUGH) YUE IS REALLY POPULAR WITH FEMALE FANS. ♡

MAGISTER NEGI MAGI

THIRD PLACE

YUE AND CHAMO MAKE A GOOD DUO~♡ I HOPE YOU CONTINUE TO CHEER THEM ON!

(AKAMATSU)

夕映！大〜好き！

3-D BACKGROUNDS EXPLANATION CORNER

THE STORY HAS MOVED TO THE FLOATING ISLAND OSTIA!
AND NEW CREATIONS HAVE APPEARED AS BACKGROUNDS.

• OSTIA'S BIG ARENA

SCENE NAME: LARGE ARENA POLYGON COUNT: 876,469

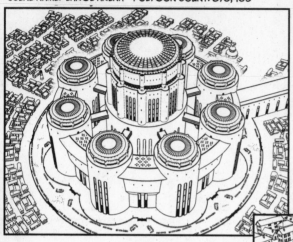

THE BIG ARENA IN OSTIA, WHERE THEY'RE HOLDING THE TOURNAMENT TO COMMEMORATE THE 20TH ANNIVERSARY OF THE END OF THE WAR. MADE UP OF EIGHT SUB-ARENAS COMPARABLE IN SIZE TO GRANICUS' ARENA AND A GIGANTIC MAIN ARENA IN THE CENTER, ITS CIRCUMFERENCE IS APPROXIMATELY TWO KILOMETERS AND... ANYWAY, ITS SIZE IS NOTHING TO BE SNEEZED AT. I PUT CROWDS IN PLACES HERE AND THERE, BUT THEY'RE SO SMALL, YOU CAN HARDLY SEE THEM. (LAUGH)

HOPES GET HIGHER AS YOU WONDER IF NEGI AND FRIENDS CAN REALLY COME OUT VICTORIOUS IN THIS PLACE.

• THE SURROUNDING TOWN.

THE SMALL HOUSES SURROUNDING IT ARE 3-D, TOO, BUT ENLARGED, THEY LOOK LIKE THIS. IT'S PRETTY HALF-HEARTED (LAUGH)

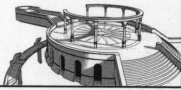

• OBSERVATORY

SCENE NAME: OBSERVATORY POLYGON COUNT: 10,746

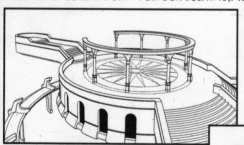

THE OBSERVATORY WHERE NEGI AND ASUNA REUNITED. IT'S IN PART OF THE NATURE PARK LOCATED ON THE EDGE OF OSTIA, AND IT OVERLOOKS A GIANT PANORAMA ABOVE THE SEA OF CLOUDS.

IT'S BUILT WITH THE SAME RING-SHAPED PARTS AS THE GATE PORT IN MEGALO-MESEMBRIA, AND GETS ITS ABILITY TO FLOAT FROM THE SAME PRINCIPLES.

FURTHERMORE, THERE ARE PANELS WHERE I ADDED SHADOWS WITH 3-D TO REPRODUCE THEM REALISTICALLY. THE PICTURE TO THE RIGHT SHOWS THOSE SHADOWS. WE WOULD TREAT THIS PICTURE BY ADDING CLOUD AND SKY TONE BY HAND, THUS COMPLETING THE PANEL.

LEXICON NEGIMARIUM

[*Negima!* 217th Period Lexicon Negimarium]

■ Form of the Dark Night

(Actus Noctis Erebeae)

A way of practicing dark magic. In Latin, it means "gesture of dark night." The translation of "gesture" into "form" refers to the series of actions in which those gestures come together.

■ Clairvoyance

(clara visibilitas)

A type of ESP (extrasensory perception); it perceives objects, places, and current events that can't be seen with the naked eye, as if actually witnessing them. Negi's ability to find the location of his wand when he closes his eyes (see *Negima!* volume 3, 21st Period) is another type of this ability.

[*Negima!* 218th Period Lexicon Negimarium]

■ Breasts [NOTE: This entry is narrated by Paio Zi, the hunter known for his obsession with breasts.]

(mamma)

German Jewish psychologist E. Neumann (1905–60) said: "Just as do the priestesses, who are put on par with the goddess, the goddess leaves her breasts exposed. Breasts are a symbol of the flow of cultivation, nourishment, and life." (*The Great Mother,* 9.Kap.) In magical cultures, too (especially matriarchal societies), women's breasts—along with the abdomen, buttocks, and genitals—are said to hold extremely sacred meaning, yes? This is because the breasts are the symbol of the fertility that leads to human life. This should be well understood from archaeological artifacts, yes? Neumann said: "Because they are in the central region of the woman's torso, the abdomen and the breasts, often very large breasts, become 'the only realistic thing.' In these statues, the richness of feminine parts is expressed primitively and in a superhuman manner." (ebd.8.Kap.) Thus, women's breasts, especially enormous breasts, are said to have the character of bringing forth and protecting physical life, yes? This is called "a woman's elementary character." This is made evident by the fact that, for example, the Latin word for physical substance, *materia,* comes from the word *mater*, meaning mother, yes?

But a woman's breasts are not only endowed with the "elementary character" of procreation and protection. A woman's breasts, or rather,

her chest area, also has the important element called the "transformative character," yes? "Indeed, many figures emphasize the genitals and breasts, and indicate only the elementary character, only the symbol of procreation and nurturing. However, in other statues, we see that the transformative character and the abdomen, genitals, and buttocks are emphasized, while the chest area is ignored. In these, the contradiction of the feminine parts themselves appears in the contradiction of the paradoxical shapes of the upper and lower halves of the body. The underside of a woman with child is connected to a heterogeny that almost never unifies with it; in other words, the upper body of a young maiden who has not yet become a woman. (...) It becomes clear when viewed from the side that the thin and leaf-like, fleshless physique of the upper body combines with the fully fleshed torso in the form of one statue, and the typical order of the elementary character in the 'lower body' and the transformative character of the 'upper body,' become an example of a pattern of divine physique." (ebd.8.Kap.) According to Neumann, the thin chest seen in ancient female statues symbolizes a woman's "transformative character," yes?[1] This "transformative character" signifies maidenly youth, a more advanced mentality, and, most important, the dynamism to shift toward individual characteristics. (vgl.ebd.3.Kap.)

Indeed, based on this analysis, it seems possible to accurately describe the personalities of the members of "Ala Alba," yes? For example, let's look at Nagase and Sakurazaki. Both of them have wonderful breasts, one with enormous breasts and one with meager breasts, but in Nagase, as indicated by her large breasts, we can see the "woman's elementary character"—a tendency to protect those around her, yes? On the other hand, from someone such as Sakurazaki, we see the "transformative character"—a recklessness that comes from youth. That is exactly why both of them fell so easily into a trap in order to save a hostage, yes?

[*Negima!* 219th Period Lexicon Negimarium]

■ Right Arm Release

(dextra emittam)

"*Dextra*" is a Latin ablative meaning "right hand." An "ablative" indicates a place or a method. "*Emittam*" is in the first-person-singular present-active subjunctive mood. Therefore, this phrase means "may I release from my right hand."

This spell is incanted in order to release delayed magic and the like from the right hand. In the 219th Period, Negi incants the spell to release the magic loaded into his hand through his use of dark magic.

■ Lightning Speed

[AGILITAS FULMINIS]

One of the practical uses of dark magic, it takes the magic power from "Thunderous Gale (Jovis Tempestas Fulguriens)" into one's flesh and fuses it with the spirit. In doing so, it gives the caster exceedingly great mobility. But if it fails, not only is there a danger that the gusts and lightning from "Thunderous Gale" will damage the caster's flesh, but there are cases when the wind spirits (spritus) violate the caster's mind (spiritus) and make him go mad.

Why would loading the magic power of "Thunderous Gale" into oneself give the caster such extreme mobility? It is because premodern cultural systems that use spells have a prelogical mentality (mentalité prélogique)[2], so to speak. The French social scientist and anthropologist, L. Lévy-Brühl (1857–1939), states the following: "The mentality of primitive people could be called prelogical just as easily as it could be called mystic." (*How Natives Think*, ch. II, II)[3]

It is believed that the language systems in premodern and prelogical cultures tended to dislike abstract linguistic activity. Therefore, their linguistic activity is made up of extremely specific forms. "The closer the mentality of a societal group comes to prelogical forms, the more power their literal thoughts have. Their language proves that. The typical vocabulary, vocabulary that deals with accurate, general ideas, is almost completely lacking, and their special vocabulary, or in other words, their vocabulary that indicates existences or objects that bring a special, specific image to mind when called by name, is plentiful. (...) [For example] the Tasmanians did not have any words that reproduced abstract ideas. (...) They could not even express properties in abstract ways such as hard, soft, hot, cold, long, short, round, etc. To express "hard," they would say, "*like* a stone;" for "high," they would say, "*big legs*," and for "round," they would say "*like* a ball" or "*like* the moon." (ibid. ch. IV, V, emphasis added)

As it says here, prelogical languages expressed abstract ideas—whether by simile or by metaphor—through specific things. This, too, is because abstract ideas and specific objects are linked in various ways through a law called the "law of participation (loi de participation)."

Therefore, the spell that produces gales and lightning, "Thunderous Gale," also implies the "rapidity" of a gale and the "swiftness" of lightning, and, as words imbued with the power of a spell, it can also bring about those effects.

■ "Ruler of the shadow land, Scathach, grant into my hands thirty thorn-bearing spirit lances. 'Throwing Thunder'"

(locos umbrae regnans, Scathach, in manum meam det jaculum daemonium cum spinis triginta. JACULATIO FULGORIS)

A spell that attacks by releasing electrically charged magical javelins. Because the missiles released are javelins and not arrows, each one of them is stronger than a magic arrow made of lightning, and has greater physical destructive power. However, because they mimic the shape of a javelin, they are easier to dodge than the direct lightning attack "White Lightning (Fulguratio Albicans)."

■ "Load"

(supplementum)

A spell that uses dark magic to take magical power into oneself and fuse it with the spirit.

■ **ब**
   (ba)
   The Sanskrit character for the voiced unaspirated labial sound. It means "baku" or "bind."

[*Negima!* 221st Period Lexicon Negimarium]

■ **Svanhvít**
   The flagship of Megalo-Mesembria's international tactical fleet. It was newly made and put in service as a battle cruiser in the middle stages of the Great War. With its long cruising range, its high fire power, and its mobility, it achieves great results in battle. After the previous flagship sustained heavy damage and retired from military service toward the end of the Great War, it was remodeled as the battle mother ship, equipped with a new type of main cannon called the "divine retribution cannon" as well as a crew of Demon-God soldiers, provisions, and maneuvering capabilities, and became the flagship of Megalo-Mesembria's international tactical fleet. In the campaign to retake the Great Bridge, it crushed the Hellas Empire's summon beasts and dealt fatal damage to the enemy's war potential. After the Great War, Megalo-Mesembria's international tactical military underwent a large-scale disarmament, but this flagship is still in service.
   "Svanhvít" is the name of a Valkyrie who appears in Völundr's poem supplied in the Elder Edda, and according to the translator of the Reclam edition, A. Klause, it is Old Norse for "a person (woman) who is white like a swan."

■ **Dragon's Tree**
   (vṛkṣo nagasya)
   A dragon with advanced spiritual character, with much higher intelligence than humans, who lived a long, long time ago. As it is patterned after the gods, like Ryōmen Sukuna no Kami, it will not be destroyed even if its flesh is. It is currently unknown why such a being would be serving as guardian of the Hellas Empire's capital city.
   Vṛkṣo nagasya comes from the Sanskrit *vṛkṣas* (tree) and *nagasya* (the singular genitive of naga [snake or dragon]), and according to the law of sandhi (the law of pronunciation change in Sanskrit), the suffix of *vṛkṣas* changes from *-as* to *-o* (when the chapter was published in the magazine, the law was not applied). The name means "dragon's tree."

■ **Coffee**
   (قهوة)
   There are roughly three legends as to the origin of coffee. One is that the mufti of Aden, Abu 'Abd Allah Muhammad ibn Sa'id (?–1470?) learned of the custom of drinking coffee on his travels (most likely in Ethiopia). Another is that the saint of Mocha and ascetic priest Ali Ibn Umar (?–1418)[4] staved off hunger when he found the coffee bean in the mountains of Yemen. The last is a legend called "The Dancing Goats."

The first person to leave a record of the legend of the dancing goats was the Syrian academic priest Antonius Faustus Naironus Banesius[5], who taught in Rome in the seventeenth century. The following is an excerpt from that record.

> It stands to reason that I should relate evidence concerning a coincidental experience about how this medicine came to be known as *kahve* (in Turkish) or *café* (in Romantic languages). (...) In truth, for example, a common tradition of the Asian people is explained thus: In the Yemen region of Happy Arabia, at the home of monks of a certain monastery, a camel herder, or in another version, a goat herder, had a certain complaint. His complaint was that a few times a week, his herd would stay awake all night and dance furiously, to an abnormal level. The imam at the monastery was moved with curiosity, and when he found the place where the herd came from their pasture, that night, he and his fellows performed a thorough investigation to see where and in what manner the goats, or the camels, danced and ate grass. When they did, the imam came across a certain bush. The camels had been filling their bellies with the fruit from that bush—or rather the juice from it. The imam wanted to test the moral character of this fruit himself. And thus, the imam boiled the fruit in hot water, partook of the drink at night, and experienced a state of wakefulness. It is from this event that the monks determined to use this fruit to stay awake every night. Thus it is said that this handy fruit is more useful for nighttime prayer. (*A Discourse on Coffee: Its Description and Virtues,* 1671)

The root for the Latin referring to this state of wakefulness that can be brought about by taking coffee, *vigilantia* (as well as "to be awake [*vigilare, vigilia*]"), VEG, has sister-relationships with words in Indo-European etymology, such as the Greek *ygieinos,* or "healthy" or the Sanskrit *ugra* (powerful). Thus, according to this legend, the effects of coffee are not only to bring about a simple state of sleeplessness (*exsomnis*), but to bring about a state that includes a strong vitality. This can also be seen in *vigere,* a word akin to *vigilare* (to be awake), which means "to be powerfully lively." This is likely exactly why Naironus believed coffee to be "the best medicine for health." But the drinking of seven cups a day is somewhat questionable.

---

1. When Neumann interpreted the statue of a woman with a thin chest as symbolizing the "transformative character," the historical artifact he referenced was the goddess statue (Venus of Lespugue) excavated in Lespugue in the Haute-Garonne province of France. (But for some reason, in Neumann's original German, it is written as Lespugne.) It is a famous piece, so even if you have no interest in breasts, I recommend looking at it in art history or archaeology photo collections, yes? Those who can use the Internet can do a search on "Venus of Lespugue." But while this goddess statue is damaged, she has large breasts that hang all the way down to her abdomen, yes? Actually, in chapter eight of this same book, Neumann references this goddess statue as a historical example of a woman statue with large breasts. It's just that the breasts on this statue are so large that they hang down to her abdomen and her

chest area becomes flat, yes? Taking all this into account, there is doubt as to whether or not Neumann used appropriate material to support his arguments.

2. "*Shinsei*" is an anthropological term meaning "disposition." To express it in English, the most appropriate word would be "mentality."

3. Lévy-Brühl, in the preface of the Japanese translation of his work, amends his theory by stating that it is not necessarily true that any peoples or societies that are absolutely differentiated from civilization actually exist.

4. It is sometimes written as "Omar," but in Arabic, the O sounds like the U, so it is read "Umar."

5. Also called by Antoine Faust Naironi.

魔法先生ネギま!
MAGISTER NEGI MAGI

赤松 健 SHONEN MAGAZINE COMICS
KEN AKAMATSU

24

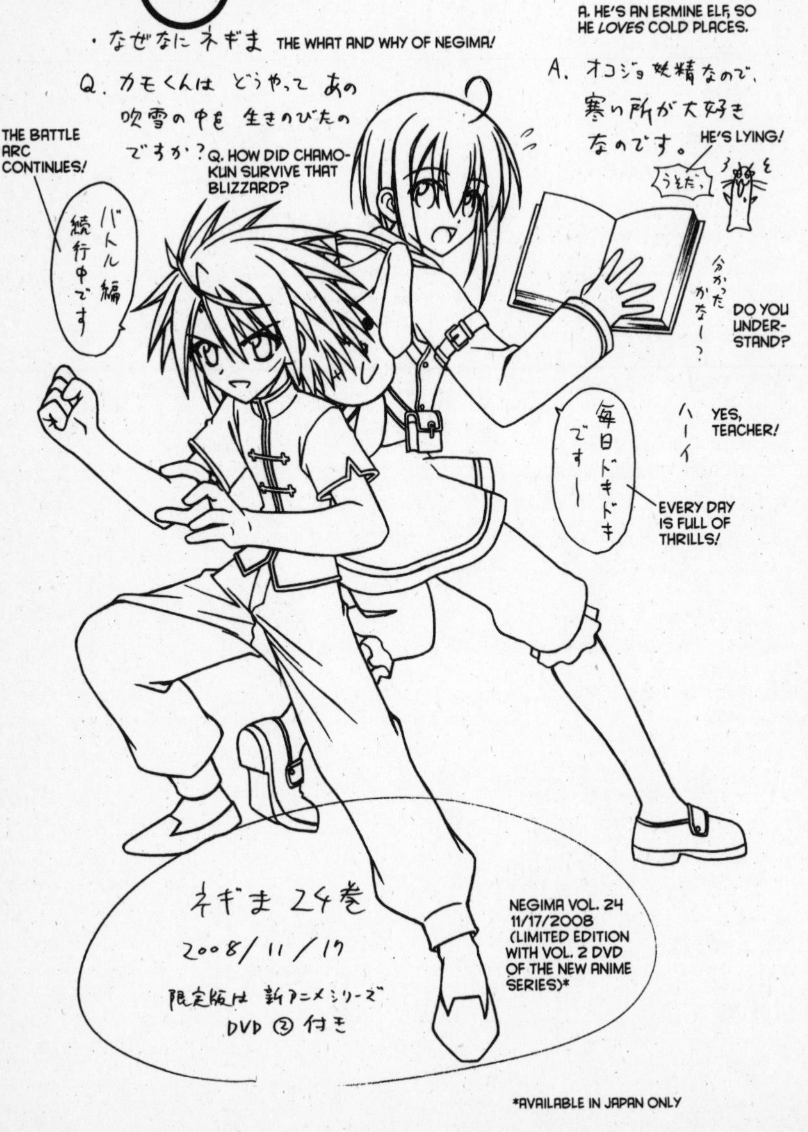

・なぜなにネギま THE WHAT AND WHY OF NEGIMA!
Q. カモくんは どうやって あの吹雪の中を 生きのびたのですか?
Q. HOW DID CHAMO-KUN SURVIVE THAT BLIZZARD?
A. オコジョ妖精なので、寒い所が大好きなのです。
A. HE'S AN ERMINE ELF, SO HE LOVES COLD PLACES.
うそだ。
HE'S LYING!
バトル編続行中です
THE BATTLE ARC CONTINUES!
分かったかなー?
DO YOU UNDER-STAND?
ハーイ
YES, TEACHER!
毎日ドキドキですー
EVERY DAY IS FULL OF THRILLS!
ネギま 24巻
2008/11/17
限定版は 新アニメシリーズ DVD ② 付き
NEGIMA VOL. 24
11/17/2008
(LIMITED EDITION WITH VOL. 2 DVD OF THE NEW ANIME SERIES)*

*AVAILABLE IN JAPAN ONLY

キャラ解説
CHARACTER PROFILE

㉒ 鳴滝風香
㉒ FŪKA NARUTAKI

双子ちゃんの元気な方。(笑)
THE HYPER ONE OF THE TWINS. (LAUGH)
いわゆる「ボクっ娘」で、妹より
SHE'S THE SO-CALLED BOKUKKO, AND SHE'S TOUGHER, HAS
強気でツリ目でボーイッシュなん
SLANTIER EYES, AND IS MORE BOYISH THAN HER YOUNGER
ですが、オバケがこわかったりする
SISTER, BUT THEY'RE THE SAME IN THAT THEY'RE BOTH
ところは同じです。
SCARED OF GHOSTS AND THINGS.

かわいーよね♡
AREN'T THEY CUTE♡

何か小学生みたいですけど、中3です。
SHE LOOKS LIKE AN ELEMENTARY SCHOOL GIRL, BUT SHE'S A
高校生や大学生になった姿を想像
THIRD-YEAR IN JUNIOR HIGH. I CAN'T IMAGINE WHAT SHE'LL LOOK
できないな・・・(笑)
LIKE WHEN SHE'S IN HIGH SCHOOL OR COLLEGE... (LAUGH)

アニメ版CVはこやまきみこさん。
IN THE ANIME, SHE IS VOICED BY KIMIKO KOYAMA-SAN. SHE'S
「陸上防衛隊まおちゃん」からお世話になってます。
HELPED ME OUT SINCE *MAO-CHAN.* SHE'S THE AUTHORITY ON
ロリ声のオーソリティです！歌もうまいよ。
LOLITA VOICES! AND SHE'S A GOOD SINGER.

ドラマ版は片岡沙耶ちゃん♡
IN THE DRAMA, SHE IS PLAYED BY SAYA KATAOKA-CHAN♡
撮影当時は元気少女だったけど、
WHILE FILMING, SHE WAS AN ENERGETIC YOUNG
最近かなり女らしくなってきた
GIRL, BUT RECENTLY I GET THE FEELING SHE'S BECOME
ような・・・(^^)
MORE OF A WOMAN... (^^)
そのうちグラビアアイドルになっちゃうんじゃ
MAYBE SHE'LL BE A BIKINI MODEL
ないかな?!
SOON?!

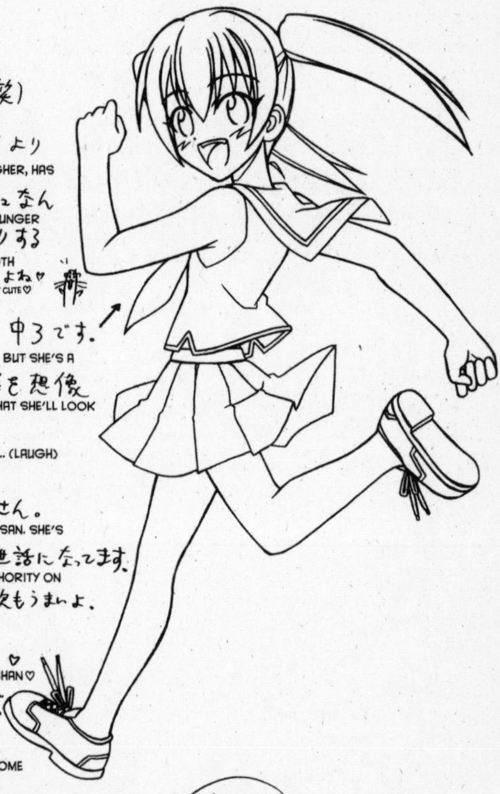

赤松
AKAMATSU

About the Creator

Negima! is only Ken Akamatsu's third manga, although he started working in the field in 1994 with *AI Ga Tomaranai* (released in the United States with the title *A.I. Love You*). Like all of Akamatsu's work to date, it was published in Kodansha's *Shonen Magazine*. *AI Ga Tomaranai* ran for five years before concluding in 1999. In 1998, however, Akamatsu began the work that would make him one of the most popular manga artists in Japan: *Love Hina*. *Love Hina* ran for four years, and before its conclusion in 2002, it would cause Akamatsu to be granted the prestigious Manga of the Year award from Kodansha, as well as going on to become one of the bestselling manga in the United States.

Translation Notes

Japanese is a tricky language for most Westerners, and translation is often more art than science. For your edification and reading pleasure, here are notes on some of the places where we could have gone in a different direction with our translation of the work, or where a Japanese cultural reference is used.

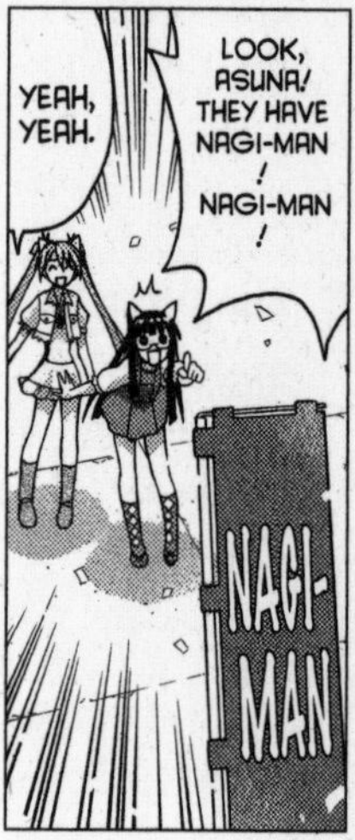
LOOK, ASUNA! THEY HAVE NAGI-MAN! NAGI-MAN!
YEAH, YEAH.
NAGI-MAN

Nagi-man, page 7

Nagi-man is short for "Nagi *manjū*." A *manjū* is a steamed yeast bun with filling. In this case, they probably have Nagi's face printed on them to commemorate the great war hero.

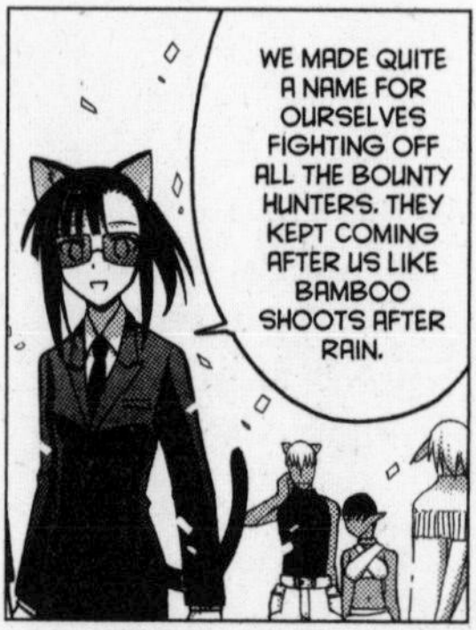
WE MADE QUITE A NAME FOR OURSELVES FIGHTING OFF ALL THE BOUNTY HUNTERS. THEY KEPT COMING AFTER US LIKE BAMBOO SHOOTS AFTER RAIN.

Bamboo shoots after rain, page 8

This is a figure of speech in Japan referring to the same thing happening over and over very quickly, like how bamboo shoots grow like crazy after it has rained. We can only imagine how many bounty hunters Setsuna and the others had to fight off.

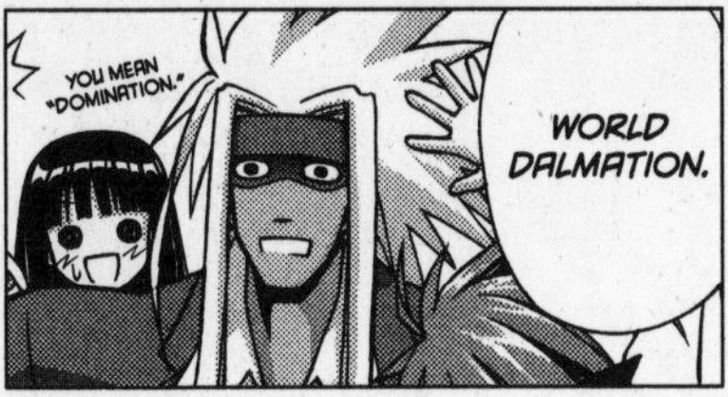
WORLD DALMATION.
YOU MEAN "DOMINATION."

World uniforms, page 38

Rakan's mistake isn't quite as random as it may seem at first. In Japanese, the word *seifuku* can mean "domination" (as in world domination) or "uniform" (as in high school uniform), depending on which Chinese characters are used. Rakan uses the characters for "uniforms," though whether he did it on purpose or because he's always thinking about girls in cute outfits remains a mystery.

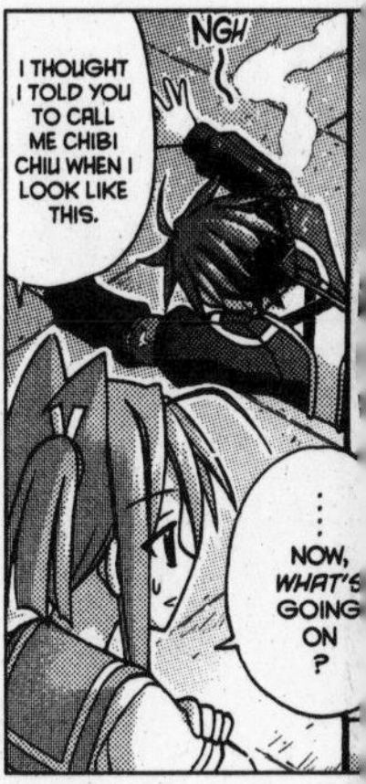
NGH
I THOUGHT I TOLD YOU TO CALL ME CHIBI CHIU WHEN I LOOK LIKE THIS.
...... NOW, WHAT'S GOING ON ?

Chibi Chiu, page 58

Chibi is a Japanese word referring to someone small, and is usually not very flattering. But in this case, because it sounds so nice with Chisame's nickname, Chiu, she wants Negi to use it because it's so cute.

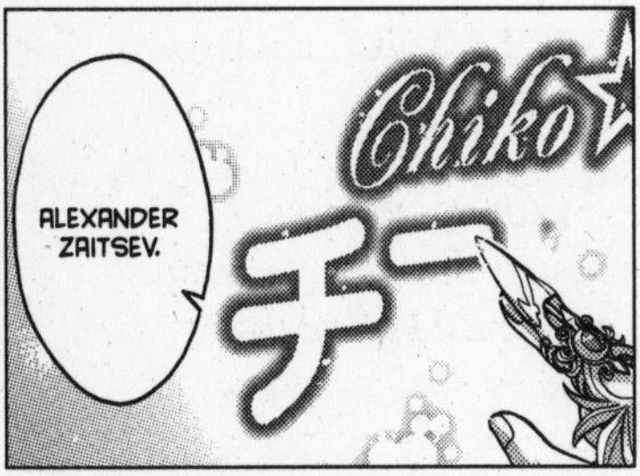
Chiko☆
チー
ALEXANDER ZAITSEV.

Alexander Zaitsev, page 81

While this is the name that Chiko☆Tan chose out of shame for his real name, it may be interesting to note that he gets it from a Russian figure-skating champion.

Kai●-ken, page 108

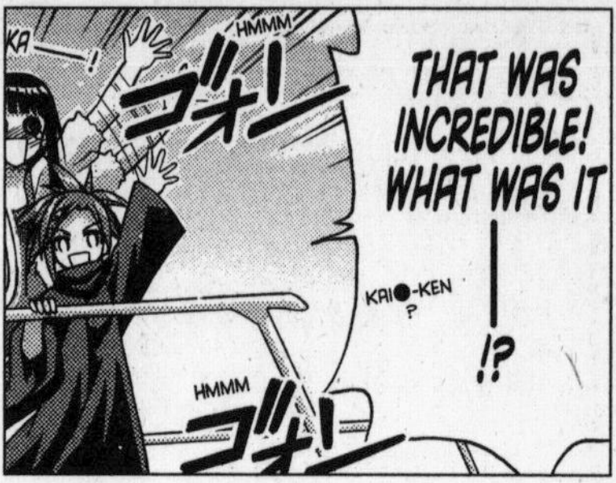
KA—!
HMMM
THAT WAS INCREDIBLE! WHAT WAS IT —!?
KAI●-KEN?
HMMM

Asakura is being censored as she tries to use the copyrighted name Kaio-ken, a technique Dragonball fans will recognize as the one Goku learns from King Kai. Like Negi's technique, it gives the user an enormous boost in strength, but can also damage the user's body.

La●uta, page 118

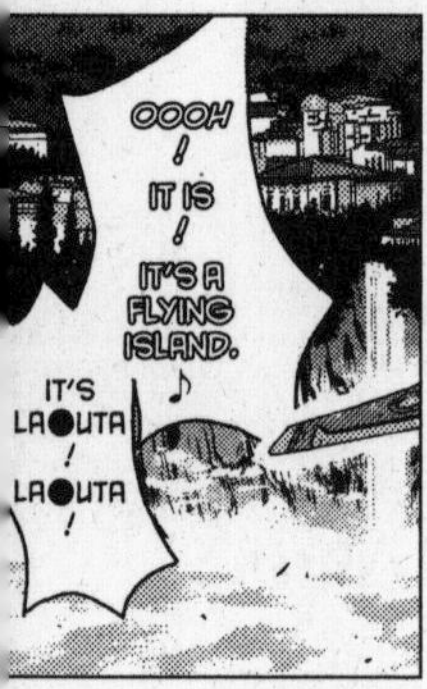
OOOH! IT IS! IT'S A FLYING ISLAND. ♪
IT'S LA●UTA! LA●UTA!

Studio Ghibli fans may be able to tell that what Yūna and Makie are comparing Ostia to is the Castle in the Sky, Laputa.

Nagi-Koji, page 138

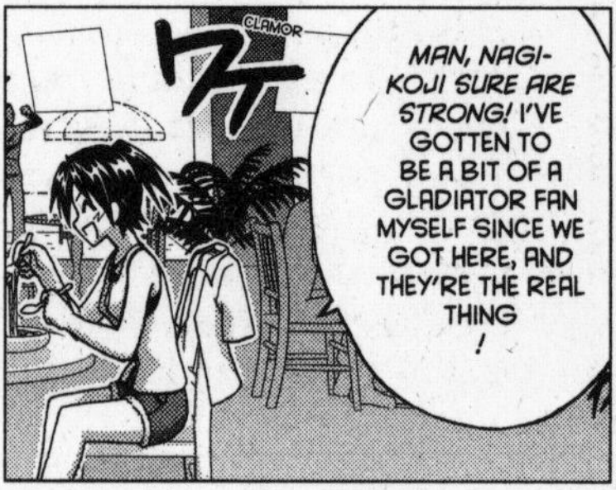
CLAMOR
MAN, NAGI-KOJI SURE ARE STRONG! I'VE GOTTEN TO BE A BIT OF A GLADIATOR FAN MYSELF SINCE WE GOT HERE, AND THEY'RE THE REAL THING!

Maybe because of the way their writing system works in Japan, instead of using initials to shorten things, they'll use the first two syllables of each thing in the phrase. For example, "personal computer" becomes "perso-com (or *pasocon,* for Japanese pronunciation)" instead of PC. In this case, they're using it to refer to pairs of people, like Nagi-Koji for Nagi and Kojirō, or Kono-Setsu for Konoka and Setsuna.

Bokukko, page 178

In Japanese, there are several different ways to say "I," many of which are used mainly by one gender. *Boku* is a first-person pronoun that is usually used by men, but there are some girls who use it, too, like Fūka, and they are called *bokukko,* or "*boku* girls."

NEGIMA!? NEO

MAGISTER NEGI MAGI

STORY BY KEN AKAMATSU
ART BY TAKUYA FUJIMA

BASED ON THE POPULAR ANIME!

Negi Springfield is only ten years old, but he's already a powerful wizard. After graduating from his magic school in England, the prodigy is given an unusual assignment: teach English at an all-girl school in Japan. Now Negi has to find a way to deal with his thirty-one totally gorgeous (and completely overaffectionate) students—without using magic! Based on the *Negima!* anime, this is a fresh take on the beloved *Negima!* story.

NEGIMA!? NEO
MAGISTER NEGI MAGI
Story by KEN AKAMATSU
Creator of Negima!
Art by TAKUYA FUJIMA
1
BASED ON THE POPULAR ANIME!

Available anywhere books or comics are sold!

VISIT WWW.DELREYMANGA.COM TO:

- Read sample pages
- View release date calendars for upcoming volumes
- Sign up for Del Rey's free manga e-newsletter
- Find out the latest about new Del Rey Manga series

RATING OT AGES 16+

DEL REY MANGA デルレイ

www.delreymanga.com

TOMARE!

[STOP!]

You're going the wrong way!

Manga is a completely different type of reading experience.

To start at the *beginning*, go to the *end*!

That's right! Authentic manga is read the traditional Japanese way—from right to left, exactly the *opposite* of how American books are read. It's easy to follow: Just go to the other end of the book, and read each page—and each panel—from right side to left side, starting at the top right. Now you're experiencing manga as it was meant to be.